# POLITICAL IDEOLOGIES

**Also by Andrew Heywood**

POLITICAL IDEAS AND CONCEPTS

# Political Ideologies

## An Introduction

Second Edition

Andrew Heywood

WORTH PUBLISHERS

Political Ideologies

Second Edition

© Andrew Heywood 1992, 1998

Foreword © Andrew Gamble 1992

All rights reserved

Printed in Great Britain

Library of Congress Catalog Card Number: 98–84777

ISBN: 1–57259–723–2

Worth Publishers

33 Irving Place

New York, NY 10003

*To Jean*

# Contents

# Boxes

## Thinkers

# Foreword

Ideology has had a strange history. It is inseparable from the political experience of the modern world, yet few major theorists of politics have a good word for it. Figures as diverse as Karl Marx, Michael Oakeshott and Talcott Parsons all condemned it, for different reasons. To its opponents ideology is the opposite of such wholesome things as truth, science, rationality, objectivity and philosophy. It signifies beliefs and doctrines that are either dogmas beyond the reach of criticism or cloaks for individual and group interests.

It is hardly surprising, given the influence of this negative conception, that it should at times have been fashionable to bury ideology and declare it at an end. But like similar efforts to bury history and politics, ideology has a habit of coming back. The politics of the modern world have been shaped by the key ideological traditions. Ideologies are a crucial resource for ordering, defining and evaluating political reality and establishing political identities.

The great merit of Andrew Heywood's book is that he takes ideology seriously, and explores patiently and with admirable clarity the different characteristics of the classic western ideologies, as well as the new themes and directions of recent ideological thought. He has produced one of the best available introductions to the subject anywhere in print.

The western ideological tradition, which originated in the French and American revolutions of the eighteenth century, does not exhaust ways of understanding politics, nor does it eclipse many non-western traditions of political thought. But it is an indispensable tradition nonetheless, and an ability to understand its key terms and internal development is a basic requirement for citizenship in the modern world. Andrew Heywood is the ideal guide.

*University of Sheffield*                                          ANDREW GAMBLE

# Preface to the Second Edition

The first edition of *Political Ideologies* was written against the backdrop of the east European revolutions of 1989–91. It therefore reflected on many of the issues and developments of that remarkable period. However, rather than history settling down into new and stable post-Cold-War patterns, in certain respects the pace of political and ideological change has subsequently increased. Indeed the end of the century and the advent of a new millennium appear to have generated their own range of hopes and fears. This second edition thus attempts to take account of a new set of challenges and uncertainties. These include the ramifications of the collapse of communism (and, some would argue, the death of socialism), the emergence of a global capitalist system, the shift from anticolonial to postcolonial sensibilities in the developing world, the rise of particularist creeds such as ethnic nationalism and religious fundamentalism, and the advent of postmodernity or postmodernism.

Throughout the book an attempt has been made to update material and revise judgements in the light of contemporary developments. Boxes have been added to allow for a closer examination of particular thinkers and important ideas, and to highlight the different ways in which the various ideologies have understood and used key political concepts. There are also a number of major changes. The most important of these are the following.

Chapter 1 has been expanded to include a more thorough and detailed examination of the concept of ideology and the nature of ideological thought. The issue of democracy has been moved to Chapter 2, where it is now discussed in relation to liberalism, which means that democracy no longer features as a separate chapter. The section on classical Marxism in Chapter 4 has been expanded, partly on the ground that the collapse of orthodox communism has helped to disentangle Marx from Lenin and Stalin. The treatment of nationalism in Chapter 5 has been revised, insofar as nationalism is no longer portrayed as a narrow political doctrine associated with self-determination, but as a broader collection of doctrines and movements. Chapter 9, now entitled ecologism rather than environmentalism, has been refocused to give greater attention to the implications of adopting an ecocentric political perspective. Ecofeminism is also given greater attention as one of the schools of environmentalist thought.

Chapter 10 is a new chapter on religious fundamentalism. This reflects the fact that it is increasingly difficult to classify fundamentalism as merely a subspecies of nationalism, and it also allows account to be taken of the range and importance of fundamentalist creeds around the world. Chapter 11 has been expanded to encompass a specific discussion of postmodernism. In addition, the last section of each chapter now examines the twenty-first-century prospects for the ideology in question. Finally, I would like to thank all those who commented on or gave me feedback about the first edition of the book, and hope that the second edition goes some way to addressing the issues and suggestions they made.

ANDREW HEYWOOD

# Chapter 1

# Introduction: Understanding Ideology

The role of ideas
What is ideology?
Left, centre and right
The rise and fall of ideologies
Further reading

All people are political thinkers. Whether they know it or not, people use political ideas and concepts whenever they express their opinions or speak their mind. Everyday language is littered with terms such as 'freedom', 'fairness', 'equality', 'justice' and 'rights'. In the same way, words such as 'conservative', 'liberal', 'socialist', 'communist' and 'fascist' are regularly employed by people either to describe their own views, or those of others. However, even though such terms are familiar, even commonplace, they are seldom used with any precision or a clear grasp of their meaning. What, for instance, is 'equality'? What does it mean to say that all people are equal? Are people born equal, should they be treated by society as if they are equal? Should people have equal rights, equal opportunities, equal political influence, equal wages? Similarly, words such as 'communist' or 'fascist' are commonly misused. What does it mean to call someone a 'fascist'? What values or beliefs do fascists hold, and why do they hold them? How do communist views differ from those of, say, liberals, conservatives or socialists? This book examines the substantive ideas and beliefs of the major political ideologies. Three preliminary issues must be addressed, however. First, what role do ideas and theories play in politics? Second, what is the nature of the belief systems within which these ideas have developed and, in a sense, are packaged? In other words, what is political ideology? Third, how useful is the conventional terminology of left and right in classifying these ideas and ideologies?

## The role of ideas

Not all political thinkers have accepted that ideas and ideologies are of much importance. Politics has sometimes been thought to be little more than a naked struggle for power. If this is true, political ideas are mere

1

propaganda, a form of words or slogans designed to win votes or attract popular support. Ideas and ideologies are therefore simply 'window dressing', used to conceal the deeper realities of political life. This is certainly a position supported by behaviourism, the school of psychology associated with John B. Watson (1878–1958) and B. F. Skinner (1904–90). From the perspective of behaviourism, human beings are little more than biological machines, conditioned to act (or, more correctly, react) to external stimuli. The thinking subject, together with their ideas, values, feelings and intentions, is simply an irrelevance. A very similar view also informed 'dialectical materialism', the crude form of Marxism that dominated intellectual enquiry in the Soviet Union and other orthodox communist states. This held that political ideas can only be understood in the light of the economic or class interests of those who express them. Ideas have a 'material basis', they have no meaning or significance on their own. Orthodox Marxists therefore analyse politics strictly in terms of social class and treat political ideologies as nothing more than an expression of the interests of particular classes.

The opposite argument has also been put. The UK economist John Maynard Keynes (see p. 61), for example, argued that the world is ruled by little other than the ideas of economists and political philosophers. As he put it in the closing pages of his *General Theory*:

> Practical men, who believe themselves to be quite exempt from any intellectual influences, are usually the slaves of some defunct economist. Madmen in authority, who hear voices in the air, are distilling their frenzy from some academic scribbler of a few years back. (Keynes [1936] 1963, p. 383)

Far from dismissing ideas as being conditioned responses to practical circumstances, this position highlights the degree to which beliefs and theories provides the wellspring of human action. The world is ultimately ruled by 'academic scribblers'. Such a view suggests, for instance, that modern capitalism, in important respects, developed out of the classical economics of Adam Smith (see p. 52) and David Ricardo (1772–1823), that Soviet communism was significantly shaped by the writing of Karl Marx (see p. 126) and V. I. Lenin (see p. 132), and that the history of Nazi Germany can only be understood by reference to the doctrines advanced in Hitler's *Mein Kampf*.

In reality, both these accounts of political life are one-sided and inadequate. Political ideas are not merely a passive reflection of vested interests or personal ambition, but have the capacity to inspire and guide political action itself and so can shape material life. At the same time, political ideas do not emerge in a vacuum: they do not drop from the sky like rain. All political ideas are moulded by the social and historical circumstances in which they develop and by the political ambitions they serve. Quite simply, political theory and political practice are inseparably linked. Any balanced and persuasive account of political life must therefore acknowledge the constant interplay between ideas and ideologies on the one hand, and historical and material forces on the other.

Ideas and ideologies influence political life in a number of specific ways. In the first place, they provide a perspective through which the world is understood and explained. People do not see the world as it is, but only as they expect it to be; in other words, they see it through a veil of ingrained beliefs, opinions and assumptions. Whether consciously or unconsciously, everyone subscribes to a set of political beliefs and values that guide their behaviour and influence their conduct. Political ideas and ideologies thus set goals that inspire political activity. In this respect politicians are subject to two very different influences. Without doubt, all politicians want power. This forces them to be pragmatic (see p. 11), to adopt those policies and ideas that are electorally popular or win favour with powerful groups such as business or the army. However politicians seldom seek power simply for its own sake. They also possess beliefs, values and convictions about what to do with power when it is achieved.

The balance between pragmatic and ideological considerations clearly varies from politician to politician, and also at different stages in a politician's career. Some, for example Adolf Hitler (see p. 219), have been fiercely, even fanatically, committed to a clear set of ideological goals. Hitler's writings are shot through with virulent anti-Semitism (see p. 230) and openly discuss his desire to found a German-dominated, racial empire in Eastern Europe. Marxist revolutionaries such as Lenin have been dedicated to the goal of building a classless, communist society. However, no politician can afford to be blinded by ideological conviction: at the very least, strategic compromises have to be made if power is to won and retained. Anti-Semitic attacks undoubtedly increased in Germany after Hitler's appointment as Chancellor in 1933, but it was not until the war years that Hitler embarked upon the policy of racial extermination that some have believed was always his goal. In Lenin's case, despite a distaste for capitalism, in 1921 he introduced the New Economic Policy, which permitted the reemergence of limited private enterprise in Russia. Other politicians, notably but by no means exclusively those in the United States, have come to be regarded as little more than political commodities. They have been packaged and have sold themselves on the basis of image and personality, paying little or no attention to ideas or policies. Nevertheless US politicians are not simply power-seeking pragmatists. The importance of ideas and values in US politics is concealed by the fact that the two major parties, the Republicans and the Democrats, share the same broad ideological goals. Most US politicians subscribe to what has been called the 'American ideology', a set of liberal-capitalist values about the virtues of a free market economy and respect for the principles embodied in the US Constitution.

Political ideas also help to shape the nature of political systems. Systems of government vary considerably throughout the world and are always associated with particular values or principles. Absolute monarchies were based upon deeply established religious ideas, notably the divine right of kings. The political systems in most contemporary western countries are founded upon a set of liberal democratic principles. Western states typically respect the ideas of limited and constitutional government, and also believe that government should be representative, based upon regular and competitive elections. In the same way traditional communist political systems conformed to the principles of Marxism–Leninism. Communist states were dominated by a single party, a ruling Communist Party, whose authority rested upon Lenin's belief that the Communist Party alone represents the interests of the working class. Even the fact that the world is divided into a collection of nation-states and that government power is usually located at the national level reflects the impact of political ideas, in this case of nationalism and, more specifically, the principle of national self-determination.

Finally, political ideas and ideologies can act as a form of social cement, providing social groups, and indeed whole societies, with a set of unifying beliefs and values. Political ideologies have commonly been associated with particular social classes, for example liberalism with the middle classes, conservatism with the landed aristocracy, socialism with the working class and so forth. These ideas reflect the life experiences, interests and aspirations of a social class, and therefore help to foster a sense of belonging and solidarity. However ideas and ideologies can also succeed in binding together divergent groups and classes within a society. For instance there is a unifying bedrock of liberal-democratic values in most western states, while in Moslem countries Islam has established a common set of moral principles and beliefs. In providing society with a unified political culture, political ideas help to promote order and social stability.

A unifying set of political ideas and values can develop naturally within a society. However it can also be enforced from above in an attempt to manufacture obedience and thereby operates as a form of social control. The values of elite groups such as political and military leaders, government officials, landowners or industrialists may diverge significantly from those of the masses. Ruling elites may use political ideas to contain opposition and restrict debate through a process of ideological manipulation. This was most obvious in regimes that possessed 'official' ideologies such as Nazi Germany and the Soviet Union. In both cases official or politically 'reliable' beliefs, those of national socialism and Marxism–Leninism respectively, dominated political life and indeed all social institutions, art, culture, education, the media and so on. Opposing views and beliefs were simply censored or suppressed. Some argue that a more subtle form of ideological manipulation occurs in all societies. This can be seen in the Marxist belief, examined in the next section, that the culture of capitalist societies is dominated by ideas that serve the interests of the economically dominant class.

## What is ideology?

This book is primarily a study of political ideologies, rather than an analysis of the nature of ideology. Much confusion stems from the fact that, though obviously related, 'ideology' and 'ideologies' are quite different things to study. To examine 'ideology' is to consider a particular *type* of political thought, distinct from, say, political science or political philosophy. To study political ideology is to analyse the nature, role and significance of this category of thought, and to reflect on questions such as which sets of political ideas and arguments should be classified as ideologies. For instance, is ideology liberating or oppressive, true or false, and so forth. Similarly, are conservatism and nationalism ideologies in the same sense as liberalism and socialism? On the other hand, to study 'ideologies' is to be concerned with analysing the *content* of political thought, to be interested in the ideas, doctrines and theories that have been advanced by and within the various ideological traditions. For example, what can liberalism tell us about freedom? Why have socialists traditionally supported equality? How do anarchists defend the idea of a stateless society? Why have fascists regarded struggle and war as healthy? In order to examine such 'content' issues, however, it is necessary to consider the 'type' of political thought we are dealing with. Before discussing the characteristic ideas and doctrines of the so-called ideologies, we need to reflect on why these sets of ideas have been categorised as ideologies. More importantly, what does the categorisation tell us? What can we learn about, for example, liberalism, socialism, feminism and fascism, from the fact that they are classified as ideologies?

### Concepts of ideology

The first problem confronting any discussion of the nature of ideology is the fact that there is no settled or agreed definition of the term, only a collection of rival definitions. As David McLellan (1986, p. 1) put it, 'Ideology is the most elusive concept in the whole of the social sciences'. Few political terms have been the subject of such deep and impassioned controversy. This has occurred for two reasons. In the first place, as all concepts of ideology acknowledge a link between theory and practice, the term uncovers highly contentious debates, considered in the previous section, about the role of ideas in politics and the relationship between beliefs and theories on the one hand, and material life or political conduct on the other. Secondly, the concept of ideology has not been able to stand apart from the ongoing struggle between and amongst political ideologies. For much of its history the term ideology has been used as a political weapon, a device with which to condemn or criticise rival sets of ideas or belief systems. Not until the second half of the twentieth century was a neutral and apparently objective concept of ideology widely employed, and even then disagreements persisted over the social role and political significance of ideology. Among the meanings that have been attached to ideology are the following:

- A political belief system.
- An action-orientated set of political ideas.
- The ideas of the ruling class.
- The world view of a particular social class or social group.
- Political ideas that embody or articulate class or social interests.
- Ideas that propagate false consciousness amongst the exploited or oppressed.
- Ideas that situate the individual within a social context and generate a sense of collective belonging.
- An officially sanctioned set of ideas used to legitimise a political system or regime.
- An all-embracing political doctrine that claims a monopoly of truth.
- An abstract and highly systematic set of political ideas.

The origins of the term are nevertheless clear. The word ideology was coined during the French Revolution by Antoine Destutt de Tracy (1754–1836), and was first used in public in 1796. For de Tracy, *idéologie* referred to a new 'science of ideas', literally an idea-ology. With a rationalist zeal typical of the Enlightenment, he believed that it was possible objectively to uncover the origins of ideas, and proclaimed that this new science would come to enjoy the same status as established sciences such as biology and zoology. More boldly, since all forms of enquiry are based on ideas, de Tracy suggested that ideology would eventually come to be recognised as the queen of the sciences. However, despite these high expectations, this original meaning of the term has had little impact on later usage.

The career of ideology as a key political term stems from the use made of it in the writings of Karl Marx. Marx's use of the term, and the interest shown in it by later generations of Marxist thinkers, largely explains the prominence ideology enjoys in modern social and political thought. Yet the meaning Marx ascribed to the concept is very different from the one usually accorded it in mainstream political analysis. Marx used the term in the title of his early work *The German Ideology* ([1846] 1970), written with his lifelong collaborator Friedrich Engels (1820–95). This also contains Marx's clearest description of his view of ideology:

> The ideas of the ruling class are in every epoch the ruling ideas, i.e. the class which is the ruling *material* force of society, is at the same time the ruling *intellectual* force. The class which has the means of material production at its disposal, has control at the same time over the means of mental production, so that thereby, generally speaking, the ideas of those who lack the means of mental production are subject to it. (Marx and Engels, 1970, p. 64)

Marx's concept of ideology has number of crucial features. First, ideology is about delusion and mystification; it perpetrates a false or mistaken view of the world, what Engels later referred to as 'false consciousness'. Marx used ideology as a critical concept, whose purpose is to unmask a process of systematic mystification. His own ideas he classified as scientific, because they were designed accurately to uncover the workings of history and society. The contrast between ideology and science, between falsehood and truth, is thus vital to Marx's use of the term. Secondly, ideology is linked to the class system. Marx believed that the distortion implicit in ideology stems from the fact that it reflects the interests and perspective on society of the ruling class. The ruling class is unwilling to recognise itself as an oppressor and, equally, is anxious to reconcile the oppressed to their oppression. The class system is thus presented upside down, a notion Marx conveyed through the image of the *camera obscura*, the inverted picture that is produced by a camera lens or the human eye. Liberalism, which portrays rights that can only be exercised by the propertied and privileged as universal entitlements, is therefore the classic example of ideology.

Thirdly, ideology is a manifestation of power. In concealing the contradictions upon which capitalism, in common with all class societies, is based, ideology serves to disguise from the exploited proletariat the fact of its own exploitation, and thereby upholds a system of unequal class power. Ideology literally constitutes the 'ruling' ideas of the age. Finally, Marx treated ideology as a temporary phenomenon. Ideology will only continue so long as the class system that generates it survives. The proletariat, in Marx's view the 'grave digger' of capitalism, is destined not to establish another form of class society, but rather to abolish class inequality altogether by bringing about the collective ownership of wealth. The interests of the proletariat thus coincide with those of society as a whole. The proletariat, in short, does not need ideology because it is the only class that needs no illusions.

Later generations of Marxists have, if anything, shown greater interest in ideology than Marx did himself. This largely reflects the fact that Marx's confident prediction of capitalism's doom proved to be highly optimistic, encouraging later Marxists to focus on ideology as one of the factors explaining the unexpected resilience of the capitalist mode of production. However, important shifts in the meaning of the term also took place. Most importantly, all classes came to be seen to possess ideologies. In *What is to be Done* ([1902] 1988) Lenin thus described the ideas of the proletariat as 'socialist ideology', a phrase that would have been absurd for Marx. For Lenin and most twentieth-century Marxists, ideology referred to the distinctive ideas of a particular social class, ideas that advance its interests regardless of its class position. However as all classes, the proletariat as well as the bourgeoisie, have an ideology, the term was robbed of its negative or pejorative connotations. Ideology no longer implied necessary falsehood and mystification, and no longer stood in contrast to science; indeed 'scientific socialism' (Marxism) was recognised as form of proletarian ideology. Nevertheless, although Lenin's concept of ideology was essentially neutral, he was well aware of the role ideology played in upholding the capitalist system. Enslaved by 'bourgeois ideology', the proletariat, Lenin argued, would never achieve class consciousness on its own, hence he pointed to the need for a 'vanguard' party to guide the working masses towards the realisation of their revolutionary potential.

The Marxist theory of ideology was perhaps developed furthest by Antonio Gramsci. Gramsci ([1935] 1971) argued that the capitalist class system is upheld not simply by unequal economic and political power, but by what he termed the 'hegemony' of bourgeois ideas and theories. Hegemony means leadership or domination, and in the sense of ideological hegemony it refers to the capacity of bourgeois ideas to displace rival views and become, in effect, the commonsense of the age. Gramsci highlighted the degree to which ideology is embedded at every level in society, in its art and literature, in its education system and mass media, in everyday language and popular culture. This bourgeois hegemony, Gramsci insisted, could only be challenged at the political and intellectual level, which means through the establishment of a rival 'proletarian hegemony', based on socialist principles, values and theories.

The capacity of capitalism to achieve stability by manufacturing legitimacy was also a particular concern of the Frankfurt School, a group of mainly German neo-Marxists who fled the Nazis and later settled in the United States. Its most widely known member, Herbert Marcuse (see p. 139), argued in *One Dimensional Man* (1964) that advanced industrial society has developed a 'totalitarian' character in the capacity of its ideology to manipulate thought and deny expression to oppositional views.

## Antonio Gramsci (1891–1937)

Italian Marxist and social theorist. The son of a minor public official, Gramsci joined the Socialist Party in 1913, becoming in 1921 the general secretary of the newly formed Italian Communist Party. He was elected to the Italian Parliament in 1924, but was imprisoned by Mussolini in 1926. He remained incarcerated until his death.

In *Prison Notebooks* (Gramsci, 1971), written between 1929 and 1935, Gramsci tried to redress the emphasis within orthodox Marxism upon economic or material factors. He rejected any form of 'scientific' determinism by stressing, through the theory of hegemony, the importance of the political and intellectual struggle. Though proponents of Eurocommunism have claimed him as an influence, he remained throughout his life a Leninist and a revolutionary. His stress on revolutionary commitment and 'optimism of the will' also endeared him to the new left.

By manufacturing false needs and turning humans into voracious consumers, modern societies are able to paralyse criticism through the spread of widespread and stultifying affluence. According to Marcuse, even the apparent tolerance of liberal capitalism serves a repressive purpose in that it creates the impression of free debate and argument, thereby concealing the extent to which indoctrination and ideological control take place.

One of the earliest attempts to construct a non-Marxist concept of ideology was undertaken by the German sociologist Karl Mannheim (1893–1947). Like Marx, he acknowledged that people's ideas are shaped by their social circumstances, but, in contrast to Marx, he strove to rid ideology of its negative implications. In *Ideology and Utopia* ([1929] 1960) Mannheim portrayed ideologies as thought systems that serve to defend a particular social order, and that broadly express the interests of its dominant or ruling group. Utopias, on the other hand, are idealised representations of the future that imply the need for radical social change, invariably serving the interests of oppressed or subordinate groups. He further distinguished between 'particular' and 'total' conceptions of ideology. 'Particular' ideologies are the ideas and beliefs of specific individuals, groups or parties, while 'total' ideologies encompass the entire *Weltanschauung*, or 'world-view', of a social class, society or even historical period. In this sense Marxism, liberal capitalism and Islamic fundamentalism can each be regarded as 'total' ideologies. Mannheim nevertheless held that *all* ideological systems, including utopias, are distorted, because each offers a partial and necessarily self-interested view of social reality. However he argued that the attempt to uncover objective truth need not be abandoned altogether. According to Mannheim, objectivity is strictly the preserve of the 'socially unattached intelligentsia', a class of intellectuals who alone can engage in disciplined and dispassionate enquiry because they have no economic interests of their own.

The subsequent career of the concept was deeply marked by the emergence of totalitarian dictatorships in the interwar period, and by the heightened ideological tensions of the Cold War of the 1950s and 1960s. Liberal theorists in particular portrayed the regimes that developed in Fascist Italy, Nazi Germany and Stalinist Russia as historically new and uniquely oppressive systems of rule, and highlighted the role played by 'official' ideologies in suppressing debate and criticism and promoting regimented obedience. Writers as different as Karl Popper (1902–94), Hannah Arendt (1906–75), J. L. Talmon and Bernard Crick, and the 'end of ideology' theorists examined in Chapter 11, came to use the term ideology in a highly restrictive manner, seeing fascism and communism as its prime examples. According to this usage, ideologies are 'closed' systems of thought, which, by claiming a monopoly of truth, refuse to tolerate opposing ideas and rival beliefs. Ideologies are thus 'secular religions'; they possess a 'totalising' character and serve as instruments of social control, ensuring compliance and subordination. However not all political creeds are ideologies by this standard. For instance liberalism, based as it is on a fundamental commitment to freedom, tolerance and diversity, is the clearest example of an 'open' system of thought (Popper, 1945).

A distinctively conservative concept of ideology can also be identified. This is based on a long-standing conservative distrust of abstract principles and philosophies, born out of a sceptical attitude towards rationalism and progress. The world is viewed as infinitely complex and largely beyond the capacity of the human mind to fathom. The foremost modern exponent of this view was the British political philosopher Michael Oakeshott (1901–90). 'In political activity', Oakeshott famously argued in *Rationalism in Politics* (1962), 'men sail a boundless and bottomless sea'. From this perspective ideologies are seen as abstract systems of thought, sets of ideas that are destined to simplify and distort social reality because they claim to explain what is, frankly, incomprehensible. Ideology is thus equated with dogmatism, fixed or doctrinaire beliefs that are divorced from the complexities of the real world. Conservatives have therefore rejected the 'ideological' style of politics, based on attempts to reshape the world in accordance with a set of abstract principles or pre-established theories. Until infected by the highly ideological politics of the new right, conservatives had preferred to adopt what Oakeshott called a 'traditionalist stance', which spurns ideology in favour of pragmatism, and looks to experience and history as the surest guides to human conduct.

## Pragmatism

Pragmatism refers generally to a concern with practical circumstances rather than theoretical beliefs, with what *can* be achieved in the real world, as opposed to what *should* be achieved in an ideal world. As a philosophical doctrine (most commonly associated with philosophers such as William James (1842–1910) and John Dewey (1859–1952) pragmatism holds that the meaning and justification of beliefs should be judged by their practical consequences. Though by definition a pragmatic style of politics is non-ideological, it does not amount to unprincipled opportunism. Pragmatism suggests a cautious attitude towards change that rejects sweeping reforms and revolution as a descent into the unknown, and prefers instead incremental adjustments and, perhaps, evolutionary progress.

Since the 1960s, however, the term ideology has gained a wider currency through being refashioned according to the needs of conventional social and political analysis. This has established ideology as a neutral and objective concept, the political baggage once attached to it having been removed. Martin Seliger (1976, p. 14), for example, defined an ideology as 'a set of ideas by which men posit, explain and justify the ends and means of organised social action, irrespective of whether such action aims to preserve, amend, uproot or rebuild a given social order'. An ideology is therefore an action-orientated system of thought. So defined, ideologies are neither good nor bad, true nor false, open nor closed, liberating nor oppressive – they can be all these things.

The clear merit of this social-scientific concept is that it is inclusive, in the sense that it can be applied to all 'isms', to liberalism as well as Marxism, to conservatism as well as fascism, and so on. The drawback of any negative concept of ideology is that it is highly restrictive. Marx saw liberal and conservative ideas as ideological but regarded his own as scientific; liberals classify communism and fascism as ideologies but refuse to accept that liberalism is one as well; traditional conservatives condemn liberalism, Marxism and fascism as ideological but portray conservatism as merely a 'disposition'. However, any neutral concept of ideology also has its dangers. In particular, in off-loading its political baggage the term may be rendered so bland and generalised that it loses its critical edge altogether. If ideology is interchangeable with terms such as 'belief system', 'world-view', 'doctrine' or 'political philosophy', what is the point of continuing to pretend that it has a separate and distinctive meaning? Two questions are especially important in this respect: what is the relationship between ideology and truth, and in what sense can ideology be seen as a form of power?

## Ideology, truth and power

Any short or single-sentence definition of ideology is likely to stimulate more questions than it answers. Nevertheless, it provides a useful and necessary starting point. In this book, ideology is understood as the following:

> An ideology is a more or less coherent set of ideas that provides the basis for organised political action, whether this is intended to preserve, modify or overthrow the existing system of power. All ideologies therefore (a) offer an account of the existing order, usually in the form of a 'world view', (b) provide the model of a desired future, a vision of the 'good society', and (c) outline how political change can and should be brought about.

This definition is neither original nor novel, and it is entirely in line with the social-scientific usage of the term. It nevertheless draws attention to some of the important and distinctive features of the phenomenon of ideology. In particular it emphasises that the complexity of ideology derives from the fact that it straddles the conventional boundaries between descriptive and normative thought, and between political theory and political practice. Ideology, in short, brings about two kinds of synthesis: between understanding and commitment, and between thought and action.

In relation to the first synthesis, the fusion of understanding and commitment, ideology blurs the distinction between what 'is' and what 'should be'. Ideologies are descriptive in that, in effect, they provide individuals and groups with an intellectual map of how their society works and, more broadly, with a general view of the world. This, for instance, helps to explain the important integrative capacity of ideology, its ability to 'situate' people within a particular social environment. However such descriptive understanding is deeply embedded within a set of normative or prescriptive beliefs, both about the adequacy of present social arrangements and about the nature of any alternative or future society. Ideology therefore has a powerful emotional or affective character: it is a means of expressing hopes and fears, sympathies and hatreds, as well as of articulating beliefs and understanding.

As (a) and (b) above are linked, 'facts' in ideologies inevitably tend to merge into and become confused with 'values'. One of the implications of this is that no clear distinction can be made between ideology and science. In this light it is helpful to treat ideologies as paradigms, in the sense employed by Thomas Kuhn in *The Structure of Scientific Revolutions* (1962). An ideology, then, can be seen as a set of principles, doctrines and theories that help to structure the process of intellectual enquiry. In effect it constitutes a framework within which the search for political knowledge takes place, a language of political discourse. For instance much of academic political science and, still more clearly, mainstream economics draws upon individualist and rationalist assumptions that have an unmistakable liberal heritage. The notion of ideology as an intellectual framework or political language is also important because it highlights the depth at which ideology structures human understanding. The tendency to deny that one's own beliefs are ideological (often while condemning other people for committing precisely this sin) can be explained by the fact that, in providing the very concepts through which the world becomes intelligible, our ideology is effectively invisible. We fail or refuse to recognise that we look at the world through a veil of theories, presuppositions and assumptions that shape what we see and thereby impose meaning on the world.

The second synthesis, the fusion of thought and action, reflected in the linkage between (b) and (c) above, is no less significant. Seliger (1976) drew attention to this when referring to what he called the 'fundamental' and 'operative' levels of ideology. At a fundamental level, ideologies resemble political philosophies in that they deal with abstract ideas and theories, and their proponents may at times seem to be engaged in dispassionate enquiry. Although the term 'ideologue' is often reserved for crude or self-conscious supporters of particular ideologies, respected political philosophers such as John Locke (see p. 38), John Stuart Mill (see p. 30) and Friedrich Hayek (see p. 94) each worked within and contributed to ideological traditions. At an operative level, however, ideologies take the form of broad political movements, engaged in popular mobilisation and the struggle for power. Ideology in this guise may be expressed in sloganising, political rhetoric, party manifestos and government policies. While ideologies must, strictly speaking, be both idea-orientated and action-orientated, certain ideologies are undoubtedly stronger on one level than the other. For instance fascism has always emphasised operative goals and, if you like, the politics of the deed. Anarchism, on the other hand, especially since the mid-twentieth century, has largely survived at a fundamental or philosophical level.

Nevertheless ideologies invariably lack the clear shape and internal consistency of political philosophies; they are only more or less coherent. This apparent shapelessness stems in part from the fact that ideologies are not hermetically sealed systems of thought; rather they are, typically, fluid sets of ideas that overlap with other ideologies and shade into one another. This not only fosters ideological development but also leads to the emergence of hybrids in the form of liberal conservatism, socialist feminism, conservative nationalism and so on. Moreover each ideology contains a range of divergent, even rival traditions and viewpoints. Not uncommonly, disputes between supporters of the same ideology are more passionate and bitter than arguments between supporters of rival ideologies, because what is at stake is the true nature of the ideology in question – what is 'true' socialism, 'true' liberalism or 'true' anarchism? Such conflicts, both between and within ideological traditions, are made more confusing by the fact that they are often played out with the use of the same political vocabulary, each side investing terms such as 'freedom', 'democracy', 'justice' and 'equality' with their own meanings. This highlights the problem of what W. B. Gallie (1955–6, p. 169) termed 'essentially contested concepts'. These are concepts about which there is such deep controversy that no settled or agreed definition can ever be developed. In this sense, the concept of ideology is certainly 'essentially contested', as indeed are the other terms examined in the 'Perspectives on. . .' boxes.

Clearly, however, there must be a limit to the incoherence or shapelessness of ideologies. There must be a point at which, by abandoning a particularly cherished principle or embracing a previously derided theory, an ideology loses its identity or, perhaps, is absorbed into a rival ideology. Could liberalism remain liberalism if it abandoned its commitment to liberty? Would socialism any longer be socialism if it developed an appetite for violence and war? One way of dealing with this problem, following Michael Freeden (1996, pp. 75–91), is to highlight the morphology, the form and structure, of an ideology in terms of its key concepts, in the same way that the arrangement of furniture in a room helps us to distinguish between a kitchen, a bedroom, a lounge and so on. Each ideology is therefore characterised by a cluster of core, adjacent and peripheral concepts, not all of which need be present for a theory or a doctrine to be recognised as belonging to that ideology. A kitchen, for instance, does not cease to be a kitchen simply because the sink or the cooker is removed. Similarly a kitchen remains a kitchen over time despite the arrival of new inventions such as dishwashers and microwave ovens. Individualism, liberty and human rationality, for example, could be identified as liberalism's nexus of core concepts. The absence of any one of them need not compromise a doctrine's liberal credentials, but the absence of two of them would suggest the emergence of a new ideological configuration.

What does this tell us about the relationship between ideology and truth? For Marx, as we have seen, ideology was the implacable enemy of truth. Falsehood is implicit in ideology because, being the creation of the ruling class, its purpose is to disguise exploitation and oppression. Nevertheless, as Mannheim recognised, to follow Marx in believing that the proletariat needs no illusion or ideology is to accept a highly romanticised view of the working masses as the emancipators of humankind. However Mannheim's own solution to this problem, a faith in free-floating intellectuals, does not get us much further. All people's views are shaped, consciously or unconsciously, by broader social and cultural factors, and while education may enable them to defend these views more fluently and persuasively, there is little evidence that it makes those views any less subjective or any more dispassionate.

This implies that there exists no objective standard of truth against which ideologies can be judged. Indeed to suggest that ideologies can be deemed to be either true or false is to miss the vital point that they embody values, dreams and aspirations that are, by their very nature, not

---

**Perspectives on . . .**

## Ideology

**Liberals**, particularly during the Cold War period, have viewed ideology as an officially sanctioned belief system that claims a monopoly of truth, often through a spurious claim to be scientific. Ideology is therefore inherently repressive, even totalitarian; its prime examples are communism and fascism.

**Conservatives** have traditionally regarded ideology as a manifestation of the arrogance of rationalism. Ideologies are elaborate systems of thought that are dangerous or unreliable because, being abstracted from reality, they establish principles and goals that lead to repression or are simply unachievable. In this light, socialism and liberalism are clearly ideological.

**Socialists**, following Marx, have seen ideology as a body of ideas that conceal the contradictions of class society, thereby promoting false consciousness and political passivity amongst subordinate classes. Liberalism is the classic ruling-class ideology. Later Marxists adopted a neutral concept of ideology, regarding it as the distinctive ideas of any social class, including the working class.

**Fascists** are often dismissive of ideology as an oversystematic, dry and intellectualised form of political understanding that is based on mere reason rather than passion and the will. The Nazis preferred to portray their own ideas as a *Weltanschauung* or 'world view', not as a systematic philosophy.

**Ecologists** have tended to regard all conventional political doctrines as part of a super-ideology of industrialism. Ideology is thus tainted by its association with arrogant humanism and growth-orientated economics – liberalism and socialism being its most obvious examples.

**Fundamentalists** have treated key religious texts as ideology, on the grounds that, by expressing the revealed word of God, they provide a programme for comprehensive social reconstruction. Secular ideologies are therefore rejected because they are not founded on religious principles and so lack moral substance.

susceptible to scientific analysis. No one can 'prove' that one theory of justice is preferable to any other, any more than rival conceptions of human nature can be tested by surgical intervention to demonstrate once and for all that human beings possess rights, are entitled to freedom, or are naturally selfish or naturally sociable. At the end of the day, ideologies are embraced less because they stand up to scrutiny and logical analysis, and more because they help individuals, groups and societies to make sense of the world in which they live. As Andrew Vincent (1995, p. 20) put it, 'We examine ideology as fellow travellers, not as neutral observers'.

Nevertheless ideologies undoubtedly embody a claim to uncover truth; in this sense they can be seen as 'regimes of truth'. By providing us with a language of political discourse, a set of assumptions and presuppositions about how society does and should work, ideology structures both what we think and how we act. As a 'regime of truth', ideology is always linked to power. In a world of competing truths, values and theories, ideologies seek to prioritise certain values over others, and to invest legitimacy in particular theories or sets of meanings. Furthermore, as ideologies provide an intellectual maps of the social world, they help to establish the relationship between individuals and groups on the one hand and the larger structure of power on the other. Ideologies therefore play a crucial role in either upholding the prevailing power structure, by portraying it as fair, natural, rightful or whatever, or in weakening or challenging it, by highlighting its iniquities or injustices and drawing attention to the attractions of alternative power structures.

## Left, right and centre

Many attempts have been made to categorise political ideas and ideologies, and to relate them to one another. The most familiar and firmly established method of doing this is the left–right political spectrum. This is a linear spectrum that locates political beliefs at some point between two extremes, the far left and the far right. Terms such as 'left wing' or 'right wing' are widely used to sum up a person's political beliefs or position, and groups of people are referred to collectively as 'the left', 'the right' and indeed 'the centre'. There is also broad agreement about where different ideas and ideologies are located along this spectrum. Most people would recognise the spectrum depicted in Figure 1.1.

Although familiar, it is far more difficult to establish precisely what the spectrum means and how helpful it is in defining and describing political views. The origin of the terms 'left' and 'right' dates back to the French Revolution and the seating arrangements adopted by the different groups at the first meeting of the Estates-General in 1789. Aristocrats who

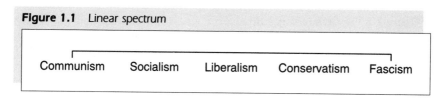

**Figure 1.1**   Linear spectrum

Communism    Socialism    Liberalism    Conservatism    Fascism

supported the king sat to his right, while radicals, members of the Third Estate, sat to his left. A similar seating pattern was followed in the subsequent French Assemblies. The term 'right' was soon understood to mean reactionary or monarchist, and the term 'left' implied revolutionary or egalitarian sympathies. In contemporary politics, however, the left–right divide has become increasingly complex and no longer reflects a simple choice between revolution and reaction. For example, although right-wing views may often be reactionary and preach a return to an earlier and better time, fascism, on the extreme right, has also been revolutionary, and in the case of Italian fascism, positively forward-looking. Similarly, although left-wing views have usually been progressive or revolutionary, socialists and communists have at times resisted change. For instance they have sought to defend the welfare state, or to prevent centrally planned economies from being reformed or abolished.

The linear spectrum is commonly understood to reflect different political values or contrasting views about economic policy. In terms of values, the spectrum is sometimes said to reflect different attitudes towards equality. Left-wingers are committed to equality and are optimistic about the possibility of achieving it. Right-wingers typically reject equality as either undesirable or impossible to achieve. This is closely related to different attitudes towards the economy, and in particular the ownership of wealth. Communists, on the far left, have believed in a state planned economy; socialists and modern liberals have defended the mixed economy and government regulation; right-wing conservatives are committed to free-market capitalism and private property. All such interpretations, however, involve inconsistencies. For instance, fascist regimes have practised economic management and state control, despite being on the far right of the spectrum. Moreover it is unclear where anarchism should be placed on the linear spectrum. Anarchists are strongly committed to the idea of equality, which would normally place them on the far left of the spectrum, but their opposition to all forms of economic management and any form of government may suggest that they should be on the far right.

The weakness of the linear spectrum is that it tries to reduce politics to a single dimension, and suggests that political views can be classified according to merely one criterion, be it one's attitude to change, view of equality or economic philosophy. Political ideologies are in fact highly complex collections of beliefs, values and doctrines, which any kind of

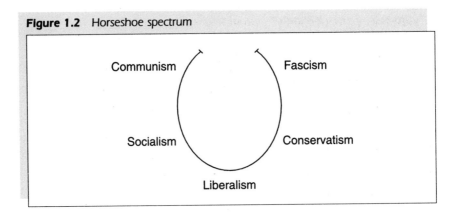

**Figure 1.2**  Horseshoe spectrum

spectrum is forced to oversimplify. Attempts have nevertheless been made to develop more sophisticated political spectrums that embody two or more dimensions. The linear spectrum, for example, has sometimes been criticised because the ideologies at its extremes, communism and fascism, exhibit similarities. In particular, communist and fascist regimes have both developed repressive, authoritarian forms of political rule, which some have described as 'totalitarian' (see p. 233). As a result, an alternative political spectrum might be horseshoe-shaped, indicating that the extreme points on the left and the right tend to converge, distinguishing both from the 'democratic' beliefs of liberalism, socialism and conservatism (Figure 1.2).

This spectrum, however, has also been criticised. The similarities between communism and fascism may be more apparent than real. Certainly the values for which the two ideologies stand are fundamentally different. Communism extols the virtues of cooperation, common owner-ship and classlessness, while fascism proclaims the importance of disci-pline, order and unquestioning obedience. Also, in some respects Nazi Germany was very different from Stalinist Russia: for example capitalism thrived under Hitler, at least until the final years of the war, while it was swiftly and brutally eradicated under Stalin. From this point of view the horseshoe spectrum can perhaps be seen as one of the products of Cold War ideology, in other words, as an attempt to condemn communism by equating it with its 'totalitarian' partner, fascism.

Another spectrum was proposed by Hans Eysenck in *Sense and Nonsense in Psychology* (1964). Eysenck took the conventional left–right spectrum as the horizontal axis of his spectrum, but added a vertical axis that measured political attitudes that were at one extreme 'tough minded' or authoritarian, and at the other 'tender minded' or democratic. Political ideas can therefore be positioned on both the left–right axis and the 'tough' and 'tender' axis. In this case the differences between, for instance, Nazism

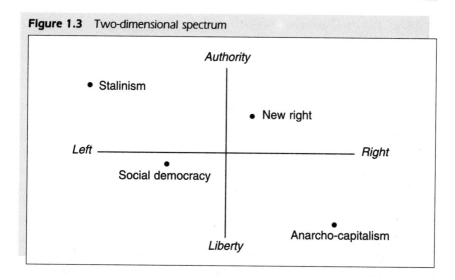

**Figure 1.3** Two-dimensional spectrum

and Stalinism can be made clear by placing these at opposite extremes of the left–right axis, while their similarities can be emphasised by placing both firmly at the 'tough minded' extreme of the vertical axis (Figure 1.3).

However all such spectrums raise difficulties because they tend to simplify and generalise highly complex sets of political ideas. At best, they are a shorthand method of describing political ideas or beliefs, and must always be used with caution. In fact a growing body of literature advocates abandoning the left–right divide altogether. As Giddens (1994) pointed out, the emergence of new political issues such as feminism, animal rights and the environment has rendered the conventional ideas of left and right largely redundant. The green movement stated this boldly in adopting slogans such as 'not left or right but ahead'. The shift away from old class polarities has also furthered this process, leading to a situation in which, for instance, conservatives have developed a growing taste for radicalism and ideological politics, and socialists have evinced an enthusiasm for competition and the market. In sharp contrast, however, Norberto Bobbio (1996) has argued that, since left and right essentially reflect different attitudes towards equality, the terms are far from irrelevant in a world characterised by new patterns of societal inequality and widening global inequalities.

## The rise and fall of ideologies

This book examines the principal ideas and doctrines of modern political thought. It is organised around the major ideologies that have dominated political life during the last two hundred years, and considers each ideology in turn. Each chapter starts with an introduction, which looks at the origins and development of the ideology and considers both its historical and contemporary significance. The second section examines the central themes of the ideology, its core values, principles and theories. In so doing it attempts to distinguish liberals from socialists, conservatives from a fascists and so on. Subsequent sections analyse the divergent and sometimes conflicting traditions that have emerged within the ideology, or explore in greater detail themes or issues that have been particularly crucial to the ideology.

The ideologies considered in this book are, in origin at least, 'western ideologies', that is, they arose first in Europe and North America as a result of the process of modernisation. They have, however, subsequently become 'world ideologies', largely because of the struggle against colonial rule and the desire for material and political progress in the developing world. The process of modernisation in the West, out of which these ideologies emerged, was simultaneously economic, political and cultural. Society had previously been simple and agricultural, based upon a feudal social order in which land was the principal source of wealth. Social positions were fixed and largely determined by birth; at the top was a landed aristocracy and beneath them the mass of 'bonded' serfs or peasants. Political power was vested in the hands of absolute monarchs, who ruled in association with powerful landed interests. Life in such societies was understood in terms of unchanging and usually natural relationships. The dominant influence on intellectual life in feudal times was religion. The right of the king to rule, for example, was rarely challenged because it was accepted that he had been chosen by God and so ruled with divine authority.

Between the sixteenth and nineteenth centuries the structures and certainties of feudal life broke down in the face of a series of revolutions. The first of these was a commercial revolution, in which food and other goods started to be produced not to satisfy a particular estate or village, but to be sold in the marketplace. This led to the emergence of an increasingly market-orientated capitalist economy. By the mid eighteenth century, starting in Britain, an industrial revolution had commenced in which traditional craft skills and manual labour were gradually replaced by more efficient and technological methods of machine and factory production. The productive capacity of society was enormously expanded and the social order became progressively more complex and diverse. A rising middle class of businessmen and industrialists developed, as did a new class of industrial workers. These social and economic upheavals were accompanied by a series of political revolutions. The English Revolution of the seventeenth century divested the king of absolute power and led to the emergence of the first ideas of constitutional government. The American

Revolution of 1776 overthrew British rule and produced a republican system of government based upon federal and constitutional principles. The most significant revolution of all, the French Revolution of 1789, swept aside monarchical absolutism in the name of the modern ideas of 'liberty, equality and fraternity'.

These political and social upheavals were accompanied by major cultural changes, notably the spread of Enlightenment ideas and views. The Enlightenment was an eighteenth-century intellectual movement that challenged traditional beliefs in religion, politics and learning in general, and sought to establish the supremacy of science and reason. It threw up new ways of thinking about society, and in particular it offered the prospect of onward and upward progress based upon supposedly universal values such as democracy and freedom. By the early nineteenth century most of the modern political ideologies had emerged. The major ideologies considered in Chapters 2–4 – liberalism, conservatism and socialism – developed as contrasting responses to the process of modernisation. Although liberalism and socialism were both very clearly children of the Enlightenment, they offered starkly contrasting interpretations of the emerging industrial society. While liberals supported the growth of industrial capitalism, socialists argued that capitalism was merely another class-based society, founded upon injustice. Conservatives, for their part, sought to defend and uphold the traditional social order. The ideas of nationalism, anarchism and feminism were also born out of this period of political, social and cultural transformation. Although fascism and Soviet communism did not emerge until the First World War, both drew heavily upon nineteenth-century ideas and doctrines. Even the most 'modern' ideology considered here, ecologism, has roots in the nineteenth-century backlash against industrialisation.

The expansion of colonial rule between 1870 and 1914 gave these western ideologies a worldwide significance. In much of the developing world, twentieth-century politics have been shaped by the struggle against colonialism and the subsequent tasks of nation building, which have been conducted in language largely inherited from the West. However ideologies such as socialism and nationalism, and ideas such as democracy and revolution, have not retained their original meanings. Western ideas have been reinterpreted and reapplied in very different circumstances and linked to very different political ends. For instance African and Arab socialism owe as much to traditional social and religious values as they do to classical socialist doctrines. In other cases, developing-world ideologies have been non-western and even anti-western, as reflected in the rising importance of political Islam, which now stands as a major rival to both liberalism and socialism in many parts of Africa and Asia. At the same time western ideologies have been reinvigorated by the growing impact of developments in what used to be called the Third World. For example in the 1960s the new left was profoundly influenced by national liberation struggles in Asia, Africa and Latin America, and by the theories of guerrilla warfare developed by Mao Zedong and Che Guevara. Similarly, modern ecologism has been inspired by Gandhi's philosophy of non-violence and the self-sufficiency of traditional Indian village life.

If the age of ideologies can be said to date from 1789 and the outbreak of the French Revolution, some would argue that it lasted precisely 200 years and culminated with the collapse of communism in the eastern European revolutions of 1989. The idea of the end of ideology is examined in the final chapter. What cannot be doubted, however, is that as the century, indeed the millennium, draws to an end, the various ideological traditions have been confronted by a daunting range of new challenges. For instance globalisation has diminished the importance of political and ideological projects built around the needs of the nation. The emergence of global capitalism has resulted in intensified marketisation, as reflected in the remorseless advance of commercialisation and technological change. The weakening of class and other social solidarities and the decline of deference and respect for authority have led to a process of individualisation. The impact such challenges will have on the major ideologies is far from certain. For example, while some have proclaimed the worldwide triumph of western liberal democracy, others have announced the collapse of the entire Enlightenment project and looked to sources such as Islamic fundamentalism, Confucianism or Buddhism for future ideological developments. Similarly some commentators subscribe to a form of millenarianism and look to the new century to bring widening understanding and deepening harmony, while others see only the prospect of conflict and bloodshed, particularly through the spread of ethnic nationalism and other particularisms. The final section of each chapter attempts to shed some light on such matters by reflecting on the prospects for the ideology in the twenty-first century.

## Millenarianism

Millenarianism (sometimes called chiliasm) is the belief in a future thousand-year period of divine rule on Earth, which will be inaugurated by Christ's second coming. As such it is associated with heightened expectations and great religious excitement. Extended to politics, millenarianism refers to any doctrine that promises sudden and complete emancipation, in particular release from political oppression and social misery. The Marxist belief in a classless, communist society and the anarchist goal of a stateless society can both be seen as examples of millenarianism, as can certain kinds of nationalism. Political millenarianism is a form of utopianism (see p. 193).

# Further reading

Freeden, M., *Ideologies and Political Theory: A Conceptual Approach* (Oxford: Clarendon Press, 1996). An examination of the major ideologies that pays particular attention to their conceptual morphology.

*Journal of Political Ideologies* (Abingdon, UK and Cambridge, Mass., USA: Carfax). A journal, published since 1996, that analyses the nature of political ideology and examines concrete ideological traditions; demanding but wide-ranging and authoritative.

Larrain, J., *Marxism and Ideology* (London: Macmillan, 1983). A very useful analysis of the use of the concept within the Marxist tradition.

McLellan, D., *Ideology* (Milton Keynes: Open University, 1986). A clear and short yet comprehensive discussion of this elusive concept.

Seliger, M., *Ideology and Politics* (London: Allen & Unwin, 1976). A very thorough account of ideology, considered by some to be the classic treatment of the subject.

Thompson, J. B., *Studies in the Theory of Ideology* (Cambridge: Polity Press, 1984). A good introduction to debates about the nature and significance of ideology.

# Chapter 2

# Liberalism

Origins and development
The primacy of the individual – central themes
Liberalism and democracy
Classical liberalism
Modern liberalism
Liberalism in the twenty-first century

## Origins and development

The term 'liberal' has been in use since the fourteenth century but has had a wide variety of meanings. The Latin *liber* referred to a class of free men, in other words, men who were neither serfs nor slaves. It has meant generous, as in 'liberal' helpings of food and drink; or, in reference to social attitudes, it has implied openness or open-mindedness. It also came to be increasingly associated with ideas of freedom and choice. The term 'liberalism' to denote a political allegiance made its appearance much later: it was not used until the early part of the nineteenth century, being first employed in Spain in 1812. By the 1840s the term was widely recognised throughout Europe in relation to a distinctive set of political ideas. However it was taken up more slowly in the UK: although the Whigs started to call themselves Liberals during the 1830s, the first distinctly Liberal government was not formed until Gladstone took office in 1868.

As a systematic political creed, liberalism may not have existed before the nineteenth century, but it was based upon ideas and theories that had developed during the previous three hundred years. Liberal ideas resulted from the breakdown of feudalism in Europe and the growth, in its place, of a market or capitalist society. In many respects liberalism reflected the aspirations of the rising middle classes, whose interests conflicted with the established power of absolute monarchs and the landed aristocracy. Liberal ideas were radical, they sought fundamental reform and even, at times, revolutionary change. The English Revolution of the seventeenth century and the American and French Revolutions of the late eighteenth century each embodied elements that were distinctively liberal, even though the word 'liberal' was not at the time used in a political sense.

Liberals challenged the absolute power of the monarchy, supposedly based upon the doctrine of the 'divine right of kings'. In place of absolutism they advocated constitutional and, later, representative government. Liberals criticised the political and economic privileges of the landed aristocracy and the unfairness of a feudal system in which social position was determined by the 'accident of birth'. They also supported the movement towards freedom of conscience in religion and questioned the authority of the established church.

The nineteenth century was in many ways the liberal century. As industrialisation spread throughout western countries, liberal ideas triumphed. Liberals advocated an industrialised and market economic order 'free' from government interference, in which businesses would be allowed to pursue profit and nations encouraged to trade freely with one another. Such a system of industrial capitalism developed first in the UK from the mid eighteenth century onwards, and was well-established by the early nineteenth century. It subsequently spread to North America and throughout Europe, initially into western Europe and then, more gradually, into eastern Europe. During the twentieth century industrial capitalism exerted a powerful appeal for developing countries in Africa, Asia and Latin America, especially when social and political development was defined in essentially western terms. However developing-world states have sometimes been resistant to the attractions of liberal capitalism because their political cultures have emphasised community rather than the individual. In such cases they have provided more fertile ground for the growth of socialism or nationalism rather than western liberalism. Where capitalism has been successfully established, as in Japan, it has tended to assume a corporate rather than an individualistic character. Japanese industry, for example, is motivated more by traditional ideas of group loyalty and duty than by the pursuit of individual self-interest.

Western political systems have also been shaped by liberal ideas and values, so much so that they are commonly classified as liberal democracies. These systems are constitutional in that they seek to limit government power and safeguard civil liberties, and are representative in the sense that political office is gained through competitive elections. Developing first in western Europe and North America, liberal democracy subsequently took root in parts of the developing world and, after the revolutions of 1989–91, in eastern Europe too. In some cases western-style liberal regimes were bequeathed to African or Asian countries upon achieving independence, but with varying degrees of success. India remains the world's largest liberal democracy. Elsewhere, however, liberal democratic systems have sometimes collapsed in the absence of industrial capitalism or because of the nature of the indigenous political culture. In contrast the political cultures of most western countries are built upon a bedrock of liberal-capitalist values. Ideas such as freedom of speech, freedom of religious worship and the right to own property, all drawn from liberalism, are so deeply ingrained in western societies that they are seldom challenged openly or even questioned.

In effect liberalism has come to be the dominant ideology of the industrialised West. Some political thinkers have even argued that there is a necessary and inevitable link between liberalism and capitalism. This has been suggested by liberalism's critics as well as its supporters. Marxists, for instance, have suggested that liberal ideas simply reflect the economic interests of a 'ruling class' of property owners within capitalist society; they portray liberalism as the classic example of 'bourgeois ideology'. On the other hand thinkers such as Friedrich Hayek (see p. 94) have argued that economic freedom – the right to own, use and dispose of private property – is an essential guarantee of political liberty. Hayek therefore claimed that a liberal democratic political system and respect for civil liberties can only develop in the context of a capitalist economic order.

Nevertheless historical developments in the nineteenth and twentieth centuries clearly influenced the substance of liberal ideology. The character of liberalism changed as the 'rising middle classes' succeeded in establishing their economic and political dominance. The radical, even revolutionary edge of liberalism faded with each liberal success. Liberalism thus became increasingly conservative, standing less for change and reform, and more for the maintenance of existing – largely liberal – institutions. Liberal ideas, too, could not stand still. From the late nineteenth century onwards the progress of industrialisation led liberals to question, and in some ways to revise, the ideas of early liberalism.

Whereas early liberals had wanted government to interfere as little as possible in the lives of its citizens, modern liberals came to believe that government should be responsible for delivering welfare services such as health, housing, pensions and education, as well as for managing, or at least regulating, the economy. This led to the development of two traditions of thought within liberalism, commonly called classical liberalism and modern liberalism. As a result, some commentators have argued that liberalism is an incoherent ideology, embracing contradictory beliefs, notably about the desirable role of the state. On the other hand, in common with all political ideologies, liberalism has been subject to change as its basic principles have been applied to changing historical circumstances. No political ideology is rigid or monolithic, all encompass a range of views and even rival traditions. There is nevertheless an underlying coherence and unity at the heart of liberal thought in the form of a fundamental commitment to the importance of individual freedom and to the principles that flow from individualism.

## The primacy of the individual – central themes

Liberalism is, in a sense, the ideology of the industrialised West. So deeply have liberal ideas permeated political, economic and cultural life that their influence can become hard to discern, liberalism appearing to be indistinguishable from 'western civilisation' in general. Indeed it became fashionable to portray liberalism not simply as an ideology but as a 'meta-ideology', that is, as a body of rules that lays down the grounds upon which political and ideological debate can take place. This reflects the belief that liberalism gives priority to 'the right' over 'the good'. In other words liberalism strives to establish the conditions in which people and groups can pursue the good life as each defines it, but it does not prescribe or try to promote any particular notion of what is good. By portraying liberalism as morally neutral, such a view suggests that its ideas and values have a potentially universal appeal. No one, it appears, needs to fear the advance of liberalism, as liberals treat the interests of all members of society as equal. This does not, however, mean that liberalism is simply a philosophy of 'do your own thing'. While liberalism undoubtedly favours openness, debate and self-determination, it is also characterised by a powerful moral thrust. The moral and ideological stance of liberalism is embodied in a commitment to a distinctive set of values and beliefs. The most important of these are the following:

- The individual
- Freedom
- Reason
- Justice
- Toleration.

### The individual

In the modern world the concept of the individual is so familiar that its political significance is often overlooked. In the feudal period there was little idea of individuals having their own interests or possessing personal and unique identities. Rather people were seen as members of the social groups to which they belonged: their family, village, local community or social class. Their lives and identities were largely determined by the character of these groups in a process that changed little from one generation to the next. However as feudalism broke down, individuals were confronted by a broader range of choices and social possibilities. They were encouraged, perhaps for the first time, to think for themselves, and to think of themselves in personal terms. A serf, for example, whose family may always have lived and worked on the same piece of land, became a 'free man' and acquired some ability to choose who to work for, or maybe the opportunity to leave the land altogether and look for work in the growing towns or cities.

As the certainties of feudal life broke down a new intellectual climate emerged. Rational and scientific explanations gradually displaced traditional religious theories, and society was increasingly understood from the viewpoint of the human individual. Individuals were thought to possess personal and distinctive qualities: each was of special value. This was evident in the growth of natural rights theories in the seventeenth and eighteenth centuries. These suggested that individuals were invested with a set of God-given, natural rights, defined by John Locke (see p. 38) as 'life, liberty and property'. The individual alone possesses such rights, and in that sense is more important than any social group. Natural rights theorists therefore argued that society should be constructed so as to afford protection to individual interests and needs. The German philosopher Immanuel Kant (1724–1804) expressed a similar belief in the dignity and equal worth of human beings in his conception of individuals as 'ends in themselves' and not merely as means for the achievement of the ends of others.

This belief in the primacy of the individual is the characteristic theme of liberal ideology and has had important implications for liberal thought. It has led some liberals to view society as simply a collection of individuals, each seeking to satisfy his or her own needs and interests. Such a view has been called atomistic, in that it conceives of individuals as 'isolated atoms' within society; indeed it can lead to the belief that 'society' itself does not exist, but is merely a collection of self-sufficient individuals. Such extreme individualism is based upon the assumption that the individual is egotistical, essentially self-seeking and largely self-reliant. C. B. Macpherson (1973, p. 199) characterised early liberalism as 'possessive individualism' because, he argued, it regarded the individual as 'the proprietor of his own

---

### Individualism

Individualism is the belief in the supreme importance of the individual over any social group or collective body. In the form of methodological individualism, this suggests that the individual is central to any political theory or social explanation – all statements about society should be made in terms of the individuals who compose it. Ethical individualism, on the other hand, implies that society should be constructed so as to benefit to the individual, giving moral priority to individual rights, needs or interests. Classical liberals and the new right subscribe to a form of egoistical individualism that emphasises self-interestedness and self-reliance. Modern liberals and socialists, though, may temper this by acknowledging the importance of social responsibility and altruism.

person or capacities, owing nothing to society for them'. In contrast later liberals have held a more optimistic view of human nature, and have been more prepared to believe that individuals possess a social responsibility for one another, especially for those who are unable to look after themselves. Whether human nature is conceived of as being egoistical or altruistic, liberals are united in their desire to create a society in which each person is capable of developing and flourishing to the fullness of his or her potential.

## Freedom

A belief in the supreme importance of the individual leads naturally to a commitment to individual freedom. Individual liberty (liberty and freedom being interchangeable) is for liberals the supreme political value, and in many ways the unifying principle within liberal ideology. For early liberals, liberty was a natural right, an essential requirement for leading a truly human existence. It also gave individuals the opportunity to pursue their own interests by exercising choice: the choice of where to live, who to work for, what to buy and so forth. Later liberals have seen liberty as the only condition in which people are able to develop their skills and talents and fulfil their potential.

Nevertheless liberals do not accept that individuals have an absolute entitlement to freedom. If liberty is unlimited it can become 'licence', the right to abuse others. In *On Liberty* ([1859] 1972, p. 73) John Stuart Mill (see p. 30) argued that 'the only purpose for which power can be rightfully exercised over any member of a civilised community, against his will, is to prevent harm to others'. Mill's position is libertarian (see p. 89) in that it accepts only the most minimal restrictions on individual freedom, and then in order to prevent 'harm to others'. He distinguished clearly between actions that are 'self-regarding', over which individuals should exercise absolute freedom, and those that are 'other-regarding', which can restrict the freedom of others or do them damage. Mill did not accept any restrictions on the individual that are designed to prevent a person from damaging himself or herself, either physically or morally. Such a view suggests, for example, that laws forcing car drivers to put on seat belts or motor cyclists to wear crash helmets are as unacceptable as any form of censorship that limits what an individual may read or listen to. Radical libertarians may defend the right of people to use addictive drugs such as heroin and cocaine on the same grounds. Although the individual may be sovereign over his or her body and mind, each must respect the fact that every other individual enjoys an equal right to liberty. This has been expressed by the modern liberal John Rawls (see p. 35) in the principle that everyone is entitled to the widest possible liberty consistent with a like liberty for all.

## John Stuart Mill (1806–73)

UK philosopher, economist and politician. Mill was subjected to an intense and austere regime of education by his father, the utilitarian theorist James Mill, resulting in a mental collapse at the age of 20. He went on to found and edit the *London Review* and was MP for Westminster from 1865 to 1881.

Mill's varied and complex work was crucial to the development of liberalism because in many ways it straddled the divide between classical and modern theories. His opposition to collectivist tendencies and traditions was firmly rooted in nineteenth-century principles, but his emphasis on the quality of individual life, reflected in a commitment to 'individuality', as well as his sympathy for causes such as female suffrage and, later, workers' cooperatives, looked forward to twentieth-century developments. Mill's major writings include *On Liberty* (1859), *Considerations on Representative Government* (1861) and *The Subjection of Women* (1869).

Although liberals agree about the value of liberty, they have not always agreed about what it means for an individual to be 'free'. In his 'Two Concepts of Liberty' ([1958] 1969), Isaiah Berlin distinguished between a 'negative' theory of liberty and a 'positive' one. Early or classical liberals have believed that freedom consists in each person being left alone, free from interference and able to act in whatever way they may choose. This conception of liberty is 'negative' in that it is based upon the absence of external restrictions or constraints upon the individual. Modern liberals, on the other hand, have been attracted to a more 'positive' conception of liberty, defined by Berlin as the ability to be one's own master, to be autonomous. Self-mastery requires that the individual is able to develop skills and talents, broaden his or her understanding, and gain fulfilment. For John Stuart Mill, for example, liberty meant much more than simply being free from outside constraints: it involved the capacity of human beings to develop and ultimately achieve self-realisation. These rival conceptions of liberty have not merely stimulated academic debate within liberalism, but have led liberals to hold very different views about the desirable relationship between the individual and the state.

### Reason

The liberal case for freedom is closely linked to a faith in reason. Liberalism is, and remains, very much part of the Enlightenment project. The central theme of the Enlightenment was the desire to release humankind from its bondage to superstition and ignorance, and unleash an 'age of reason'. Key Enlightened thinkers included Jean-Jacques

## Perspectives on . . .

### Freedom

**Liberals** give priority to freedom as the supreme individualist value. While classical liberals support negative freedom, understood as the absence of constraints or freedom of choice, modern liberals advocate positive freedom in the sense of personal development and human flourishing.

**Conservatives** have traditionally endorsed a weak view of freedom as the willing recognition of duties and responsibilities, negative freedom posing a threat to the fabric of society. The new right, however, endorses negative freedom in the economic sphere, freedom of choice in the marketplace.

**Socialists** have generally understood freedom in positive terms to refer to self-fulfilment achieved through either free creative labour or cooperative social interaction. Social democrats have drawn close to modern liberalism in treating freedom as the realisation of individual potential.

**Anarchists** regard freedom as an absolute value, believing it to be irreconcilable with any form of political authority. Freedom is understood to mean the achievement of personal autonomy, not merely being 'left alone' but being rationally self-willed and self-directed.

**Fascists** reject any form of individual liberty as a nonsense. 'True' freedom, in contrast, means unquestioning submission to the will of the leader and the absorption of the individual into the national community.

**Ecologists**, particularly deep ecologists, treat freedom as the achievement of oneness, self-realisation through the absorption of the personal ego into the ecosphere or universe. In contrast with political freedom, this is sometimes seen as 'inner' freedom, freedom as self-actualisation.

**Fundamentalists** see freedom as essentially an inner or spiritual quality. Freedom means conformity to the revealed will of God, spiritual fulfilment being associated with submission to religious authority.

Rousseau (see p. 163), Immanuel Kant, Adam Smith (see p. 52) and Jeremy Bentham (see p. 51). Enlightenment rationalism influenced liberalism in a number of ways. In the first place it strengthened its faith in both the individual and in liberty. To the extent that human beings are rational, thinking creatures, they are capable of defining and pursuing their own best interests. By no means do liberals believe that individuals are infallible in this respect, but the belief in reason builds into liberalism a strong bias against paternalism. Not only does paternalism prevent individuals from making their own moral choices and, if necessary, from learning from their

---

### Rationalism

Rationalism is the belief that the world has a rational structure, and that this can be disclosed through the exercise of human reason and critical enquiry. As a philosophical theory, rationalism is the belief that knowledge flows from reason rather than experience, and thus contrasts with empiricism. As a general principle, however, rationalism places a heavy emphasis on the capacity of human beings to understand and explain their world, and to find solutions to problems. While rationalism does not dictate the ends of human conduct, it certainly suggests how these ends should be pursued. It is associated with an emphasis on principle and reason-governed behaviour, as opposed to reliance on custom or tradition, or non-rational drives and impulses.

---

own mistakes, but it also creates the prospect that those invested with responsibility for others will abuse their position for their own ends.

A further legacy of rationalism is that liberals are strongly inclined to believe in progress. Progress literally means advance, a movement forward. In the liberal view, the expansion of knowledge, particularly through the scientific revolution, enabled people not only to understand and explain their world but also to help shape it for the better. In short the power of reason gives human beings the capacity to take charge of their own lives and fashion their own destinies. Rationalism thus emancipates humankind from the grip of the past and from the weight of custom and tradition. Each generation is able to advance beyond the last as the stock of human knowledge and understanding progressively increases. This also explains the characteristic liberal emphasis upon education. People can better or improve themselves through the acquisition of knowledge and the abandonment of prejudice and superstition. Education is thus a good in itself. It is a vital means of promoting personal self-development and, if extended widely, of achieving historical and social advancement.

Reason, moreover, is significant in highlighting the importance of discussion, debate and argument. While liberals are generally optimistic about human nature, seeing people as reason-guided creatures, they have seldom subscribed to the utopian creed of human perfectibility because they recognise the power of self-interest and egoism. The inevitable result of this is rivalry and conflict. Individuals battle for scarce resources, businesses compete to increase profits, nations struggle for security or strategic advantage, and so forth. The liberal preference is clearly that such conflicts be settled through debate and negotiation. The great advantage of reason is that it provides a basis upon which rival claims and demands can be evaluated – do they 'stand up' to analysis, are they 'reasonable'?

Moreover it highlights the cost of not resolving disputes peacefully, namely violence, bloodshed and death. Liberals therefore deplore the use of force and aggression; for example, war is invariably seen as an option of the very last resort. Not only does violence mark the failure of reason, but all too often it also unleashes irrational blood lusts and the desire for power for its own sake. Liberals may believe that the use of force is justified either on the grounds of self-defence or as a means of countering oppression, but always and only after reason and argument have failed.

## Justice

Justice denotes a particular kind of moral judgement, in particular one about the distribution of rewards and punishment. In short justice is about giving each person what he or she is 'due'. The narrower idea of social justice refers to the distribution of material rewards and benefits in society, such as wages, profits, housing, medical care, welfare benefits and so on. The liberal theory of justice is based upon a firm commitment to formal equality. If human beings are thought of first and foremost as individuals, they must be entitled to the same rights and the same respect. Liberals believe in universalism, that is, that individuals everywhere possess common or universal features; they are of equal moral worth. For example liberals believe that all individuals are endowed with equal rights, which they enjoy by virtue of being human; these are 'natural rights' or 'human rights'. Rights should not be reserved for any particular class of person, such as men, whites, Christians or the wealthy. Consequently liberals fiercely disapprove of any social privileges or advantages that are enjoyed by some but denied to others on the basis of factors such as gender, race, colour, creed, religion or social background. Individuals should be 'equal before the law' and should enjoy equal political or civil rights.

The equality to which liberals subscribe is equality of opportunity. Each and every individual should have the same chance to rise or fall in society. The game of life, in that sense, must be played on an even playing field. This is not to say that there should be absolute equality, that living conditions and social circumstances should be the same for all. Liberals believe absolute equality to be undesirable because people are not born equal. They possess different talents and skills, and some are prepared to work much harder than others. Liberals believe that it is right to reward merit, ability and the willingness to work – indeed they think it essential to do so if people are to have an incentive to realise their potential and develop the talents they were born with. Equality, for a liberal, means that individuals should have an equal opportunity to develop their unequal skills and abilities.

This leads to a belief in meritocracy – literally, rule by the talented or able. A meritocratic society is one in which inequalities of wealth and social position solely reflect the unequal distribution of merit or skills amongst human beings, or are based upon factors beyond human control, for example luck or chance. Such a society is socially just because individuals are judged not by their gender, the colour of their skin or their religion, but according to their talents and willingness to work, or on what Martin Luther King called 'the content of their character'.

Wealth, therefore, should reflect merit. Liberals believe that property is gained by hard work and the exercise of abilities. Those with more ability or who have worked hard, have 'earned' their wealth and deserve to be more prosperous than the lazy or incapable. However wealth is not only earned by individual hard work but can also be acquired by the accident of birth. Although the idea of inherited wealth does not conform to strict meritocratic principles, most liberals have been prepared to accept it in the belief that its restriction would interfere with an individual's right to dispose of his or her property according to personal choice, and would thus amount to an offence against freedom.

However, liberal thinkers have sometimes disagreed about how this principle of social justice should be applied in practice. In *A Theory of Justice* (1970), John Rawls accepted the need for people to be rewarded for the work they do because he recognised that some measure of economic inequality is essential to provide an incentive for people to work. Nevertheless he argued that economic inequality is only justifiable if it works to the benefit of the poorest and the least advantaged in society. He suggested that social justice should be understood to mean 'fairness', which for him meant a presumption in favour of equality. Consequently Rawls concluded that a just society would be one in which wealth is redistributed through some form of welfare system for the benefit of the less-well-off. A very different conception of social justice was developed by Robert Nozick (see p. 97) in *Anarchy, State and Utopia* (1974). Nozick's libertarian views echo those advanced by John Locke in the seventeenth century. Nozick claimed that any distribution of wealth, however unequal, is socially just provided that certain 'justice preserving' rules have been observed. These rules include the requirement that property is 'justly' acquired in the first place – acquired without being stolen or infringing the rights of others – and that it is transferred 'justly' by one responsible person to another. Nozick therefore argued that the right to property should not be violated in the name of social equality, and he rejected the very notion of redistributing wealth, and with it all forms of social welfare.

Such different views of social justice reflect an underlying disagreement within liberalism about the conditions that can best achieve a just society. Classical liberals believe that the replacement of feudalism by a market or

## John Rawls (born 1921)

US academic and political philosopher. Rawls' major work, *A Theory of Justice* (1971), is regarded as the most important work of political philosophy written in English since the Second World War, and it has had a crucial influence on both modern liberal and social democratic thought.

Rawls used a form of social contract theory to reconcile liberal individualism with the principles of redistribution and social justice. His notion of 'justice as fairness' is based upon the belief that behind a 'veil of ignorance' (that is, not knowing our own social position and circumstances) most people would favour two basic principles: (a) that the liberty of each person should be compatible with a like liberty for all, and (b) that social inequality should only exist if it works to the benefit of the poorest in society. The universalist presumptions of his early work were somewhat modified in *Political Liberalism* (1993).

capitalist society created the social conditions in which each individual could prosper according to his or her merits. Provided individuals are equal in the eyes of the law, they are thought to enjoy an equal opportunity to rise or fall in society. Modern liberals, in contrast, believe that unrestrained capitalism has led to new forms of social injustice that have privileged some and disadvantaged others. As a result they favour government intervention in social and economic life, designed to promote greater equality of opportunity and thereby achieve a socially just society.

## Toleration

The liberal social ethic is very much characterised by a willingness to accept, even celebrate, moral, cultural and political diversity. Liberals have often echoed the famous words of Voltaire (1694–1778): 'I detest what you say but will defend to the death your right to say it'. The cherished civil liberties that underpin liberal-democratic political systems – freedom of speech, association, religious worship and so forth – are all, in effect, guarantees of toleration. Most commentators therefore agree that liberalism goes hand in hand with pluralism, a multiplicity of values, views and interests being seen as a good in itself. Since diversity in its various forms is natural, it can only be removed by political repression or, perhaps liberals have feared, by the spread of dull conformism. Thus in principle liberals oppose censorship or any attempt to prevent the free expression of views in society. This is why the western liberal conscience was so deeply offended by the *fatwa*, or religious order, by which Ayatollah Khomeini (see p. 306) in 1989 passed the sentence of death on the UK writer Salman Rushdie upon the publication of his book *The Satanic Verses*.

## Pluralism

Pluralism, in its broadest sense, is a belief in or commitment to diversity or multiplicity, the existence of many things. As a descriptive term, pluralism may denote the existence of party competition (political pluralism), a multiplicity of ethical values (moral pluralism), a variety of cultural beliefs (cultural pluralism) and so on. As a normative term it suggests that diversity is healthy and desirable, usually because it safeguards individual liberty and promotes debate, argument and understanding. More narrowly, pluralism is a theory of the distribution of political power. As such it holds that power is widely and evenly dispersed in society, not concentrated in the hands of an elite or ruling class. In this form pluralism is usually seen as a theory of 'group politics', implying that group access to government ensures broad democratic responsiveness.

Underlying this liberal preference for a diversity of views and interests in society is the value of toleration. Toleration means forbearance, a willingness to allow people to think, speak and act in ways of which we disapprove. As such it is both an ethical ideal and a social principle. On the one hand it represents the goal of personal autonomy, on the other it establishes a set of rules about how human beings should behave towards one another. The liberal case for toleration first emerged in the seventeenth century in the attempt by writers such as John Milton (1608–74) and John Locke to defend religious freedom. In *A Letter Concerning Toleration* ([1689] 1963), Locke argued that since the proper function of government is to protect life, liberty and property, it has no right to meddle in 'the care of men's souls'. This highlights what for liberals is the vital distinction between 'public' and 'private' life. Toleration should be extended to all matters regarded as private on the grounds that, like religion, they concern moral questions that should be left to the individual.

J. S. Mill, in *On Liberty* ([1859] 1972), suggested that toleration is of fundamental importance to both the individual and society. From the individual's point of view, tolerance is primarily a guarantee of personal autonomy and is thus a condition for moral self-development. Mill warned that this is particularly threatened by the spread of democracy and what he called the 'despotism of custom'. Nevertheless toleration is just as important for the health of society as a whole. Only a free market of ideas will enable 'truth' to emerge, as good ideas displace bad ones and ignorance is progressively banished. Mill was therefore able to argue as follows:

> If all mankind minus one, were of one opinion, and only one person were of the contrary opinion, mankind would be no more justified in silencing that one person, than he, if he had the power, would be justified in silencing mankind ([1859] 1972, p. 85).

No liberal, however, would endorse unlimited toleration. For example Locke was not prepared to extend the principle of toleration to Roman Catholics, who in his view were a threat to national sovereignty as they gave allegiance to a foreign pope. More commonly, toleration may be qualified in relation to views that are in themselves intolerant. Liberals may thus be prepared to support laws forbidding the expression of, for instance, racist opinions or laws that ban undemocratic political parties, on the grounds that the spread of such opinions or the success of such parties is likely to spell the demise of liberal toleration. While liberals would support the right of Islamic fundamentalists to criticise the content of *The Satanic Verses*, they may nevertheless advocate the prosecution of those who publicly endorse the death sentence on Salman Rushdie.

Sympathy for toleration and diversity is also linked to the liberal belief in a balanced society, one not riven by fundamental conflict. Although individuals and social groups pursue very different interests, liberals hold that there is a deeper harmony or balance amongst these competing interests. For example the interests of workers and employers differ: workers want better pay, shorter hours and improved working conditions; employers wish to increase their profits by keeping their production costs – including wages – as low as possible. Nevertheless these competing interests also complement one another: workers need jobs, and employers need labour. In other words each group is essential to the achievement of the other group's goals. Individuals and groups may pursue self-interest but a natural equilibrium will tend to assert itself. This principle of balance has influenced liberal thought in a variety of ways. It has led some liberals to believe that a natural and unregulated equilibrium will tend to emerge in economic life. It encourages liberals to believe in a balance of interests amongst competing groups within the political system, and it disposes them to believe in the possibility of peace and harmony amongst the nations of the world.

This emphasis on diversity and toleration has also attracted criticism, however. Both liberals and their critics have portrayed liberalism as morally neutral, in that it seeks not to impose one set of values or beliefs but to create conditions in which people with different moral and material priorities can live together both peacefully and profitably. In that sense liberalism eschews fundamental values, values held to be authoritative and unquestionable. The only restriction placed on diversity is the qualification that each party must tolerate the views and actions of others; in that sense toleration can be seen as the sole fundamental value of liberalism. The danger of this position, however, is that it can create a society devoid of moral structure and incapable of restraining greed and egoism. Conservatives, for instance, have condemned liberalism for promoting moral and cultural relativism, arguing that in the absence of authoritative values, orderly and civilised social interaction is impossible. Individuals end up knowing only their rights and do not acknowledge any duties or responsibilities. In the final decades of the twentieth century this led to a growing communitarian critique of liberal individualism, which is examined in the final section of this chapter.

## Liberalism and democracy

### The liberal state

Liberals do not believe that a balanced and tolerant society will develop naturally out of the free actions of individuals and voluntary associations. This is where liberals disagree with anarchists, who believe that both law and government are unnecessary. Liberals fear that free individuals may wish to exploit others, steal their property or even turn them into slaves if it is in their interests to do so. They may also break or ignore their contracts when it is to their advantage. The liberty of one person is always therefore in danger of becoming a licence to abuse another; each person can be said to be both a threat to and under threat from every other member of society. Our liberty requires that they are restrained from encroaching upon our freedom, and in turn their liberty requires that they are safeguarded from us. Liberals have traditionally believed that such protection can only be provided by a sovereign state, capable of restraining all individuals and groups within society. Freedom can therefore only exist 'under the law'; as John Locke put it, 'where there is no law there is no freedom'.

### John Locke (1632–1704)

English philosopher and politician. Born in Somerset, Locke studied medicine at Oxford before becoming secretary to Anthony Ashley Cooper, first Earl of Shaftsbury. His political views were developed against the background of and were shaped by the English Revolution.

A consistent opponent of absolutism and often portrayed as the philosopher of the 'Glorious Revolution' of 1688, which established a constitutional monarchy, Locke is usually seen as a key thinker of early liberalism. Although he accepted that by nature humans are free and equal, the priority he accorded property rights prevented him from endorsing political equality or democracy in the modern sense. Locke's most important political works are *A Letter Concerning Toleration* (1689) and *Two Treatises of Government* (1690).

This argument is the basis of the social contract theory, developed by seventeenth-century writers such as Thomas Hobbes (see p. 72) and John Locke, which, for liberals, explains the individual's political obligations towards the state. Hobbes and Locke constructed a picture of what life had been like before government was formed, in a stateless society or what they called a 'state of nature'. As individuals are selfish, greedy and power-seeking, the state of nature would be characterised by an unending civil war of each against all, in which, in Hobbes' words, human life would be 'solitary, poor, nasty, brutish and short'. As a result, they argued, rational individuals would enter into an agreement, or 'social contract', to establish a sovereign government, without which orderly and stable life would be impossible. All individuals would recognise that it is in their interests to sacrifice a portion of their liberty in order to set up a system of law; otherwise their rights, and indeed their lives, would constantly be under threat. Hobbes and Locke were aware that this 'contract' is a historical fiction. In reality states are rarely formed through a formal agreement amongst citizens wishing to escape from the dangers of anarchy. The purpose of the social contract argument, however, is to highlight the value of the sovereign state to the individual. In other words Hobbes and Locke wished individuals to behave as if the historical fiction were true, by respecting and obeying government and law, in gratitude for the safety and security that only a sovereign state can provide.

The social contract argument embodies several important liberal attitudes towards the state in particular and political authority in general. In the first place, it suggests that in a sense political authority comes 'from below'. The state is created by individuals and for individuals; it exists in order to serve *their* needs and interests. Government arises out of the agreement or consent of the governed. Political authority must therefore be legitimate, it must be rightful or acceptable in the eyes of those who are subject to it. This implies that citizens do not have an absolute obligation to obey all laws or accept any form of government. If government is based upon a contract, made by the governed, government itself may break the terms of this contract. When the legitimacy of government evaporates, the people have the right of rebellion. This principle was developed by Locke in *Two Treaties of Government* ([1690] 1962) and was used to justify the Glorious Revolution of 1688, which deposed James II and established a constitutional monarchy in Britain under William and Mary. It was also clearly expressed by Thomas Jefferson (see p. 49) in the American Declaration of Independence (1776), which declares that when government becomes an absolute despotism 'it is the right of the people to alter or abolish it'.

Secondly, social contract theory portrays the state as an umpire or neutral referee in society. The state is not created by a privileged elite, wishing to exploit the masses, but out of an agreement amongst all the people. The state therefore embodies the interests of all its citizens and acts as a neutral arbiter when individuals or groups come into conflict with one another. For example if individuals break contracts made with others the state applies the 'rules of the game' and enforces the terms of the contract, provided, of course, each party had entered into the contract voluntarily and in full knowledge. The essential characteristic of any such umpire is that its actions are, and are seen to be, impartial. Liberals thus regard the state as a neutral arbiter amongst the competing individuals and groups within society.

Some liberals, however, have seen the state as rather more than an umpire prepared to intervene in civil society only when strife or injustice threaten. This is particularly evident in the work of the German philosopher Hegel (1770–1831). In *The Philosophy of Right* ([1821] 1942) Hegel argued that the state is an ethical idea that embodies the collective aspirations of society. The state is a realm of 'universal altruism' which promotes loyalty and commitment to higher national ideals, in contrast to civil society which is a realm of individualism and self-interested behaviour. Hegel went as far as to identify the progress of humanity with the development of the modern state, which he referred to as the 'march of God on earth'. This belief in the state as a positive good rather than merely a necessary evil had a particular impact on emergent modern liberalism, helping to foster support for welfarism and interventionism. In sharp contrast, however, fascists used these Hegelian ideas to defend strong, authoritarian government.

## Constitutional government

Although liberals are convinced of the need for government, they are also acutely aware of the dangers that government embodies. Government exercises sovereign power and therefore poses a constant threat to individual liberty. All governments therefore threaten to become a tyranny against the individual. Early liberalism developed very largely out of a critique of absolutist rule. In the twentieth century liberals were re-alerted to the dangers inherent in government power by the growth of totalitarian dictatorships, especially during the interwar period.

Liberals have traditionally feared arbitrary government. When political power can be exercised according to the personal whim or prejudice of the ruler it is apt to be despotic or dictatorial. Indeed liberals have typically believed that political power is corrupting in itself, encouraging those who possess it to subjugate and exploit those who do not. This was expressed in Lord Acton's famous warning: 'Power tends to corrupt and absolute power corrupts absolutely'. As a result liberals have sought to establish

## Constitutionalism

Constitutionalism, in a narrow sense, is the practice of limited government brought about by the existence of a constitution. Constitutionalism in this sense can be said to exist when government institutions and political processes are effectively constrained by constitutional rules. More broadly, constitutionalism refers to a set of political values and aspirations that reflect the desire to protect liberty through the establishment of internal and external checks on government power. It is typically expressed in support for constitutional provisions that establish this goal, notably a codified constitution, a bill of rights, separation of powers, bicameralism and federalism or decentralisation. Constitutionalism is thus a species of political liberalism.

limited government. This has traditionally been embodied in the principle of constitutionalism. A constitution is a set of rules that seek to allocate duties, powers and functions amongst the various institutions of government. It therefore constitutes the rules that govern the government itself. As such it both defines the extent of government power and limits its exercise.

Constitutional constraints upon government have taken two forms. In the first place, the powers of government bodies and politicians can be limited by the introduction of external and usually legal constraints. For example all liberal democracies, with the exception of the UK, Israel and New Zealand, possess written constitutions, which codify the major powers and responsibilities of government institutions within a single document. The first such document was the United States Constitution, written in 1787. In many cases bills of rights also exist, which entrench individual rights by providing a legal definition of the relationship between the individual and the state. The first ten amendments of the US Constitution, for example, list individual rights and are collectively called the 'Bill of Rights'. A similar 'Declaration of the Rights of Man' (1789) was adopted during the French Revolution. Where neither written constitutions nor bills of rights exist, as in the UK, liberals have stressed the importance of statute law in checking government power through the principle of the rule of law. This was most clearly expressed in nineteenth-century Germany in the concept of the *Rechtsstaat*, a state ruled by law.

Secondly, constitutionalism can be established by the introduction of internal constraints which disperse political power among a number of institutions and create a network of 'checks and balances'. As the French political philosopher Montesquieu (1689–1775) put it, 'power should be a check to power'. All liberal political systems exhibit some measure of internal fragmentation. This can be achieved by applying the doctrine of the separation of powers, proposed by Montesquieu himself. This is the belief that the legislative, executive and judicial powers of government should be exercised by three independent institutions, thus preventing any individual or small group from gaining dictatorial power. US government, for example, is based upon a strict separation of powers between Congress, the presidency and the Supreme Court. Particular emphasis has also been placed upon the principle of judicial independence. The judiciary interprets the meaning of law, both constitutional and statutory, and therefore reviews the powers of government itself. If the judiciary is going to check the power of the legislature and the executive, it must enjoy formal independence and be politically impartial. A similar division of powers also exists between central and local government in most liberal states. This is achieved most radically by federalism, as exists in the United States, Canada, Australia, India and Germany, in which each level of government is allocated a range of sovereign powers, defined and guaranteed by the constitution.

## Democratic rule

The origins of the term 'democracy' can be traced back to Ancient Greece. Like other words ending in 'cracy' – autocracy, aristocracy, bureaucracy and so on – democracy is derived from the Greek word *kratos*, meaning power or rule. Democracy thus stands for 'rule by the *demos*', *demos* meaning 'the people', though it was originally taken to imply 'the poor' or 'the many'. However the very popularity of democracy has threatened its undoing as a meaningful political term. In being almost universally regarded as 'a good thing', democracy has come to be used as little more than a 'hurrah' word, implying approval of a particular set of ideas or system of rule. In Bernard Crick's (1962, p. 56) words, 'Democracy is perhaps the most promiscuous word in the world of public affairs'. In reality, democracy is a contested concept: there is no agreed or settled definition of the term, only a number of rival definitions. The most influential of these have been direct and representative democracy.

In his Gettysburg address of 1864, Abraham Lincoln extolled the virtues of what he called 'government of the people, by the people and for the people'. Given that all government is *of* the people, this suggests two alternative forms of rule: government *by* the people and government *for* the people. Direct democracy reflects the former; it is based upon the direct, unmediated and continuous participation of citizens in the tasks of government. This was achieved in the classical democracy of ancient Athens in a form of government by mass meeting, and is manifest in modern politics in the use of the referendum. Since in direct or participatory democracy the people literally govern themselves, the distinction between government and the governed and between the state and civil society is effectively obliterated. However the drawback of direct democracy is that it is most appropriate to relatively small communities, meaning that representative democracy is widely considered to be the only practicable form of democracy in modern circumstances. Representative democracy is a limited and indirect form of democracy. It is limited in that political participation is reduced to the act of voting every few years; it is indirect in that the public do not exercise power themselves but merely select who will rule on their behalf. By placing government in the hands of a class of professional politicians, albeit publicly accountable ones, representative democracy comes closer to the ideal of government *for* the people.

Liberal attitudes to democracy have been distinctly ambivalent. In the nineteenth century liberals often saw democracy as threatening or dangerous. In this respect, they echoed the ideas of earlier political theorists such as Plato and Aristotle, who viewed democracy as a system of rule by the masses at the expense of wisdom and property. The central liberal concern has been that democracy can become the enemy of individual liberty. This arises from the fact that 'the people' are not a single entity but rather a collection of individuals and groups, possessing different opinions and opposing interests. The 'democratic solution' to conflict is a recourse to numbers and the application of majority rule, the principle that the will of the majority or greatest number should prevail over that of the minority. In other words, democracy comes down to the rule of the 51 per cent, a prospect that Alexis de Tocqueville (1805–59) famously described as 'the tyranny of the majority'. Individual liberty and minority rights can thus be crushed in the name of the people. James Madison (see p. 44) articulated similar views at the US Constitutional Convention in Philadelphia in 1787. Madison argued that the best defence against majoritarian tyranny is a network of checks and balances that would make government responsive to competing minorities and also safeguard the propertied few from the propertyless masses.

Liberals have expressed particular reservations about democracy not merely because of the danger of majority rule but also because of the make-up of the majority in modern, industrial societies. As far as J. S. Mill was concerned, for instance, political wisdom is unequally distributed and is largely related to education. The uneducated are more liable to act according to narrow class interests, whereas the educated are able to use their wisdom and experience for the good of others. He therefore insisted that elected politicians should speak for themselves rather than reflect the views of their electors, and he proposed a system of plural voting that would disenfranchise the illiterate and allocate one, two, three or four votes to people depending upon their level of education or social position.

## James Madison (1751–1836)

US statesman and political theorist. Madison was a Virginian who was a keen advocate of American nationalism at the Continental Congress, 1774 and 1775. He helped to set up the Constitutional Convention in 1778, and played a major role in writing the Constitution. Madison served as Jefferson's Secretary of State, 1801–9, and was the fourth President of the United States, 1809–17.

Madison was a leading proponent of pluralism and divided government, urging the adoption of federalism, bicameralism and the separation of powers as the basis of US government. Madisonianism thus implies a strong emphasis upon checks and balances as the principal means of resisting tyranny. Nevertheless, when in office, Madison was prepared to strengthen the powers of national government. His best-known political writings are his contributions to *The Federalist* (1787–8), which campaigned for Constitutional ratification.

Ortega y Gasset (1883–1955), the Spanish social thinker, expressed such fears more dramatically in *The Revolt of the Masses* (1930). Gasset warned that the arrival of mass democracy had led to the overthrow of civilised society and the moral order, paving the way for authoritarian rulers to come to power by appealing to the basest instincts of the masses.

By the twentieth century, however, a large proportion of liberals had come to see democracy as a virtue, although this was based upon a number of arguments and doctrines. The earliest of liberal justifications for democracy was that it provides a means of checking the power of government. In the seventeenth century John Locke developed a limited theory of protective democracy by arguing that voting rights should be extended to the propertied, who could then defend their natural rights against government. If government, through taxation, possesses the power to expropriate property, citizens are entitled to protect themselves by controlling the composition of the tax-making body – the legislature. In other words democracy came to mean 'government by consent', operating through the mechanism of a representative assembly. This idea was developed into the notion of universal suffrage by utilitarian theorists such as Jeremy Bentham and James Mill (1773–1836). The utilitarian case for democracy is based upon the need to protect or advance individual interests. Bentham came to believe that, since all individuals seek pleasure and the avoidance of pain, a universal franchise (conceived in his day as manhood suffrage) is the only way of promoting 'the greatest happiness for the greatest number'. However to justify democracy on protective grounds is to provide only a qualified endorsement of democratic rule. Ultimately, protective democracy aims to give citizens the greatest scope to live their lives as they choose, and thus tends to be associated with minimum government intervention.

A more radical endorsement of democracy is linked to the virtues of political participation. This has been associated with the ideas of J.-J. Rousseau but received a liberal interpretation in the writings of J. S. Mill. In a sense Mill encapsulates the ambivalence of the liberal attitude towards democracy. In its unrestrained form democracy leads to tyranny, but in the absence of democracy ignorance and brutality will prevail. For Mill, the central virtue of democracy is that it promotes the 'highest and most harmonious' development of human capacities. By participating in political life citizens enhance their understanding, strengthen their sensibilities and achieve a higher level of personal development. In short, democracy is essentially an educational experience. As a result, although he rejected political equality, Mill believed that the franchise should be extended to all but those who are illiterate and, in the process, suggested (radically for his time) that suffrage should also be extended to women. In addition he advocated strong and independent local authorities in the belief that this would broaden people's opportunity to hold public office.

However liberal theories about democracy in the twentieth century tended to focus less on consent and participation and more on the need for consensus in society. This can be seen in the democratic elitism of the US economist and sociologist Joseph Schumpeter (1883–1950). Schumpeter's (1976, p. 269) 'realistic' model of democracy was summed up as follows:

> The democratic method is that institutional arrangement for arriving at political decisions in which individuals acquire the power to decide by means of a competitive struggle for the people's vote.

As Schumpeter put it, 'democracy is the rule of the politician'. Its importance, however, is in no way diminished: electoral competition creates a political market that forces politicians to take account of the various interests operating in society. Pluralist theorists such as the US political scientist Robert Dahl (b. 1915) and Charles Lindblom have termed modern democratic systems 'polyarchies', meaning rule by the many as distinct from all citizens. A polyarchy is characterised by the extension of citizenship to a relatively high proportion of adults and the right of those citizens to oppose government officials by voting them out of office. Whilst this may fall a long way short of the classical ideal of popular self-government, it has the crucial advantage of maintaining a consistent level of accountability and popular responsiveness. From this point of view, the attraction of democracy is that it is the only system of rule capable of maintaining equilibrium within complex and fluid modern societies.

Liberal-democratic political systems thus have a hybrid character: they embody two distinct features, one liberal, the other democratic. The liberal element in liberal democracy is the belief in limited government, the idea that the individual should enjoy some protection from the arbitrary action of public officials. The democratic element reflects the belief that government should in some way be accountable or sensitive to the people. In combination, the elements create a model of democracy that has three central features. First, liberal democracy is an indirect and representative form of democracy. Political office is gained through success in regular elections, conducted on the basis of formal political equality – 'one person, one vote; one vote, one value'. Second, it is based upon competition and electoral choice. This is ensured by political pluralism, a tolerance of a wide range of contending beliefs, conflicting social philosophies and rival political movements and parties. Third, liberal democracy is characterised by a clear distinction between the state and civil society. This is maintained both by internal and external checks on government power and the existence of autonomous groups and interests, and by the market or capitalist organisation of economic life.

## Classical liberalism

Classical liberalism was the earliest liberal tradition. Classical liberal ideas developed during the transition from feudalism to capitalism, and reached their high point during the early industrialisation of the nineteenth century. As a result classical liberalism has sometimes been called 'nineteenth-century liberalism'. The cradle of classical liberalism was the UK, where the capitalist and industrial revolutions were most advanced. Its ideas have always been more deeply rooted in Anglo-Saxon countries, particularly the UK and the United States, than in other parts of the world.

Classical liberal ideas have taken a variety of forms but their common characteristic is a belief in negative freedom. The individual is free insofar as he or she is left alone, not interfered with or coerced by others. As stated earlier, freedom in this sense is the absence of external constraints upon the individual. Such a conception of liberty establishes a very clear distinction between the state and the individual. The state is oppressive: it has the power to punish citizens, it can take away their property by fines, their liberty through imprisonment and even, at times, their lives by capital punishment. The creation of a state, even through a social contract, inevitably involves the sacrifice of individual liberty: the individual is no longer able to act simply as he or she wishes.

Classical liberals therefore see civil society as a 'realm of freedom', while the state is a 'realm of coercion'. The state is at best a necessary evil. It is

## Perspectives on . . .

### Democracy

**Liberals** understand democracy in individualist terms as consent expressed through the ballot box, democracy being equated with regular and competitive elections. Whilst democracy constrains abuses of power, it must always be conducted within a constitutional framework in order to prevent majoritarian tyranny.

**Conservatives** endorse liberal-democratic rule but with qualifications about the need to protect property and traditional institutions from the untutored will of 'the many'. The new right, however, has linked electoral democracy to the problems of overgovernment and economic stagnation.

**Socialists** traditionally endorsed a form of radical democracy based on popular participation and the desire to bring economic life under public control, dismissing liberal democracy as simply capitalist democracy. Nevertheless modern social democrats are now firmly committed to liberal-democratic structures.

**Anarchists** endorse direct democracy and call for continuous popular participation and radical decentralisation. Electoral or representative democracy is merely a facade that attempts to conceal elite domination and reconcile the masses to their oppression.

**Fascists** embrace the ideas of totalitarian democracy, holding that a genuine democracy is an absolute dictatorship as the leader monopolises ideological wisdom and is alone able to articulate the true interests of the people. Party and electoral competition are thus corrupt and degenerate.

**Ecologists** have often supported radical or participatory democracy. 'Dark' greens have developed a particular critique of electoral democracy that portrays it as a means of imposing the interests of the present generation of humans on (unenfranchised) later generations, other species and nature as a whole.

*necessary* in that, at the very least, it establishes order and security and ensures that contracts are enforced; civil society could not exist in a 'state of nature'. The state is *evil* in the sense that it imposes a collective will upon society and limits the freedom and responsibilities of the individual. Classical liberalism is therefore characterised by a belief in a minimal state, which would act, using Locke's metaphor, as a 'nightwatchman', its role being limited to the protection of individuals from one another. All other responsibilities should then be placed in the hands of sovereign individuals.

The wish to restrict, as far as possible, the collective power of government and thereby expand the private responsibilities of the individual had a particular appeal during the nineteenth century. It was thought that the arrival of industrial capitalism had created social conditions that allowed individuals to pursue their own interests and to take responsibility for their own lives. If individuals were largely self-reliant they had little need for the state, except to guarantee basic public order. Classical liberalism, however, is not merely a nineteenth-century form of liberalism, whose ideas are now only of historical interest. Its principles and theories in fact found growing appeal in the second half of the twentieth century, and once again its influence was greatest in the UK and the United States. The contemporary revival of classical liberalism, in the form of neoclassical liberalism or neoliberalism, largely occurred as a reaction to growing state involvement in economic and social life, particularly in the early postwar period. This was most evident in relation to the ideas of the new right, examined in Chapter 3.

## Natural rights

The natural rights theorists of the seventeenth and eighteenth centuries, such as John Locke in England and Thomas Jefferson in America, have had a considerable influence upon liberal ideology. Modern political debate is littered with references to 'rights' and claims to possess 'rights'. A bewildering range of rights have been claimed by individuals, described variously as 'natural' rights, 'human' rights, 'civil' rights, 'political' rights and so on. The rights claimed range from freedom of speech and religious worship, to the right to work or receive free medical treatment. In 1948 the United Nations established a Universal Declaration of Human Rights, and a European Convention on Human Rights was introduced in 1953. Rights have also been claimed by groups of people, as in the idea of 'trade union rights' or the 'right of national self-determination'. Moreover ecological theorists have extended the notion of rights to non-humans, for example 'animal rights' or the 'rights of the planet'.

A right is a claim that someone or something is entitled to act or be treated in a particular way. For Locke and Jefferson rights were natural, in that they are invested in human beings by nature or God. Natural rights are now more commonly called human rights. They are, in Jefferson's words, 'inalienable' because human beings are entitled to them by virtue of being human: they cannot, in that sense, be taken away. Natural rights are thus thought to be the essential conditions for leading a truly human existence. For Locke there were three such rights: 'life, liberty and property'. Jefferson did not accept that property was a natural or God-given right, but rather one that had developed for human convenience. In the American Declaration of Independence he therefore described inalienable rights as those of 'life, liberty and the pursuit of happiness'.

## Thomas Jefferson (1743–1826)

US political philosopher and statesman. Jefferson was a wealthy Virginian planter who was a delegate to the Second Continental Congress, 1775, and Governor of Virginia, 1779–81. He served as the first Secretary of State, 1789–94, and was the third President of the United States, 1801–9. Jefferson was the principal author of the Declaration of Independence and wrote a vast number of addresses and letters.

Jefferson developed a democratic form of agrarianism that sought to blend a belief in rule by a natural aristocracy with a commitment to limited government and *laissez-faire*. He also exhibited sympathy for social reform, favouring the extension of public education, the abolition of slavery and greater economic equality. In the United States, Jeffersonianism stands for resistance to strong central government and a stress upon individual freedom and responsibility, and states' rights.

The idea of natural or human rights has affected liberal thought in a number of ways. For example the weight given to such rights distinguishes authoritarian thinkers such as Thomas Hobbes from early liberals such as John Locke. As explained earlier, both Hobbes and Locke believed that government was formed through a 'social contract'. However in *Leviathan* ([1631] 1968), written at the time of the English Civil War, Hobbes argued that only a strong government, preferably a monarchy, would be able to establish order and security in society. He was prepared to invest the king with sovereign or absolute power, rather than risk a descent into a 'state of nature'. The citizen should therefore accept any form of government because even repressive government is better than no government at all. Hobbes therefore placed the need for order above the desire for liberty. Locke, on the other hand, argued against arbitrary or unlimited government. Government is established in order to protect the three basic rights of 'life, liberty and property'. When these are protected by the state, citizens should respect government and obey the law. However if government violates the rights of its citizens, they in turn have the right of rebellion. Unlike Hobbes, Locke approved of the English Revolution of the seventeenth century and applauded the establishment of a constitutional monarchy in 1688. In later centuries liberals have often used the idea of individual rights to justify popular revolt against government tyranny.

For Locke, moreover, the contract between state and citizens is a specific and limited one: its purpose is to protect a set of defined natural rights. As a result Locke believed in limited government. The legitimate role of government is limited to the protection of 'life, liberty and property'. Therefore the functions of governments should not extend beyond the 'minimal' functions of preserving public order and protecting property, providing defence against external attack and ensuring that contracts are enforced. Other issues and responsibilities are properly the concern of private individuals. Thomas Jefferson expressed the same sentiment a century later when he argued, 'That government is best which governs least'.

## Utilitarianism

Natural rights theories were not the only basis of early liberalism. An alternative and highly influential theory of human nature was put forward in the early nineteenth century by the utilitarians, notably Jeremy Bentham and James Mill. Bentham regarded the idea of rights as 'nonsense' and called natural rights 'nonsense on stilts'. In their place, he proposed what he believed to be the more scientific and objective idea that individuals are motivated by self-interest and that these interests can be defined as the desire for pleasure, or happiness, and the wish to avoid pain. Bentham and Mill argued that individuals calculate the quantities of pleasure and pain that each possible action would generate, and choose whichever course promises the greatest amount of pleasure over the pain. Utilitarian thinkers believe that it is possible to quantify happiness and pain in terms of utility, taking into account their intensity, duration and so forth. Human beings are therefore thought to be utility maximisers, seeking the greatest possible pleasure and the least possible pain or unhappiness.

The principle of utility is furthermore a moral principle in that it suggests that the 'rightness' of an action, policy or institution can be established by its tendency to promote happiness. Just as each individual can calculate what is morally good by the quantity of pleasure an action will produce, so the principle of 'the greatest happiness for the greatest number' can be used to establish which policies will benefit society at large. In early-nineteenth-century Britain a group of thinkers and writers gathered around Bentham. Called the philosophic radicals, they proposed a range of social, political and legal reforms on the basis of this notion of general utility.

Utilitarian ideas have had a considerable impact upon liberalism. In particular they have provided a moral philosophy that explains how and why individuals act as they do. The utilitarian conception of human beings as rationally self-interested creatures was adopted by later generations of liberal thinkers. Furthermore each individual is thought to be able to perceive his or her own best interests. This cannot be done on their behalf by some paternal authority, for instance the state. Bentham argued that individuals act so as to gain pleasure or happiness in whatever way they choose. No one else can judge the quality or degree of their happiness. If

## Jeremy Bentham (1748–1832)

UK philosopher, legal reformer and founder of utilitarianism. Bentham's ideas formed the basis of philosophical radicalism, which was responsible for many of the reforms in social administration, law, government and economics in Victorian Britain.

Bentham developed a supposedly scientific alternative to natural rights theory, in the form of a moral and philosophical system based upon the belief that human beings are rationally self-interested creatures, or utility maximisers. Using the 'greatest happiness' principle, he developed a justification for *laissez-faire* economics, constitutional reform and, in later life, political democracy. Bentham's utilitarian creed was developed in *Fragments on Government* (1776) and more fully in *Principles of Morals and Legislation* (1789).

each individual is the sole judge of what will give him or her pleasure, then the individual alone can determine what is morally right.

On the other hand utilitarian ideas can also be illiberal. Bentham held that the principle of utility could be applied to society at large and not merely to individual human behaviour. Institutions and legislation can be judged by the yardstick of 'the greatest happiness'. However this formula has majoritarian implications because it uses the happiness of 'the greatest number' as a standard of what is morally correct, and therefore allows that the interests of the majority outweighs those of the minority. Liberals, in contrast, believe that each and every individual should be entitled to pursue his or her own interests, not just those who happen to be in the majority. The strict application of Benthamite principles can therefore, liberals fear, result in majoritarian tyranny. Nevertheless this concern with 'the greatest number' also explains why in the late nineteenth and early twentieth centuries socialist thinkers were also drawn to utilitarianism.

## Economic liberalism

The late eighteenth and early nineteenth centuries witnessed the development of classical economic theory in the work of political economists such as Adam Smith (see p. 52) and David Ricardo (1770–1823). Smith's *The Wealth of Nations* ([1776] 1976) was in many respects the first economics text book. His ideas drew heavily upon liberal and rationalist assumptions about human nature and made a powerful contribution to the debate about the desirable role of government within civil society. As with many other aspects of early liberalism, classical political economics developed first in Britain, and its ideas have been embraced with greatest enthusiasm in the UK and the United States.

Adam Smith wrote at a time of wide-ranging government restrictions upon economic activity. Mercantilism, the dominant economic idea of the sixteenth and seventeenth centuries, had encouraged governments to intervene in economic life in an attempt to encourage the exportation of goods and restrict imports. Smith's economic writings were designed to attack mercantilism, arguing instead for the principle that the economy works best when it is left alone by government.

Smith thought of the economy as a market, indeed as a series of interrelated markets. He believed that the market operates according to the wishes and decisions of free individuals. Freedom within the market means freedom of choice: the ability of the businesses to choose what goods to make, the ability of workers to choose an employer, and the ability of consumers to choose what goods or services to buy. Relationships within such a market, between employers and employees, between buyers and sellers, are therefore voluntary and contractual. Indeed classical economists assumed that individuals are materially self-interested, motivated by the desire to gain pleasure or happiness by acquiring and consuming wealth. Economic theory is largely based upon the idea of 'economic man', the notion that human beings are utility maximisers, bent upon material acquisition.

The attraction of classical economics was that, although each individual is materially self-interested, the economy itself is thought to operate according to a set of impersonal pressures – market forces – that tend naturally to promote economic prosperity and well-being. For example, no single producer can set the price of a commodity – prices are set by the market, by the number of goods offered for sale and the number consumers are willing to buy. These are the forces of supply and demand.

## Adam Smith (1723–90)

Scottish economist and philosopher, usually seen as the founder of the 'dismal science'. After holding the chair of logic and then moral philosophy at Glasgow University, Smith became tutor to the Duke of Buccleuch, which enabled him to visit France and Geneva and develop his economic theories.

In *The Theory of Moral Sentiments* (1759) Smith developed a theory of motivation that tried to reconcile human self-interestedness with unregulated social order. His most famous work, *The Wealth of Nations* (1776), was the first systematic attempt to explain the workings of the economy in market terms, emphasising the importance of a division of labour. Though often seen as a free-market theorist, Smith was nevertheless aware of the limitations of *laissez-faire*.

The market is a self-regulating mechanism, it needs no guidance from outside. The market should be 'free' from government interference because it is managed by what Adam Smith referred to as 'an invisible hand'. This idea of a self-regulating market reflects the liberal belief in a naturally existing harmony amongst the conflicting interests within society. Employers, workers and consumers all act in their own best interests, but market forces ensure that these interests are compatible: businesses, for example, can only make profits by producing what consumers are willing to buy.

The 'invisible hand' has been used by later economists to explain how economic problems such as unemployment, inflation or balance of payments' deficits can be removed by the mechanisms of the market. For instance unemployment occurs when there are more people prepared to work than there are jobs available: in other words the supply of labour exceeds the demand for it. As a result market forces push down the 'price' of labour, that is, wages. As wages fall, employers are able to recruit more workers and unemployment drops. Market forces can therefore eradicate unemployment without the need for government interference, provided that wage levels, like other prices, are flexible. A free market will also lead to economic efficiency. Each firm is disciplined by the profit motive, which forces producers to keep their costs low. Waste and inefficiency cannot be tolerated. On the other hand the possibility of excessively high profits is prevented by competition. If profits are unusually high in a particular industry, this will simply encourage other producers to enter the industry, thereby expanding output and bringing down both prices and profit levels. Economic resources will be attracted to their most profitable use, which means that they will be attracted to growing industries and away from declining ones. The market is also responsive because it is constantly driven by the desires of the consumer. The consumer is sovereign: to remain profitable firms are forced to identify the consumers' needs and wishes, and to satisfy them. Therefore market forces will naturally tend to promote a vigorous and efficient economy that responds automatically to any change in consumer demand.

Free market ideas became economic orthodoxy in the UK and the United States during the nineteenth century. The high point of free market beliefs was reached with the doctrine of *laissez-faire*, literally meaning 'to leave to be'. This is the idea that the state should have no economic role, but should simply leave the economy alone and allow businesspeople to act however they please. *Laissez-faire* ideas oppose all forms of factory legislation, including restrictions upon the employment of children, limits to the number of hours worked and any regulation of working conditions. Such economic individualism is usually based upon a belief that the unrestrained pursuit of profit will ultimately lead to general benefit. *Laissez-faire* ideas remained strong in the UK throughout much of the nineteenth century, and in the United States they were not seriously challenged until the 1930s. In the late twentieth century, faith in the free market was revived by the Reagan administration in the United States and the Thatcher and Major governments in the UK. Both administrations expected to promote efficiency and growth by releasing the 'dead hand' of government from the economy and allowing the natural vigour of the market mechanism to reassert itself. The other manifestation of economic liberalism, a commitment to free trade, is discussed in Chapter 6 in relation to liberal internationalism.

## Social Darwinism

One of the distinctive features of classical liberalism is its attitude to poverty and social equality. An individualistic political creed will tend to explain social circumstances in terms of the talents and hard work of each individual human being. Individuals make what they want, and what they can, of their own lives. The free market, in allowing all individuals to pursue their own interests, is therefore a guarantee of social justice. Those with ability and a willingness to work will prosper, while the incompetent or the lazy will not. This idea was memorably expressed in the title of Samuel Smiles' book *Self-Help* ([1859] 1986) which begins by reiterating the well-tried maxim that 'Heaven helps those who help themselves'. Such ideas of individual responsibility were widely employed by supporters of *laissez-faire* in the nineteenth century. For example Richard Cobden (1804–65), the UK economist and politician, advocated an improvement of the conditions of the working classes, but argued that it should come about through 'their own efforts and self-reliance, rather than from law'. He advised them to 'look not to Parliament, look only to yourselves'.

Ideas of individual self-reliance reached their boldest expression in Herbert Spencer's *The Man Versus The State* ([1884] 1940). Spencer (1820–1904), the UK philosopher and social theorist, developed a vigorous defence of the doctrine of *laissez-faire*, drawing upon ideas that the British scientist Charles Darwin (1809–82) had developed in *On the Origin of Species* ([1859] 1972). Darwin presented a theory of evolution that explained the diversity of species found on Earth. He proposed that each species undergoes a series of random physical and mental changes, or mutations. Some of these changes enable a species to survive and prosper: they are pro-survival. Other mutations are less favourable and make survival more difficult or even impossible. A wide range of living species have therefore developed on Earth, while many other species have become extinct. A process of 'natural selection' decides which species are fitted to survive by nature, and which are not.

Although Darwin himself applied these ideas only to the natural world, they were soon employed in constructing social and political theories as well. Spencer, for example, argued that a process of natural selection also exists within human society, which is characterised by the principle of 'the survival of the fittest'. Society was therefore portrayed as a struggle for survival amongst individuals. Those who are best suited by nature to survive rise to the top, while the less fit fall to the bottom. Inequalities of wealth, social position and political power are therefore natural and inevitable, and no attempt should be made by government to interfere with them. Indeed any attempt to support or help the poor, unemployed or disadvantaged is an affront to nature itself. Spencer's American disciple William Sumner (1840–1910) stated this principle boldly in 1884 when he asserted that 'the drunkard in the gutter is just where he ought to be'.

Social Darwinian liberalism stands in stark contrast to the idea of social welfare. If the state provides pensions, benefits, free education and free healthcare, the individual is encouraged to be lazy and is deprived of self-respect. If, however, people are encouraged to 'stand on their own two feet', they enjoy dignity and become productive members of society. Such ideas have not been restricted to the nineteenth century but also influenced new right thinking in the late twentieth century. The Reagan administration sought to promote a 'frontier ideology', which emphasised self-reliance and enterprise, while the Thatcher and Major governments in the UK attacked the 'dependency culture' that they believed the welfare state had encouraged, and tried to foster in its place an American-style 'enterprise culture'.

## Modern liberalism

Modern liberalism is sometimes described as 'twentieth-century liberalism'. Just as the development of classical liberalism was closely linked to the emergence of industrial capitalism in the nineteenth century, so modern liberal ideas were related to the further development of industrialisation. Industrialisation had brought about a massive expansion of wealth for some, but was also accompanied by the spread of slums, poverty, ignorance and disease. Moreover social inequality became more difficult to ignore as a growing industrial working class was seen to be disadvantaged by low pay, unemployment and degrading living and working conditions. These developments had an impact on British liberalism from the late nineteenth century onwards, but in other countries they did not take effect until much later; for example American liberalism was not affected until the depression of the 1930s. In these changing historical circumstances, liberals found it progressively more difficult to maintain the belief that the arrival of industrial capitalism had brought with it general prosperity and liberty for all. Consequently many came to revise the early liberal expectation that the unrestrained pursuit of self-interest produced a socially just society. As the idea of economic individualism came increasingly under attack, liberals rethought their attitude towards the state. The minimal state of classical theory was quite incapable of rectifying the injustices and inequalities of civil society. Consequently modern liberals were prepared to advocate the development of an interventionist or enabling state.

## Individuality

John Stuart Mill's ideas have been described as 'the heart of liberalism'. This is because he provided a 'bridge' between classical and modern liberalism: his ideas look both backwards to the early nineteenth century and forward to the twentieth century. Mill's interests ranged from political economy to the campaign for female suffrage, but it was the ideas developed in *On Liberty* ([1859] 1972) that most clearly show Mill as a contributor to modern liberal thought. This work contains some of the boldest liberal statements in favour of individual freedom. Mill suggested that 'Over himself, over his own body and mind, the individual is sovereign' (1972, p. 73), a conception of liberty that is essentially negative for it portrays freedom as the absence of restrictions upon an individual's 'self-regarding' actions. Mill believed this to be a necessary condition for liberty, but not in itself a sufficient one. He thought that liberty was a positive and constructive force. It gave individuals the ability to take control of their own lives, to gain autonomy or achieve self-realisation.

Mill was strongly influenced by European romanticism and found the notion of human beings as utility maximisers both shallow and unconvincing. He believed passionately in individuality, the distinctiveness, even uniqueness, of each individual human being. The value of liberty is that it enables individuals to develop, to gain talents, skills and knowledge and to refine their sensibilities. Mill disagreed with Bentham's utilitarianism insofar as Bentham believed that actions could only be distinguished by the quantity of pleasure or pain they generated. For Mill there were 'higher' and 'lower' pleasures. Mill was concerned to promote those pleasures that develop an individual's intellectual, moral or aesthetic sensibilities. He was clearly not concerned with simple pleasure-seeking, but with personal self-development, and declared that he would rather be 'Socrates dissatisfied than a fool satisfied'. As such he laid the foundation for a positive theory of liberty. Nevertheless Mill did not draw the conclusion that the state should step in and guide individuals towards personal growth and 'higher' pleasures because, like Tocqueville, he feared the spread of conformism in society. For example, although he encouraged the spread of education as perhaps the best way by which individuals could gain fulfilment, he feared that state education would simply mean that everyone shared the same views and beliefs.

## Positive freedom

The clearest break with early liberal thought came in the late nineteenth century with the work of the UK philosopher T. H. Green (1836–82), whose writing influenced a generation of so-called 'new liberal' thinkers such as L. T. Hobhouse (1964–1929) and J. A. Hobson (1854–1940). Green believed that the unrestrained pursuit of profit, as advocated by classical liberalism, had given rise to new forms of poverty and injustice. The economic liberty of the few had blighted the life chances of the many. Following J. S. Mill, he rejected the early liberal conception of human beings as essentially self-seeking utility maximisers, and suggested a more optimistic view of human nature. Individuals, according to Green, have sympathy for one another; they are capable of altruism. The individual possesses social responsibilities and not merely individual responsibilities, and is therefore linked to other individuals by ties of caring and empathy. Such a conception of human nature was clearly influenced by socialist ideas that emphasised the sociable and cooperative nature of humankind. As a result, Green's ideas have been described as 'socialist liberalism'.

Green also challenged the classical liberal notion of liberty. Negative liberty merely removes external constraints upon the individual, giving the individual freedom of choice. In the case of the businesses which wish to maximise profits, negative freedom would justify their ability to hire the cheapest labour possible, for example to employ children rather than adults, or women rather than men. Economic freedom can therefore lead to exploitation. Green argued that contracts of work are not made by free or equal individuals. Workers are sometimes coerced into accepting employment because poverty and starvation are the only alternatives, while employers usually have the luxury of choosing from amongst a number of workers. Freedom of choice in the market place is therefore an inadequate conception of individual freedom.

In the place of negative freedom, Green proposed the idea of positive freedom. Freedom is the ability of the individual to develop and attain individuality; it involves the ability of the individual to realise his or her potential, attain skills and knowledge and achieve fulfilment. Unrestrained capitalism does not give each individual the same opportunities for self-realisation. The working class, for example, is held back by the disadvantages of poverty, sickness, unemployment and ignorance. In removing external constraints from the individual, negative freedom might amount to no more than the freedom to starve, while positive freedom aims to empower the individual and safeguard people from the social evils that threaten to cripple their lives. Such a notion of positive freedom has had an important place in twentieth-century liberal thought. When, in the Atlantic Charter of 1941, Franklin Roosevelt and Winston Churchill described the 'four freedoms' for which they fought the Second World War, they included 'freedom from fear' and 'freedom from want'. The Beveridge Report of 1942, the foundation of the welfare state in the UK, also advocated positive freedoms, this time from the 'five giants' of want, disease, ignorance, squalor and idleness.

If market society does not provide individuals with equal opportunities to grow and develop, modern liberals have argued that this can only be achieved through collective action, undertaken by government. Influenced by Hegel, Green believed that the state is invested with social responsibility for its citizens; it is seen not merely as a threat to individual liberty, but, in a sense, as its guarantor. Unlike early liberals, modern liberals have been prepared to view the state positively as an enabling state, exercising an increasingly wide range of social and economic responsibilities.

Although this has clearly involved a revision of classical liberal ideas, it does not amount to the abandonment of basic liberal thinking. Modern liberalism has drawn closer to socialism, but it has not placed society before the individual. For T. H. Green, for example, freedom ultimately consisted in individuals acting morally. The state cannot force people to be good, it can only provide conditions in which they can make more responsible moral decisions. The balance between the state and the individual has been altered, but the underlying commitment to the needs and interests of the individual remains. Modern liberals share the classical liberal preference for self-reliant individuals who take responsibility for their own lives; the essential difference is the recognition that this can only occur if social conditions are conducive to it. The central thrust of modern liberalism is therefore to help individuals to help themselves.

## Social liberalism

The twentieth century has witnessed the growth of state intervention in most western states and in many developing ones. Much of this intervention has taken the form of social welfare: attempts by government to provide welfare support for its citizens by overcoming poverty, disease and ignorance. If the minimal state was typical of the nineteenth century, during the twentieth century the modern state became a welfare state. This occurred as a consequence of a variety of historical and ideological factors. Governments, for example, sought to achieve national efficiency, more healthy work forces and stronger armies. They also came under electoral pressure for social reform from newly enfranchised industrial workers and in some cases the rural peasantry. The political argument for welfarism has not been the prerogative of any single ideology. It has been put, in different ways, by socialists, liberals, conservatives, feminists and even at times by fascists. Within liberalism the case for social welfare has been made by modern liberals, in marked contrast to classical liberals, who extolled the virtues of self-help and individual responsibility.

Modern liberals have defended welfarism on the basis of equality of opportunity. If particular individuals or groups are disadvantaged by their social circumstances, then the state possesses a social responsibility to reduce or remove these disadvantages. This responsibility is reflected in the development of the welfare state. Such an expansion of the responsibilities of government has not, however, diminished individual rights, but rather broadened them. Citizens have acquired a range of welfare or social rights, such as the right to work, the right to education and the right to decent housing. Classical liberals believe that the only rights to which the citizen is entitled are negative rights, those that depend upon the restraint of government power. This applies to most of the traditional civil liberties respected by liberals, such as freedom of speech, religious worship and assembly. These rights constitute a 'private sphere', which should be untouched by government. Welfare rights, however, are positive rights because they can only be satisfied by the positive actions of government, through the provision of state pensions, benefits and, perhaps, publicly funded health and education services.

During the twentieth century liberal parties and liberal governments have usually championed the cause of social welfare. The foundations of the welfare state in the UK were laid before the First World War by the Asquith Liberal government, which introduced old age pensions and a limited system of health and unemployment insurance. The Liberal Party, now the Liberal Democrats, has remained a modern liberal party in its continuing commitment to the principles of social welfare. When the UK welfare state was expanded after the Second World War by the Attlee Labour government, it was according to the 1942 Beveridge Report, a blueprint provided by the modern liberal William Beveridge (1879–1963). This promised to create a comprehensive system of social security that would cover all citizens 'from the cradle to the grave'. The Liberal Party of Canada has similarly campaigned for the adoption of universal welfare policies, whilst the Progressive Conservative Party advocates individual responsibility and free enterprise.

In the United States liberal welfarism developed in the 1930s during the administration of F. D. Roosevelt. Ideas of economic individualism and self-help remained dominant well into the twentieth century, but under Roosevelt's 'New Deal' public relief was introduced for the unemployed, the old, children, widows and the blind. New Deal liberalism survived the death of Roosevelt in 1945, and reached its height in the 1960s with the

'New Frontier' policies of John Kennedy and Lyndon Johnson's 'Great Society' programme. The latter concentrated on improving the civil rights of US blacks and countering poverty and squalor in US cities. The idea of positive discrimination, called 'affirmative action' in the United States, in which individuals and groups are entitled to special considerations to compensate for social disadvantage, also developed out of a liberal commitment to equal opportunities. In the USA, for example, the principle has been widely employed since the 1960s to broaden social opportunities for blacks in the light of low income levels, high rates of unemployment and poor housing. Black students in the United States are often able to gain access to higher education with lower qualifications than their white counterparts. The principle of positive discrimination need not, of course, only apply to racial disadvantage: it could equally be employed to compensate for social disadvantages that arise as a result of gender, age or physical disability.

## Keynesianism

In addition to providing social welfare, in the twentieth century western governments also sought to deliver prosperity by 'managing' their economies. This once again involved rejecting classical liberal thinking, in particular its belief in a self-regulating free market and the doctrine of *laissez-faire*. The abandonment of *laissez-faire* came about because of the increasing complexity of industrial capitalist economies and their apparent inability to guarantee general prosperity if left to their own devices. The Great Depression of the 1930s, sparked off by the Wall Street Crash of 1929, led to high levels of unemployment throughout the industrialised world and in much of the developing world. This was the most dramatic demonstration of the failure of the free market. After the Second World War virtually all western states adopted policies of economic intervention in an attempt to prevent a return to the pre-war levels of unemployment.

To a large extent these interventionist policies were guided by the work of John Maynard Keynes. In *The General Theory of Employment, Interest and Money* ([1936] 1963), Keynes challenged classical economic thinking and rejected its belief in a self-regulating market. Classical economists had argued that there was a 'market solution' to the problem of unemployment, and indeed all other economic problems. According to them, unemployment will fall if wages are allowed to drop; it will only persist if, usually because of trade union pressure, wage levels are inflexible. Workers, according to this view, literally 'price themselves out of jobs'. Keynes argued, however, that the level of economic activity, and therefore of employment, is determined by the total amount of demand – aggregate demand – in the economy. He suggested that if wage levels are cut,

## John Maynard Keynes (1883–1946)

UK economist. Keynes was an adviser to Lloyd George at the Paris Peace Conference of 1919, and later led the British delegation at the Bretton Woods Conference, which set up the International Monetary Fund in 1944.

In his major work, *The General Theory of Employment, Interest and Money* (1936), Keynes developed a critique of neoclassical economics that highlights the 'economic anarchy' of *laissez-faire* capitalism. He argued for an enlarged economic role for government in the form of 'demand management', operating largely through the control of savings and investment. Though an opponent of the free market, Keynes' principal concern was to make capitalism work, rather than to endorse a socialist alternative.

purchasing power within the economy will fall and with it aggregate demand. If people have less money in their pockets to spend, firms will produce fewer goods, with the result that unemployment will continue to rise. A free market might consequently spiral downwards into depression and be incapable of reviving itself, which is what Keynes believed had occurred in the 1930s. Unlike previous trade cycles, the Great Depression did not end with a 'natural' upturn in economic fortunes.

Keynes suggested that governments can 'manage' their economies by influencing the level of aggregate demand. Government spending is, in effect, an 'injection' of demand into the economy. By building a school the government creates employment for construction workers and demand for building materials, the effects of which will ripple throughout the economy, as construction workers, for example, have the money to buy more goods. This is what Keynes called the 'multiplier effect'. Taxation, on the other hand, is a 'withdrawal' from the economy, it reduces aggregate demand and dampens down economic activity. At times of high unemployment, Keynes recommended that the government should 'reflate' the economy by either increasing public spending or cutting taxes. Unemployment can therefore be solved, not by the invisible hand of capitalism, but by government intervention, in this case by running a budget deficit, meaning that the government literally 'overspends'. Keynesian demand management thus promised to give governments the ability to manipulate employment and growth levels and hence to secure general prosperity.

As with the provision of social welfare, modern liberals have seen economic management as constructive in promoting prosperity and harmony in civil society. Keynes was not opposed to capitalism; indeed in many ways he was its saviour. He simply argued that *unrestrained* private enterprise is unworkable within complex industrial societies. The first, if limited, attempt to apply Keynes' ideas was undertaken in the United States during Roosevelt's 'New Deal'. However Roosevelt's commitment to a balanced budget and his consequent refusal to allow increased government spending on public works projects to exceed taxation revenues resulted in only a very gradual decline in unemployment. The Great Depression was in fact brought to an end by a widespread and substantial expansion of government expenditure in the form of increased military spending in preparation for war, rather than a deliberate attempt to cure unemployment. This was most evident in Germany where unemployment was halved within eighteen months of Hitler's appointment as Chancellor in 1933. The unemployment of the inter-war period was therefore cured by inadvertent Keynesianism.

However, by the end of the Second World War Keynesian ideas were widely established as an economic orthodoxy in the West, displacing the older belief in *laissez-faire*. Virtually all countries employed the idea of economic management in carrying out post-war economic reconstruction and planning for future growth. Keynesianism was credited with being the key to the 'long boom', the historically unprecedented economic growth of the 1950s and 1960s, which witnessed the achievement of widespread affluence, at least in western countries. During this period Keynesian ideas stood triumphant, drawing support from conservative and socialist parties as well as liberal ones.

Keynesianism remained largely unchallenged in the industrialised West until the re-emergence of economic difficulties in the 1970s, which generated renewed sympathy for the theories of classical political economy. This led to a shift away from Keynesian priorities, particularly full employment, to monetarist ones, notably low or zero inflation. Indeed, by fuelling public spending, Keynesianism was held responsible for persistently high levels of inflation, which in turn strangled economic growth. Keynesian ideas were nevertheless revived in the 'new' political economy, or neo-Keynesianism, which developed out of the failure of the free market revolution of the 1980s to reverse long-term economic decline. Although this recognised that the 'crude' Keynesianism of the 1950s and 1960s had been rendered redundant as a result of globalisation, it also marked a renewed awareness of the fact that unregulated capitalism tends to bring low investment, short-termism and social fragmentation or breakdown.

## Liberalism in the twenty-first century

The twentieth century appears to be culminating with the worldwide triumph of liberalism. The liberal model of representative government combined with market-based economics that has dominated political and social development in the West since the nineteenth century is spreading remorselessly throughout the globe. This view was most memorably articulated by the US social theorist Francis Fukuyama (1989), who proclaimed that 'We are witnessing . . . the end of history as such: that is, the end point of mankind's ideological evolution and the universalisation of Western liberal democracy as the final form of human government'. Evidence to support this thesis is easy to find. After the collapse of fascism in 1945, the principal alternative to western liberalism was Soviet-style communism. However this too collapsed spectacularly in the eastern European revolutions of 1989–91, undermining, in the process, the very ideas of planning and interventionism. In Africa, Asia and Latin America a process of 'democratisation' was underway that involved the spread of competitive party systems and a growing enthusiasm for market reforms. Whether this continuing process reflects the manifest superiority of liberalism over its ideological rivals (as 'end of history' theorists suggest), or is a consequence of the emergence of a global capitalist system dominated by multinational corporations (as critics warn), the shape of the future seems to be predetermined. Economic and political differences will progressively diminish as all societies, at different rates, converge on an essentially liberal model of development.

However this liberal triumphalism needs to be tempered by the recognition of new challenges, both internal and external. Internally, within western society liberalism faces criticism from thinkers who have rediscovered the importance of community. These communitarian theorists have taken particular issue with the implications of liberal individualism. Alisdair MacIntyre (1981) and Michael Sandel (1982), for example, have rejected individualism as facile, on the grounds that it suggests that the self is 'unencumbered', drawing its identity entirely from within rather than from its social, historical or cultural context. In their view the self is better viewed as 'embedded' in existing social practices and relations. The flaw this exposes in liberalism is its inability to construct a 'politics of the common good', committed as it is to the belief that each individual should pursue the good life as he or she defines it. This moral vacuum can allow society, quite literally, to disintegrate; unconstrained by social duty and moral responsibility, individuals are concerned only with their own interests and their own rights. Therefore, in the long run, liberal society may lack the cultural resources either to check unrestrained egoism or to promote cooperation and collective endeavour.

The external challenge to liberalism comes from outside its western homeland. There is as much evidence that the end of the bipolar world order, dominated by the clash between a capitalist West and the communist East, has unleashed new and non-liberal political forces as there is of the advance of liberal democracy. In eastern Europe resurgent nationalism, whose popular appeal is based upon strength, certainty and security, has often proved more potent than equivocal liberalism. Moreover this nationalism is more commonly associated with ethnic purity and authoritarianism than with liberal ideals such as self-determination and civic pride. Various forms of fundamentalism (see p. 299), quite at odds with liberal culture, have also arisen in the Middle East and parts of Africa and Asia. Indeed political Islam may prevail over liberalism in much of the developing world precisely because of its capacity to offer a non-western, indeed anti-western, stance. Furthermore, where successful market economies have been established they have not always been founded on the basis of liberal values and institutions. For instance the resurgence of East Asia may owe more to Confucianism's ability to maintain social stability than to the influence of liberal ideas such as competition and self-striving.

Far from moving towards a unified, liberal world, political development in the twenty-first century may be characterised by growing ideological diversity. Islam, Confucianism and even authoritarian nationalism may yet prove enduring rivals to western liberalism. John Gray (1995a) argued that this prospect stems from a larger development: the effective collapse of the Enlightenment project, of which liberalism had always been a part. This project was based upon the assumption that a set of universally applicable rational principles can lay down conditions that allow individuals to pursue incommensurable ends. The task of liberalism, in short, is to construct institutions that are likely to achieve this goal. Representative government, party competition, market economies and so forth were thus designed to allow people to pursue the good life in their own way without leading to disorder and social breakdown. The problem liberalism has to face, however, is what happens when individuals embrace value systems and world views, such as religious fundamentalism, that call for the construction of non-liberal institutions. Gray therefore suggested that as political and cultural diversity deepen the true successor to liberalism will be pluralism, the strength of which is that it accepts both liberal and non-liberal values and institutions as equally legitimate.

## Further reading

Arblaster, A., *The Rise and Decline of Western Liberalism* (Oxford: Basil Blackwell, 1984). A wide-ranging and very stylish account of liberal doctrines, emphasising their individualist character.

Bellamy, R., *Liberalism and Modern Society: An Historical Argument* (Cambridge: Polity Press, 1992). An analysis of the development of liberalism that focuses on the adaptations necessary to apply liberal values to new social realities.

Gray, J., *Liberalism*, 2nd edn (Milton Keynes: Open University Press, 1995). A short and not uncritical introduction to liberalism as the political theory of modernity; contains a discussion of postliberalism.

Hall, J. A., *Liberalism: Politics, Ideology and the Market* (London: Paladin, 1988). A thoughtful and accessible account of liberal thought and the development of liberal ideas.

Holden, B., *Understanding Liberal Democracy*, 2nd edn (Hemel Hempstead: Harvester Wheatsheaf, 1993). An accessible introduction to the concept and nature of liberal democracy, looking at criticisms and justifications.

Ramsay, M., *What's Wrong with Liberalism? A Radical Critique of Liberal Political Philosophy* (London: Leicester University Press, 1997). A thoughtful and accessible account of liberal theory and practice from a variety of critical perspectives.

Ruggiero, G. de, *The History of European Liberalism* (Boston: Beacon, 1959). A classic study of the development of liberal ideas and movements; written in 1925 but still worth consulting.

# Chapter 3

# Conservatism

## Origins and development

In everyday language the term 'conservative' has a variety of meanings. It can refer to moderate or cautious behaviour, a life-style that is conventional, even conformist, or a fear of or refusal to change. 'Conservatism' was first used to describe a distinctive political ideology in the early nineteenth century. Its ideas arose in reaction to the growing pace of political and economic change, which in many ways had commenced with the French Revolution in 1789. One of the earliest and perhaps the classic statement of conservative principles is contained in Edmund Burke's (see p. 71) *Reflections on the Revolution in France* ([1790] 1968), which deeply regretted the revolutionary challenge to the *ancien régime* that had occurred the previous year. During the nineteenth century, western states were transformed by the pressures unleashed by industrialisation and reflected in the growth of liberalism, socialism and nationalism. While these ideologies preached reform and at times supported revolution, conservatism stood in defence of an increasingly embattled traditional social order.

Conservative thought has varied considerably as it has adapted itself to existing traditions and national cultures. British conservatism, for instance, has drawn heavily upon the ideas of Burke, who advocated not blind resistance to change, but rather a prudent willingness to 'change in order to conserve'. In the nineteenth century British conservatives defended a political and social order that had already undergone profound change, in particular the overthrow of the absolute monarchy, as a result of the English Revolution of the seventeenth century. Such pragmatic principles have also influenced the Conservative parties established in other Commonwealth countries. The Canadian Conservative Party adopted the title Progressive Conservative precisely to distance itself from reactionary ideas.

In continental Europe, where some autocratic monarchies persisted throughout much of the nineteenth century, a very different and more authoritarian form of conservatism developed, which defended monarchy and rigid autocratic values against the rising tide of reform. Only with the formation of christian democratic parties after the Second World War did continental conservatives, notably in Germany and Italy, fully accept political democracy and social reform. The United States, on the other hand, has been influenced relatively little by conservative ideas. The United States was formed as a result of a successful colonial war against the British crown. The US system of government and its political culture reflect deeply established liberal and progressive values, and politicians of both major parties – the Republicans and the Democrats – have typically resented being labelled 'conservative'. It is only since the 1960s that overtly conservative views have been expressed by elements within both parties, notably by southern Democrats and the wing of the Republican party that was associated in the 1960s with Senator Barry Goldwater, and which in the 1970s and 1980s supported Ronald Reagan, first as governor of California and then as president, 1981–9.

As conservative ideology arose in reaction against the French Revolution and the process of modernisation in the West, it is less easy to identify political conservatism outside Europe and North America. In Africa, Asia and Latin America political movements have developed that sought to resist change and preserve traditional ways of life, but they have seldom employed specifically conservative arguments and values. An exception to this is perhaps the Japanese Liberal-Democratic Party, which has dominated politics in Japan since 1955. The Liberal-Democratic Party has close links with business interests and is committed to promoting a healthy private sector. At the same time it has attempted to preserve traditional Japanese values and customs, and has therefore supported distinctively conservative principles such as loyalty, duty and hierarchy. In other countries conservatism has exhibited a marked authoritarian character. Perón in Argentina and Khomeini (see p. 306) in Iran, for instance, both established regimes based upon strong central authority, but which also mobilised mass popular support on issues such as nationalism, economic progress and the defence of traditional values.

Although conservatism is the most intellectually modest of political ideologies, it has also been remarkably resilient, perhaps precisely because of this fact. Conservatism has prospered because it has been unwilling to be tied down to a fixed system of ideas. A significant revival of conservative fortunes has in fact been evident since the 1970s with the political right regaining power in a number of countries, including Germany, Canada, Denmark and the UK. Particularly prominent in this respect were the Thatcher and Major governments in the UK and the Reagan administration in the United States, which all practised an unusually radical and ideological brand of conservatism, commonly termed the 'new right'. New right ideas have drawn heavily upon free-market economics and in so doing have exposed deep divisions within conservatism. Some commentators have questioned whether 'Reaganism' or 'Thatcherism' even belong within conservative ideology at all. For example the US free-market economist Milton Friedman (b. 1912) described Margaret Thatcher as a 'nineteenth century liberal', rather than a 'Tory' (see p. 86).

Although the new right has challenged traditional conservative views about economic policy, it nevertheless remains part of conservatism. In the first place it has not abandoned traditional conservative social principles such as belief in order, authority and discipline – in some respects it has strengthened them. Furthermore the new right's enthusiasm for the free market has exposed the extent to which conservatism had already been influenced by liberal ideas. As with all political ideologies, conservatism contains a range of traditions. In the nineteenth century it was closely associated with an authoritarian defence of monarchy and aristocracy, which has survived in the form of authoritarian populist movements in the developing world. In the twentieth century western conservatives have been divided between paternalistic support for state intervention and a libertarian commitment to the free market. The significance of the new right is that it has sought to revive the electoral fortunes of conservatism by readjusting the balance between these traditions in favour of libertarianism (see p. 89).

## The desire to conserve – central themes

The character of conservative ideology has been the source of particular argument and debate. For example it is often suggested that conservatives have a clearer understanding of what they oppose than of what they favour. In that sense conservatism has been portrayed as a negative philosophy, its purpose being simply to preach resistance to, or at least suspicion of, change. However, if conservatism were to consist of no more than a knee-jerk defence of the *status quo*, it would be merely a political attitude rather than an ideology. In fact many people or groups can be considered 'conservative' in the sense that they resist change, but certainly cannot be said to subscribe to a conservative political creed. For example communists in the Soviet Union who opposed the dismantling of the collectivised economy, and socialists who campaign in defence of the welfare state or nationalised industries, can both be classified as conservative in terms of their actions, but certainly not in terms of their political principles. The desire to resist change may be the recurrent theme within conservatism, but what distinguishes conservatives from supporters of rival political creeds is the distinctive way they uphold this position.

A second problem is that to describe conservatism as an ideology is to risk irritating conservatives themselves. They have often preferred to describe their beliefs as an 'attitude of mind' or 'common sense', as opposed to an 'ism' or ideology. Lord Hugh Cecil (1912), for example, described conservatism as 'a natural disposition of the human mind'. Others have argued that what is distinctive about conservatism is its emphasis on history and experience, and its distaste for rational thought. As discussed in Chapter 1, conservatives have typically eschewed the 'politics of principle' and adopted instead a traditionalist political stance. Their opponents have also lighted upon this feature of conservatism, sometimes portraying it as little more than an unprincipled apology for the interests of a ruling class or elite. However both conservatives and their critics ignore the weight and range of theories that underpin conservative 'common sense'. For example conservatives may prefer to base their thinking upon experience and history rather than abstract principles, but this preference is itself based upon specific beliefs, in this case about the limited rational capacities of human beings. Conservatism is neither simple pragmatism (see p. 11) nor mere opportunism. It is founded upon a particular set of political beliefs about human beings, the societies they live in and the importance of a distinctive set of political values. As such, like liberalism and socialism it can rightfully be described as an ideology. The most significant of its central beliefs are the following:

- Tradition
- Human imperfection
- Organic society
- Authority
- Property

## Tradition

Conservatives have argued against change on a number of grounds. A central and recurrent theme of conservatism is its defence of tradition, its desire to maintain established customs and institutions. Liberals, in contrast, argue that social institutions should not be evaluated according to how long they have survived, but how far they fulfil the needs and interests of individuals. If institutions fail this test they should be reformed, or perhaps removed. For example in many countries liberals have reached the conclusion that monarchy is a redundant institution in the modern world and should be abolished. Conservatives, however, fiercely disagree, and for a number of reasons they believe that customs and institutions should be preserved precisely because they have succeeded in enduring through history.

For some conservatives this conclusion reflects their religious faith. If the world is thought to have been fashioned by God the Creator, traditional customs and practices in society will be regarded as 'God given'. Burke thus believed that society was shaped by 'the law of our Creators', or what he also called 'natural law'. If human beings tamper with the world they are challenging the will of God, and as a result they are likely to make human affairs worse rather than better. Since the eighteenth century it has become increasingly difficult to maintain that tradition reflects the will of God. It was possible for Burke to believe that the institution of monarchy had been ordained by God because it had been so long-established and was still almost universally accepted. As the pace of historical change accelerated, however, old traditions were replaced by new ones, and these new ones, for example free elections and universal suffrage, were clearly seen to be man-made rather than in any sense 'God given'. Nevertheless the religious objection to change has been kept alive by modern fundamentalists, who believe that God's wishes have been revealed to humankind in the literal truth of their religious texts. The US new right, for example, has been deeply influenced by the 'born again' Christian movement. Its campaigns against abortion and for the reintroduction of prayers in schools are ultimately based upon its interpretation of the Bible. Islamic fundamentalists in various parts of the Middle East and North Africa similarly base their beliefs on Sharia law, according to which women may be stoned to death for adultery, in line with the words of Allah revealed in the Koran. The relationship between conservatism and religious fundamentalism is discussed more fully in Chapter 10.

Most conservatives, however, support tradition without needing to argue that it has divine origins. Burke, for example, described society as a partnership between 'those who are living, those who are dead and those who are to be born'. G. K. Chesterton, the British novelist and essayist, expressed this idea as follows: 'Tradition means giving votes to the most obscure of all classes: our ancestors. It is a democracy of the dead. Tradition refuses to submit to the arrogant oligarchy of those who merely happen to be walking around.' Tradition in this sense reflects the accumulated wisdom of the past. The institutions and practices of the past have been 'tested by time' and should therefore be preserved for the benefit of the living and for generations to come. This notion of tradition reflects an almost Darwinian belief that those institutions and customs that

## Edmund Burke (1729–97)

Dublin-born British statesmen and political theorist, often seen as the father of the Anglo-American conservative tradition. A Whig politician, Burke was sympathetic towards the American Revolution of 1776 but earned his reputation through the staunch criticism of the 1789 French Revolution that he presented in *Reflections on the Revolution in France* (1790).

Burke was deeply opposed to the attempt to recast French politics in accordance with abstract principles such as liberty, equality and fraternity, arguing that wisdom resides largely in experience, tradition and history. Nevertheless he held that the French monarchy was in part responsible for its own fate, as it had obstinately refused to 'change in order to conserve'. Burke had a gloomy view of government, recognising that, although it can prevent evil, it rarely promotes good. He also supported the classical economics of Adam Smith (see p. 52) and regarded market forces as 'natural law'.

have survived have only done so because they have worked and been found to be of value. They have been endorsed by a process of 'natural selection' and demonstrated their fitness to survive. Conservatives in the UK, for instance, argue that the institution of monarchy should be preserved because it embodies historical wisdom and experience. In particular the crown has provided the UK with a focus of national loyalty and respect 'above' party politics; quite simply, it has worked.

Conservatives also venerate tradition because it gives the individual a sense of belonging and identity. Established customs and practices are ones that individuals can recognise; they are familiar and reassuring. Tradition thus provides people with a feeling of 'rootedness', an historical sense of who they are. The institution of monarchy, for example, links people to the past and provides them with a sense of who they are. Change, on the other hand, is a journey into the unknown, it creates uncertainty and insecurity and so endangers our happiness. Tradition therefore consists of rather more than political institutions that have stood the test of time. It encompasses all those customs and social practices that are familiar and generate security and belonging, ranging from the judiciary's insistence upon wearing traditional robes and wigs to campaigns to preserve, for example, the traditional colour of letter boxes or telephone boxes.

## Human imperfection

In many ways conservatism is, a 'philosophy of human imperfection' (O'Sullivan, 1976). Other ideologies assume that human beings are naturally 'good', or that they can be made 'good' if their social circumstances are improved. In their most extreme form, such beliefs are utopian and envisage the perfectibility of humankind in an ideal society. Conservatives dismiss these ideas as, at best, idealistic dreams, and base their theories instead on the belief that human beings are both imperfect and unperfectible.

Human imperfection is understood in several ways. In the first place, human beings are thought to be psychologically limited and dependent creatures. In the view of conservatives, people fear isolation and instability. They are drawn psychologically to the safe and the familiar, and above all seek the security of knowing 'their place'. Such a portrait of human nature is very different from the image of the self-reliant, enterprising, 'utility maximiser' proposed by early liberals. The belief that individuals desire security and belonging has led conservatives to emphasise the importance of social order, and to be suspicious of the attractions of liberty. Order ensures that human life is stable and predictable; it provides security in an uncertain world. Liberty, on the other hand, presents individuals with choices and can generate change and uncertainty. Conservatives have often echoed the views of Thomas Hobbes in being prepared to sacrifice liberty in the cause of social order.

Whereas other political philosophies trace the origins of immoral or criminal behaviour to society, conservatives believe it is rooted in each individual. Human beings are thought to be morally imperfect. Conservatives hold a pessimistic even Hobbesian view of human nature. Humankind is thought to be innately selfish and greedy, anything but perfectible. For some conservatives this is explained by a religious belief in the doctrine of 'original sin'. Crime is not the product of social conditions such as

## Thomas Hobbes (1588–1679)

English political philosopher. Hobbes – the son of a minor clergyman who subsequently abandoned his family – became tutor to the exiled Prince of Wales, Charles Stewart, and lived under the patronage of the Cavendish family. Writing at a time of uncertainty and civil strife, precipitated by the English Revolution, Hobbes was the first since Aristotle to develop a comprehensive theory of nature and human behaviour.

Hobbes' classic work, *Leviathan* (1651), defended absolutist government as the only alternative to anarchy and disorder, and proposed that citizens have an unqualified obligation towards their state. In so doing he provided a rationalist defence for authoritarianism (see p. 82), which nevertheless disappointed supporters of the divine right of kings. Hobbes' individualist methodology, and the use he made of social contract theory, prefigured early liberalism.

poverty or inequality, rather it is the consequence of natural instincts and appetites. Human beings can only be persuaded to behave in a civilised fashion if they are deterred from expressing their violent and antisocial impulses. The only effective deterrent is law, backed up by the knowledge that it will be strictly enforced. Law breaking can only be deterred by a fear of punishment, and conservatives may therefore argue in favour of long prison sentences and the use of corporal or even capital punishment. For conservatives the role of law is not to uphold liberty, but to preserve order. The concepts of 'law' and 'order' are so closely related in the conservative mind that they have almost become a single, fused concept.

Humankind's intellectual powers are also thought to be limited. Conservatives believe that the world is simply too complicated for human reason fully to grasp. The political world, as the UK political philosopher Michael Oakeshott (1901–90) put it, is 'boundless and bottomless'. This explains why conservatives are so suspicious of abstract ideas and systems of thought that claim to understand what is, they argue, simply incomprehensible. Conservatives prefer to ground their ideas in experience and history; they adopt a cautious, moderate and above all pragmatic approach to the world, avoiding, if at all possible, doctrinaire or dogmatic beliefs. Rationalist ideologies such as liberalism and socialism advocate reform or even revolution in the belief that human beings are able to understand their world, and can therefore see how it can be improved. Conservatives believe such rationalism (see p. 32) to be both arrogant and misguided. High-sounding political principles such as the 'rights of man', 'equality' and 'social justice' become very dangerous when they are thought to provide a blueprint for the reform or remodelling of the world. This is why, conservatives suggest, reform and revolution often lead to greater suffering rather than less. For example they have often pointed out that both the French and the Russian Revolutions resulted in new forms of terror and oppression that were very different from the utopian dreams that inspired the revolutionaries themselves. For a conservative, to do nothing may be preferable to doing something, and a conservative will always wish to ensure, as Oakeshott said, that 'the cure is not worse than the disease'.

## Organic society

The conservative view of society is very different from that of liberalism. Liberals believe that society arises from the actions of individuals, each intent upon pursuing self-interest. Social groups and associations are 'contractual' in that they are entered into voluntarily. Libertarian conservatives, who are attracted to liberal, free market ideas, have some sympathy with this view. Margaret Thatcher, for instance, suggested that 'there is no such thing as society, only individuals and their families'.

## Human nature

**Liberals** view human nature as a set of innate qualities intrinsic to the individual, placing little or no emphasis on social or historical conditioning. Humans are self-seeking and largely self-reliant creatures; but they are also governed by reason and are capable of personal development, particularly through education.

**Conservatives** believe that human beings are essentially limited and security-seeking creatures, drawn to the known, the familiar, the tried and tested. Human rationality is unreliable, and moral corruption is implicit in each human individual. The new right nevertheless embraces a form of self-seeking individualism.

**Socialists** regard humans as essentially social creatures, their capacities and behaviour being shaped more by nurture than by nature, and particularly by creative labour. Their propensity for cooperation, sociability and rationality means that the prospects for human development and personal growth are considerable.

**Anarchists** view human nature in highly optimistic terms. Humans are either seen to have a powerful inclination towards sociable, gregarious and cooperative behaviour, being capable of maintaining order through collective effort alone, or to be basically self-interested but rationally enlightened.

**Fascists** believe that humans are ruled by the will and other non-rational drives, most particularly by a deep sense of social belonging focused on nation or race. Although the masses are fitted only to serve and obey, elite members of the national community are capable of personal regeneration as 'new men' through dedication to the national or racial cause.

**Feminists** usually hold that men and women share a common human nature, gender differences being culturally or socially imposed. Separatist feminists nevertheless argue that men are genetically disposed to domination and cruelty, while women are naturally sympathetic, creative and peaceful.

**Ecologists**, particularly deep ecologists, see human nature as part of the broader ecosystem, even as part of nature itself. Materialism, greed and egoism therefore reflect the extent to which humans have become alienated from the oneness of life and thus from their own true nature. Human fulfilment requires a return to nature.

Traditional conservatives, on the other hand, believe that this is an 'atomistic' picture of society, based upon the pretence that individuals can be or want to be self-reliant. Conservatives believe, as explained earlier, that human beings are dependent and security-seeking creatures. They do not and cannot exist outside society, but desperately need to belong, to have 'roots' in society. The individual cannot be separated from society, but is part of the social groups that nurtures him or her: family, friends or peer group, workmates or colleagues, local community and even the nation. These groups provide individual life with security and meaning. As a result traditional conservatives are reluctant to understand freedom in terms of 'negative freedom', in which the individual is 'left alone'. Freedom is rather a willing acceptance of social obligations and ties by individuals who recognise their value. Freedom involves 'doing one's duty'. When, for example, parents instruct children how to behave, they are not constraining their liberty, but providing guidance for their children's benefit. To act as a dutiful son or daughter and conform to parental wishes is to act freely, out of a recognition of one's obligations. Conservatives believe that a society where individuals know only their rights and do not acknowledge their duties would be atomistic and rootless. Indeed it is the bonds of duty and obligation that hold society together.

Social groups are thought to be formed 'naturally' rather than through any form of conscious or voluntary contract. Society arises out of natural necessity. The most basic and most important social institution, the family, develops out of the simple need to bear and bring up children. In no sense can the children in a family be said to have agreed to a 'contract' when joining the family, they simply grow up within it and are nurtured and guided by it. Society exists before the individual, it helps to form the individual's character and personality. Society is thought of by conservatives as a living thing, an organism, whose parts work together just as the brain, heart, lungs and liver do within a human organism. Each part of this organic society – family, church, business, government and so on – plays a particular role in sustaining the whole and maintaining the 'health' of society. Society is not, as liberals think it to be, a 'machine' that is constructed by rational individuals and can be tampered with and improved. If society is organic, its structure and institutions have been shaped by natural forces and its fabric should be preserved and respected by the individuals who live within it.

The family is both the most basic institution of society and in many ways a model for all other social institutions. The family should be protected, and if necessary strengthened. The family has not been fashioned by any social thinker or political theorist, but is the product of 'natural' social impulses such as love, caring and responsibility. The family provides all its members, and particularly children, with safety and security, and teaches individuals about the value of duty and the need to respect others. Conservatives have therefore viewed a healthy family life as essential to the stability of society. Indeed one of the distinctive themes of modern conservative thought is the 'defence of the family' and the need for a return to 'family values' in the face of the twin threats of permissiveness and materialism.

Conservatism also differs from other political ideologies in stressing the social value of religion. Religion may be understood not only as a spiritual phenomenon but also as the essential 'social cement' of society. Conservatives think that all societies need to be held together by a set of shared values and beliefs, and that religion provides society with such a moral fabric. As a result a close relationship has developed between conservatism and religion. The Church of England has been traditionally described as 'the Conservative Party at prayer', though the relationship between the two was strained by the Thatcher and Major governments' adoption of free-market principles. Christian democratic parties throughout continental Europe openly promote the virtues of the Christian faith, and the Italian Christian Democratic Party enjoys a particularly close relationship with the Vatican.

Conservatives are reluctant to leave moral questions to the individual, as was suggested, for example, by libertarians such as John Stuart Mill (see p. 31). If morality becomes an issue of personal choice, the moral fabric of society is brought into question and with it the cohesion upon which social order is based. Morality is therefore a social issue, not simply a matter of personal preference. Consequently society has the right to protect itself by upholding a set of shared beliefs and values. This can be achieved by promoting respect for religion and the church, but if necessary may also involve the force of law. Conservatives believe that law should not only maintain public order, but should also defend and uphold moral principles. Laws that liberals would object to, for example prohibiting blasphemy or imposing censorship, may be justified by conservatives on precisely these grounds. In their view, what people watch on television or read in books and newspapers should be subject to the guidance of laws because society must be protected against immorality.

Another example of a social institution for which conservatives reserve particular respect is the nation. Nations, like families, are formed naturally, in this case out of a natural affinity that develops amongst people who share the same language, history, culture and traditions. Conservatives argue that people are drawn towards others who are similar to themselves in a search for security and a sense of belonging. Patriotism (see p. 165) is therefore both a natural and a healthy instinct. At the same time, according to conservatives, suspicion of and even prejudice against foreigners may also be regarded as natural, as people from alien cultures may

**Perspectives on . . .**

## Society

**Liberals** regard society not as an entity in its own right but as a collection of individuals. To the extent that society exists, it is fashioned out of voluntary and contractual agreements made by self-interested human beings. Nevertheless there is a general balance of interests in society that tends to promote harmony and equilibrium.

**Conservatives** see society as an organism, a living entity. Society thus has an existence outside the individual, and in a sense is prior to the individual; it is held together by the bonds of tradition, authority and a common morality. The new right nevertheless subscribes to a form of liberal atomism.

**Socialists** have traditionally understood society in terms of unequal class power, economic and property divisions being deeper and more genuine than any broader social bonds. Marxists believe that society is characterised by class struggle, and argue that the only stable and cohesive society is a classless one.

**Anarchists** believe that society is characterised by unregulated and natural harmony, based on the natural human disposition towards cooperation and sociability. Social conflict and disharmony are thus clearly unnatural, a product of political rule and economic inequality.

**Nationalists** view society in terms of cultural or ethnic distinctiveness. Society is thus characterised by shared values and beliefs, ultimately rooted in a common national identity. This may imply that multinational societies are inherently unstable.

**Fascists** regard society as a unified organic whole, meaning that individual existence is meaningless unless it is dedicated to the common good rather than the private good. Nevertheless membership of society is strictly restricted on national or racial grounds.

**Feminists** have understood society in terms of patriarchy and an artificial division between the 'public' and 'private' spheres of life. Society may therefore be seen as an organised hypocrisy designed to routinise and uphold a system of male power.

threaten social cohesion. Burke was amongst the first to argue that such irrational sentiments and prejudices are natural and also constructive, insofar as they help to 'bind society together'. Conservative campaigns against immigration have been motivated by precisely such beliefs, as in the case of Enoch Powell's warnings in the late 1960s that further black Commonwealth immigration into the UK would provoke growing hostility in the (white) host community and the likelihood of racial violence. Whereas liberals welcome social and cultural pluralism (see p. 36), conservatives have doubts about the very idea of a multicultural or multiracial society. Clearly conservatives do not share the internationalist beliefs held by liberals and socialists. Humanity is not thought to be universal, each member sharing a common human identity, but is seen as a collection of nations, each one seeking to maintain its distinctive and unique character, and harbouring natural suspicions about the intentions and behaviour of other nations. This has been evident in the growth of so-called Euroscepticism within the British Conservative Party, provoked by moves towards political and economic union within the European Union.

## Authority

A further distinguishing theme of conservatism is its stress upon the importance of authority. Conservatives do not accept the liberal belief that authority arises out of a contract made by free individuals. In liberal theory, authority is thought to be established by individuals for their own benefit. According to social contract theory, citizens in effect agree to be governed. In contrast conservatives believe that authority, like society, develops naturally. Parents have authority over children, they control virtually every aspect of their young lives, but without any contract or agreement having been undertaken. Authority develops, once again, from natural necessity, in this case the need to ensure that children are cared for, kept away from danger, have a healthy diet, go to bed at sensible times and so on. Such authority can only be imposed 'from above', quite simply because children do not know what is good for them. It does not and cannot arise 'from below'; in no sense can children be said to have agreed to be governed.

Authority is thought to be rooted in the nature of society and all social institutions. In schools, authority should be exercised by the teacher, in the workplace, by the employer, and in society at large, by government. Conservatives believe that authority is necessary and beneficial as everyone needs the guidance, support and security of knowing 'where they stand' and what is expected of them. Authority thus counters rootlessness and anomie. This has led conservatives to place special emphasis upon leadership and discipline. Leadership is a vital ingredient in any society because it is the capacity to give direction and provide inspiration for others. Discipline is not just mindless obedience but a willing and healthy respect for authority. Authoritarian conservatives go further and portray authority as absolute and unquestionable. Most conservatives, however, believe that authority should be exercised within limits and that these limits are imposed not by an artificial contract but by the natural responsibilities that authority entails. Parents should have authority over their children, but not the right to treat them in any way they choose. The authority of a parent reflects an obligation to nurture, guide and, if necessary, punish their children, but it does not empower a parent to abuse a child or, for example, sell the child into slavery.

Conservatives believe the natural structure of society to be hierarchic, and therefore reject any commitment to social equality. They think, as liberals do, that people are born unequal in the sense that talents and skills are distributed unequally amongst people. For liberals, however, this leads to a belief in meritocracy, in which individuals rise or fall according to their abilities and willingness to work. Traditionally, conservatives have believed that inequality is more deep-rooted: it is an inevitable feature of an organic society, not merely a consequence of individual differences. Pre-democratic conservatives such as Burke were in this way able to embrace the idea of a 'natural aristocracy'. Just as the brain, the heart and the liver all perform very different functions within the body, the various classes and groups that make up society also have their own specific roles. There must be leaders and there must be followers; there must be managers and there must be workers; for that matter, there must be those who go out to work and those who stay at home and bring up children. Genuine social equality is therefore a myth; in reality there is a natural inequality of wealth and social position, justified by a corresponding inequality of social responsibilities. The working class may not enjoy the same living standards and life chances as their employers, but at the same time they do not have the livelihoods and security of many other people resting on their shoulders.

The conservative defence of authority also influences its attitude towards the state. In some ways citizens are seen as children within the family: they need guidance and discipline. Citizens must be taught an awareness of their duties and obligations, and not merely of their rights. The classical liberal model of a minimal state has usually been rejected by conservatives in favour of the idea of a strong state. Public order and the moral fabric of society must be upheld by a clear and enforceable set of laws. Wrongdoing can only be deterred by a system of punishment, administered by government. Furthermore, within conservatism there is a strong paternalistic tradition that portrays government as a father figure within society. This implies that the authority of the state, as with that of the father, is a natural necessity, and that it is exercised for the benefit of its citizens. Nevertheless conservatives have been quick to warn against the improper use of government power. Government should be limited in the sense that it cannot and should not try to change human beings. Politics should be restricted to the central task of reconciling conflicts between individuals and groups, and should not be concerned with moral rights and wrongs. Michael Oakeshott expressed the typically conservative view of politics as a limited activity when he pointed out that government was 'not designed to make men good or even better'.

## Property

Property is an asset that possesses a deep and at times almost mystical significance for conservatives. Liberals believe that property reflects merit: those who work hard and possess talent will and should acquire wealth. Property, therefore, is 'earned'. This doctrine has an attraction for those conservatives who regard the ability to accumulate wealth as an important economic incentive. Nevertheless conservatives also hold that property has a range of psychological and social advantages. For example it provides security. In an uncertain and unpredictable world, property ownership gives people a sense of confidence and assurance, something to 'fall back on'. Property, whether the ownership of a house or savings in the bank, provides individuals with a source of protection. Conservatives therefore believe that thrift – caution in the management of money – is a virtue in itself and have sought to encourage private savings and investment in property.

Property ownership also promotes a range of important social values. Those who possess and enjoy their own property are more likely to respect the property of others. They will also be aware that property must be safeguarded from disorder and lawlessness. Property owners therefore have a 'stake' in society, they have an interest in maintaining law and order. In this sense property ownership can promote what can be thought of as the 'conservative values' of respect for law, authority and social order. This is reflected in the desire of conservative parties to create 'property owning democracies'. In the UK in the 1980s the Thatcher government attempted to foster 'popular capitalism' by legalising the sale of council houses and by sweeping privatisation, continued by Major in the 1990s.

A deeper and more personal reason why conservatives support property ownership is that it can almost be regarded as an extension of an individual's personality. People 'realise' themselves, even see themselves, in what they own. Possessions are not merely external objects, valued because they are useful – a house to keep one warm and dry, a car to provide transport and so on – but also reflect something of the owner's personality and character. This is why, conservatives point out, burglary is a particularly unpleasant crime: its victims suffer not only the loss of or damage to their possessions, but also the sense that they have been personally violated. A home is the most personal and intimate of possessions, it is decorated and organised according to the tastes and needs of its owner and therefore reflects his or her personality. The proposal of some socialists that property should be 'socialised', owned in common rather than by private individuals, thus strikes conservatives as particularly appalling because it threatens to create a soulless and depersonalised society.

Conservatives, however, are not prepared to go as far as *laissez-faire* liberals in believing that each individual has an absolute right to use their property however they may choose. While libertarian conservatives may support an essentially liberal view of property, most conservatives argue that all rights, including property rights, entail obligations. Property is not an issue for the individual alone, but is also of importance to society. The rights of the individual must be balanced against the well-being of society or the nation. If, for example, conservatives believe that the national interest is served by government intervention in the economy, then the freedom of the businesspeople must be curtailed. Furthermore property is not merely the creation of the present generation. Much of it – land, houses, works of art – has been passed down from earlier generations. The present generation is, in that sense, the custodian of the wealth of the nation and has a duty to preserve and protect it for the benefit of future generations. Lord Stockton, formerly Harold Macmillan, expressed just such a position in the 1980s when he objected to the Thatcher government's policy of privatisation and described it as 'selling off the family silver'.

## Authoritarian conservatism

Whereas all conservatives would claim to respect the concept of authority, few modern conservatives would accept that their views are authoritarian. Nevertheless, although contemporary conservatives are keen to demonstrate their commitment to democratic, particularly liberal-democratic, principles, there is a tradition within conservatism that has favoured authoritarian rule, especially in continental Europe. The authoritarian tradition dates back to Plato, who proposed that government be entrusted to a small class of philosopher-kings, the Guardians, whose authority was absolute and unquestionable because it was based upon their superior wisdom and understanding. At the time of the French Revolution the principal defender of autocratic rule was the French political thinker Joseph de Maistre (1753–1821). De Maistre was a fierce critic of the French Revolution, but in contrast to Burke he wished to restore absolute power to the hereditary monarchy. He was a reactionary and was quite unprepared to accept any reform of the *ancien régime,* which had been overthrown in 1789. His political philosophy was based upon willing and

### Authoritarianism

Authoritarianism is belief in or the practice of government 'from above', in which authority is exercised over a population with or without its consent. Authoritarianism thus differs from authority. The latter rests on legitimacy, and in that sense arises 'from below'. Authoritarian thinkers typically base their views on either a belief in the wisdom of established leaders or the idea that social order can only be maintained by unquestioning obedience. However authoritarianism is usually distinguished from totalitarianism (see p. 233). The practice of government 'from above', which is associated with monarchical absolutism, traditional dictatorships and most forms of military rule, is concerned with the repression of opposition and political liberty, rather than the more radical goal of obliterating the distinction between the state and civil society. Authoritarian regimes may therefore tolerate a significant range of economic, religious and other freedoms.

complete subordination to 'the master'. In *Du Pape* (1817) de Maistre went further and argued that above the earthly monarchies a supreme spiritual power should rule in the person of the pope. De Maistre believed deeply that society was organic, and would fragment or collapse if it were not bound together by the twin principles of 'throne and altar'. His central concern was therefore the preservation of order, which alone, he believed, could provide people with safety and security. Revolution, and even reform, would weaken the chains that bound people together and would lead to a descent into chaos and oppression. Even the cruel ruler should be obeyed because once the established principle of authority was questioned, infinitely greater suffering would result.

Throughout the nineteenth century, conservatives in continental Europe remained faithful to the rigid and hierarchical values of autocratic rule, and stood unbending in the face of rising liberal, nationalist and socialist protest. Nowhere was authoritarianism more entrenched than in Russia, where Tsar Nicholas I, 1825–55, proclaimed the principles of 'orthodoxy, autocracy and nationality', in contrast to the values that had inspired the French Revolution: 'liberty, equality and fraternity'. Nicholas's successors stubbornly refused to allow their power to be constrained by constitutions or the development of parliamentary institutions. In Germany, constitutional government did develop, but Bismarck, the imperial chancellor from 1871 to 1890, ensured that it remained a sham. Elsewhere, authoritarianism remained particularly strong in Catholic countries. The papacy suffered not only the loss of its temporal authority with the achievement of Italian unification, which led Pius IX to declare himself a 'prisoner of the Vatican', but also an assault upon its doctrines with the rise of secular political ideologies. In 1864 the pope condemned all radical or progressive ideas, including those of nationalism, liberalism and socialism, as 'false doctrines of our most unhappy age', and when confronted with the loss of the papal states and Rome he proclaimed in 1870 the edict of papal infallibility. The unwillingness of continental conservatives to come to terms with reform and democratic government extended well into the twentieth century. In the aftermath of the First World War, for example, conservative elites in Italy and Germany helped to overthrow parliamentary democracy and bring Mussolini and Hitler to power by providing support for and giving respectability to the rising fascist movements.

In other cases, conservative-authoritarian regimes have looked to the newly enfranchised masses for political support. This happened in France, where universal manhood suffrage was introduced in 1848. Louis Napoleon succeeded in being elected president, and he later established himself as Emperor Napoleon III by appealing to the smallholding peasantry, the largest element of the French electorate. The Napoleonic regime fused authoritarianism with the promise of economic prosperity and social reform in the kind of plebiscitary dictatorship more commonly found in the twentieth century. Bonapartism has clear parallels with modern Perónism. Juan Perón was dictator of Argentina from 1946 to 1955 and proclaimed the familiar authoritarian themes of obedience, order and national unity. However he based his political support not upon the interests of traditional elites, but upon the impoverished masses, the 'shirtless ones' as Perón called them. The Perónist regime was populist (see p. 301) in that it moulded its policies according to the instincts and wishes of the common people, in this case popular resentment against 'Yankee imperialism', and a widespread desire for economic and social progress. Similar regimes have developed in parts of Africa and the Middle East, notably Khomeini's Islamic Republic in Iran. In contrast to military dictatorships, which typically suppress all forms of political activity, authoritarian-populist regimes have sought to mobilise active public support, usually through elections, plebiscites or mass demonstrations, and typically base their appeal upon a potent blend of nationalism and modernisation.

Authoritarian-populism does not, however, have a clear political character. Although nationalism is a common component of their ideological appeal, some of these regimes, as in the case of Khomeini's Iran, have been conservative or reactionary, while others, especially in Africa, have embraced socialist or even Marxist principles. Populism proclaims that the attitudes or aspirations of the masses, whatever they might be, should be the only legitimate guide for political leaders. However in mobilising popular support for dictatorial rule, authoritarian-populist regimes such as Perón's perhaps exhibit features that are more closely associated with fascism than conservatism.

## Paternalistic conservatism

Although continental conservatives adopted an attitude of uncompromising resistance to change, a more flexible and ultimately more successful Anglo-American tradition can be traced back to Edmund Burke. The lesson that Burke drew from the French Revolution was that change can be natural or inevitable, in which case it should not be resisted. 'A state without the means of some change', he suggested, 'is without the means of its conservation' ([1790] 1975, p. 285). The characteristic style of Burkean conservatism is cautious, modest and pragmatic; it reflects a suspicion of fixed principles, whether revolutionary or reactionary. As Ian Gilmour (1978) put it, 'the wise Conservative travels light'. The values that conservatives hold most dear – tradition, order, authority, property and so on – will be safe only if policy is developed in the light of practical circumstances and experience. Such a position will rarely justify dramatic or radical change but accepts a prudent willingness to 'change in order to conserve'. Pragmatic conservatives support neither the individual nor the state in principle, but are prepared to support either, or, more frequently, recommend a balance between the two, depending upon 'what works'. In practice the reforming impulse in conservatism has also been closely associated with the survival into the nineteenth and twentieth centuries of neo-feudal paternalistic values.

## One nation conservatism

The paternalistic conservative tradition is often related to Benjamin Disraeli (1804–81), UK prime minister in 1868 and again from 1874 to 1880. Disraeli developed his political philosophy in two novels, *Sybil* (1845) and *Coningsby* (1844), written before he assumed ministerial responsibilities. These novels emphasised the principle of social obligation, in stark contrast to the extreme individualism then dominant within the Liberal Party. Disraeli wrote against a background of growing industrialisation, economic inequality and, in continental Europe at least, revolutionary upheaval. He tried to draw attention to the danger of Britain being divided into 'two nations: the Rich and the Poor'. In the best conservative tradition, Disraeli's argument was based upon a combination of prudence and principle.

On the one hand growing social inequality contains the seed of revolution. A poor and oppressed working class, Disraeli feared, would not simply accept its misery. The revolutions that had broken out in Europe in 1830 and 1848 seemed to bear out this belief. Reform would therefore be sensible because, in stemming the tide of revolution, it would ultimately be in the interests of the rich. On the other hand Disraeli also appealed to moral values. He suggested that wealth and privilege brought with them social obligations, in particular a responsibility for the poor or less-well-off. In so doing Disraeli emphasised the traditional conservative belief that society is held together by an acceptance of duty and obligations. He believed that society is naturally hierarchic, but also held that inequalities of wealth or social privilege give rise to an inequality of responsibilities. The wealthy and powerful must shoulder the burden of social responsibility, which in effect is the price of privilege. These ideas were based upon the feudal principle of *noblesse oblige*, the obligation of the aristocracy to be honourable and generous. For example the landed nobility claimed to exercise a paternal responsibility for their peasants, as the king did in relation to the nation. Disraeli recommended that these obligations should not be abandoned, but should be expressed, in an increasingly industrialised world, in social reform. Such ideas came to be represented by the slogan 'one nation'. In office, Disraeli was responsible both for the Second Reform Act of 1867, which for the first time extended the right to vote to the working class, and for the social reforms that improved housing conditions and hygiene.

Disraeli's ideas had a considerable impact upon conservatism and contributed to a radical and reforming tradition that still appeals both to the pragmatic instincts of conservatives and to their sense of social duty. In the UK these ideas provide the basis of what is called 'one nation conservatism', whose supporters sometimes style themselves as 'Tories' to denote their commitment to preindustrial, hierarchic and paternal values. Disraeli's ideas were subsequently taken up in the late nineteenth century by Randolph Churchill in the form of 'Tory democracy'. In an age of widening political democracy, Churchill stressed the need for traditional institutions – for example the monarchy, the House of Lords and the church – to enjoy a wider base of social support. This could be achieved by winning working-class votes for the Conservative Party by continuing Disraeli's policy of social reform. Such ideas were also supported by Joseph Chamberlain, whose Liberal Unionists split with Gladstone over the issue of home rule for Ireland and were integrated into the Conservative Party during the 1890s. Chamberlain campaigned for 'tariff reform', which he believed would bring both international and social benefits. He hoped that the establishment of tariff barriers against trade from outside the Empire – 'imperial preference' – would strengthen Britain's links with her Empire, and in so doing bolster her economic and strategic position. Furthermore tariffs would generate government revenues, which he recommended should be devoted to social reform. Chamberlain had achieved fame in 1875 when, as Lord Mayor of Birmingham, he had pioneered a radical programme of slum clearance and urban development.

## Toryism

'Tory' was used in eighteenth-century Britain to refer to a parliamentary faction that (as opposed to the Whigs) supported monarchical power and the Church of England, and represented the landed gentry; in the United States, it implied loyalty to the British crown. Although in the mid-nineteenth century the British Conservative Party emerged out of the Tories, and in the UK 'Tory' is still widely (but unhelpfully) used as a synonym for Conservative, Toryism is best understood as a distinctive ideological stance within broader conservatism. Its characteristic features are a belief in hierarchy, tradition, duty and organicism. While 'high' Toryism articulates a neo-feudal belief in a ruling class and a predemocratic faith in established institutions, the Tory tradition is also hospitable to welfarist and reformist ideas, providing these serve the cause of social continuity. One nation conservatism can thus be seen as a form of 'welfare Toryism' or 'Tory democracy'.

Pragmatic and reforming ideas were also evident in nineteenth-century Germany under Bismarck. Bismarck was particularly alarmed by the growth of socialism, which he associated with revolution and terrorism. He sought to combat the 'socialist menace' by a combination of repression – banning socialist meetings and newspapers – and social reform. From 1879 onwards he also supported protectionism, partly because he, like Chamberlain, saw it as a way of financing social welfare expenditure. During the 1880s Germany constructed the first, if limited, welfare state, which featured a system of medical and accident insurance, sick pay and old age pensions. Bismarck's experiment in what has been described as 'state socialism' was designed to wean the working class away from revolution, but it also reflected the neofeudal sense of paternal duty that was deeply ingrained in the Junker landed nobility, from which he came.

The fact that both Bismarck and Chamberlain came to champion the cause of protectionism rather than free trade reflects their essentially pragmatic attitude towards economic policy. The liberal case for free trade is based upon a combination of economic theory and political principle. In contrast conservatives, who are typically cautious about systematic theories or abstract principles, have preferred to recommend 'what works' in the prevailing circumstances. Neither free trade nor protectionism is preferred in principle; either policy can be advocated by conservatives according to what is thought to serve the national interest at any particular time. A similarly pragmatic attitude has been adopted by conservatives confronted with a choice between government intervention and the free market.

## The middle way

In the post-1945 period, conservative governments in various parts of the world came to accept that government should not only provide social welfare, but should also 'manage' the economy. Conservatives, like modern liberals, embraced Keynesianism, but for rather different reasons. Conservative parties tried to pursue what they regarded as a non-ideological, 'middle way' between the extremes of *laissez-faire* liberalism and socialist state planning. Conservatism was therefore the way of moderation, and sought to draw a balance between rampant individualism and overbearing collectivism. In the UK, the depression and high unemployment of the 1930s reinforced the idea that economic policy should not simply be left to the market. In *The Middle Way* ([1938] 1966, p. 185) Harold Macmillan, who was to be prime minister from 1957 to 1963, advocated what he called 'planned capitalism', which he described as 'a mixed system which combines state ownership, regulation or control of certain aspects of economic activity with the drive and initiative of private enterprise'. At the time, Macmillan was MP for Stockton, an area seriously afflicted by unemployment, and he possessed the privileged social background and sense of moral obligation that have often characterised one nation or paternalistic conservatives.

During the 1950s paternalistic values became dominant within the British Conservative Party. By the time the Conservative Party was returned to government in 1951, it had come to accept the major and radical reforms that had been enacted by the Attlee Labour government of 1945–51. These reforms included the achievement of full employment through the use of Keynesian economics, a mixed economy brought about through nationalising major industries, and a significant expansion of the welfare state, including the creation of the National Health Service. The common feature of these reforms was an expansion of state intervention into social and economic life. Whereas the Labour government believed that intervention was designed to promote social equality, and therefore build socialism, conservatives accepted these reforms on the grounds of paternalism. State intervention did not seek to abolish hierarchy and authority, but rather to promote the values of compassion and obligation that the one nation tradition stood for. During the 1950s the policies of the Labour and Conservative parties converged to such an extent that the term 'Butskellism' was coined, which underlined the similarity of views between the Conservative Chancellor of the 1950s, R. A. Butler, and his Labour predecessor and leader of the party 1955–61, Hugh Gaitskell. The Conservatives therefore came to subscribe to a post-war 'social democratic' consensus, whose principal architects had been the modern liberals, Keynes (see p. 61) and Beveridge. However, after Margaret Thatcher's appointment as prime minister in 1979, Tory paternalism was progressively marginalised as new right ideas and values gained ascendency with UK conservatism.

Interventionist policies were also adopted by christian democratic parties in continental Europe after 1945. In the aftermath of the Second World War, continental conservatives abandoned their authoritarian beliefs. This new form of conservatism was committed to political democracy and influenced by the paternalistic social traditions of Catholicism. Protestant social theory has often been associated with the rise of capitalism because it extols the value of hard work and individual responsibility. Catholic social theory, in contrast, has traditionally focused upon the social group rather than the individual, and stressed a harmony of interest amongst social classes. During the nineteenth and early twentieth centuries, despite the papacy's firm commitment to autocracy, Catholic parties, such as the Centre Party in Germany, supported constitutional government, political democracy and social reform. After 1945 this Catholic social ethic was reflected in the willingness of christian democratic parties to embrace Keynesian welfarist policies. The Christian Democratic Union in Germany, for example, championed the cause of the 'social-market economy', which has been widely influential across much of continental Europe. A social market is an economy that is structured by market principles and largely free from government control, operating in the context of a society in which cohesion is maintained through a comprehensive welfare system and effective public services. The market is thus not so much an end in itself as a means of generating wealth in order to achieve broader social goals.

The Progressive Conservative Party (PCP) in Canada also contains various shades of opinion. Ideologically it favours greater orthodoxy in government finance and less government involvement in social affairs than the Liberal Party. However the difference between Canada's two major parties is a matter of emphasis rather than principle: PCP policies are usually determined by political expediency, local issues and practical needs, rather than by ideology. In Japan the Liberal-Democratic Party has dominated government since it was founded in 1955. Its name 'Liberal-Democratic' was adopted to highlight the LDP's acceptance of the democratic constitution imposed upon Japan after its defeat in 1945, but in other respects the party can be regarded as a paternalistic conservative party. It has attempted to preserve respect for Japanese culture and traditions, despite the rapid economic growth of the post-war period. The Japanese government, and especially its Finance Ministry, has been the architect of the Japanese 'economic miracle'. Japanese government works closely with the country's major corporations in targeting export markets and planning investment policy, and it certainly does not leave such economic decisions to the 'invisible hand' of capitalism.

## Libertarian conservatism

Although conservatism draws heavily upon pre-industrial ideas such as organicism, hierarchy and obligation, the ideology has also been much influenced by liberal ideas, especially classical liberal ideas. This is sometimes seen as a late-twentieth-century development, the new right having in some way 'hijacked' conservatism in the interests of classical liberalism. Nevertheless liberal doctrines, especially those concerning the free market, have been advanced by conservatives since the late eighteenth century and can be said to constitute a rival tradition to conservative paternalism. These ideas are libertarian in that they advocate the greatest possible economic liberty and the least possible government regulation of social life. Libertarian conservatives have not simply converted to liberalism but believe liberal economics to be compatible with a more traditional, conservative social philosophy, based upon values such as authority and duty. This is evident in the work of Edmund Burke, in many ways the founder of traditional conservatism, but also a keen supporter of the liberal economics of Adam Smith (see p. 52).

The libertarian tradition has been strongest in those countries where classical liberal ideas have had the greatest impact, once again the UK and the United States. As early as the late eighteenth century, Burke expressed a strong preference for free trade in commercial affairs and a competitive, self-regulating market economy in domestic affairs. The free market is efficient and fair, but it is also, Burke believed, natural and necessary. It is 'natural' in that it reflects a desire for wealth, a 'love of lucre', that is part of human nature. The laws of the market are therefore 'natural laws'. He accepted that working conditions dictated by the market are, for many, 'degrading, unseemly, unmanly and often most unwholesome', but insisted that they would suffer further if the 'natural course of things' were

---

### Libertarianism

Libertarianism refers to a range of theories that give strict priority to liberty (understood in negative terms) over other values, such as authority, tradition and equality. Libertarians thus seek to maximise the realm of individual freedom and minimise the scope of public authority, typically seeing the state as the principle threat to liberty. The two best-known libertarian traditions are rooted in the idea of individual rights (as with Robert Nozick, see p. 97) and in *laissez-faire* economic doctrines (as with Friedrich Hayek, see p. 94), although socialists have also embraced libertarianism. Libertarianism is sometimes distinguished from liberalism on the ground that the latter, even in its classical form, refuses to give priority to liberty over order. However it differs from anarchism in that libertarians generally recognise the need for a minimal or nightwatchman state, sometimes styling themselves as 'minarchists'.

disturbed. Burke saw no tension between his support for a market economy and his defence of a traditional social order, because he believed that by the late eighteenth century the traditional order in Britain had ceased to be feudal and had instead become capitalist. The capitalist free market could therefore be defended on grounds of tradition, just like the monarchy and the church.

During the nineteenth century support for the free market was pushed to the margins within the British Conservative Party by the dominance of Disraelian paternalistic ideas, but it was never eradicated. Support for libertarian views grew towards the turn of the century in reaction to growing government intervention in social and economic life. The British Constitutional Association (BCA), 1905–18, supported largely by Conservatives, was portrayed as 'the new Canute', because of its opposition to the programme of social welfare introduced by the Asquith Liberal government. In contrast to the paternalistic ideas spreading within the Conservative Party, the BCA advocated an extreme *laissez-faire* position, strongly influenced by the social Darwinian views of Herbert Spencer (1820–1903). As A. V. Dicey – the noted constitutional authority and BCA member – said, paraphrasing Samuel Smiles, 'State help kills self help'. The further expansion of the state in the post-1945 period once again stimulated a libertarian backlash within conservatism. One nation values, which had dominated British conservatism in the 1950s, came under growing pressure from the 1970s onwards as free-market ideas, associated with economic theorists such as Friedrich Hayek and Milton Friedman, displaced Keynesian orthodoxy. This and similar trends elsewhere in the world are considered in more detail in relation to the new right.

Libertarian conservatives are not, however, consistent liberals. They believe in economic individualism and 'getting government off the back of business', but they are less prepared to extend this principle of individual liberty to other aspects of social life. Early liberals such as Richard Cobden (1804–65) and John Stuart Mill were prepared to place social and moral responsibility in the hands of the individual, not merely economic responsibility. As Hayek emphasised in *The Constitution of Liberty* (1960), liberalism can be distinguished from both conservatism and, in his view, socialism by its belief that moral decisions should be left to the individual, unless they lead to conduct that threatens other people. The individual therefore needs as little guidance as possible from the state. Conservatives, even libertarian conservatives, have a more pessimistic view of human nature. A strong state is required to maintain public order and ensure that authority is respected. Indeed in some respects libertarian conservatives are attracted to free-market theories precisely because they promise to secure social order. Whereas liberals have believed that the market economy preserves individual liberty and freedom of choice, conservatives have at times been attracted to the market as an instrument of social discipline. Market forces regulate and control economic and social activity. For example they may deter workers from pushing for higher wage increases by threatening them with unemployment. As such the market can be seen as an instrument that maintains social stability and works alongside the more evident forces of coercion: the police and the courts. While some conservatives have feared that market capitalism can lead to endless innovation and restless competition, upsetting social cohesion, others have been attracted to it in the belief that it can establish a 'market order', sustained by impersonal 'natural laws' rather than the guiding hand of political authority.

## New right

During the early post-1945 period, pragmatic and paternalistic ideas dominated conservatism throughout much of the western world. The remnants of authoritarian conservatism collapsed with the overthrow of the Portuguese and Spanish dictatorships in the 1970s. Just as conservatives had come to accept political democracy during the nineteenth century, after 1945 they came to embrace a Keynesian and welfarist form of social democracy. This tendency was confirmed by the rapid and sustained economic growth of the post-war years, the 'long boom', which appeared to bear out the success of 'managed capitalism'. During the 1970s, however, a set of more radical ideas developed within conservatism, directly challenging the Keynesian welfarist orthodoxy. These new right ideas had their greatest impact in the UK and the United States, but were also influential in continental Europe, notably in France and Germany, and had some kind of effect upon western states across the globe.

The 'new right' is a broad term and has been used to describe ideas that range from the demand for tax cuts to calls for greater censorship of television and films, and even campaigns against immigration or in favour of repatriation. Two principal themes can nevertheless be identified within it. The first is revived support for classical liberal economics, in particular for the free-market ideas of Adam Smith. This feature of the new right can be called the liberal new right, or neoliberalism. The second theme also draws upon nineteenth-century ideas, but those of traditional conservatism, especially its defence of order, authority and discipline. Such ideas constitute the conservative new right, or neoconservatism. Not all thinkers or politicians who subscribe to new right ideas hold both neoliberal and neoconservative views: for example Roger Scruton, a noted British neoconservative, argued in *The Meaning of Conservatism* (1984) that a principled commitment to the free market has no place within conservatism. On the other hand it is clear that neoliberal and neoconservative views often coincide. The two governments most clearly influenced by new right ideas, the Reagan and Thatcher administrations, supported, if to different degrees, both the liberal and the conservative new right. 'Thatcherism' in the UK and 'Reaganism' in the United States were the forms that new right ideas assumed in these countries. These terms can be misleading, however, because they have been used to refer to the very individual political styles associated with Margaret Thatcher and Ronald Reagan, as well as to the ideas to which they were committed.

New right ideas were the product of various historical factors. Perhaps most importantly, the long boom of the post-war period ended in recession in the early 1970s, with rising unemployment coinciding with high inflation, a phenomenon that economists call 'stagflation'. The renewal of economic difficulties had greatest impact in those countries already subject to relative decline. The United States, for example, became increasingly aware of competition from the reconstructed Japanese and German economies, while the UK economy had declined markedly, especially in relation to those countries that had joined the European Community at its creation in 1957. In these circumstances, Keynesian ideas of economic management came under considerable pressure on the political right. New right thought was also influenced by social factors, especially the spread of a liberal social philosophy. Conservatives feared that this had led to the twin evils of 'permissiveness' and widespread welfare dependency. Conservatism in the United States received a considerable boost from the recruitment of a number of former liberal intellectuals, led by Irving Kristol and Norman Podhoretz, who became outspoken critics of 'big' government. Finally, international factors strengthened nationalist sentiments within conservatism and heightened its fear of communism. The US new right was alarmed at what it believed to be the growing military might of the Soviet Union and loss of national prestige in Vietnam and Iran. In the UK there was concern about the loss of great power status and the threat to sovereignty posed, after 1973, by membership of the European Community.

## Neoliberalism

The liberal aspects of new right thinking are most definitely drawn from classical rather than modern liberalism, and amount to a restatement of the case for a minimal state. This has been summed up as 'private, good; public, bad'. The liberal new right is antistatist. The state is regarded as a realm of coercion and unfreedom; collectivism restricts individual initiative and saps self-respect. Government, however benignly disposed, invariably has a damaging effect on human affairs. Instead faith is placed in the individual and the market. Individuals should be encouraged to be self-reliant and to make rational choices in their own interests. The market is respected as a mechanism through which the sum of individual choices can lead to progress and general benefit. As such, the liberal new right has attempted to establish the dominance of libertarian ideas over paternalistic ones within conservative ideology.

The dominant theme within this antistatist doctrine is an ideological commitment to the free market. The new right has resurrected the classical economics of Smith and Ricardo (1772–1823), as it has been presented in the work of modern economists such as Friedrich Hayek and Milton Friedman. Free market ideas, which had been abandoned in favour of Keynesianism during the early twentieth century, gained renewed credibility during the 1970s. Governments experienced increasing difficulty in delivering economic stability and sustained growth. Doubts consequently developed about whether it was in the power of government at all to solve economic problems. Hayek and Friedman, for example, challenged the very idea of a 'managed' or planned' economy. They pointed to the inefficiency of the centrally planned economies of the Soviet Union and eastern Europe, arguing that the task of allocating resources in a complex, industrialised economy was simply too difficult for any set of state bureaucrats to achieve successfully. The inevitable results of collectivisation were shortages of vital goods and the need to queue for the bare necessities of life. The virtue of the market, on the other hand, is that it acts as the central nervous system of the economy, reconciling the supply of goods and services with the demand for them. It allocates resources to their most profitable use and thereby ensures that consumer needs are satisfied. In the light of the re-emergence of unemployment and inflation in the 1970s, Hayek and Friedman argued that government was invariably the cause of economic problems, rather than the cure. Government had progressively ignored market forces in the mistaken, if well-intentioned, belief that state intervention was necessary and desirable.

The ideas of John Maynard Keynes were one of the chief targets of new-right criticism. Keynes had argued that capitalist economies were not self-regulating. He placed particular emphasis upon the 'demand side' of the economy, believing that the level of economic activity and employment were dictated by 'aggregate demand' in the economy. Keynes' solution to the problem of unemployment was that governments should 'manage demand' by running a budget deficit: government should 'inject' more money into the economy through public spending than it 'withdraws' through taxation. Milton Friedman, however, argued that there was a 'natural rate of unemployment' that was beyond the ability of government to influence, and that the attempts of government to eradicate unemployment by employing Keynesian techniques had merely caused other, more damaging, economic problems.

## Friedrich von Hayek (1899–1992)

Austrian economist and political philosopher. Hayek, an academic, taught at the London School of Economics and the Universities of Chicago, Freiburg and Salzburg. He was awarded the Nobel Prize for economics in 1974.

An exponent of the so-called Austrian School, Hayek was a firm believer in individualism and market order, and an implacable critic of socialism. *The Road to Serfdom* (1948) was a pioneering work that attacked economic interventionism as implicitly totalitarian; later works such as *The Constitution of Liberty* (1960) and *Law, Legislation and Liberty* (1979) supported a modified form of traditionalism and upheld an Anglo-American version of constitutionalism (see p. 41). Hayek's writings had a considerable impact upon the emergent new right.

Whereas Keynesianism is based upon a belief that unemployment is the most serious of economic problems, free market economists are more concerned about the problem of inflation. Inflation is a rise in the general price level, which leads to a decline in the value of money, that is, the same amount of money buys fewer goods. The market is based upon a process of buying and selling, made possible by the existence of money, which acts as a convenient means of exchange. The alternative to money, a barter system, makes exchange very cumbersome because it is difficult to establish the relative values of different goods. The health of a market economy therefore requires that money has a sound and stable value. If people lose faith in a means of exchange because its value fluctuates unpredictably, they will be discouraged from undertaking commercial or economic activity. In its most extreme case – hyperinflation – money falls so dramatically in value that it becomes worthless and the economy reverts to a barter system, as occurred during the German economic crisis of 1923.

Both Hayek and Friedman placed special emphasis upon 'sound money' and argued that the principal economic responsibility of government is to ensure the financial stability of the market economy by lowering or, as Hayek hoped, eradicating inflation altogether. They suggested that governments pursuing Keynesian policies had unknowingly fuelled inflation and generated the 'stagflation' of the 1970s. This was explained by monetarism, the theory that the price level is determined by the quantity of money in the economy: the money supply. If the money supply grows more quickly than the number of goods and services in the economy, the value of money will fall and the price of goods will rise. In other words inflation occurs when 'too much money chases too few goods'. This is precisely what monetarists have claimed Keynesian policies had brought about. In allowing their spending to exceed tax revenues, governments in effect 'print money'. They expand the money supply and thereby fuel inflation, without, in the process, having any beneficial effect upon the 'natural rate' of unemployment. The economic policies of both the Reagan and the Thatcher administration during the 1980s were guided by these free-market and monetarist theories. Both administrations allowed unemployment to rise sharply in the early 1980s in the belief that only the market could solve the problem. Similarly, they placed emphasis upon cutting inflation by reducing government expenditure. In the United States, Reagan gave support to the idea of a Balanced Budget Amendment, advocated by Milton Friedman.

Free market economists also believe that high-spending, Keynesian welfarist policies damage economic performance by pushing up tax levels. Instead of giving attention to the 'demand side' of the economy, free market economists preach supply-side economics. This means that governments attempt to foster conditions that encourage producers to produce, rather than consumers to consume. Keynesian policies burden producers with high levels of taxation and complex regulations. Taxes discourage enterprise and infringe property rights. Supply-side economics was the central feature of what was called 'Reaganomics' in the United States. Reagan introduced the most dramatic cuts in personal and corporate taxation ever witnessed in the United States (even though his successor, George Bush, failed to keep his 'no new taxes' promise). Under Thatcher in the UK, levels of direct taxation were progressively reduced to near US levels, the highest rate of income tax being reduced from 83 pence in the pound in 1979 to 40 pence in the pound by 1988.

The new right was also critical of the mixed economy. After 1945 many western states nationalised their basic industries in order to facilitate the management of their economies. This created economies that were a mixture of state-owned 'public sector' and individually owned 'private sector' industries. The new right wished to reverse this trend. Under Thatcher and Major in the UK and, to an extent, the Chirac government in France, a policy of privatisation was pursued that transferred industries such as telecommunications, water, gas and electricity from public to private ownership. Nationalised industries were criticised as being inherently inefficient because, unlike private firms and industries, they are not disciplined by the profit motive. Waste and inefficiency in the public sector can be tolerated, the new right argue, because the taxpayer will always pick up the bill.

In the United States, where a mixed economy had never developed, new right pressure focused upon the deregulation of the private sector. Independent regulatory agencies, which were introduced in the late nineteenth century and had proliferated since the 1960s, had been set up by Congress with the intention of regulating private enterprise in accordance with the public interest. The Reagan administration believed that such agencies were disrupting the efficiency of the private economy and argued that the public interest was more likely to be guaranteed by the market mechanism itself rather than any government agency, however ably staffed and hardworking. Consequently the funding of these agencies was dramatically reduced during the Reagan years, for example the Environmental Protection Agency suffered a 50 per cent cut in its budget. In addition personnel were appointed to these agencies who had greater sympathy for the free market than they had for government regulation.

The liberal new right is not only antistatist on grounds of economic efficiency and responsiveness, but also because of its political principles, notably its commitment to individual liberty. Freedom is a theme that recurs throughout neoliberal writing: Friedrich Hayek's critique of the growing power of the state in 1944 was called *The Road to Serfdom*, while Milton Friedman's expositions of liberal economics were entitled *Capitalism and Freedom* (1962) and *Free to Choose* (1980). The new right claims to be defending freedom against 'creeping collectivism'. At the extreme, these ideas lead in the direction of anarcho-capitalism, discussed in Chapter 7, which believes that all goods and services, including the courts and public order, should be delivered by the market. Government is deprived not only of its economic role, but also of those 'minimal' functions that are considered necessary by classical liberals.

The freedom defended by the liberal, libertarian and even anarchist elements of the new right is negative freedom: the removal of external restrictions upon the individual. As the collective power of government is seen as the principal threat to the individual, freedom can only be ensured by 'rolling back the state'. In the twentieth century, however, the state has expanded surreptitiously by developing into a welfare state, claiming to protect its citizens from the threat of poverty, unemployment and other social ills. The new right critique of welfare has been most radically developed in the United States. Robert Nozick (1974) condemned all policies of welfare and redistribution as a violation of property rights. In *Losing Ground* (1984), Charles Murray argued that welfare creates a 'culture of dependency' because it saps independence, initiative and enterprise. Welfare is thus the cause of disadvantage, not its cure. Such a theory clearly resurrects the notion of the 'undeserving poor'. From this perspective, welfare is a matter of individual responsibility; it is not a social responsibility invested in the state. Margaret Thatcher expressed this idea graphically by proclaiming that 'there is no such thing as society'. Murray also argued that, as welfare relieves women of dependency on 'breadwinning' men, it is a major cause of family breakdown, creating an underclass largely composed of single mothers and fatherless children. In *The Bell Curve* (1995), written with Richard Herrnstein, Murray went further still and explained social deprivation in terms of the innate inferiority of US blacks in particular.

### Robert Nozick (born 1938)

US academic and political philosopher. Nozick's major work *Anarchy, State and Utopia* (1974) is widely seen as one of the most important modern works of political philosophy, and it has profoundly influenced new right theories and beliefs.

Nozick developed a form of libertarianism that was close to Locke's and was clearly influenced by nineteenth-century US individualists such as Lysander Spooner (1808–87) and Benjamin Tucker (1854–1939). He argued that property rights should be strictly upheld, provided the property was justly purchased or justly transferred from one person to another. This position means support for minimal government and minimal taxation, and undermines the case for welfare and redistribution. Nozick's rights-based theory of justice was developed in response to the ideas of John Rawls (see p. 35).

## Neoconservatism

Consistent libertarians such as Nozick and the anarcho-capitalists have no sympathy for conservative social theory. However, many supporters of new right economics also hold profoundly conservative social views. Although they support freedom, they understand freedom in essentially economic terms. It is market freedom: freedom of choice in economic life supported by strict individual responsibility. Economic liberty must nevertheless be balanced against the need for social order. It is therefore possible for the new right to defend the expansion of liberty in economic affairs and simultaneously call for the restoration of authority in social life. The dual character of Thatcherism in the UK was summed up by Andrew Gamble (1988) as a commitment to 'the free economy and the strong state'. Neoconservatism is in some ways a reaction against the 'permissive 1960s'. By the 1960s, rising affluence in the post-war period had led to a growing willingness, especially amongst the young, to question and criticise conventional moral and social standards. Manifestations of this post-materialism were evident in the flowering of a youth 'counterculture' that emphasised personal choice in moral and life-style issues, and in the growth of a diverse range of political movements, including student radicalism, anti-Vietnam War protests, civil rights demonstrations, feminism and environmental activism. The new right regarded these developments as evidence of the collapse of traditional moral principles. In the face of permissiveness, Thatcher in the UK proclaimed her support for 'Victorian values', and in the United States organisations such as Moral Majority campaigned for a return to 'family values'.

David Edgar (1988) has argued that the conservative new right has been prepared to place 'the good' before 'the free'. Neoconservatives see two dangers in permissiveness. In the first place, the freedom to choose one's own morals or life-style could lead to the choice of immoral or 'evil' views. There is a significant religious element in the conservative new right, especially in the United States. During the 1970s and 1980s various US groups sprang up that expressed concern about the decline of 'traditional values'. Many of these were associated with the 'born again' Christian movement and in effect constituted a 'Christian new right'. Moral Majority, founded by Jerry Falwell in 1979 and supported by Ronald Reagan and powerful Southern senators such as Jessie Helms, acted as an umbrella organisation for this movement. During the 1980s and into the 1990s its principal energies were devoted to the campaign against abortion, and in particular the attempt to overturn the 1973 Supreme Court judgement on Roe vs Wade, which legalised abortion in the United States. Similar so-called 'pro-life' groups have sprung up in the UK and other western countries. They argue that women should not have the right to an abortion because the act is, quite simply, morally wrong. Abortion is equated with any other kind of murder. Homosexuality, pornography, premarital sex and, in the United States at least, the teaching of Darwinian theories of evolution rather than Biblical 'creationism' have also been castigated as morally 'bad'.

The second danger of permissiveness is not so much that people may adopt the wrong morals or life-styles, but may simply choose *different* moral positions. For a liberal, moral pluralism is healthy because it promotes diversity and rational debate, but for a neoconservative it is deeply threatening because it undermines the cohesion of society. A permissive society is a society that lacks ethical norms and unifying moral standards. It is a 'pathless desert', which provides neither guidance nor support for individuals and their families. If individuals merely do as they please, civilised standards of behaviour will be impossible to maintain.

Neoconservatives argue that this has been evident in rising delinquency and crime since the 1960s and in a general decline of authority. People need and want to know where they stand, and what is expected of them. This security is provided by the exercise of authority, in the family by the father, at school by the teacher, at work by the employer, and in society at large by a system of 'law and order'. Permissiveness undermines the roots of authority by permitting, even encouraging, the questioning of authority. As respect for authority breaks down, disorder and instability escalate. The conservative new right therefore stands for the restoration of authority. This can be seen in its call for the strengthening of 'family values'. The 'family', however, is understood in strictly traditional terms. It is thought to be naturally hierarchical: children should listen to, respect and obey their parents; and it is naturally patriarchal: the husband is the provider and the wife the home-maker. If these authority relationships are weakened, children will be brought up without a set of decent moral values and with little respect for their elders. A permissive society is therefore a breeding ground for antisocial behaviour, delinquency and crime.

Social order can also be strengthened by making punishment more severe, both to express the revulsion of society towards crime and to serve as a deterrent, discouraging criminal behaviour in others. In the United States, neoconservatives campaigned for restoration of the death penalty, which had been denounced as a 'cruel and unusual punishment' by the Supreme Court in the 1960s. By the late 1980s capital punishment had been reinstated in majority of the states. Similarly the US new right has campaigned to maintain the right to own firearms, as enshrined in the Second Amendment of the US Constitution. In the UK in the 1980s, a 'short, sharp shock' regime was introduced in youth custody centres, and in the 1990s, under Major, support was given to minimum sentences and US-style 'boot camps' for young offenders.

Such views about the need for order and discipline in society contrast strongly with the call for initiative and enterprise in the economy. Outside the economic sphere, the new right has generally supported a strong state. Stuart Hall interpreted Thatcherism in the UK as a form of 'authoritarian populism', reflecting and responding to widespread popular anxiety about the relaxation of moral standards and the weakening of authority in society (Hall and Jacques, 1983). The new right's case for a stronger state comes from its belief that order and social stability have increasingly been under threat. During the miners' strike of 1984–5, Thatcher referred to trade union militants as an 'enemy within', against which the nation needed to be protected. Neoconservatives fear that the growth of crime, vandalism, demonstrations and strikes all constitute a challenge to public order, against which only government can safeguard us.

At the same time the new right perceived a growing threat from an 'enemy without'. In the 1970s and 1980s this threat principally came from the Soviet Union, which was viewed by Ronald Reagan as 'an evil empire'. During this period the new right was distinguished by its fierce anti-communism, which in both the UK and the United States found expression in campaigns for greater defence expenditure. This was also linked to what the new right believed to be a weakening of national ties and identities. Reagan sought to rekindle American national pride, which had been badly damaged by the ignominy of its withdrawal from Vietnam in 1975 and the humiliation of the seizure of American hostages in Iran in 1979. The military build-up of the 1980s was designed to re-establish US predominance on the world stage, and it was hoped that the invasion of Granada and bombing of Libya would underline its willingness to use this power. In the UK, the Thatcher government too was associated with resurgent nationalism, particularly in its triumphalist response to the Falklands

War in 1982. However this tendency within neoconservatism was most clearly manifested in the growth of Euroscepticism in the 1980s and 1990s. Intensified hostility towards the EU within the Conservative Party not only reflected fears about the loss of sovereignty, but also, at a deep level, highlighted anxieties about a crisis of national identity. Euroscepticism is thus a typically conservative form of nationalism in that it has an insular and exclusive character. Conservative nationalism is discussed more fully in Chapter 5.

However, the degree to which neoconservatism is compatible with neoliberalism has been the source of considerable debate. Gamble's (1988) analysis emphasises key political linkages between the 'free market' and the 'strong state', in that in a context of widening inequality and weakening state supports there is a greater need to police the market order and uphold social and political authority. New right theorists themselves nevertheless hold that neoliberalism and neoconservatism are compatible at a deeper, ideological level. For instance Letwin (1992) portrayed Thatcherism in the UK as a moral crusade committed to a set of so-called 'vigorous virtues' – uprightness, self-sufficiency, energy, independent mindedness, loyalty and robustness – which in economic life require the rolling back of the state, but in social life imply greater intervention to maintain law and order, uphold national ideals and strengthen defence. For Willetts (1992) the apparent tension within the new right reflects nothing more than the basic and enduring concern of conservatism, which is to balance its commitment to the individual against its commitment to community.

Nevertheless it is difficult to view the new right as fully coherent in either ideological or political terms. Neoliberalism upholds values such as freedom, choice, rights and competition that are rooted in a conception of human nature that stresses robust individualism and self-reliance. Neo-conservatism champions value such as authority, discipline, respect and duty that are rooted in a conception of human nature that stresses fragility, fallibility and social dependence. Politically this tension is manifest in the tendency of neoliberalism to unleash forces and pressures that run directly counter to the fondest hopes of neoconservatism. For example the relentless dynamism of unregulated capitalism strains social cohesion and weakens the authority of established values and traditional institutions. Similarly, as markets are no respecters of national borders, consistent neoliberalism helps to undermine the nation as a meaningful economic and political entity.

## Conservatism in the twenty-first century

The late twentieth century has provided considerable fuel for conservative optimism if not triumphalism. Conservatism appears to have succeeded in overthrowing the 'pro-state' tendency that has characterised government throughout much of the twentieth century, especially since 1945, and in establishing an alternative 'pro-market' tendency. However, perhaps the major achievement of conservatism has been the vanquishing of its major rival, socialism. Parliamentary socialists in states ranging from New Zealand and Australia to Spain, Sweden and the UK have increasingly sought to maintain electoral credibility by embracing the values and philosophy of the market, accepting that there is no economically viable alternative to capitalism. More dramatically, the collapse of communism in eastern Europe and elsewhere produced, at least initially, a flowering of traditionalist political doctrines and free-market economics ones. What is more, conservatism's contribution to this process lay largely in its capacity to recreate itself as an ideological project. Distancing itself from its organicist, hierarchical and non-ideological instincts, conservatism, in the guise of the new right, aligned itself with market individualism and social authoritarianism. Although the 'heroic' phase of new right politics, associated with figures such as Thatcher and Reagan and the battle against the 'nanny state', may have passed and given way to a 'managerial' phase, this should not disguise the fact that market values have come to be accepted across the spectrum of conservative beliefs. Having exposed the twentieth-century 'socialist' mistakes of central planning and welfare capitalism, public policy in the twenty-first century looks set to be dominated by the 'new' conservative blend of the free market and the strong state.

However conservatism is also confronted by a number of challenges. One of these is that the very collapse of socialism creates problems in itself. As the twentieth century progressed, conservatism increasingly defined itself through its antipathy towards socialism. Indeed this may have been the real significance of the emergence of new right ideas and values. However if conservatism has become a critique of central planning and economic management, what role will it have once these have disappeared? In other words, how can conservatism remain relevant in a post-socialist age? A further problem stems from the long-term economic viability of the free-market philosophy. Faith in the free market has been historically and culturally limited. Enthusiasm for unregulated capitalism has been a largely Anglo-American phenomenon that peaked during the nineteenth century in association with classical liberalism, and was revived in the late twentieth century in the form of the new right. 'Rolling back the state' in economic life may sharpen incentives, intensify competition and promote entrepreneurialism, but sooner or later the disadvantages become apparent, notably short-termism, low investment, widening inequality and social exclusion. Just as liberals eventually came to recognise that the free market is an economic dead end, conservatives in the twenty-first century may have to learn the same lesson.

The prospects for conservatism are also tied up with the irony that neoliberal economics are at odds with the values that conservative ideology has historically been associated with, as well as with the social interests and electoral coalitions that have in the past supported conservative parties. Radical free-market policies create an economic free-for-all that strengthens self-seeking and egoistical behaviour, and promotes restless competition and social flux and instability. The neoliberal utopia is, after all, a society that is strictly individualist and endlessly dynamic. However such dynamism can only be achieved at the expense of tradition, continuity and organic order. It is, moreover, a prospect that is deeply unattractive to traditional elites and supporters of established institutions.

However, despite the economic and ideological drawbacks of the free market, conservatives may find that its more difficult to ditch neoliberalism than it was to embrace it in the first place. While the adoption of new right principles may have been essentially a pragmatic response to declining conservative electoral and political fortunes, they brought with them a distinctively unconservative passion for principle and established an unmistakably ideological style of politics. With this inevitably comes greater intellectual rigidity. Conservatives, in other words, may no longer 'travel light' in ideological terms. The danger is that whereas in the past conservatism encountered little internal resistance to its attempts to recreate itself as a viable ideological project, this may not be the case in the future.

## Further reading

Barry, N. P., *The New Right* (London: Croom Helm, 1987). A thorough and comprehensive introduction to the emergence of the new right and its major ideas and doctrines.

Eatwell, R. and N. O'Sullivan (eds), *The Nature of the Right: European and American Politics and Political Thought since 1789* (London: Pinter, 1989). An authoritative and thoughtful collection of essays on approaches to right-wing thought and the variety of conservative and rightist traditions.

Gamble, A., *The Free Economy and the Strong State* (London: Macmillan, 1988). An influential examination of the new right project that focuses specifically on Thatcherism in Britain.

Honderich, T., *Conservatism* (London: Hamish Hamilton, 1991). A distinctive and rigorously unsympathetic account of conservative thought; closely argued and interesting.

O'Sullivan, N., *Conservatism* (London: Dent; New York: St Martin's, 1976). A classic account of conservatism that lays particular stress upon its character as a 'philosophy of imperfection'.

Scruton, R., *The Meaning of Conservatism*, 2nd edn (Basingstoke: Macmillan, 1984). A stylish and openly sympathetic study that develops its own view of the conservative tradition.

# Chapter 4

# Socialism

## Origins and development

The term 'socialist' derives from the Latin *sociare*, meaning to combine or to share. Its earliest known usage was in 1827 in Britain, in an issue of the *Co-operative Magazine*. By the early 1830s the followers of Robert Owen (1771–1858) in Britain and Saint-Simon (1760–1825) in France had started to refer to their beliefs as 'socialism', and by the 1840s the term was familiar in a range of industrialised countries, notably France, Belgium and the German states.

Socialism is the broadest of political ideologies, encompassing a bewildering range of theories and traditions. Indeed it is tempting to refer to 'socialisms' rather than simply 'socialism', as a common ideological heritage is claimed by groups as disparate as communist revolutionaries, African nationalists, western social democrats and even some fascists, in particular national socialists. In their attempt to establish 'true' socialism, it was not uncommon for these traditions to be more hostile towards one another, than towards other ideologies. Such confusion largely arises from the success of socialism in establishing itself as a major political force in virtually every part of the globe, with the exception of North America. As socialist ideas have spread they have been moulded and sometimes transformed by the very different social, cultural and historical forces encountered in western and eastern Europe, Asia, Africa and Latin America.

Although socialists have sometimes claimed an intellectual heritage that goes back to Plato's *Republic* or Thomas More's *Utopia* (1516), like liberalism and conservatism the origins of socialism lie in the nineteenth century. Socialism arose as a reaction against the social and economic conditions generated in Europe by the growth of industrial capitalism. The birth of socialist ideas was closely linked to the development of a new but growing class of industrial workers, who suffered the poverty and degradation that were so often a feature of early industrialisation.

The character of early socialism was influenced by the harsh and often inhuman conditions in which the industrial working class lived and worked. The *laissez-faire* policies of the early nineteenth century gave factory owners a free hand when setting wage levels and factory conditions. Wages were typically low, child and female labour were commonplace, the working day often lasted up to twelve hours and the threat of unemployment was ever-present. In addition the new working class was disorientated, being largely composed of first-generation urban dwellers, unfamiliar with the conditions of industrial life and work and possessing few of the social institutions that could give their lives stability or meaning. As a result, early socialists often sought a radical, even revolutionary alternative to industrial capitalism. For instance Charles Fourier (1772–1837) in France and Robert Owen in Britain advocated the establishment of utopian communities based upon cooperation and love, rather than competition and greed. The Germans Karl Marx (see p. 126) and Friedrich Engels (1820–95) developed more complex and systematic theories, which claimed to uncover the 'laws of history' and proclaimed that the revolutionary overthrow of capitalism was inevitable.

In the late nineteenth century the character of socialism was transformed by a gradual improvement in working-class living conditions. The growth of trade unions, working-class political parties and sports and social clubs served to provide greater economic security and to integrate the working class into industrial society. In the advanced industrial societies of western Europe it became increasingly difficult to continue to see the working class as a revolutionary force. Socialist political parties progressively adopted legal and constitutional tactics, encouraged by the gradual extension of the vote to working-class men. By the First World War the socialist world was clearly divided between those socialist parties that had sought power through the ballot box and preached reform, and those, usually in more backward countries such as Russia, that proclaimed a continuing need for revolution. The Russian Revolution of 1917 entrenched this split: revolutionary socialists, following the example of Lenin (see p. 132) and the Bolsheviks, usually adopted the title 'communist', while reformist socialists retained the name 'socialist' or 'social democrat'.

The twentieth century has witnessed the spread of socialist ideas into African, Asian and Latin American, countries with little or no experience of industrial capitalism. Socialism in these countries often developed out of the anticolonial struggle, rather than a class struggle. The idea of class exploitation was replaced by that of colonial oppression, creating a potent fusion of socialism and nationalism, which is examined more fully in Chapter 5. The Bolshevik model of communism was adopted in China after the revolution of 1949 and subsequently spread to North Korea, Vietnam, Cambodia and Laos. More moderate forms of socialism have been practised elsewhere, for example by the Congress Party, which has ruled India for much of the period since independence in 1947. Distinctive forms of African and Arab socialism have also developed, being influenced respectively by the communal values of traditional tribal life and the moral principles of Islam. In South and Central America, socialist revolutionaries have waged war against military dictatorships, often seen to be operating in the interests of US imperialism. The Castro regime, which came to power after the Cuban revolution of 1959, developed close links with the Soviet Union, while the Sandinista guerrillas, who seized power in Nicaragua in 1979, remained non-aligned. In Chile, in 1970 Salvador Allende became the world's first democratically elected Marxist head of state, but was overthrown and killed in a CIA-backed coup in 1973.

In the late twentieth century socialism suffered a number of spectacular reverses, leading some to proclaim the 'death of socialism'. The most dramatic of these reverses was of course the collapse of communism in the eastern European revolutions of 1989–91. However, rather than socialists uniting around the principles of western social democracy, these principles were thrown into doubt as parliamentary socialist parties in many parts of the world embraced ideas and policies that are more commonly associated with liberalism or even conservatism. The final section of this chapter looks at the various challenges that confront modern socialism, and examines whether socialism any longer has future as a distinctive ideology.

## No man is an island – central themes

One of the difficulties of analysing socialism is that the term has been understood in at least three distinctive ways. From one point of view, socialism is seen as an economic model, usually linked to some form of collectivisation and planning. Socialism in this sense stands as an alternative to capitalism, the choice between these two fundamentally different productive systems being the most crucial of all economic questions. However the choice between 'pure' socialism' and 'pure' capitalism was always an illusion, as all economic forms have, in different ways, blended features of both systems. Indeed modern socialists tend to see socialism not so much as an alternative to capitalism, but as a means of harnessing capitalism to broader social ends. The second approach treats socialism as an instrument of the labour movement. Socialism, in this view, represents the interests of the working class and offers a programme through which the workers can acquire political or economic power. Socialism is thus really a form of 'labourism'. From this perspective, the significance of socialism fluctuates with the fortunes of the working-class movement worldwide. Nevertheless, although the historical link between socialism and organised labour cannot be doubted, socialist ideas have also been associated with skilled craftsmen, the rural peasantry and, for that matter, with political and bureaucratic elites. That is why, in this book, socialism is understood in a third and broader sense as a political creed or ideology, characterised by a particular cluster of ideas, values and theories. The most significant of these are the following:

- Community
- Cooperation
- Equality
- The satisfaction of need
- Common ownership.

## Community

At its heart, socialism possesses a unifying vision of human beings as social creatures, capable of overcoming social and economic problems by drawing upon the power of the community rather than simply individual effort. This is a collectivist vision because it stresses the capacity of human beings for collective action, their willingness and ability to pursue goals by working together, as opposed to striving for personal self-interest. Most socialists, for instance, would be prepared to echo the words of the English metaphysical poet, John Donne:

> No man is an Island entire of itself;
> every man is a piece of the Continent, a part of the main;. . .
> any man's death diminishes me, because I am involved in Mankind;
> and therefore never send to know for whom the bell tolls;
> it tolls for thee.

Human beings are therefore 'comrades', 'brothers' or 'sisters', tied to one another by the bonds of a common humanity.

Socialists are far less willing than either liberals or conservatives to believe that human nature is unchanging and fixed at birth. Rather they believe that human nature is 'plastic', moulded by the experiences and circumstances of social life. In the long-standing philosophical debate about whether 'nurture' or 'nature' determines human behaviour, socialists resolutely side with nurture. From birth – perhaps even while in the womb – each individual is subjected to experiences that shape and condition his

### Collectivism

Collectivism is, broadly, the belief that collective human endeavour is of greater practical and moral value than individual self-striving. It thus reflects the idea that human nature has a social core, and implies that social groups, whether 'classes', 'nations', 'races' or whatever, are meaningful political entities. However the term is used with little consistency. Bakunin (see p. 195) and other anarchists used collectivism to refer to self-governing associations of free individuals. Others have treated collectivism as strictly the opposite of individualism (see p. 28), holding that it implies that collective interests should prevail over individual ones. It is also sometimes linked to the state as the mechanism through which collective interests are upheld, suggesting that the growth of state responsibilities marks the advance of collectivism.

or her personality. All human skills and attributes are learnt from society, from the fact that we stand upright to the language we speak. Whereas liberals draw a clear distinction between the 'individual' and 'society', socialists believe that the individual is inseparable from society. Human beings are neither self-sufficient nor self-contained; to think of them as separate or atomised 'individuals' is absurd. Individuals can only be understood, and understand themselves, through the social groups to which they belong. The behaviour of human beings therefore tells us more about the society in which they live and have been brought up, than it does about any abiding or immutable human nature.

Liberals and conservatives often argue that, at heart, human beings are essentially self-seeking and egoistical. Socialists, on the other hand, regard selfish, acquisitive, materialistic or aggressive behaviour as socially conditioned rather than natural. Such characteristics are the product of a society that encourages and rewards selfish and acquisitive behaviour. This is precisely the allegation that socialists have traditionally made against capitalism. Human beings are not utility maximisers, but they are encouraged to act as such by the mechanism of the capitalist market, geared as it is to the pursuit of profit.

The radical edge of socialism derives not from its concern with what people are like, but with what they have the capacity to become. This has led socialists to develop utopian visions of a better society in which human beings can achieve genuine emancipation and fulfilment as members of a community. African and Asian socialists have often stressed that their traditional, preindustrial societies already emphasise the importance of social life and the value of community. In these circumstances, socialism has sought to preserve traditional social values in the face of the challenge from western individualism. As Julius Nyerere, president of Tanzania from 1964 to 1985, pointed out, 'We, in Africa, have no more real need to be "converted" to socialism, than we have of being "taught" democracy'. He therefore described his own views as 'tribal socialism'.

In the West, however, the social dimension of life has had to be 'reclaimed' after several generations of industrial capitalism. This was the goal of nineteenth-century utopian socialists such as Fourier and Owen, who organised experiments in communal living. Charles Fourier encouraged the founding of model communities, each containing about 1800 members, which he called 'phalansteries'. Robert Owen also set up a number of experimental communities, the best known being New Harmony in Indiana, 1824–9. The most enduringly successful communitarian experiment has been the kibbutz system in Israel, which consists of a system of cooperative, usually rural, settlements that are collectively owned and run by their members. The first kibbutz was founded in 1909 and now about 3 per cent of Israeli citizens live on kibbutzim, while a further 5 per cent live in rather less strict Moshav settlements.

## Cooperation

If human beings are social animals, socialists believe that the natural relationship amongst them is one of cooperation rather than competition. Liberals and conservatives regard competition amongst human beings as natural and, in some respects, healthy. It is natural because human beings are thought to be self-interested, and healthy insofar as it encourages individuals to work hard and develop whatever skills or abilities they may possess. Individuals should be rewarded for their personal achievements, whether it is running faster than anyone else, gaining higher marks in an exam or working harder than their colleagues.

Socialists, on the other hand, believe that competition pits one individual against another, encouraging each of them to deny or ignore their social nature rather than embrace it. As a result competition fosters only a limited range of social attributes and instead promotes selfishness and aggression. Cooperation, however, makes moral and economic sense. Individuals who work together rather than against each other will develop bonds of sympathy, caring and affection. Furthermore the energies of the community rather than those of the single individual can be harnessed. The Russian anarchist Peter Kropotkin (see p. 200), for example, suggested that the principal reason why the human species had survived and prospered was because of its capacity for 'mutual aid'. Socialists believe that human beings can be motivated by moral incentives and not merely by material incentives. In theory, capitalism rewards individuals for the work they do: the harder they work, or the more abundant their skills, the greater their reward will be. The moral incentive to work hard, however, is the desire to contribute to the common good, which develops out of a sympathy or sense of responsibility for fellow human beings. Although few modern social democrats would contemplate the outright abolition of material incentives, they nevertheless insist on the need for a balance of some kind between material and moral incentives. For example socialists would argue that an important incentive for achieving economic growth is that it helps to finance the provision of welfare support for the poorest and most vulnerable elements in society.

The socialist commitment to cooperation has stimulated the growth of cooperative enterprises, designed to replace the competitive and hierarchic businesses that have proliferated under capitalism. Both producers' and consumers' cooperatives have attempted to harness the energies of groups of people working for mutual benefit. In the UK, cooperative societies sprang up in the early nineteenth century. These societies bought goods in bulk and sold them cheaply to their working-class members. The 'Rochdale Pioneers' set up a grocery shop in 1844 and their example was soon taken up throughout industrial England and Scotland. Producer cooperatives, owned and run by their workforce, are common in parts of northern Spain and former Yugoslavia, where industry is organised according to the principle of workers' self-management. Collective farms in the Soviet Union were also designed to be cooperative and self-managing, though in practice they operated within a rigid planning system and were usually controlled by local party bosses.

## Equality

A commitment to equality is in many respects the defining feature of socialist ideology, equality being the political value that most clearly distinguishes socialism from its rivals, notably liberalism and conservatism. Conservatives believe society to be naturally hierarchic, and therefore reject the idea of social equality as quite absurd. Liberals, however, are committed to equality, but on the grounds that all individuals are of equal moral worth and are therefore entitled to equal rights and respect. They are nevertheless born with very different talents and skills and are entitled to be rewarded accordingly: those who work hard and possess abilities deserve to be wealthier than those who do not. Liberals therefore favour equality of opportunity, but see no reason why this should, or will, lead to social and economic equality.

In contrast socialists are far more reluctant to explain the inequality of wealth in terms of innate differences of ability amongst individuals. Socialists believe that just as capitalism has fostered competitive and selfish behaviour, human inequality very largely reflects the unequal structure of society. They do not hold the naive belief that all people are born identical, possessing precisely the same capacities and skills. An egalitarian society would not, for instance, be one in which all students gain the same mark in their mathematics examinations. Nevertheless socialists believe that the most significant forms of human inequality are a result of unequal treatment by society, rather than unequal endowment by nature. For example, despite natural differences in academic ability, educational performance is more usually a reflection of social factors such as access to full-time schooling, the quality of teaching, encouragement and support from the family and the availability of resources such as libraries, books and the space and time in which to study. As a result socialists are not satisfied simply to allow individuals an equal opportunity to develop their unequal skills or talents. Socialists demand social equality as an essential guarantee that all individuals, and not merely the privileged, are able to develop themselves to their fullest potential.

Once individual differences are understood to be socially produced, social equality is seen as being both possible and desirable. Social inequality is not only unjust, being based very largely upon an accident of birth, but also fosters rivalry, resentment and social divisions. Equality, on the other hand, enables human beings to work together cooperatively and harmoniously: equality is the essential underpinning of a genuine community. Perhaps the most extreme example of the socialist commitment to egalitarianism was in China during the so-called Cultural Revolution, 1966–9. Fearful that the Chinese Revolution was in danger of taking a 'capitalist road' and falling under the influence of rightist elements, the Chinese leader Mao Zedong (1893–1976) launched a radical campaign against privilege and inequality. An army of 'Red Guards' attacked and deposed 'capitalist roaders' within the government service, in schools and universities, and in the Communist Party itself. Wage differentials were swept away and even competitive sports such as football were banned.

Although socialists agree about the virtue of social and economic equality, they disagree about the extent to which this should be brought about. Marxists believe that inequality springs from the existence of private property, which has led to an unequal distribution of economic power between the property-owning bourgeoisie and the propertyless proletariat. For Marx, equality could only be achieved by the complete abolition of private property and the achievement of a classless society. Social equality will only be established when productive wealth is owned in common by all, in other words, when absolute equality is achieved.

Social democrats, however, seek to tame capitalism rather than abolish it. They believe that inequality reflects not the unequal ownership of wealth, but the fact that wealth is unequally distributed in society in terms of wages and salaries. Private property need not therefore be abolished but, less radically, simply be distributed more equally within society. Social democrats thus advocate greater distributive equality rather than absolute equality. In their view equality can be brought about by the redistribution of wealth from rich to poor, for example by expanding the welfare state or introducing a progressive system of taxation.

## Equality

**Liberals** believe that people are 'born' equal in the sense that they are of equal moral worth. This implies formal equality, notably legal and political equality, as well as equality of opportunity; but social equality is likely to be purchased at the expense of freedom and through the penalising of talent.

**Conservatives** have traditionally viewed society as naturally hierarchical and have thus dismissed equality as an abstract and unachievable goal. Nevertheless the new right evinces a strongly individualist belief in equality of opportunity while emphasising the economic benefits of material inequality.

**Socialists** regard equality as a fundamental value. Despite shifts within social democracy towards the liberal view, social equality, whether in its relative or absolute sense, has been seen as essential to ensuring social cohesion and fraternity, establishing justice or equity, and enlarging freedom in a positive sense.

**Anarchists** place a particular stress upon political equality, understood as an equal and absolute right to personal autonomy, implying that all forms of political inequality amount to oppression. Anarcho-communists believe in absolute social equality achieved through the collective ownership of productive wealth.

**Fascists** believe that humankind is marked by radical inequality, both between leaders and followers and between the various nations or races of the world. Nevertheless the emphasis on the nation or race implies that all members are equal at least in terms of their core social identity.

**Feminists** take equality to mean sexual equality, in the sense of equal rights, equal opportunities or equal social outcomes irrespective of gender. However, radical feminists have argued that the demand for equality may simply lead to women being 'male-identified'.

**Ecologists** advance the notion of biocentric equality, which emphasises that all life forms have an equal right to 'live and blossom'. Conventional notions of equality are therefore seen as anthropocentric, in that they exclude the interests of all organisms and entities other than humankind.

## Needs

The egalitarian tendencies of socialism are firmly linked to theories about the proper distribution of material benefits or rewards in society. Liberals generally argue that such rewards should be distributed according to individual abilities: what a person is entitled to should reflect his or her talents and willingness to work. Rights-based theories tend to justify material inequality by reference to natural inequality amongst humankind. Conservatives, for their part, have usually been reluctant to apply moral principles to the question of material distribution, preferring to accept that, whether we like it not, such matters are largely determined by luck and birthright. Socialists, in contrast, are more likely to argue that material benefits should be distributed on the basis of need, an idea that is sometimes regarded as the socialist theory of justice.

Needs differ from both wants and preferences. A 'need' is a necessity, it *demands* satisfaction; it is not simply a frivolous wish or a passing fancy. For this reason socialists regard needs as 'basic' to human beings, and their satisfaction is the foundation of full human existence. While 'wants' are a matter of personal judgement, shaped by social and cultural factors, needs are objective and universal, belonging to all people regardless of gender, nationality, religion, social background and so forth. The attraction of a needs-based theory of social justice is therefore that it addresses the most fundamental requirements of the human condition. This also explains why, in stark contrast to liberalism, socialists do not regard freedom and equality as conflicting principles. The socialist view of freedom is distinctly positive in that it takes freedom to mean human fulfilment or self-realisation. For socialists, this means not only the satisfaction of basic physiological needs such as food, water, shelter and so on, but also a range of higher needs, including the need for fellowship and love and the satisfaction that comes from creative labour. Since such needs are the same the world over, material resources should clearly be distributed so as to satisfy at least the basic needs of each and every person. From the socialist perspective, therefore, the drive for equality is in effect a means of enlarging liberty.

The most famous expression of the need-based theory of social justice is Marx's assertion that a fully communist society will inscribe on its banners the following formula: 'From each according to his ability, to each according to his needs!'. It would be a mistake, however, to reduce socialist conceptions of social justice to a simplistic theory of need satisfaction. For example Marx himself distinguished between the distributive principle that would be appropriate to full communism and the one that should be adopted in the transitional 'socialist' society. Marx accepted that capitalist practices could not be swept away overnight, and that many of them, for example material incentives, would linger on in a socialist society. He therefore recognised that under socialism labour would be paid according to its individual contribution and that this would vary according to the worker's physical or mental capacities. The 'socialist' principle of justice was therefore, 'to each according to his *work*'. The criterion of need can be said to be the basis of the communist principle of justice because, according to Marx, it is appropriate only to a future society of such material abundance that questions about the distribution of wealth become almost irrelevant. Modern social democrats concur with this view in holding that the satisfaction of needs is only one of the purposes of material distribution and that its significance is largely confined to the attempt to eradicate poverty.

A needs-based theory of justice does not, however, always lead to the equal distribution of resources, because needs themselves may sometimes be unequal. For example if need is the criterion, the only proper basis for distributing healthcare is ill-health. The sick should receive a greater proportion of the nation's resources than the healthy, simply because they are sick. Whereas socialists may accept, as an incentive to work, the accumulation of wealth well beyond what is reasonably needed, they are likely to regard as flagrantly obscene the failure to satisfy basic needs such as health and hunger. To allow people, wherever in the world they may live, to be hungry, thirsty, homeless or sick, or to live in fear, when the resources exist to make them otherwise, is therefore immoral. However the idea that the needs of one person constitute a moral imperative upon another, encouraging him or her to forego material benefits, is based on moral and philosophical assumptions that are not shared by liberalism and conservatism. Liberals may argue that redistributing wealth to satisfy the needs of the poor merely violates the rights of the rich. Conservatives have pointed out that if needs exist they are conditioned by historical, social and cultural factors, making the notion of universal 'human' needs as meaningless as the idea of universal 'human' rights.

## Common ownership

Socialists have often traced the origins of competition and inequality to the institution of private property, by which they usually mean productive wealth or 'capital' rather than personal belongings such as clothes, furniture or houses. This attitude to property sets socialism apart from liberalism and conservatism, which both regard property ownership as natural and proper. Socialists criticise private property for a number of reasons. In the first place property is unjust: wealth is produced by the collective effort of human labour and should therefore be owned by the community, not by private individuals. Secondly, socialists believe that property breeds acquisitiveness. Private property encourages people to be materialistic, to believe that human happiness or fulfilment can be gained through the pursuit of wealth. Those who own property wish to accumulate more, while those who have little or no wealth dream of acquiring it. Finally, property is divisive, it fosters conflict in society, for example between owners and workers, employers and employees, or simply the rich and the poor. Socialists have therefore proposed that the institution of private property either be abolished and replaced by the common ownership of productive wealth or, more modestly, that the right to property be balanced against the interests of the community.

Karl Marx envisaged the abolition of private property and hence the creation of a classless, communist society in place of capitalism. He clearly believed that property should be owned collectively and used for the benefit of humanity. However he said little about how this goal could be achieved in practice. When Lenin and the Bolsheviks seized power in Russia in 1917 they believed that socialism could be built through nationalisation, the extension of direct state control over the economy. This process was not completed until the 1930s, when Stalin's 'second revolution' witnessed the construction of a centrally planned economy, a system of state collectivisation. 'Common ownership' came to mean 'state ownership', or what the Soviet constitution described as 'socialist state property'. The Soviet Union thus developed a form of state socialism. Such an economic system was also thought to be more efficient than capitalism because it was based upon rational planning rather than the arbitrary pursuit of profit. All economic enterprises in the Soviet Union were directed by a sprawling network of government ministries and planning committees, which set output targets, fixed prices and controlled all exchange.

Social democrats have also been attracted to the state as an instrument through which wealth can be collectively owned and the economy rationally planned. However in the West nationalisation has been applied more selectively, its objective not being full state collectivism but the construction of a mixed economy, in which some industries would remain in private hands while others would be publicly owned. In the UK, for example, the Attlee Labour government, 1945–51, nationalised what it called the 'commanding heights' of the economy: major industries such as coal, steel, electricity and gas. Through these industries the government hoped to regulate the entire economy without the need for comprehensive collectivisation. However this selective commitment to common or public ownership was one of the chief casualties of the so-called 'new' revisionism of the 1980s and 1990s. Influenced by the image of nationalised industries as inefficient and unresponsive, modern social democrats have increasingly viewed the politics of ownership as redundant, and instead have shown enthusiasm for a 'dynamic market economy'.

Other socialists have remained faithful to the goal of common owner-ship, but believe that it could be achieved without expanding the powers of the state. Although socialism has often been associated with state owner-ship, nationalisation and planning, it also possesses a strong libertarian tradition. Marx, for instance, predicted that in a communist society the state would 'wither away', and he certainly did not envisage the highly bureaucratic systems of central planning that developed in communist states during the twentieth century. Small, self-managing communities

## Perspectives on . . .

### Economy

**Liberals** see the economy as a vital part of civil society and have a strong preference for a market or capitalist economic order based on property, competition and material incentives. However, while classical liberals favour *laissez-faire* capitalism, modern liberals recognise the limitations of the market and accept limited economic management.

**Conservatives** show clear support for private enterprise but have traditionally favoured pragmatic if limited intervention, fearing the free-for-all of *laissez-faire* and the attendant risks of social instability. The new right, however, endorses unregulated capitalism.

**Socialists** in the Marxist tradition have expressed a preference for common ownership and absolute social equality, which in orthodox communism was expressed in state collectivisation and central planning. Social democrats, though, support welfare or regulated capitalism, believing that the market is a good servant but a bad master.

**Anarchists** reject any form of economic control or management. However, while anarcho-communists endorse common ownership and small-scale self-management, anarcho-capitalists advocate an entirely unregulated market economy.

**Fascists** have sought a 'third way' between capitalism and communism, often expressed through the ideas of corporatism, supposedly drawing labour and capital together into an organic whole. Planning and nationalisation are supported as attempts to subordinate profit to the (alleged) needs of the nation or race.

**Ecologists** condemn both market capitalism and state collectivism for being growth-obsessed and environmentally unsustainable. Economics, therefore, must be subordinate to ecology, and the drive for profit at any cost must be replaced by a concern with long-term sustainability and harmony between humankind and nature.

have often been thought to be more appropriate units of common ownership than the state. Anarcho-communists, such as Peter Kropotkin, envisaged a stateless society made up of largely self-sufficient communes, in which people would work cooperatively and harmoniously. Other socialists have advocated the idea of 'workers' self-management', which became a central feature of the Yugoslav model of socialism after 1948.

## Roads to socialism

Competing traditions and tendencies within socialism have been divided by two major issues, the first of which concerns the goals or ends for which socialists should strive. Socialists have held very different conceptions of what a socialist society should look like; in effect there have been competing definitions of 'socialism'. These disagreements are discussed in the next two sections of this chapter. Second, socialists have disagreed about the appropriate means to achieve their ends, the various 'roads' that may lead to socialism. This concern with means follows from the fact that socialism developed as a radical or revolutionary ideology that was critical of its host society: industrial capitalism in the West and colonialism in the developing world. Socialists have consequently been concerned with change: the reform or overthrow of existing society. Which particular 'road to socialism' is chosen is of crucial significance because it both determines the character of the socialist movement and influences the form of socialism eventually achieved. In other words, 'means' and 'ends' are often very difficult to distinguish. The nature of socialism in the twentieth centry was deeply affected by the choice between the revolutionary and the evolutionary roads to its achievement.

### Revolutionary socialism

Many early socialists believed that socialism could only be introduced by the revolutionary overthrow of the existing political system and accepted that violence would be an inevitable feature of such a revolution. One of the earliest advocates of revolution was the French socialist August Blanqui (1805–81), who proposed the formation of a small band of dedicated conspirators to plan and carry out a revolutionary seizure of power. Marx and Engels, on the other hand, envisaged a 'proletarian revolution', in which the class-conscious working masses would rise up to overthrow capitalism. The first successful socialist revolution did not, however, take place until 1917, when a dedicated and disciplined group of revolutionaries, led by Lenin and the Bolsheviks, seized power in Russia in what was more a *coup d'état* than a popular insurrection. In many ways the Bolshevik Revolution served as a model for subsequent generations of socialist revolutionaries.

During the nineteenth century, revolutionary tactics were attractive to socialists for two reasons. First, the early stages of industrialisation produced stark injustice as the working masses were afflicted by grinding poverty and widespread unemployment. Capitalism was viewed as a system of naked oppression and exploitation, and the working class was thought to be on the brink of revolution. When Marx wrote in 1848 that 'A spectre is haunting Europe – the spectre of Communism' he was writing against a background of revolt and revolution in many parts of the continent. Second, the working classes had few alternative means of political influence, indeed almost everywhere they were excluded from political life. Where autocratic monarchies persisted throughout the nineteenth century, as in Russia, these were dominated by the landed aristocracy. Where constitutional and representative government had developed, the right to vote was usually restricted by a property qualification to the middle classes. In the exceptional cases where universal manhood suffrage was introduced much earlier, as in France in 1848, it was in predominantly agricultural and still deeply religious countries where the majority of the electorate, the small-holding peasantry, were politically conservative. In such cases the French anarchist Proudhon (see p. 199) warned that 'universal suffrage is counter-revolution'. For the unenfranchised working masses the only realistic prospect of introducing socialism lay with political revolution.

Revolution has, however, not merely been a tactical consideration for socialists, it also reflects their analysis of the state and its function. Whereas liberals believe the state to be a neutral body, responding to the interests of all citizens and acting in the common good, revolutionary socialists believe the state to be an agent of class oppression, acting in the interests of 'capital' and against those of 'labour'. Marxists, for example, believe that political power reflects class interests, that the state is a 'bourgeois state', inevitably biased in favour of capital. Political reform and gradual change are clearly pointless. The proletariat has no alternative: in order to build socialism it has first to overthrow the bourgeois state through political revolution. Marx believed that this revolution would be followed by a temporary period called the 'dictatorship of the proletariat', during which the revolution would need to be protected against the danger of counterrevolution carried out by the dispossessed bourgeoisie. Eventually, as socialism was established, the state would 'wither away' because there would be no call for class oppression in a classless society.

The class bias of the modern state was undeniable during the period when the working class was excluded from voting and political influence.

However revolutionary socialists believe that the 'bourgeois state' has not been reformed by the advent of political democracy. Lenin was the fiercest advocate of this view and of the continuing need for revolution. 'The real essence of bourgeois parliamentarianism', Lenin proclaimed in *The State and Revolution* ([1917] 1964, p. 54), is 'deciding every few years which member of the ruling class is to repress and crush the people through Parliament'. Parliamentary democracy is thus a mere facade concealing the reality of class rule, it is 'bourgeois democracy'. Modern Marxists have tended to revise this simplistic theory of the state and to acknowledge that at times the state can enjoy 'relative autonomy' from the class system. Nevertheless, a class bias continues to operate. In the first place the personnel of the state – civil servants, judges, police chiefs and so on – are drawn predominantly from privileged social backgrounds and will thus seek to defend capitalism, as Ralph Miliband argued in *The State in Capitalist Society* (1969). Secondly, governments are usually judged by how far they can maintain growth and prosperity in the economy, which forces them to serve the interests of business and industry. Finally, Marxists such as Nicos Poulantzas (1968) have argued that it is the role of the state to support the social system within which it operates, which means – whatever the party in power – upholding the capitalist system.

In the second half of the twentieth century, faith in revolution was most evident amongst socialists in the developing world. In the post-1945 period many national liberation movements embraced the 'armed struggle' in the belief that colonial rule could neither be negotiated nor voted out of existence. In Asia the Chinese Revolution of 1949 was the culmination of a long military campaign against both Japan and the Chinese Nationalists, the Kuomintang. Vietnamese national unity was achieved in 1975 after a prolonged war fought first against France and subsequently against the United States. Until his death in 1967, Che Guevara, the Argentine revolutionary, led guerrilla forces in various parts of South America and commanded troops during the Cuban revolution of 1959, which overthrew the US-backed Batista regime and brought Fidel Castro to power. Similar revolutionary struggles have taken place in Africa, for example the bitter war through which Algeria eventually gained independence from France in 1962. In the light of the Algerian experience, the French revolutionary theorist Frantz Fanon (1925–61) argued in *The Wretched of the Earth* ([1961] 1965) that violent insurrection was not merely a political necessity, but was also a psychologically desirable feature of the anticolonial struggle. Fanon believed that years of colonial rule had engendered a paralysing sense of inferiority and impotence amongst the black peoples of Africa, which could only be purged by the experience of revolt and the shedding of blood.

## Evolutionary socialism

Although early socialists supported the idea of revolution, as the nineteenth century progressed enthusiasm for popular revolt waned, at least in the advanced capitalist countries of western and central Europe. Capitalism itself had matured and by the late nineteenth century the urban working class had lost its revolutionary character and been integrated into society. Wages and living standards had started to rise, partly as a result of colonial expansion into Africa and Asia after 1875. The working class had also begun to develop a range of institutions – working men's clubs, trade unions, political parties and so on – which both protected their interests and nurtured a sense of security and belonging within industrial society. Furthermore, the gradual advance of political democracy led to the extension of the franchise (the right to vote) to the working classes. For example a limited number of working-class men were enfranchised in the UK in 1867, their number was expanded in 1884, and universal manhood suffrage, together with limited female suffrage, was achieved in 1918. The combined effect of these factors was to shift the attention of socialists away from violent insurrection and to persuade them that there was an alternative evolutionary, or 'democratic', road to socialism. It is notable, for example, that towards the end of his life Marx was prepared to speculate about the possibility of a peaceful transition to socialism in the advanced capitalist countries of western Europe, and Engels openly approved of the electoral tactics increasingly employed by the German Social Democratic Party (SPD). Where revolutionary doctrines continued to dominate it was usually in economically and politically backward countries such as Russia.

In the UK, for instance, Marxist ideas had little impact and socialists were more influenced by the Fabian Society, formed in 1884. The Fabians, led by Beatrice Webb (1858–1943) and Sidney Webb (1859–1947) and including noted intellectuals such as George Bernard Shaw and H. G. Wells, took their name from the Roman General Fabius Maximus, who was noted for the patient and defensive tactics he had employed to defeat Hannibal's invading armies. In their view socialism would develop naturally and peacefully out of liberal capitalism via a very similar process. This would occur through a combination of political action and education. Political action required the formation of a socialist party, which would compete for power against established parliamentary parties rather than prepare for violent revolution. They therefore accepted the liberal theory of the state as a neutral arbiter, rather than the Marxist belief that it was an agent of class oppression. The Webbs were actively involved in the formation of the British Labour Party and helped to write its 1918 constitution. The Fabians also believed that elite groups such as politicians of all parties, civil servants, scientists and academics could be converted to socialism through education. These elite groups would be 'permeated' by socialist ideas as they would recognise that socialism is morally superior to capitalism, being based upon Biblical principles, as well as being more rational and efficient. A socialist economy, for instance, could avoid the debilitating effects of class conflict and poverty.

Fabian ideas also had an impact upon the SPD, formed in 1875. The SPD quickly became the largest socialist party in Europe, and in 1912 the largest party in the German Reichstag. Although committed in theory to a Marxist strategy, in practice it adopted a reformist approach, influenced by the ideas of Ferdinand Lassalle (1825–64). Lassalle had argued that the extension of political democracy could enable the state to respond to working-class interests, and he envisaged socialism being established through a gradual process of social reform, introduced by a benign state. Such ideas were developed more thoroughly by Eduard Bernstein (see p. 143), whose *Evolutionary Socialism* (1898) contained the first comprehensive revision of Marxist thought. Bernstein was particularly impressed by the development of the democratic state, which he believed made the Marxist call for revolution redundant. The working class could use the ballot box to introduce socialism, which would therefore develop as an evolutionary outgrowth of capitalism. Bernstein was therefore largely pragmatic, his favourite maxim being that 'the movement is everything and the goal is nothing'.

The evolutionary principles of parliamentary socialism dominated the working-class political parties that sprang up around the turn of the century: the Australian Labour Party was founded in 1891, the British Labour Party in 1900, the Italian Socialist Party in 1892, its French counterpart in 1905, and so on. In the early years of the twentieth century the Second International was split by disagreements between revolutionary socialists such as Lenin and socialist leaders such as the SPD theoretician Karl Kautsky (1854–1938) in Germany, who pursued reformist tactics. By the end of the First World War a deep rift had developed between the socialist and communist movements. Socialist parties, embracing a parliamentary road to socialism, employed legal and electoral methods and proclaimed their commitment to 'democratic socialism'. Communist parties, on the other hand, formed in the aftermath of the Russian Revolution, remained faithful to the insurrectionary tactics that Lenin and the Bolsheviks had successfully employed in 1917.

In the late twentieth century, however, the distinction between evolutionary socialism and revolutionary communism became increasingly blurred. In the 1970s western communist parties, led by the Spanish, Italian and French communist parties, formally abandoned violent revolution and recast themselves as parliamentary parties. The resulting Eurocommunism was committed to pursuing a democratic road to communism and the maintenance of an open, competitive political system. The momentous events of 1989 witnessed the collapse of single-party communist rule throughout eastern Europe and the establishment of political pluralism and electoral democracy. With the introduction of competitive party systems, communist parties in the Soviet Union and eastern Europe acknowledged the underlying principle of evolutionary socialism: that political power should only be gained, and retained, through success in a competitive struggle for the popular vote.

## The inevitability of gradualism?

The advent of political democracy in the late nineteenth and early twentieth centuries caused a wave of optimism to spread throughout the socialist movement, as reflected, for example, in the Fabian prophecy of 'the inevitability of gradualism'. The idea that the victory of socialism was inevitable was not new. For instance Marx had predicted the inevitable overthrow of capitalist society in a proletarian revolution. However, whereas Marx believed that history was driven by the irresistible forces of class conflict, evolutionary socialists highlighted the logic of the democratic process itself.

Their optimism was founded on a number of assumptions. First, the progressive extension of the franchise would eventually lead to the establishment of universal adult suffrage and therefore of political equality. Second, political equality would, in practice, work in the interests of the majority, that is, those who decide the outcome of elections. Socialists thus believed that political democracy would invest power in the hands of the working class, easily the most numerous class in any industrial society. Third, socialism was thought to be the natural 'home' of the working class. As capitalism was seen as a system of class exploitation, oppressed workers would naturally be drawn to socialist parties, which offered them the prospect of social justice and emancipation. The electoral success of socialist parties would therefore be guaranteed by the numerical strength of the working class. Fourth, once in power, socialist parties would be able to carry out a fundamental transformation of society through a process of social reform. In this way political democracy not only opened up the possibility of achieving socialism peacefully, it made this process inevitable. The achievement of political equality had to be speedily followed by the establishment of social equality.

Such optimistic expectations have, however, not been borne out in reality. Some have even argued that democratic socialism is founded upon a contradiction: in order to respond successfully to electoral pressures, socialists have been forced to revise or 'water down' their ideological beliefs. Socialist parties have enjoyed periods of power in virtually all liberal democracies, with the exception of North America. However they have certainly not been guaranteed power. The Swedish Social Democratic Labour Party (SAP) has been the most successful in this respect, having been in power alone or as the senior partner in a coalition in all but two of the years between 1951 and 1993. However even the SAP has only once achieved 50 per cent of the popular vote (in 1968). The British Labour Party gained its greatest support (49 per cent) in 1951, equalled by the Spanish Socialist Workers' Party in 1982. The SPD in Germany got 46 per cent of the vote in 1972 and the combined socialist and communist vote in Italy in 1976 amounted to 44 per cent. Moreover, although these parties have undoubtedly introduced significant social reforms when in power, usually involving the expansion of welfare provision and economic management, they have certainly not presided over any fundamental social transformation. At best capitalism has been reformed, not abolished.

Democratic socialism has in fact encountered a number of problems not envisaged by its founding fathers. In the first place, does the working class any longer constitute the majority of the electorate in advanced industrial societies? Socialist parties have traditionally focused their electoral appeal upon urban manual workers, the 'factory fodder' of capitalist societies. Modern capitalism, however, has become increasingly technological, demanding a skilled workforce that is often engaged in technical rather than manual tasks. The 'traditional' working class, engaged in regimented manual labour and working in established heavy industries, has given way to a growing 'new' working class, composed of skilled workers, usually better paid and working in expanding light industries, service industries or 'sunrise' industries. In *The Culture of Contentment* (1992) J. K. Galbraith drew attention to the emergence in modern societies, or at least amongst the politically active, of a 'contented majority' whose material affluence and economic security encourage them to be politically conservative. If working-class support no longer offers socialist parties the prospect of an electoral majority, they are either forced to appeal more broadly for support to other social classes, or to share power as a coalition partner with middle-class parties. Both options require socialist parties to modify their ideological commitments in order to appeal to electors who have little or no interest in socialism, or to work with parties that seek to uphold capitalism.

Furthermore, is the working class socialist at heart? Is socialism genuinely in the interests of the working class? Socialist parties have been forced to acknowledge the ability of capitalism to 'deliver the goods', especially during the 'long boom' of the post-1945 period, which brought growing affluence to all classes in western societies. During the 1950s socialist parties, once committed to fundamental change, revised their policies in an attempt to appeal to an increasingly affluent working class. A similar process took place in the 1980s and 1990s, as socialist parties struggled to come to terms with changes in the class structure of capitalism as well as the pressures generated by economic globalisation. In effect socialism came to be associated with attempts to make the market economy work, rather than with the attempt to re-engineer the social structure of capitalism. Such shifts are examined in more detail later, in connection with the changing character of social democracy.

Left-wing socialists, on the other hand, have been reluctant to accept that the working class has abandoned fundamentalist socialism. Rather they believe that the working class has been deprived of the ability to make independent political judgements that reflect their own interests. Marxists, for example, have argued that capitalism is supported by a process of ideological manipulation. 'Bourgeois ideology' pervades society, preventing the working class perceiving the reality of its own exploitation. For example Lenin proclaimed that without the leadership of a revolutionary party the working class would only be able to gain 'trade union consciousness', a desire for material improvement within the capitalist system, but not full revolutionary 'class consciousness'. Gramsci (see p. 9), emphasised that the bourgeoisie dominates capitalism not only through its economic power but also by a process of 'ideological hegemony'. Criticism has also focused upon the role of the mass media in forming the views and values of the electorate. Although the media in capitalist countries usually enjoys independence from government, socialists would strongly deny that it is politically impartial. For instance Tony Benn (1980) suggested that the mass media in the UK and other capitalist countries possesses an antisocialist bias, largely because newspaper ownership lies in the hands of a small number of powerful individuals or major multinational companies.

Finally, can socialist parties, even if elected to power, carry out socialist reforms? Socialist parties have formed single-party governments in a number of western countries, including France, Sweden, Spain, the UK, Australia and New Zealand. Once elected, however, they have been confronted with entrenched interests in both the state and society. In 1902 Karl Kautsky argued that 'the capitalist class rules but it does not govern, it contents itself with ruling the government'. Elected governments operate within what Miliband (1983) has called a 'state system' – the administration, courts, police and military – whose personnel are not elected and come from similar social backgrounds to businesspeople. These groups reflect a class bias and are capable of blocking, or at least diluting, radical socialist policies. Moreover elected governments, of whatever ideological inclination, must respect the power of big business, which is the major employer and investor in the economy as well as the wealthiest contributor to party funds. In other words, although democratic socialist parties may succeed in forming elected governments, there is the danger that they will merely win office without necessarily acquiring power.

## Communism

The term 'communism' originated amongst the secret revolutionary societies of Paris in the mid 1830s. However its use in political debate causes confusion because it is understood in at least three different ways. First, it refers to a future society based on the common ownership of wealth and, possibly, the communal organisation of social existence. As such, thinkers as different as Plato and Thomas More can be said to have subscribed to communism, although the term is more commonly associated with the writings of Marx and Engels. Second, it denotes a political movement aimed at establishing such a society, usually by drawing on the revolutionary potential of the working class. This movement came into existence in the years after the First World War with the formation of communist parties, modelled, initially at least, on the Russian Bolsheviks. Third, the term communism came to be used to describe the regimes that communist parties established when they gained power, for example in the Soviet Union, eastern Europe, China, Cuba and elsewhere. Communism thus came to mean 'actually existing socialism', sometimes seen as orthodox communism. This section attempts to straddle these various definitions by examining both the theory and the practice of Marxism. However the term Marxism is no less beset by difficulties than is communism.

Strictly speaking, 'Marxism' as a codified body of thought only came into existence after Marx's death in 1883. It was the product of the attempt, notably by Marx's lifelong collaborator, Engels, the German socialist leader Karl Kautsky and the Russian theoretician Georgie Plekhanov (1856–1918), to condense Marx's ideas and theories into a systematic and comprehensive world view that suited the needs of the growing socialist movement. Engels' *Anti-Dühring*, written in 1876 while Marx was still alive, is sometimes seen as the first work of Marxist orthodoxy, emphasising the need for adherence to an authoritative interpretation of Marx's work. This orthodox Marxism, which is often portrayed as 'dialectical materialism' (a term coined by Plekhanov and not used by Marx), later formed the basis of Soviet communism. This 'vulgar' Marxism undoubtedly placed heavier stress on mechanistic theories and historical inevitability than did Marx's own writings. The matter, however, is further complicated by the breadth and complexity of Marx's own writings and the difficulty of establishing the 'Marxism of Marx'. Some, for instance, see Marx as an economic determinist, while others proclaim him to be a humanist socialist. Moreover distinctions have also been drawn between his early and later writings, sometimes presented as the distinction between the 'young Marx' and the 'mature Marx'. It is nevertheless clear that Marx himself believed that he had developed a new brand of socialism that was scientific in the sense that it was primarily concerned with disclosing the nature of social and historical development, rather than with advancing an essentially ethical critique of capitalism.

## Classical Marxism

### Philosophy

The core of classical Marxism – the Marxism of Marx – is a philosophy of history that outlines why capitalism is doomed and why socialism is destined to replace it. This is, however, philosophy of a particular kind. As Marx put it in his 'Thesis on Feueurbach' ([1845] Marx and Engels, 1968): 'The philosophers have only *interpreted* the world, in various ways; the point, however, is to *change* it'. He therefore saw his work as both a theory of society and a socialist political project. Indeed the sophistication and complexity of Marx's writings derive in part from his unwillingness to separate theory from practice and his belief that as human beings shape their world, in the process they are also helping to shape themselves. But in what sense did Marx believe his work to be scientific? Marx criticised earlier socialist thinkers such as Saint-Simon, Fourier and Owen as 'utopians' on the ground that their socialism was grounded in a desire for total social transformation unconnected with the necessity of class struggle and revolution. Marx, in contrast, undertook a laborious empirical analysis of history and society, hoping thereby to gain insight into the nature of future developments. However, whether with Marx's help or not, Marxism as the attempt to gain historical understanding through the application of scientific methods, later developed into Marxism as a body of scientific truths, gaining a status more akin to that of a religion. Engels' declaration that Marx had uncovered the 'laws' of historical and social development was a clear indication of this transition.

What made Marx's approach different from that of other social thinkers was that he subscribed to what Engels called the 'materialist conception of history' or historical materialism. Rejecting the idealism of the German philosopher Hegel (1770–1831), who believed that history amounted to the unfolding of the so-called 'world spirit', Marx held material circumstances to be fundamental to all forms of social and historical development. This reflected the belief that the production of the means of subsistence is the most crucial of all human activities. Since humans cannot survive without food, water, shelter and so on, the way in which these are produced conditions all other aspects of life; in short, 'social being determines

## Karl Marx (1818–83)

German philosopher, economist and political thinker, usually portrayed as the father of twentieth-century communism. After a brief career as a teacher and journalist, Marx spent the rest of his life as an active revolutionary and writer, living mainly in London and supported by his friend and life-long collaborator, Friedrich Engels.

Marx's work was derived from a synthesis of Hegelian philosophy, British political economy and French socialism. Its centrepiece was a critique of capitalism that highlights its transitional nature by drawing attention to systemic inequality and instability. Marx subscribed to a teleological theory of history that held that social development would inevitably culminate with the establishment of communism. His classic work is the three-volume *Capital* (1867, 1885 and 1894); his best-known and most accessible work is the *Communist Manifesto* (1848).

consciousness'. In the preface to *A Contribution to the Critique of Political Economy*, written in 1859, Marx gave this theory its most succinct expression by suggesting that social consciousness and the 'legal and political superstructure' arise from the 'economic base', the real foundation of society. This 'base' consists essentially of the 'mode of production' or economic system – feudalism, capitalism, socialism and so on. Although the precise nature of the relationship between the base and the superstructure has been the subject of considerable debate and speculation, it undoubtedly led Marx to conclude that political, legal, cultural, religious, artistic and other aspects of life could primarily be explained by reference to economic factors.

Although in other respects a critic of Hegel, Marx nevertheless embraced his belief that the driving force of historical change was the dialectic, a process of interaction between competing forces that leads to a higher stage of development. In effect, progress is the consequence of internal conflict. For Hegel, this explained the movement of the 'world spirit' towards self-realisation through conflict between a thesis and its opposing force, an antithesis, producing a higher level, a synthesis, which in turn constitutes a new thesis. Marx, as Engels put it, 'turned Hegel on his head' by investing this Hegelian dialectic with a materialistic interpretation. Marx thus explained historical change by reference to internal contradictions within each mode of production arising from the existence of private property. Capitalism is thus doomed because it embodies its own antithesis, the proletariat, seen by Marx as the 'grave digger of capitalism'. Conflict between capitalism and the proletariat will therefore lead to a higher stage of development in the establishment of a socialist, and eventually a communist, society.

This enabled Marx to divide history into a series of stages, each characterised by its own economic structure and class system. In *The German Ideology* ([1846] 1970) Marx identified four such stages: (1) primitive communism or tribal society, in which material scarcity provided the principal source of conflict; (2) slavery, covering classical or ancient societies and characterised by conflict between master and slave; (3) feudalism, marked by antagonism between land owners and serfs; and (4) capitalism, dominated by the struggle between the bourgeoisie and the proletariat. Human history had therefore been a long struggle between the oppressed and the oppressor, the exploited and the exploiter. Each stage of history nevertheless marked an advance on the last in that it brought about the further development of the 'forces of production': machinery, technology, labour processes and the like. However, following Hegel, Marx envisaged an end of history, which would occur when a society was constructed that embodied no internal contradictions or antagonisms. This, for Marx, meant communism, a classless society based on the common ownership of productive wealth. With the establishment of communism, the 'pre-history of mankind' will have come to an end.

## Economics

In Marx's early writings much of his critique of capitalism rests on the notion of alienation. This suggests that capitalism has separated people from their genuine or essential natures, that is, from their capacity as workers to develop skills, talents and understanding through the experience of free productive labour. Since capitalism is a system of production for exchange, it alienates humans from the product of their labour: they work to produce not what they need or what is useful, but 'commodities' to be sold for profit. They are also alienated from the process of labour, because most are forced to work under the supervision of foremen or managers. In addition the work is not social: individuals are encouraged to be self-interested and are therefore alienated from fellow human beings. Finally, workers are alienated from themselves. Labour itself is reduced to a mere commodity and work becomes a depersonalised activity instead of a creative and fulfilling one. In Marx's later work, however, capitalism is more often analysed in terms of class conflict and exploitation.

Social class designates a group of people who hold a common economic position and therefore share similar working and social experiences. However Marx did not use class in its more conventional sense to refer to occupational groups distinguished from one another by factors such as status and income level, as in the division between the 'blue collar' working class and the 'white collar' middle class. Rather he defined class in terms of economic power, specifically where people stand in relation to the ownership of the 'means of production', or productive wealth. Marx believed that capitalist society was increasingly being divided into 'two great classes facing one another: Bourgeoisie and Proletariat'. The bourgeoisie make up the capitalist class and live off the ownership of productive wealth; the proletariat constitute the propertyless masses, who are forced to subsist through the sale of their labour power and can thus be seen as 'wage slaves'. For Marx and later Marxists, the analysis of the class system provides the key to historical understanding and enables predictions to be made about the future development of capitalism: in the famous words of the *Communist Manifesto*, 'The history of all hitherto existing societies is the history of class struggle.'

Classes, rather than individuals, parties or other movements, are the chief agents of historical change. Crucially, Marx believed that the relationship between classes is one of irreconcilable antagonism, the subordinate class being necessarily and systematically exploited by the 'ruling class'. This he explained by reference to the idea of 'surplus value'. Unlike conventional economists, who estimate value in terms of price determined by market forces, Marx, in line with earlier theorists such as Locke (1632–1704), subscribed to a labour theory of value. This suggests that the value of a good reflects the quantity of labour that has been expended in its production. Capitalism's quest for profit can only be satisfied through the extraction of 'surplus value' from its workers, by paying them less than the value their labour generates. Economic exploitation is therefore basic to the capitalist mode of production, and it operates regardless of the meanness or generosity of particular employers.

Marx was concerned not only to highlight the inherent instability of capitalism, based as it is on irreconcilable class conflict, but also to analyse the nature of capitalist development. In particular he drew attention to its tendency to experience deepening economic crises. These stemmed, in the main, from cyclical crises of overproduction, plunging the economy into stagnation and bringing unemployment and immiseration to the working class. Each crisis would be more severe than the last because, Marx calculated, in the long-term the rate of profit would fall. Further tensions would result from a tendency towards monopolisation, the concentration of capital in fewer and fewer hands and the absorption of all other classes into the ranks of the proletariat. The exploited masses, united by a common economic interest, would thus come to constitute the overwhelming majority in any capitalist society.

## Politics

Marx's most important prediction was that capitalism was destined to be overthrown by a proletarian revolution. This would be not merely a political revolution that would remove the governing elite or overthrow the state machine, but a social revolution that would establish a new mode of production and culminate with the achievement of full communism. In Marx's view the epoch of social revolution would begin when the class system, the 'relations of production', became a fetter upon the further development of productive techniques and innovation, the so-called forces of production. Such a revolution, he anticipated, would occur in the most mature capitalist countries, for example Germany, Belgium, France and Britain, where the forces of production had expanded to their limit within the constraints of the capitalist system. Nevertheless revolution would not simply be determined by the development of objective conditions. The subjective element would be supplied by a 'class-conscious' proletariat, meaning that revolution would occur when both objective and subjective conditions were 'ripe'. As class antagonisms intensified, the proletariat would recognise the fact of its own exploitation and become a revolutionary force: a class-for-itself. In this sense revolution would be a spontaneous act, carried out by the proletarian class that, in effect, would lead or guide itself.

The initial target of this revolution was to be the bourgeois state. Two theories of the state can be identified in Marx's writings. The first is expressed in his often-quoted dictum from the *Communist Manifesto* 'The executive of the modern state is the committee for managing the common affairs of the bourgeoisie'. From this perspective, the state is clearly dependent upon society and acts as nothing more than an instrument of oppression wielded by the economically dominant class. A second – more complex and subtle – theory of the state is found in *The Eighteenth Brumaire of Louise Bonaparte* ([1852] Marx and Engels, 1968). This allows that the state can enjoy what has come to be seen as 'relative autonomy' from the ruling class, its principal role being to mediate between conflicting classes and so perpetuate the class system. In either case, however, the proletariat has no alternative: in order to defeat capitalism the state machine that upholds it must first be overthrown.

Marx nevertheless recognised that there could be no immediate transition from capitalism to communism. A transitionary 'socialist' stage of development would last as long as class antagonisms persisted. This would be characterised by what Marx called the 'revolutionary dictatorship of the proletariat', in effect a proletarian state whose purpose would be to safeguard the gains of the revolution by preventing counter-revolution by the dispossessed bourgeoisie. However, as class antagonisms began to fade with the emergence of full communism, the state will 'wither away' – once the class system had been abolished the state would lose its reason for existence. The resulting communist society would therefore be stateless as well as classless, and would allow a system of commodity production to give way to one geared to the satisfaction of human needs. For the first time, human beings would be able to shape their own destinies and realise their full potential, reflected in Marx's belief that 'the free development of each is the precondition of the free development of all'.

## Orthodox communism

The communist parties that developed in the twentieth century were undoubtedly founded upon the theories and beliefs of Marx and Engels; however they were also forced to adapt these ideas to the task of winning and retaining political power. In the process, classical Marxism was significantly revised and extended. Moreover when communist parties did achieve power it was not, as Marx had anticipated, in the developed capitalist countries of western Europe, but in backward, largely rural countries such as Russia and China. The resulting communist regimes were therefore shaped as much by historical circumstances and practical factors as by any ideological model. As a result communist rule in the twentieth century often diverged markedly from the utopian vision that Marx had developed in the nineteenth century.

The image of communism in the twentieth century has been dominated by the Russian Revolution and its consequences. The Bolshevik party, led by V. I. Lenin, seized power in a *coup d'état* in October 1917, and the following year adopted the name 'Communist Party'. As the first success-ful communist revolutionaries, the Bolshevik leaders enjoyed unquestion-able authority within the communist world, at least until the 1950s. Communist parties set up elsewhere accepted the ideological leadership of Moscow and joined the Communist International, or 'Comintern', founded in 1919. The communist regimes established in eastern Europe after 1945, in China in 1949 and in Cuba in 1959 were consciously modelled upon the structure of the Soviet Union. Thus Soviet communism became the dominant model of communist rule, and the ideas of Marxism-Leninism became the ruling ideology of the communist world.

However the Bolshevik model of communism owed much to the particular historical conditions of Russia in 1917. In the first place Russia was economically backward: the overwhelming majority of Russians still lived on the land and the urban proletariat was small and unsophisticated. Indeed orthodox Marxists, for example the members of the Menshevik party, believed Russia to be at the feudal stage of development and ripe for a bourgeois revolution, but many years away from a socialist one. It was not until Trotsky (see p. 182) formulated his theory of permanent revolution in 1906 that anyone conceived of the immediate prospect of achieving socialism in Russia. In Trotsky's view Russian development had been 'uneven' and its bourgeoisie was not strong enough to establish a stable capitalist society. The bourgeois stage of development could there-fore be bypassed and Russia could move immediately from capitalist society to socialist revolution, led by the small but powerful proletariat.

Secondly, political life in Russia had been stunted by repressive and autocratic tsarist rule, which had forced opponents of the regime either to live in exile abroad or to organise themselves into tightly disciplined, conspiratorial groups in the hope of escaping arrest and imprisonment. Finally, once in power the Bolsheviks confronted hostility from both within and without. 'White' armies, loyal to the tsar, waged a civil war until 1921 and were supported by foreign troops from the UK, France, the United States and Japan. As a result the emerging communist regime became accustomed to employing coercive means to maintain political stability and defend itself against 'class enemies'. Far from 'withering away', as Marx had predicted, economic backwardness combined with political instability forced the newly established 'proletarian state' to become increasingly centralised and powerful.

### Leninism

Soviet communism was also shaped by the decisive personal contribution of the first two Bolshevik leaders, Lenin and Stalin (see p. 134). Lenin was both a political leader and a major political thinker. Lenin's ideas reflected his overriding concern with the problems of winning power and establishing communist rule. He remained faithful to the idea of revolution, believing that parliamentary politics were merely a bourgeois sham, aimed at tricking the proletariat into believing that political power was exercised through the ballot box. Power had to be seized through armed insurrection, in accordance with Lenin's exhortation to 'smash the state!' Lenin also echoed Marx's call for a transitional dictatorship of the proletariat, between the overthrow of capitalism and the achievement of 'full communism'. The revolution had to be protected against the possibility of counter-revolution by 'class enemies', in particular the dispossessed bourgeoisie which wished to restore capitalism. Socialist revolution must therefore be followed by the construction of a proletarian or workers' state.

The most significant and novel of Lenin's ideas was his belief in the need for a new kind of political party, a revolutionary party or vanguard party. Unlike Marx, Lenin did not believe that the proletariat would sponta-neously develop revolutionary class consciousness, as the working class was deluded by bourgeois ideas and beliefs. Lacking any grasp of Marxist analysis, workers were failing to recognise that their real enemy was the capitalist system itself, and were instead seeking to improve their condi-tions within capitalism, for instance by achieving better pay, shorter hours

## Vladimir Ilich Lenin (1870–1924)

Russian Marxist theorist and revolutionary. Lenin was drawn into active politics by the execution of his brother in 1887, and became a Marxist in 1889. In 1903 he founded the Bolshevik Party, later masterminding the 1917 October Revolution. Lenin remained leader of the Soviet state until his death, although he effectively retired in late 1922 after a series of strokes.

Undoubtedly the most influential Marxist theorist of the twentieth century, Lenin was primarily concerned with the issues of organisation and revolution. *What is to be Done?* (1902) emphasised the central importance of a tightly-organised 'vanguard' party to lead and guide the proletarian class. In *Imperialism, the Highest Stage of Capitalism* (1916), he analysed colonialism as an economic phenomenon and highlighted the possibility of turning world war into class war. *State and Revolution* (1917) outlined Lenin's firm commitment to the 'insurrectionary road' and rejected electoral democracy as 'bourgeois parliamentarianism'.

and safer working conditions. Lenin suggested that only a 'revolutionary party' could lead the working class from 'trade union consciousness' to revolutionary class consciousness. Such a party should be composed of professional and dedicated revolutionaries. Its claim to leadership would lie in its ideological wisdom, specifically its understanding of Marxist theory, which was thought to provide a scientific explanation of social and historical development. The party could therefore act as the 'vanguard of the proletariat' because, armed with Marxism, it would be able to perceive the genuine interests of the proletariat and be dedicated to awakening the proletarian class to its revolutionary potential.

Lenin proposed that the vanguard party should be organised according to the principles of democratic centralism. The party should be composed of a hierarchy of institutions, linking grass-root cells to the party's highest organs: its central committee and politburo. 'Democracy' within the party required that each level of the party would be able to debate freely, make recommendations to higher organs and elect their delegates; however 'centralisation' meant that minorities would have to accept the views of the majority, and that lower organs of the party should obey decisions made by higher ones. The revolutionary party had to be tightly disciplined and centrally organised in order to provide the ideological leadership the proletariat needed. Lenin proclaimed that democratic centralism would achieve 'freedom of discussion and unity of action'.

When the Bolsheviks seized power in 1917 they did so as a vanguard party and therefore in the name of the proletariat. If the Bolshevik Party was acting in the interests of the working class, it followed that opposition parties must represent the interests of classes hostile to the proletariat, in particular the bourgeoisie. The dictatorship of the proletariat required that the revolution be protected against its class enemies, which effectively meant the suppression of all parties other than the Communist Party. By 1920 Russia had become a one-party state. Leninist theory therefore implies the existence of a monopolistic party, which enjoys sole responsibility for articulating the interests of the proletariat and guiding the revolution toward its ultimate goal, that of 'building communism'. Moreover the party must also be a ruling party. As the source of political authority within a communist state, the Communist Party must be the leading and guiding force within government and all other institutions. Orthodox communist states, modelled on the principles of Marxism–Leninism, should therefore invest their ruling communist parties with entrenched political power and a monopoly of ideological wisdom.

## Stalinism

Soviet communism was no less deeply influenced by the rule of Joseph Stalin than that of Lenin. Indeed more so, as the Soviet Union was more profoundly affected by Stalin's 'second revolution' in the 1930s than it had been by the October Revolution. Stalin's most important ideological innovation was the doctrine of 'Socialism in One Country', announced in 1924, which proclaimed that the Soviet Union could succeed in 'building socialism' without the need for international revolution. This clearly distinguished him from Trotsky, who maintained an unswerving commitment to internationalism. After consolidating himself in power, however, Stalin oversaw a dramatic economic and political upheaval, commencing with the announcement of the first Five Year Plan in 1928. Under Lenin's New Economic Policy, introduced in 1921, the Soviet Union had developed a mixed economy in which agriculture and small-scale industry remained in private hands, while the state controlled only what Lenin called the 'commanding heights of the economy'. Stalin's Five Year Plans, however, brought about rapid industrialisation as well as the swift and total eradication of private enterprise. From 1929 agriculture was collectivised, and Soviet peasants were forced at the cost of literally millions of lives to give up their land and join state or collective farms. Economic Stalinism therefore took the form of state collectivisation or 'state socialism'. The capitalist market was entirely removed and replaced by a system of central planning, dominated by the State Planning Committee, 'Gosplan', and administered by a collection of powerful economic ministries based in Moscow.

Major political changes accompanied this 'second revolution'. In order to achieve power, Stalin had exploited his position as general secretary of

## Joseph Stalin (1879–1953)

Russian revolutionary and leader of the Soviet Union, 1924–53. Stalin, the son of a shoemaker, was expelled from his seminary for revolutionary activities and joined the Bolsheviks in 1903. He became general secretary of the Communist Party in 1922, and after winning the struggle for power following Lenin's death he established a monolithic command–administrative system, sustained by widespread terror and a cult of personality.

Despite his voluminous writings, Stalin was not a significant theoretician, Stalinism referring more to a distinctive politico-economic system than to a body of ideas. His ideological heritage flows from the doctrine of 'Socialism in One Country', which dictated the drive for industrialisation and collectivisation, justified by the need to resist capitalist encirclement and to eliminate the *kulaks* (rich peasants) as a class. Stalin thus fused a quasi-Marxist notion of class war with an appeal to Russian nationalism.

the Communist Party by ensuring that his supporters were appointed to influential posts within the party apparatus. Party officials were appointed from above by a system known as the nomenklatura, rather than being elected from below. Democratic centralism became less democratic and more centralised, leading to a 'circular flow of power' in which the party leader acquired unrivalled authority by virtue of his control over patronage and promotion. During the 1930s Stalin used this power to brutal effect, removing anyone suspected of disloyalty or criticism in an increasingly violent series of purges carried out by the secret police, the NKVD. The membership of the Communist Party was almost halved, over a million people lost their lives, including all surviving members of Lenin's Politburo, and many millions were imprisoned in labour camps, or *gulags*. Political Stalinism was therefore a form of totalitarian dictatorship, operating through a monolithic ruling party, in which all forms of debate or criticism were eradicated by terror in what amounted to a civil war conducted against the party itself. The nature of totalitarianism (see p. 233) is discussed in more depth in Chapter 5.

### The decline and fall of communism

Until the death of Stalin in 1953, Soviet communism retained almost unquestionable authority in the communist world. The Soviet Union had succeeded in becoming a major industrial power, it had helped to defeat fascism in the Second World War, and its influence had expanded with the establishment of communist rule in eastern Europe and China. During this period the principal critic of Soviet communism was Leon Trotsky.

Although Trotsky had led the Bolshevik coup in 1917 and commanded the Red Army, he had been defeated by Stalin in the power struggle in the 1920s, was exiled from the Soviet Union in 1929, and was finally murdered by Stalin's assassins in 1940. In the 1930s Trotsky argued that the Soviet Union suffered from a 'bureaucratic degeneration', and proposed that a political revolution was necessary to overthrow a privileged strata of state bureaucrats and return the Soviet Union to the road to socialism. Although Trotsky formed a Fourth International to challenge the Soviet-dominated Communist International, he remained an outcast from the mainstream world and his ideas had little impact until long after his death.

The death of Joseph Stalin allowed a gradual process of questioning and criticism to take place within the Soviet Union and elsewhere. In 1956 Stalin's successor, Khrushchev, presented a secret speech to the Twentieth Congress of the Soviet Communist Party, which catalogued the 'crimes of Stalin', alleging that he had built up a 'cult of personality' and was personally responsible for the brutality and suffering of the 1930s. Khrushchev's allegations shocked the communist world, which held Stalin to be the legitimate heir of Lenin and Marx. A period of de-Stalinisation dawned in the Soviet Union, reflected in a 'cultural thaw' and a limited attempt to decentralise economic power. The Soviet invasion of Hungary, also in 1956, caused the first ripples of criticism of Moscow to spread within western communist parties. In 1958 Mao Zedong, the Chinese Communist leader, introduced the so-called 'Great Leap Forward' and established greater independence from Moscow, which in 1960 led to a formal break in relations with the Soviet Union. As the communist world became less monolithic, the Bolshevik model was challenged by rival conceptions of socialism in both the West and the East.

In the 1970s western communist parties, which had previously accepted the ideological leadership of Moscow, began to pursue greater independence and a distinctive brand of Eurocommunism. The break with Moscow was provoked by growing distaste for Soviet foreign and domestic policies, which under Brezhnev, 1964–82, entered a period of neo-Stalinism, and by the fact that the electoral appeal of communist parties was being damaged by their image as revolutionary parties and their acknowledged subordination to Moscow. The Italian, French and Spanish communist parties were the first to exercise greater independence, and in 1977 agreed a broadly worded declaration of Eurocommunist principles. They accepted that communism had to conform to existing national traditions and culture as the Russian experience was not always relevant to conditions in western Europe. The Italian Communist Party, for example, wished to abandon any formal link with atheism.

The central principle of Eurocommunism, however, was rejection of the Leninist idea of revolution in favour of a gradual and peaceful transition towards socialism. Western communist parties therefore became parliamentary parties, committed to constitutional and electoral politics. In accepting that power could be won through the ballot box, the Eurocommunists revised the Leninist idea that the state is merely an instrument of class rule and argued that it could enjoy at least 'relative autonomy' from the class system and be influenced by all social classes, including the proletariat. The Eurocommunist parties also reassessed the idea of the vanguard party. They no longer considered themselves to be the sole representatives of the working class and were therefore prepared to enter into alliances with other parties. For example the Italian Communist Party briefly shared power with the Christian Democrats (from 1977–8), in what was called an 'historic compromise', and French Communists served in the Socialist-dominated government of 1981–4.

Finally, Eurocommunists abandoned the idea of the dictatorship of the proletariat. If political power could be won through competitive elections, it would have to be retained in the same way. Eurocommunist parties therefore accepted the principle of political pluralism and relinquished their ambition to establish one-party communist rule. Eurocommunist principles thus departed fundamentally from those of orthodox Marxism–Leninism, and in many ways the political practice of European communist parties became indistinguishable from that of social democratic parties. This process of revision was significantly accelerated by the events of 1989–91, for example, in 1989 the Italian Communist Party formally adopted a social democratic programme and in 1990 it dropped the title 'Communist', renaming itself the Party of the Democratic Left. During the 1990s, in a trend soon followed by many other communist parties, it formally renounced Marxism, aligning itself instead with a variety of radical causes, including democratisation, feminism and ecologism.

Some communist states also took up the idea of reform. For example, during the 'Prague Spring' of 1968, the Czechoslovak communist leader, Alexander Dubcek, attempted an experiment in what he called 'socialism with a human face'. Civil liberties and political freedoms were restored, restrictions imposed upon the secret police and the first elements of a competitive party system introduced. However the experiment was abruptly terminated in August 1968 by a Warsaw Pact invasion, which led to Dubcek's removal and the reimposition of Marxist–Leninist orthodoxy. A further example was Yugoslavia, which had never fully conformed to Stalinist central planning. During the communist period, over 85 per cent of Yugoslav agricultural land remained privately owned and industry operated according to the principle of workers' self-management. Economic decentralisation was also introduced in Hungary after 1968 as part of what was called the 'New Economic Mechanism'. The Yugoslav and Hungarian reforms briefly created an alternative model of economic development to rival Soviet-style central planning, commonly called market socialism. The essence of this model was the attempt to gain the benefits of the market – efficiency, competition and responsiveness – without the reintroduction of private property or a capitalist class system. Such an economy is 'socialist' in that there is no market for labour and the economy is dominated by workers' cooperatives; these, however, operate within a competitive market environment.

The year 1989 marked a dramatic watershed in the history of communism. A wave of popular demonstrations, commencing in April with the emergence of a student-led 'democracy movement' in China, challenged communist rule in many parts of the world. Although the Tiananmen Square demonstrations were brutally suppressed in June, communist regimes collapsed throughout eastern Europe in the autumn and winter of 1989. The Berlin Wall was breached on 10 November and by the end of the year the 'Iron Curtain', which had divided Europe since 1945 into capitalist West and communist East, had ceased to exist. Where communist rule survived, the process of internal reform was immediately accelerated.

These dramatic events were made possible by a change in political leadership in the Soviet Union: the appointment of Mikhail Gorbachev as general secretary of the Communist Party in 1985. Alarmed by the stagnation and inefficiency of the Soviet economy, Gorbachev inaugurated a process of radical reform in the Russian tradition of 'revolution from above'. He established three goals: the first and most important was *perestroika* – the 'restructuring' of the economy; the second was *glasnost* – greater 'openness', freedom of political debate; and the third was democratisation – broader popular participation in public life. However Gorbachev's attempt to save communism through reforms that drew on the Yugoslav and Czech experiences merely highlighted the contradictions and weaknesses of the Stalinist system. *Perestroika* succeeded in dismantling an existing, if inefficient, economic system, but failed to establish an alternative one. *Glasnost* allowed long-suppressed anticommunist and particularly nationalist forces to rise to the surface, which in December 1991 finally tore the Soviet Union apart. And democratisation so threatened the position of entrenched communist and military elites that it precipitated the August 1991 coup, which destroyed Gorbachev's authority and allowed power to pass to Boris Yeltsin.

## Modern Marxism

While Marxism – or more usually Marxism–Leninism – was turned into a secular religion by the orthodox communist regimes of the East, a more subtle and complex form of Marxism developed in western Europe. Referred to as modern Marxism or neo-Marxism, this amounted to an attempt to revise or recast the classical ideas of Marx while remaining faithful to certain Marxist principles or aspects of Marxist methodology.

Two principal factors shaped the character of modern Marxism. First, when Marx's prediction about the imminent collapse of capitalism failed to materialise, modern Marxists were forced to re-examine conventional class analysis. In particular, they took greater interest in Hegelian ideas and in the stress upon 'Man the creator' found in Marx's early writings. In other words human beings came to be seen as makers of history, not simply puppets controlled by impersonal material forces. By insisting upon an interplay between economics and politics, between the material circumstances of life and the capacity of humans to shape their own destiny, modern Marxists were able to break free from the rigid 'base/ superstructure' straightjacket. In short the class struggle was no longer treated as the beginning and end of social analysis. Second, modern Marxists were usually at odds with, and sometimes profoundly repelled by, the Bolshevik model of orthodox communism. Not only were they critical of its authoritarian and repressive character, but they also recoiled from its mechanistic and avowedly scientific pretensions.

The Hungarian Marxist Georg Lukács (1885–1971) was one of the first to present Marxism as a humanistic philosophy, emphasising the process of 'reification', through which capitalism dehumanises workers by reducing them to passive objects or marketable commodities. Antonio Gramsci drew attention to the degree to which the class system is upheld not simply by unequal economic and political power but also by bourgeois 'hegemony', the spiritual and cultural supremacy of the ruling class, brought about through the spread of bourgeois values and beliefs via civil society – the media, churches, youth movements, trade unions and so on.

A more overtly Hegelian brand of Marxism was developed by the so-called Frankfurt School, whose leading members were Theodor Adorno (1903–69), Max Horkheimer (1895–1973) and Herbert Marcuse. Frankfurt theorists developed what was called 'critical theory', a blend of Marxist political economy, Hegelian philosophy and Freudian psychology, that came to have a considerable impact on the new left. The new left, prominent in the 1960s and early 1970s, rejected both of the 'old' alternatives – Soviet-style state socialism and deradicalised western social democracy. Influenced by the writings of the 'young' Marx but also by anarchism and radical forms of phenomenology and existentialism, new left theories were often diffuse. Common themes nevertheless included the rejection of conventional society – 'the system' – as oppressive, disillusion-ment with the working class as the agent of revolution, a commitment to

## Herbert Marcuse (1898–1979)

German political philosopher and social theorist, cofounder of the Frankfurt School. A refugee from Hitler's Germany, Marcuse lived in the United States and developed a form of neo-Marxism that drew heavily on Hegel and Freud. He came to prominence in the 1960s as a leading new left thinker and 'guru' of the student movement.

Central to Marcuse's work was the portrayal of advanced industrial society as an all-encompassing system of repression, subduing argument and debate and absorbing all forms of opposition – 'repressive tolerance'. Against this 'one-dimensional society', he held up the unashamedly utopian prospect of personal and sexual liberation, looking not to the conventional working class as a revolutionary force but to groups such as students, ethnic minorities, women and workers in the Third World. Marcuse's most important works include *Reason and Revolution* (1941), *Eros and Civilisation* (1958) and *One-Dimensional Man* (1964).

personal autonomy and self-fulfilment in the form of 'liberation', and a preference for decentralisation and participatory democracy.

In contrast a form of structural Marxism emerged from the writings of the French communist Louis Althusser (1918–90). This was based on the assumption that Marx viewed individuals as simply bearers of functions that arise from their structural location, in which case Marxism becomes a 'new science' essentially concerned with the analysis of the structure of a social totality. A very different approach has been adopted by analytical Marxists such as John Roemer (1986), who has tried to fuse Marxism with a methodological individualism more commonly associated with liberalism. Instead of believing that history is shaped by collective entities, in this case classes, analytical Marxists attempt to explain collective action in terms of the rational calculations of self-interested individuals. Others have gone further and completely abandoned the task of reinterpreting or revitalising Marxism. This, for instance, is reflected in the 'post-Marxism' of the one-time Marxist, Jean-François Lyotard (1984), who suggested that Marxism as a totalising theory of history, and for that matter all other 'grand narratives', had been made redundant by the emergence of postmodernism (see p. 324).

## Social democracy

The term 'social democracy' has been accorded a number of very different definitions. Its original meaning was associated with orthodox Marxism and was designed to highlight the distinction between the narrow goal of political democracy and the more fundamental objectives of socialism. Political democracy aimed to give all citizens an equal voice at election time by the achievement of universal adult suffrage. Social democracy, on the other hand, applied the principle of equality to social life and therefore to the possession of wealth. In its original sense, therefore, social democracy implied a commitment to the collective ownership of productive wealth and the achievement of a classless society. When parties adopted the title 'Social Democratic' – for example the German Social Democratic Party, SPD, founded in 1875, and the Russian Social Democratic Labour Party, founded in 1898 – they were acknowledging a formal commitment to Marxist doctrines.

However the term soon acquired a rather different meaning as a result of the parliamentary tactics adopted by most social democratic parties and especially by the largest of them, the SPD, under the leadership of Karl Kautsky. Marx himself criticised the SPD's Gotha Programme, adopted in 1875, because it proposed a peaceful transition to socialism. By the beginning of the twentieth century, social democracy was increasingly taken to refer to democratic socialism, in contrast to revolutionary socialism. After the Russian Revolution, those socialists who remained faithful to the principle of revolution followed the example of the Russian Bolsheviks and adopted the title 'Communist' to distance themselves from reformist social democratic parties.

The final change in the meaning of the term social democracy occurred as a result of the tendency among social democratic parties not only to adopt parliamentary strategies, but also to revise their socialist goals. In particular western social democrats no longer sought to abolish capitalism but rather to reform or 'humanise' it. The social democratic tradition has therefore come to stand for a broad balance between the market economy on the one hand, and state intervention on the other. In the process, socialists have re-examined their fundamental principles and, in effect, redefined socialism.

## Ethical socialism

The theoretical basis for social democracy in the twentieth century has been provided by moral or religious beliefs, rather than scientific analysis. Marx and Engels had described their own theories as 'scientific socialism', and rejected the 'utopian socialism' of earlier years. Marxism's claim to being scientific rested upon the belief that it uncovered the laws of social and historical development: the victory of socialism was inevitable, not because it embodied a higher moral vision, but because the class struggle would drive history through a succession of stages until the eventual achievement of a classless society. Marx's scientific method was based upon historical materialism, the belief that human thought and behaviour are conditioned by the economic circumstances of life. Social democrats have not accepted the materialist and highly systematic ideas of Marx and Engels, but rather advanced an essentially moral critique of capitalism. In short, socialism is portrayed as morally superior to capitalism because human beings are ethical creatures, bound to one another by the ties of love, sympathy and compassion. Such ideas have often given socialism a markedly utopian character.

The moral vision that underlies ethical socialism has been based upon both humanistic and religious principles. Socialism in France, the UK and other Commonwealth countries has been more strongly influenced by the utopian ideas of Fourier, Owen and William Morris (1854–96) than by the scientific creed of Karl Marx. Socialism has also drawn heavily upon Christianity. For example there is a long-established tradition of Christian socialism in the UK, reflected in the twentieth century in the work of R. H. Tawney. The Christian ethic that has inspired British socialism is that of universal brotherhood, the respect that should be accorded all individuals as creations of God, a principle embodied in the commandment 'Thou shalt love thy neighbour as thyself'. In *The Acquisitive Society* (1921), Tawney condemned unregulated capitalism because it is driven by the 'sin of avarice' rather than faith in a 'common humanity'. In *Equality* ([1931] 1969) Tawney condemned the British class system as 'particularly detestable to Christians' and called for a substantial reduction of social inequality.

## Richard Henry Tawney (1880–1962)

UK social philosopher and historian. Drawn into educational social work in London's East End by his social conscience, Tawney devoted his life to social reconstruction through his association with the Workers' Educational Association, the Labour Party and as professor of economic history at the London School of Economics.

Tawney's socialism was firmly rooted in a Christian social moralism unconnected with Marxist class analysis. The disorders of capitalism derived from the absence of a 'moral ideal', leading to unchecked acquisitiveness and widespread material inequality. The project of socialism was therefore to build a 'common culture' that would provide the basis for social cohesion and solidarity. Tawney's major works include *The Acquisitive Society* (1921), *Equality* (1931) and *The Radical Tradition* (1964).

Such religious inspiration has also been evident in the ideas of liberation theology, which has influenced many Catholic developing world states, especially in Latin America. After years of providing support for repressive regimes in Latin America, Roman Catholic bishops meeting at Medellin, Colombia, in 1968 declared a 'preferential option for the poor'. The religious responsibilities of the clergy were seen to extend beyond the narrowly spiritual and to embrace the social and political struggles of ordinary people. Despite the condemnation of Pope John Paul II and the Vatican, radical priests in many parts of Latin America campaigned against poverty and political oppression and at times even backed socialist revolutionary movements. For example the Sandinista revolution in Nicaragua in 1979 was supported, sometimes actively, by revolutionary priests. Similarly, socialist movements in the predominantly Muslim countries of North Africa, the Middle East and Asia have been inspired by religion. Islam is linked to socialism in that it exhorts the principles of social justice, charity and cooperation, and specifically prohibits usury or profiteering.

In abandoning scientific analysis in favour of moral or religious principles, however, social democracy weakened the theoretical basis of socialism. Social democracy has been primarily concerned with the notion of a just or fair distribution of wealth in society. This is embodied in the overriding principle of social democracy: social justice, implying a commitment to greater equality and reflected in values such as caring and compassion. However, what this goal means in practice is very difficult to establish with any precision. For instance just how much equality is required to 'humanise' capitalism? And what is an acceptable balance between welfare and wealth creation? Social democracy has consequently come to stand for a broad range of views, extending from a left-wing commitment to extending equality and expanding the collective ownership of wealth, to a right-wing belief in market efficiency that may become indistinguishable from modern liberalism and even overlap with paternalistic conservatism. Attempts have nevertheless been made to give social democracy a theoretical basis, usually involving a reexamination of capitalism itself and a redefinition of the goal of socialism.

## Revisionism

The original, fundamental goal of socialism was that productive wealth should be owned in common by all and therefore used for the common benefit. This required the abolition of private property and the introduction of what Marx referred to as 'social revolution', the transition from a capitalist mode of production to a socialist one. Fundamentalist socialism is based upon the belief that capitalism is unredeemable: it is a system of class exploitation and oppression that deserves to be abolished altogether, not merely reformed.

By the turn of the century some socialists had come to believe that Marx's analysis was defective. The clearest theoretical expression of this belief was found in Eduard Bernstein's *Evolutionary Socialism* ([1898] 1962), which undertook a comprehensive criticism of Marx and the first major revision of Marxist analysis. Bernstein's analysis was largely empirical; he rejected Marx's method of analysis – historical materialism – because the predictions Marx had made had proved to be incorrect. Capitalism had shown itself to be both stable and flexible. Indeed by the end of the nineteenth century there was little evidence that the 'spectre of Communism', referred to by Marx in the *Communist Manifesto*, was still haunting Europe. Rather than class conflict intensifying, dividing capitalist society into 'two great classes', the bourgeoisie and the proletariat, Bernstein suggested that capitalism was becoming increasingly complex and differentiated. In particular the ownership of wealth had widened as a result of the introduction of joint stock companies, owned by a number of shareholders, instead of a single powerful industrialist. The ranks of the middle classes had also swollen, the growing number of salaried employees, technicians, government officials and professional workers being neither capitalists nor proletarians. In Bernstein's view capitalism was no longer a system of naked class oppression. Capitalism could be reformed by the nationalisation of major industries and the extension of legal protection and welfare benefits to the working class, a process which Bernstein was confident could be achieved peacefully and democratically.

Western socialist parties have been revisionist in practice, if not always in theory, intent upon 'taming' capitalism rather than abolishing it. In

## Eduard Bernstein (1850–1932)

German socialist politician and theorist. An early member of the German Social Democratic Party, Bernstein became one of its leading intellectuals, deeply embroiled in the revisionist controversy. He left the party because of his opposition to the First World War, though he subsequently returned.

Influenced by British Fabianism and the philosophy of Kant (1724–1804), Bernstein attempted to revise and modernise orthodox Marxism. In *Evolutionary Socialism* (1898) he argued that economic crises were becoming less, not more acute, and drew attention to the 'steady advance of the working class'. He therefore called for alliances with the liberal middle class and the peasantry, and emphasised the possibility of a gradual and peaceful transition to socialism. In his later writings he abandoned all semblance of Marxism and developed a form of ethical socialism based on neo-Kantianism.

some cases they long retained a formal commitment to fundamentalist goals, as in the British Labour Party's belief in 'the common ownership of the means of production, distribution and exchange', expressed in clause IV of its constitution, which survived unaltered until 1995. Nevertheless, as the twentieth century progressed social democrats dropped their commitment to planning as they recognised the efficiency and vigour of the capitalist market. The Swedish Social Democratic Labour Party formally abandoned planning in the 1930s, as did the West German Social Democrats at the Bad Godesberg Congress of 1959, which accepted the principle, 'competition when possible; planning when necessary'. In the UK a similar bid formally to embrace revisionism in the late 1950s ended in failure when the Labour Party Conference rejected Hugh Gaitskell's attempts to abolish clause IV. Nevertheless, when in power the Labour Party never revealed any appetite for wholesale nationalisation.

The abandonment of planning left social democracy with three more modest objectives. The first of these was the mixed economy, a blend of public and private ownership that stands between free market capitalism and state collectivism. Nationalisation, when advocated by social democrats, is invariably selective and reserved for the 'commanding heights' of the economy, or industries that are thought to be 'natural monopolies'. The 1945–51 Attlee Labour government, for example, nationalised the major utilities – electricity, gas, coal, steel, the railways and so on – but left most of British industry in private hands. Second, social democrats sought to regulate or manage capitalist economies in order to maintain economic growth and keep unemployment low. After 1945 most social democratic parties were converted to Keynesian economics as a device for controlling the economy and delivering full employment. Finally, socialists were attracted to the welfare state as the principal means of reforming or humanising capitalism. The welfare state was seen as a redistributive mechanism that would help to promote social equality and eradicate poverty. Capitalism no longer needed to be abolished, only modified by the establishment of welfare capitalism.

An attempt to give theoretical substance to these developments, and in effect update Bernstein, was made by the UK politician and social theorist Anthony Crosland in *The Future of Socialism* (1956). Crosland (1918–77) argued that modern capitalism bore little resemblance to the nineteenth-century model that Marx had had in mind. Crosland was influenced by the ideas of James Burnham, who in *The Managerial Revolution* ([1941] 1960) suggested that a new class of managers, experts and technocrats had supplanted the old capitalist class and come to dominate all advanced industrial societies, both capitalist and communist. Crosland believed that the ownership of wealth had become divorced from its control. Whereas shareholders, who own businesses, are principally concerned with profit, salaried managers, who make day-to-day business decisions, have a broader range of goals, including the maintenance of industrial harmony as well as the public image of their company. Marxism had therefore become irrelevant; if capitalism could no longer be viewed as a system of class exploitation, then the fundamentalist goals of nationalisation and planning were simply outdated.

However, as a socialist Crosland remained faithful to the goal of social justice, which he understood to mean a more equal distribution of wealth. Wealth need not be owned in common, it could be redistributed through a welfare state, financed by progressive taxation. The welfare state would raise the living standards of the poor and the most vulnerable sections in society, while progressive taxation would ensure that the prosperous and strong bore the burden of expanded welfare support. Finally, Crosland recognised that economic growth plays a crucial role in the achievement of socialism. A growing economy is essential to generate the tax revenues needed to finance more generous social expenditure. In addition the prosperous will only be prepared to finance the needy if their own living standards are underwritten by economic growth.

## From social justice to community

During the early post-war period Keynesian social democracy appeared to have triumphed. Its strength was that it harnessed the dynamism of the market without succumbing to the levels of inequality and instability that Marx believed would doom capitalism. Liberal and conservative parties responded to this eagerly by developing their own forms of social democracy, the former based on equal opportunities, the latter on the paternalist or 'one nation' ideal. But moderate socialism, it seemed, had won the battle of ideas: political thought was moving inexorably to the left. Nevertheless Keynesian social democracy continued to be based on a compromise. On the one hand there was a pragmatic acceptance of the market as the only reliable means of generating wealth. This reluctant conversion to the market meant that social democrats accepted that there was no viable socialist alternative to the market, meaning that the socialist project was reborn as an attempt to reform, not replace, capitalism. On the other hand the socialist ethic survived in the form of a commitment to social justice, the idea of a morally defensible distribution of benefits or rewards in society. This in turn was linked to a weak notion of equality: the idea that poverty should be reduced and inequality narrowed through the redistribution of wealth from rich to poor. Abandoning the task of wholesale social reconstruction, socialists nevertheless wished to embark upon a programme of social engineering.

However, whereas fundamentalist socialism had a clear and well-defined goal – the abolition of capitalism – the revisionist goal of reforming capitalism was far more vague. All social democrats accepted that capitalism should be modified in accordance with the principle of social justice, but they had very different views about how this could be achieved, and even about how 'social justice' should be defined. What, for example, should be the balance between public and private ownership within a mixed economy – which industries should be nationalised and which left in private hands? How far should the welfare state be expanded before the growing tax burden became an impediment to economic growth? Should socialist governments accede to wage demands from low-paid workers when this risked stimulating inflation? Moreover, over time, social democrats came to defend intervention less in terms of traditional socialist principles and more by reference to modern liberal ideas such as equality of opportunity and positive freedom. The divide between socialism and liberalism thus became increasingly blurred (Marquand, 1992).

At the heart of Keynesian social democracy lay a conflict between its commitment to both economic efficiency and egalitarianism. During the 'long boom' of the post-war period, social democrats were not forced to confront this conflict because sustained growth, low unemployment and low inflation improved the living standards of all social groups and helped to finance more generous welfare provision. However, as Crosland had anticipated, recession in the 1970s and 1980s created strains within social democracy, polarising socialist thought into more clearly defined left-wing and right-wing positions. Recession precipitated a 'fiscal crisis of the welfare state', simultaneously increasing demand for welfare support as unemployment re-emerged, and squeezing the tax revenues that financed welfare spending, because fewer people were at work and businesses were less profitable. A difficult question had to be answered: should social democrats attempt to restore efficiency to the market economy, which might mean cutting inflation and possibly taxes, or should they defend the poor and the lower paid by maintaining or even expanding welfare spending?

Although such polarisation caused deep divisions, the clear trend in the 1980s and 1990s was to retreat from the central principles of Keynesian social democracy. This 'new' revisionism was brought about by a combination of electoral and international factors. In electoral terms, Keynesian policies had come to be associated with a 'tax and spend' approach to economic management that risked permanently high levels of inflation. The welfare state tended to be viewed as a burden on the employed in particular and on wealth creation in general; and nationalised industries were increasingly seen as unresponsive and inefficient. In short,

Keynesian social democracy was deemed to be electorally unviable. This was evident in the UK, where the Labour Party lost four successive general elections between 1979 and 1992, and in 1983 recorded its worst electoral result since the end of the First World War. After its third defeat in 1987, Neil Kinnock instigated a comprehensive policy review that brought many of the party's policies into line with those that the breakaway Social Democratic Party had endorsed in 1981. This process of 'modernisation' was subsequently extended by John Smith after the 1992 defeat but was pursued more radically and with a clearer purpose by Tony Blair from 1994 onwards. The abolition of clause IV in 1995 symbolised the extent of this ideological retreat.

Very similar developments have happened elsewhere. The German Social Democrats have been out of power since 1982, and have adopted an increasingly moderate, non-ideological political style. In France, despite François Mitterrand's presidential victories in 1981 and 1988, the Socialist Party effectively abandoned its attempt fundamentally to transform society after 1983 and suffered a crushing defeat in the 1993 presidential elections before losing the Elysée two years later. Although the Australian Labor Party managed to retain power between 1983 and 1996, it did so more by its ability to retain the confidence of the business community than through any attempt to extend social justice. The experience of socialist parties in states as different as New Zealand, Spain and Sweden tells a very similar story.

Ideological retreat has also been dictated by international factors. In the first place, economic globalisation has undermined the efficacy of Keynesian policies. Conventional Keynesianism was based on the ability of governments to manage national economies so as to secure high growth and low unemployment. However integration into a larger global system has not only undermined economic sovereignty but also deprived socialist governments of the capacity to deliver, or even promise to deliver, general prosperity. The collapse of communism in eastern Europe and the Soviet Union also had an impact. Despite the fact that social democrats had long criticised Soviet authoritarianism and long since abandoned the ideas of collectivisation and planning, they could not but be affected by the new spirit of market triumphalism. The demise of socialism as a project for the replacement of capitalism has also undermined the notion of socialism as a means of taming or reforming capitalism. Social democracy has thus become less immune to the appeal of economic individualism and more susceptible to enthusiasms normally associated with the new right. This is reflected in growing sympathy for low taxes, low inflation, greater competition and, in the words of the Labour Party's rewritten clause IV, a 'dynamic market economy'.

However, if social democracy has retreated from the politics of social justice, what has it retreated to? The answer appears to be the politics of community. Community, of course, has a long socialist heritage, drawing as it does, like fraternity and cooperation, on the idea of a social essence. However the communitarianism that social democrats have drawn from is associated with a particular critique of liberal individualism. Theorists such as Alisdair MacIntyre (1981) and Michael Sandel (1982) have argued that in conceiving of the individual as logically prior to and 'outside' the community, liberalism has merely legitimised selfish and egoistical behaviour, downgrading the very idea of the public good. The US sociologist Amitai Etzioni (1995) has further suggested that social fragmentation and breakdown has largely been the result of individuals' obsession with rights and their refusal to acknowledge reciprocal duties and moral responsibilities. Eager to translate the idea of community into a feasible, socialist political economy, social democrats have been particularly drawn to the idea of 'stakeholder capitalism', as developed in the works of Will Hutton (1995) and others. This differs from the 'shareholder' capitalism beloved by new right free marketeers, in that it acknowledges that the dynamism of capitalism can only be harnessed to the common good if all groups – workers and consumers as well as managers and shareholders – have a stake in the economy.

It is questionable, however, whether communitarianism can constitute a genuinely socialist project. Problems, for instance, stem from the fact that it deradicalises the thrust of socialist theory. This can be seen in the tendency of community to highlight the ties that bind all members of society and thus to ignore or conceal class differences and economic inequalities. Communitarians have therefore been more eager to adopt the language of duty and moral responsibility than to talk in terms of social justice and redistribution. They have emphasised cultural solutions to social breakdown rather than economic ones, in effect replacing social

---

### Communitarianism

Communitarianism is the belief that the self or person is constituted through the community, in the sense that individuals are shaped by the communities to which they belong and thus owe them a debt of respect and consideration – there are no 'unencumbered selves'. Although clearly at odds with liberal individualism, communitarianism nevertheless has a variety of political forms. Left-wing communitarianism holds that community demands unrestricted freedom and social equality (for example, anarchism). Centrist communitarianism holds that community is grounded in an acknowledgement of reciprocal rights and responsibilities (for example, social democracy/Tory paternalism). Right-wing communitarianism holds that community requires respect for authority and established values (for example, the new right).

engineering with cultural engineering. From this point of view, it is possible to argue that communitarianism has implicitly conservative implications as it tends to be associated with attempts to strengthen existing institutions such as the family, instead of with the task of making society anew. In the UK, for example, where 'new' revisionism has perhaps been most fully developed, Tony Blair and 'New Labour' have advanced the idea of 'one-nation socialism', based on a balance between economic efficiency and moral responsibility. Nevertheless, regardless of their ideological implications, it is questionable whether ideas such as community, stakeholding and moral responsibility are substantial enough to constitute a political programme in their own right. If they are not, clearly the search for an alternative to discarded Keynesian social democracy will go on.

## Socialism in the twenty-first century

Some would regard a discussion of socialism in the twenty-first century as pointless. Socialism is dead and the obituaries have been written. The evidence to sustain this view is all too familiar. The eastern European revolutions of 1989–91 removed the last vestiges of 'actually existing socialism', and where nominally socialist regimes survive, as in China, it is only because of the willingness of communist parties to introduce market reforms. Elsewhere, parliamentary socialist parties have been in flight from traditional principles, attempting to maintain electoral credibility by demonstrating growing sympathy for economic liberalism. The only serious debate has been about the cause of socialism's death. End-of-history theorists such as Francis Fukuyama (1989) have put it down to the inherent flaws in all socialist models and the manifest superiority of liberal capitalism. Others have highlighted the tendency of a globalised economy irresistibly to draw all nations into an international capitalist system. Still others have emphasised social changes that have reduced the political base of socialism, or for that matter any other system-transforming movement, from the working masses to an isolated and divided underclass. Whatever the explanation, the world has shifted dramatically and permanently to the right, consigning socialism to what Trotsky, in very different circumstances, called the 'dustbin of history'.

However socialists with a longer sense of history are unlikely to succumb to this despond. Just as predictions at the end of the nineteenth century about the inevitable victory of socialism proved to be flawed, so proclamations about the death of socialism made at the end of the twentieth century are likely to be unreliable. Indeed as recently as the 1960s it was free-market liberalism that was considered to be redundant while socialism appeared to be making irresistible progress. Hopes for the survival of socialism largely rest on the enduring and perhaps intrinsic imperfections of the capitalist system. As Ralph Miliband put it in his final work, *Socialism for a Sceptical Age* (1995), 'the notion that socialism has been thoroughly transformed and represents the best that humankind can ever hope to achieve is a dreadful slur on the human race'. In that sense socialism is destined to survive if only because it serves as a reminder that human development can extend beyond market individualism. And perhaps the collapse of top-down versions of socialism in the form of orthodox communism and, more modestly, Keynesian social democracy, represent an opportunity for socialism rather than its death knell. Michael Harrington (1993, p. 1) was thus able to look forward and proclaim that socialism is 'the hope of human freedom and justice under the unprecedented conditions of life that humanity will face in the twenty-first century'.

If socialism survives, what kind of socialism will it be? What seems clear is that it is unlikely to draw inspiration from the bureaucratic authoritarianism of the Soviet era. Marxism–Leninism may indeed be dead, and few socialist tears were shed at its passing. One of the consequences of this may be a re-examination of Marx's legacy, now disentangled from the experience of Leninism and Stalinism. However this is more likely to be Marx the humanist socialist than the more familiar twentieth-century image of Marx as an economic determinist. As far as parliamentary socialism is concerned, an important task remains. Keynesian social democracy, at least in its post-war guise, may have been discarded but a politically and electorally viable alternative to market capitalism has yet to emerge. Interest in ideas such as community, duty and moral responsibility provides evidence of the desire for 'new thinking' within socialism, rather than proof of socialism's rebirth. Meanwhile the search for the new socialist paradigm continues.

## Further reading

Berki, R., *Socialism* (London: Dent, 1975). An influential and elegantly argued analysis of socialist ideology that emphasises the contrasting tendencies within it.

Harrington, M., *Socialism Past and Future* (London: Pluto Press, 1993). A committed, passionate and insightful discussion of where socialism has been and where it is going.

Lane, D., *The Rise and Fall of State Socialism* (Oxford: Polity Press, 1997). A detailed analysis of the themes and structures of the socialist tradition that was born out of the 1917 Bolshevik Revolution.

McLellan, D., *The Thought of Karl Marx*, 2nd edn (London: Macmillan, 1980). A thorough and helpful introduction to Marx's work, supported by selective texts.

Sassoon, D., *One Hundred Years of Socialism* (London: Fontana, 1997). A very stylish and detailed account of the life and times of democratic socialist ideas and movements.

Wright, A., *Socialisms: Theories and Practices* (Oxford and New York: Oxford University Press, 1987). A good, brief and accessible introduction to the basic themes of socialism, highlighting the causes of disagreement within the socialist family.

# Chapter 5

# Nationalism

Origins and development
For the love of country – central themes
Nationalism and politics
Beyond nationalism
Nationalism in the twenty-first century

## Origins and development

The word 'nation' has been used since the thirteenth century and derives from the Latin *nasci*, meaning to be born. In the form of *natio*, it referred to a group of people united by birth or birthplace. In its original usage, 'nation' thus implied a breed of people or a racial group, but possessed no political significance. It was not until the late eighteenth century that the term acquired political overtones, as individuals and groups started to be classified as 'nationalists'. The term 'nationalism' was first used in print in 1789 by the anti-Jacobin French priest Augustin Barruel. By the mid nineteenth century nationalism was widely recognised as a political doctrine or movement, for example as a major ingredient of the revolutions that swept across Europe in 1848. In many respects nationalism developed into the most successful and compelling of political creeds, helping to shape and reshape history in many parts of the world for over two hundred years.

The idea of nationalism was born during the French Revolution. Previously countries had been thought of as 'realms', 'principalities' or 'kingdoms'. The inhabitants of a country were 'subjects', their political identity being formed by allegiance to a ruler or ruling dynasty, rather than any sense of national identity or patriotism (p. 165). However the revolutionaries in France who rose up against Louis XVI in 1789 did so in the name of the people, and understood the people to be the 'French nation'. Their ideas were influenced by the writings of Jean-Jacques Rousseau (see p. 163) and the new doctrine of popular self-government. Nationalism was therefore a revolutionary and democratic creed, reflecting the idea that 'subjects of the crown' should become 'citizens of France'.

The nation should be its own master. However such ideas were not the exclusive property of the French. During the Revolutionary and Napoleonic Wars, 1792–1815, much of continental Europe was invaded by France, giving rise to both resentment against France and a desire for independence. In Italy and Germany, long divided into a collection of states, the experience of conquest helped to forge for the first time a consciousness of national unity, expressed in a new language of nationalism, inherited from France. Nationalist ideas also spread to Latin America in the early nineteenth century, where Simon Bolivar, 'the Liberator', led revolutions against Spanish rule in what was then New Grenada, now the countries of Colombia, Venezuela and Ecuador, as well as in Peru and Bolivia.

The rising tide of nationalism redrew the map of Europe in the nineteenth century as the autocratic and multinational empires of Turkey, Austria and Russia started to crumble in the face of liberal and nationalist pressure. In 1848 nationalist uprisings broke out in the Italian states, amongst the Czechs and the Hungarians, and in Germany, where the desire for national unity was expressed in the creation of the short-lived Frankfurt parliament. The nineteenth century was a period of nation building. Italy, once dismissed by the Austrian Chancellor Metternich as a 'mere geographical expression', became a united state in 1861, the process of unification being completed with the acquisition of Rome in 1870. Germany, formerly a collection of 39 states, was unified in 1871 following the Franco-Prussian War.

Nevertheless it would be a mistake to assume that nationalism was either an irresistible or a genuinely popular movement during this period. Enthusiasm for nationalism was largely restricted to the rising middle classes, who were attracted to the ideas of national unity and constitutional government. Although middle-class nationalist movements kept the dream of national unity or independence alive, they were nowhere strong enough to accomplish the process of nation building on their own. Where nationalist goals were realised, as in Italy and Germany, it was because nationalism coincided with the ambition of rising states such as Piedmont and Prussia. For example German unification owed more to the Prussian army, which defeated Austria in 1866 and France in 1870–1, than it did to the liberal nationalist movement.

However, by the end of the nineteenth century nationalism had become a truly popular movement, with the spread of flags, national anthems, patriotic poetry and literature, public ceremonies and national holidays. Nationalism became the language of mass politics, made possible by the growth of primary education, mass literacy and the spread of popular newspapers. The character of nationalism also changed. Nationalism had previously been associated with liberal and progressive movements, but was increasingly taken up by conservative and reactionary politicians. Nationalism came to stand for social cohesion, order and stability, particularly in the face of the growing challenge of socialism, which embodied the ideas of social revolution and international working-class solidarity. Nationalism sought to integrate the increasingly powerful working class into the nation, and so to preserve the established social structure. Patriotic fervour was no longer aroused by the prospect of political liberty or democracy, but by the commemoration of past national glories and military victories. Such nationalism became increasingly chauvinistic and xenophobic. Each nation claimed its own unique or superior qualities, while other nations were regarded as alien, untrustworthy, even menacing. This new climate of popular nationalism helped to fuel policies of colonial expansion that intensified dramatically in the 1870s and 1880s and by the end of the century had brought most of the world's population under European control. It also contributed to a mood of international suspicion and rivalry, which led to world war in 1914.

The end of the First World War saw the completion of the process of nation building in central and eastern Europe. At the Paris Peace Conference, US President Woodrow Wilson advocated the principle of 'national self-determination'. The German, Austro-Hungarian and Russian empires were broken up and eight new states created, including Finland, Hungary, Czechoslovakia, Poland and Yugoslavia. These new countries were designed to be nation-states that conformed to the geography of existing national or ethnic groups. However the First World War failed to resolve the serious national tensions that had precipitated conflict in the first place. Indeed the experience of defeat and disappointment with the terms of the peace treaties left an inheritance of frustrated ambition and bitterness. This was most evident in Germany, Italy and Japan, where fascist or authoritarian movements came to power in the inter-war period by promising to restore national pride through policies of expansion and empire. Nationalism was therefore a powerful factor leading to war in both 1914 and 1939.

During the twentieth century the doctrine of nationalism, which had been born in Europe, spread throughout the globe as the peoples of Asia and Africa rose in opposition to colonial rule. The process of colonisation had involved not only the establishment of political control and economic dominance, but also the importation of western ideas, including nationalism, which began to be used against the colonial masters themselves. Nationalist uprisings took place in Egypt in 1919 and quickly spread throughout the Middle East. The Anglo-Afghan war also broke out in 1919, and rebellions took place in India, the Dutch East Indies and Indochina. After 1945 the map of Africa and Asia was redrawn as the

British, French, Dutch and Portuguese empires each disintegrated in the face of nationalist movements that either succeeded in negotiating independence or winning wars of national liberation.

Anticolonialism not only witnessed the spread of western-style nationalism to the developing world, but also generated new forms of nationalism. Nationalism in the developing world has embraced a wide range of movements. In China, Vietnam and parts of Africa, nationalism has been fused with Marxism, and 'national liberation' has been regarded not simply as a political goal but as part of a social revolution. Elsewhere, developing-world nationalism has been anti-western, rejecting both liberal democratic and revolutionary socialist conceptions of nationhood. The most important vehicle for expressing such ideas has been religious belief, and in particular Islam. The rise of Islam as a distinctive political creed has transformed political life in the Middle East and North Africa, especially since the Iranian Revolution of 1979. In some respects Islam currently represents the most significant challenge to the worldwide predominance of western liberal democracy.

It is, however, often argued that nationalism has had its day and is now an anachronism, relevant only to European nation building in the nineteenth century, or the anticolonial struggles of the post-Second-World-War period. This thesis is examined more fully in the final section of the chapter. Nevertheless there is evidence not only of the persistence of nationalism, but also of its revival. Since the 1960s apparently stable nation-states have been increasingly disrupted by nationalist tensions. In the UK, Scottish, Welsh and rival Irish nationalisms have become an established feature of political life. Separatist movements have developed in areas such as the Basque region of northern Spain and the Canadian province of Quebec. Moreover many of the world's most enduring political crises have involved nationalism, for instance the Arab–Israeli conflict, the Eritrean civil war and communal conflict in Sri Lanka and India.

Finally, the transformation of eastern Europe in 1989–91 led to a resurgence of nationalism throughout the area. The Soviet Union was seriously weakened by rising nationalism amongst its non-Russian peoples, and the collapse of communist rule allowed ancient national rivalries to surface throughout eastern Europe. Czechoslovakia ceased to exist in 1992 with the creation of separate Czech and Slovak republics, while Yugoslavia was torn apart by intensified ethnic conflict, which resulted in full-scale war between Serbia and Croatia in 1991 and a four-year civil war in Bosnia, 1992–96. The reunification of Germany also awoke long-suppressed nationalist aspirations within Germany itself, and provoked nationalist fears within neighbouring states.

## For the love of country – central themes

To treat nationalism as an ideology in its own right is to encounter at least three problems. The first is that nationalism is sometimes classified as a political doctrine rather than a fully fledged ideology. Whereas, for instance, liberalism, conservatism and socialism constitute complex sets of interrelated ideas and values, nationalism, the argument goes, is at heart the simple belief that the nation is the natural and proper unit of government. The drawback of this view is that it focuses only on what might be regarded as 'classical' political nationalism, and ignores the many other, and in some respects no less significant, manifestations of nationalism, such as cultural nationalism and ethnic nationalism. The core feature of nationalism is therefore not its narrow association with self-government and the nation-state, but its broader link to movements and ideas that in whatever way acknowledge the central importance of the nation. The second problem is that nationalism is sometimes portrayed as an essentially psychological phenomenon – usually as loyalty towards one's nation or dislike of other nations – instead of as a theoretical construct. Undoubtedly one of the key features of nationalism is the potency of its affective or emotional appeal, but to understand it in these terms alone is to mistake nationalism for patriotism.

Thirdly, nationalism has a schizophrenic political character. At different times nationalism has been progressive and reactionary, democratic and authoritarian, rational and irrational, and left wing and right wing. It has also been associated with almost all the major ideological traditions. In their different ways, liberals, conservatives, socialists, fascists and even communists have been attracted to nationalism, and perhaps only anarchism, by virtue of its outright rejection of the state, is fundamentally at odds with nationalism. Nevertheless, although nationalist doctrines have been used by a bewildering variety of political movements and associated with sometimes diametrically opposed political causes, a bedrock of nationalist ideas and theories can be identified. The most important of these are the following:

- The nation
- Organic community
- Self-determination
- Identity politics.

### The nation

In everyday language, words such as 'nation', 'state', 'country' and even 'race' are often confused or used as if they are interchangeable. The United

Nations, for instance, is clearly misnamed: it is an organisation of states, not one of national populations. It is common in international politics to hear references to 'the Americans', 'the Chinese', 'the Russians' and so on, when in fact it is the actions of these peoples' governments or states that are being discussed. In the case of the United Kingdom, there is confusion about whether it should be regarded as a nation or a state that comprises four separate nations: the English, the Scots, the Welsh and the Northern Irish. The Arab peoples of North Africa and the Middle East pose very similar problems. For example should Egypt, Lybia, Iraq and Syria be treated as nations in their own right, or merely as part of a single and united Arab nation, based upon a common language, Arabic, a common religion, Islam, and descent from a common Bedouin tribal past?

Many of the controversies surrounding the phenomenon of nationalism can be traced back to rival views about what constitutes a nation. On one level nations are cultural entities, collections of people bound together by shared values and traditions, in particular a common language, religion and history, and usually occupying the same geographical area. From this point of view the nation can be defined by 'objective' factors: people who satisfy a requisite set of cultural criteria can be said to belong to a nation, those who do not can be classified as non-nationals or members of foreign nations. However, to define a nation simply as a group of people bound together by a common culture and traditions raises some very difficult questions. Although particular cultural features are commonly associated with nationhood, notably language, religion, ethnicity, history and tradition, there is no blueprint nor any objective criteria that can establish where and when a nation exists.

Language is often taken to be the clearest symbol of nationhood. A language embodies distinctive attitudes, values and forms of expression that produce a sense of familiarity and belonging. German nationalism, for instance, has traditionally been founded upon a sense of cultural unity, reflected in the purity and survival of the German language. Nations have also been highly sensitive to any dilution of or threat to their languages. For example it is essentially language that divides the French-speaking peoples of Quebec from the rest of English-speaking Canada, and Welsh nationalism largely constitutes an attempt to preserve or revive the Welsh language. At the same time there are peoples who share the same language without having any conception of a common national identity: Americans, Australians and New Zealanders may speak English as a first language, but certainly do not think of themselves as members of an 'English nation'. Other nations have enjoyed a substantial measure of national unity without possessing a national language, as is the case in Switzerland where, in the absence of a Swiss language, three languages are spoken: French, German and Italian.

Religion is another major component of nationhood. Religion expresses common moral values and spiritual beliefs. In Northern Ireland, people who speak the same language are divided along religious lines: most Protestants regard themselves as Unionists and wish to preserve their links with the UK, while many in the Catholic community favour a united Ireland. Islam has been a major factor in forming the national consciousness in much of North Africa and the Middle East. The Iranian Revolution of 1979 was largely inspired by the fundamentalist beliefs of Shi'ite Moslems, who sought to purge Iran of western, particularly American, influence. There is also a sense in which Islam creates a higher unity than that of the nation-state, and Moslems in many parts of the world are prepared to refer to themselves as members of an 'Islamic nation'. Nevertheless religious beliefs do not always coincide with a sense of nationhood. Divisions between Catholics and Protestants in mainland UK do not inspire rival nationalisms, nor has the remarkable religious diversity found in the United States threatened to divide the country into a collection of distinct nations. At the same time countries such as Poland, Italy, Brazil and the Philippines share a common Catholic faith but do not feel that they belong to a common 'Catholic nation'.

Nations have also been based upon a sense of ethnic or racial unity. This was particularly evident in Germany during the Nazi period. The German word for 'people', *Völk*, implies both cultural unity and ties of blood. The significance of race has also been highlighted by far-right groups such as the National Fronts of both the UK and France, which have campaigned against 'non-white' immigration or even favoured repatriation on the ground that multiracialism undermines national unity. However nationalism usually has a cultural rather than a biological basis; it reflects an ethnic unity that may be based upon race, but more usually draws from shared values and common cultural beliefs. The nationalism of US blacks, for example, is based less upon colour than upon their distinctive history and culture. Black consciousness in the United States, the West Indies and parts of Europe has thus focused upon the rediscovery of black cultural roots, notably in the experience of slavery and in African society. However ethnicity does not always provide a basis for national identity. The United States prides itself upon cultural diversity, the result of centuries of immigration from Europe, Asia and Central and South America. US citizens regard themselves as 'Polish Americans', 'Japanese Americans', 'Hispanic Americans' and so on, happily retaining their own religions, traditions, food and even languages, without damaging their sense of national pride in being American.

Nations usually share a common history and traditions. National identity is often preserved by recalling past glories, national independence, the birthdays of national leaders or important military victories. The

United States celebrates Independence Day and Thanksgiving; Bastille Day is commemorated in France; in the UK, ceremonies continue to mark Dunkirk and D Day. On the other hand nationalist feelings may be based more upon future expectations than upon shared memories or a common past. This applies in the case of immigrants who have been 'naturalised', and is most evident in the United States, a 'land of immigrants'. The journey of the *Mayflower* and the War of Independence have no direct relevance for most Americans, whose families arrived centuries after these events occurred. American nationalism therefore has little to do with a common history or traditions, but has been forged out of a common commitment to the constitution and the values of liberal capitalism for which the United States stands.

The cultural unity that supposedly expresses itself in nationhood is therefore very difficult to pin down. It reflects a varying combination of cultural factors, rather than any precise formula. Ultimately therefore, nations can only be defined 'subjectively', by their members, not by any set of external factors. In this sense, the nation is a psycho-political entity, a group of people who regard themselves as a natural political community and are distinguished by shared loyalty or affection in the form of patriotism. Objective difficulties such as the absence of land, small population or lack of economic resources are of little significance if a group of people insists on demanding what it sees as 'national rights'. Latvia, for example, became an independent nation in 1991 despite having a population of only 2.6 million (barely half of whom are ethnic Lats), no source of fuel and very few natural resources. Likewise Kurdish peoples of the Middle East have nationalist aspirations, even though the Kurds have never enjoyed formal political unity and are presently spread over parts of Turkey, Iraq, Iran and Syria.

The fact that nations are formed through a combination of objective and subjective factors has two important consequences. First, it highlights the degree to which nationhood may be contested. Many of the world's most enduring political conflicts are actually disputes about whether a particular people should or should not be classified as a nation. Are the Tamils in Sri Lanka a nation, separate from the majority Sinhalese, and therefore entitled to their own homeland and state? Are the Basques in Spain and the Quebecois in Canada nations or simply ethnic or linguistic groups? Do the people of Northern Ireland belong to the British nation, the Irish nation, or indeed do they constitute a separate Ulster nation?

Second, it has given rise to different concepts of the nation. While all nationalists agree that nations are a blend of cultural and psycho-political factors, they disagree strongly about where the balance between the two lies. One the one hand 'exclusive' concepts of the nation stress the importance of ethnic unity and a shared history. By viewing national

## Perspectives on . . .

### The nation

**Liberals** subscribe to a 'civic' view of the nation that places as much emphasis on political allegiance as on cultural unity. Nations are moral entities in the sense that they are endowed with rights, notably an equal right to self-determination.

**Conservatives** regard the nation as primarily an 'organic' entity, bound together by a common ethnic identity and a shared history. As the source of social cohesion and collective identity, the nation is perhaps the most politically significant of social groups.

**Socialists** tend to view the nation as an artificial division of humankind whose purpose is to disguise social injustice and prop up the established order. Political movements and allegiances should therefore have an international, not a national, character.

**Anarchists** have generally held that the nation is tainted by its association with the state and therefore with oppression. The nation is thus seen as a myth, designed to promote obedience and subjugation in the interests of the ruling elite.

**Fascists** view the nation as an organically unified social whole, often defined by race, which gives purpose and meaning to individual existence. However nations are pitted against one another in a struggle for survival in which some are fitted to succeed and others to go to the wall.

**Fundamentalists** regard nations as, in essence, religious entities, communities of 'believers'. Nevertheless religion is seldom coextensive with conventional nations, hence the idea of transnational religious communities, such as the 'nation of Islam'.

identity as 'given', unchanging and indeed unchangeable, this implies that nations are characterised by common descent and so blurs the distinction between the nation and the race. On the other hand 'inclusive' concepts of the nation highlight the importance of civic consciousness and patriotic loyalty, suggesting that nations may be multiracial, multi-ethnic, multi-religious and so forth. Needless to say, these different concepts of the nation underpin very different forms of nationalism.

### Organic community

Although nationalists may disagree about the defining features of the nation, they are unified by their belief that nations are organic communities. Humankind, in other words, is *naturally* divided into a collection of nations, each possessing a distinctive character and separate identity. This, nationalists argue, is why a 'higher' loyalty and deeper political significance attaches to the nation than to any other social group or collective body. Whereas, for instance, class, gender, religion and language may be important in particular societies, or may come to prominence in particular circumstances, the bonds of nationhood are more fundamental. National ties and loyalties are found in all societies, they endure over time, and they operate at an instinctual, even primordial level.

Nevertheless different explanations have been provided for this. In *The Ethnic Origins of Nations* (1986) Anthony Smith highlighted the continuity between modern nations and premodern ethnic communities, which he called 'ethnies'. According to this view nations are historically embedded: they are rooted in a common cultural heritage and language that may long predate the achievement of statehood or the quest for national independence. Ernest Gellner, in contrast, emphasised the degree to which nationalism is linked to modernisation, and in particular to the process of industrialisation. In *Nations and Nationalism* (1983) he stressed that, while premodern or 'agro-literate' societies were structured by a network of feudal bonds and loyalties, emerging industrial societies promoted social mobility, self-striving and competition, and so required a new source of cultural cohesion. This was provided by nationalism. Although Gellner's theory suggests that nations coalesced in response to particular social conditions and circumstances, it also implies that the national community is deep-rooted and will be enduring, as a return to premodern loyalties and identities is unthinkable.

The national community is a particular kind of community, however. As a social or political principle, community suggests a social group that possesses a strong collective identity based on the bonds of comradeship, loyalty and duty. For example the German sociologist Ferdinand Tönnies (1855–1936) distinguished between *Gemeinschaft*, or 'community', typically found in traditional societies and characterised by natural affection and mutual respect, and *Gesellschaft*, or 'association', the looser, artificial and contractual relationships that are typically found in urban and industrialised societies. For nationalists, the nation is definitely forged out of *Gemeinschaft*-type relationships. Nevertheless, as Benedict Anderson (1983) pointed out, nations constitute only 'imagined communities'. Anderson argued that nations exist more as mental images than as genuine communities that require a degree of face-to-face interaction to sustain the notion of a common identity. Within nations, individuals only ever meet a tiny proportion of those with whom they supposedly share a national identity. If nations exist, they exist as imagined artifices, constructed for us through education, the mass media and a process of political socialisation.

The idea that nations are 'imagined', not organic, communities has been seized upon by critics of nationalism. The Marxist historian Eric Hobsbawm (1983), for instance, highlighted the degree to which nations are 'invented traditions'. Rather than accepting that modern nations have developed out of long-established ethnic communities, Hobsbawm argued that a belief in historical continuity and cultural purity is invariably a myth, and what is more, a myth created by nationalism itself. In this view, nationalism creates nations, not the other way round. A widespread consciousness of nationhood did not, for example, develop until the late nineteenth century, perhaps fashioned by the invention of national anthems and national flags, and the extension of primary education and thus mass literacy. Socialists, particularly Marxists, have linked this process to the attempt to consolidate inherently unstable class societies. From this perspective, nationalism is viewed as a device through which the ruling class counters the threat of social revolution by ensuring that national loyalty is stronger than class solidarity, thereby binding the working class to the existing power structure.

## Self-determination

Nationalism as a political ideology only emerged when the idea of national community encountered the doctrine of popular sovereignty. This occurred during the French Revolution and was influenced by the writings of Jean-Jacques Rousseau, sometimes seen as the 'father' of modern nationalism. Although Rousseau did not specifically address the question of the nation, or discuss the phenomenon of nationalism, his stress on popular sovereignty, expressed in the idea of the 'general will', was the seed from which nationalist doctrines sprang. As a result of the Polish struggle for independence from Russia, he came to believe that this is vested in a culturally unified people. The 'general will' is the common or collective interest of society, the will of all provided each acts selflessly. Rousseau argued that government should be based not upon the absolute power of a monarch, but upon the indivisible collective will of the entire community. During the French Revolution these beliefs were reflected in the assertion that the French people were 'citizens' possessed of inalienable rights and duties, no longer merely 'subjects' of the crown. Sovereign power thus resided with the 'French nation'. The form of nationalism that emerged from the French Revolution was therefore based on the vision of a people or nation governing itself. In other words the nation is not merely a natural community, it is a natural political community.

In this tradition of nationalism, nationhood and statehood are intrinsically linked. The litmus test of national identity is the desire to attain or maintain political independence, usually expressed in the principle of national self-determination. The goal of nationalism is therefore the

## Jean-Jacques Rousseau (1712–78)

Geneva-born French moral and political philosopher, perhaps the principal intellectual influence upon the French Revolution. Rousseau was entirely self-taught. He moved to Paris in 1742 and became an intimate of leading members of the French Enlightenment, especially Diderot (1713–84).

Rousseau's writings range over education, the arts, science, literature and philosophy. His philosophy reflects a deep belief in the goodness of 'natural man' and the corruption of 'social man'. Rousseau's political teaching, summarised in *Émile* (1762) and developed in *The Social Contract* (1762), advocates a radical form of democracy based on the idea of the 'general will'. It is impossible to link Rousseau to any one political tradition; his thought has influenced liberal, socialist, anarchist and, some argue, fascist thought.

founding of a 'nation-state'. To date this has been achieved in one of two ways. First, it may involve a process of unification. German history, for instance, has repeatedly witnessed unification. In medieval times the German states were united under Charlemagne in the Holy Roman Empire, referred to by later German nationalists as the 'First Reich'. Germany was not reunited until Bismarck founded his 'Second Reich' in 1871. Hitler's 'Third Reich' completed the process of unification by incorporating Austria into 'Greater Germany'. Following its defeat in the Second World War, Germany was again divided, with the founding of the two Germanies in 1949 – East Germany and West Germany – and the permanent independence of a separate Austria. The two Germanies were finally reunited in 1990.

Second, nation-states can be created through the achievement of independence, in which a nation is liberated from foreign rule and gains control over its own destiny. For example much of Polish history has witnessed successive attempts to achieve independence from the control of various foreign powers. Poland ceased to exist in 1793 when the Poles were partitioned by Austria, Russia and Prussia. Thanks to the Treaty of Versailles, Poland was revived in 1918 and became an independent republic. However, in accordance with the Nazi-Soviet Pact of 1939, Poland was invaded by Germany and repartitioned, this time between Germany and the Soviet Union. Although Poland achieved formal independence in 1945, for much of the post-war period it remained firmly under Soviet control. The election of a non-communist government in 1989 therefore marked a further liberation of the country from foreign control.

For nationalists the nation-state is the highest and most desirable form of political organisation. The great strength of the nation-state is that it offers the prospect of both cultural cohesion and political unity. When a people who share a common cultural or ethnic identity gain the right to self-government, community and citizenship coincide. Moreover nationalism legitimises the authority of government. Political sovereignty in a nation-state resides with the people or the nation itself. Consequently nationalism represents the idea of popular self-government, the idea that government is carried out either by the people or for the people, in accordance with their 'national interest'. This is why nationalists believe that the forces that have created a world of independent nation-states are natural and irresistible, and that no other social group could constitute a meaningful political community. The nation-state, in short, is the only viable political unit.

However it would be misleading to suggest that nationalism is always associated with the nation-state or is necessarily linked to the idea of self-determination. Some nations, for instance, may be satisfied with a measure of political autonomy that stops short of statehood and full independence. This can be seen in the case of Welsh nationalism in the UK and Breton and Basque nationalism in France. Nationalism is thus not always associated with separatism, the quest to secede from a larger political formation with a view to establishing an independent state, but may instead be expressed through federalism or devolution. Federalism creates legal and political structures that distribute power territorially within a state on the basis of shared sovereignty. For example European federalism is a device through which EU member states are able to 'pool' national sovereignty by investing a range of powers in supranational EU institutions. Devolution achieves a more modest form of political decentralisation in that devolved bodies have no share in sovereignty, even though, as in Spain, France and more recently the UK, they exercise a broad range of autonomous powers. Nevertheless it is unclear whether devolution establishes a sufficient measure of self-government to satisfy nationalist demands. The granting of wide-ranging powers to the Basque region of Spain has failed to end ETA's campaign of terrorism. Similarly the creation of a Scottish Parliament in the UK may, some argue, simply fuel nationalism, leading to federalist calls and eventually secession.

## Identity politics

All forms of nationalism address the issue of identity. Whatever political causes nationalism may be associated with, it advances these on the basis of a sense of collective identity, usually understood as patriotism. For the political nationalist, 'objective' considerations such as territory, religion and language are no more important than 'subjective' ones such as will, memory and patriotic loyalty. Nationalism therefore not only advances political causes but also tells people who they are: it gives people a history, forges social bonds and a collective spirit, and creates a sense of destiny larger than individual existence. Indeed it may be precisely the strength of nationalism's affective elements and the relative weakness of its doctrinal ones that accounts for the unusual success of nationalism as a political creed.

Certain forms of nationalism, however, are less closely related to overtly political demands than others. This particularly applies in the case of cultural nationalism and ethnic nationalism. Cultural nationalism is a form of nationalism that places primary emphasis on the regeneration of the nation as a distinctive civilisation, rather than as a discreet political community. Not uncommonly, cultural nationalists view the state as a peripheral if not alien entity. Whereas political nationalism is 'rational' and may be principled, cultural nationalism is 'mystical' in that it is based on a romantic belief in the nation as a unique historical and organic whole. Typically, cultural nationalism is a 'bottom-up' form of nationalism that draws more on popular rituals, traditions and legends than on elite or 'higher' culture. Though it is often antimodern in character, cultural nationalism may also serve as an agent of modernisation by enabling a people to 'recreate' itself.

The importance of a distinctive national consciousness was first emphasised in Germany in the late eighteenth century. Writers such as Herder (1744–1803) and Fichte (1762–1814) highlighted what they believed to be the uniqueness and superiority of Germanic culture, in contrast to the ideas of the French Revolution. Herder believed that each nation possesses a *Völksgeist* or 'national spirit', which provides its peoples with their creative impulse. The role of nationalism is therefore to develop an awareness and appreciation of a nation's culture and traditions. During the nineteenth century such cultural nationalism was particularly marked in Germany in a revival of folk traditions and the rediscovery of German

## Patriotism

Patriotism (from the Latin *patria*, meaning 'fatherland') is a sentiment, a psychological attachment to one's nation, literally a 'love of one's country'. The terms nationalism and patriotism are often confused. Nationalism has a doctrinal character and embodies the belief that the nation is in some way the central principle of political organisation. Patriotism provides the affective basis for that belief, and thus underpins all forms of nationalism. It is difficult to conceive of a national group demanding, say, political independence without possessing at least a measure of patriotic loyalty or national consciousness. However not all patriots are nationalists. Not all of those who identify with or even love their nation see it as a means through which political demands can be articulated.

myths and legends. The Brothers Grimm, for example, collected and published German folk tales, and the composer Richard Wagner based many of his operas upon ancient legends and myths.

Cultural nationalism has become a powerful force during the twentieth century, expressing a desire to preserve a threatened national culture rather than a demand for national self-government. This has been particularly evident in countries that contain several nationalities or ethnic groups, especially when minority traditions or ways of life are in danger of being swamped by a dominant culture. Welsh nationalism in the UK, for example, has been essentially cultural rather than political – there has been a revival of interest in the Welsh' language and Welsh culture in general. In the 1979 referendum the Welsh voted four to one against the creation of a devolved Welsh Assembly, and the 1997 devolution referendum was won by only the slimmest of majorities. In France, strong regional traditions persist in many parts of the country; for example in Brittany growing attention has been paid to Breton culture and its distinctive Celtic traditions. Once again, however, such patriotism usually stops short of political nationalism, as is demonstrated by the marked contrast between the cultural pride of the French Basques and the separatist and political ambitions of Basques living in Spain.

In some respects ethnic nationalism differs from cultural nationalism, even though the terms ethnicity and culture clearly overlap. Ethnicity is loyalty towards a distinctive population, cultural group or territorial area. The term is complex because it has both racial and cultural overtones. Members of ethnic groups are often seen, correctly or incorrectly, to have descended from common ancestors, and the groups are thus thought of as extended kinship groups, united by blood. Even when ethnicity is understood in strictly cultural terms, it operates at a deep emotional level and highlights values, traditions and practices that give a people a sense of distinctiveness. As it is not possible to 'join' an ethnic group, ethnic nationalism has a clearly exclusive character.

Black nationalism in many parts of the West has a strong ethnic character. Blacks in the United States and the West Indies are the descendants of slaves, who were brought up in a culture that emphasised their inferiority and demanded subservience. The development of black consciousness and national pride therefore required blacks to look beyond white culture and rediscover their cultural roots in Africa. The Jamaican political thinker and activist Marcus Garvey (1887–1940) was one of the first to argue that blacks in America and the Caribbean should look upon Africa as their homeland. Garvey founded the African Orthodox Church in the hope of inculcating a distinctive black consciousness, and advocated segregation between blacks and whites. Eventually, he hoped, blacks throughout the world would be able to return to Africa, once it was liberated from colonial rule. In the 1960s black politics in the United States took a more radical turn with the emergence of the Black Power movement and with the growth, under the leadership of Malcolm X (1926–65), of the Black Muslims, later renamed the Nation of Islam. However, while black nationalism has generally emphasised consciousness-raising and cultural pride, ethnic nationalism also has a darker side. Heightened ethnic consciousness is not uncommonly fuelled by atavistic fears and hatreds, focused on foreign peoples. Ethnic nationalism is therefore often associated with chauvinism and racialism (see p. 228), and is expressed through aggression and conquest. This face of nationalism is discussed more fully later in the chapter in connection with expansionist nationalism.

## Nationalism and politics

Political nationalism is a complex phenomenon. On the one hand it appears to be a progressive or liberating force, that offers the prospect of national unity or independence. On the other hand it can be irrational and reactionary, allowing political leaders to adopt policies of military expansion and war in the name of the nation. Its political character is shaped by a variety of cultural and historical factors. For instance a country's concept of nationhood is deeply influenced by its cultural heritage: French nationalism was not only fashioned by the French Revolution but also bears its lasting imprint: an attachment to the revolutionary values of 'liberty, equality and fraternity'. US nationalism has been affected by the heritage of colonial rule and independence. The United States has therefore traditionally regarded itself as an ally of oppressed peoples, a position represented by Woodrow Wilson at the Paris Peace Conference and, after the Second World War, in its role as leader of what it believed to be the 'Free World'. Japanese nationalism, on the other hand, has been deeply affected by the traditions and values of its imperial past. In Japan nationalism is closely linked to respect for the emperor, the ancient Shinto religion and the traditional values of obedience and discipline.

The character of nationalism is also moulded by the circumstances in which nationalist aspirations arise and the political causes that nationalism articulates. When nationalism is a reaction against the experience of foreign domination or colonial rule, it tends to have a liberating character and is linked to the goals of liberty, justice and democracy. Nationalism takes the form of a quest for 'national liberation' and popular self-government. However nationalist sentiments can also be generated by international rivalry and conflict. In such circumstances other nations may be regarded with distrust, fear or hatred, and nationalism can assume a chauvinistic and expansionist character. Nationalism has also been a product of social dislocation and demographic change. A nationalist backlash can be provoked, for example, when the cultural identity of a people is weakened or threatened by the creeping influence of a foreign culture. Nationalism has therefore sometimes been a reaction against immigration or even the pace of social and economic change. In such cases nationalism can become a vehicle for racial prejudice or xenophobia, a hatred of foreigners.

Finally, nationalism has been shaped by the political philosophies of those who espouse it. Nationalism has often dwarfed more precise and systematic political ideologies because of its capacity to articulate such a broad range of aspirations and goals. It has therefore attracted the attention of liberals, conservatives, socialists, communists and fascists. It is also a political creed that is sufficiently broad and theoretically modest to be incorporated into diametrically opposed ideologies. As a result it is perhaps more helpful to study a range of 'nationalisms' than it is to pretend that nationalism is a single or coherent political phenomenon.

## Liberal nationalism

Liberal nationalism is the oldest form of nationalism, dating back to the French Revolution and embodying many of its values. Its ideas spread quickly through much of Europe and were expressed most clearly by Guiseppe Mazzini, often thought of as the 'prophet' of Italian unification. They also influenced the remarkable exploits of Simon Bolivar, who led the Latin American independence movement in the early nineteenth century and expelled the Spanish from much of Hispanic America. Woodrow Wilson's 'Fourteen Points', proposed as the basis for the reconstruction of Europe after the First World War, were also based upon liberal nationalist principles. Moreover many twentieth-century anti-colonial leaders were inspired by liberal ideas, as in the case of Sun Yat-Sen, one of the leaders of China's 1911 Revolution, and Jawaharlal Nehru, the first prime minister of India.

The ideas of liberal nationalism were clearly shaped by J.-J. Rousseau's defence of popular sovereignty, expressed in particular in the notion of the 'general will'. As the nineteenth century progressed, the aspiration for popular self-government was progressively fused with liberal principles. This fusion was brought about by the fact that the multinational empires against which nationalists fought were also autocratic and oppressive. Mazzini, for example, wished the Italian states to unite, but this also entailed throwing off the influence of autocratic Austria. For many European revolutionaries in the mid nineteenth century, liberalism and nationalism were virtually indistinguishable. Indeed their nationalist creed

## Guiseppe Mazzini (1805-72)

Italian nationalist. Mazzini, the son of a doctor, was born in Genoa, Italy. He came into contact with revolutionary politics as a member of the patriotic secret society, the Carbonari. During the 1848 revolutions Mazzini helped to liberate Milan from Austrian influence and became head of the short-lived Roman Republic.

Mazzini's nationalism fused a belief in the nation as a distinctive linguistic and cultural community with the principles of liberal republicanism. Above all, Mazzini's was a principled form of nationalism that treated nations as sublimated individuals endowed with the right to self-government. Mazzini was confident that assertion of the principle of national self-determination would eventually bring about perpetual peace.

was largely forged by applying liberal ideas, initially developed in relation to the individual, to the nation and to international politics.

Liberalism was founded upon a defence of individual freedom, traditionally expressed in the language of rights. Nationalists believed nations to be sovereign entities, entitled to liberty, and also possessing rights, most importantly the right of self-determination. Liberal nationalism is therefore a liberating force in two senses. First, it opposes all forms of foreign domination and oppression, whether by multinational empires or colonial powers. Second, it stands for the ideal of self-government, reflected in practice in a belief in constitutionalism (see p. 41) and representation. Woodrow Wilson, for example, argued in favour of a Europe composed not only of nation-states, but also one in which political democracy rather than autocracy ruled. For him, only a democratic republic, on the US model, could be a genuine nation-state.

Moreover liberal nationalists believe that nations, like individuals, are equal, at least in the sense that they are equally entitled to the right of self-determination. The ultimate goal of liberal nationalism is therefore the construction of a world of independent nation-states, not merely the unification or independence of a particular nation. John Stuart Mill (see p. 30) expressed this as the principle that 'the boundaries of government should coincide in the main with those of nationality'. Mazzini formed the clandestine organisation 'Young Italy' to promote the idea of a united Italy, but he also founded 'Young Europe' in the hope of spreading nationalist ideas throughout the continent. At the Paris Peace Conference, Woodrow Wilson advanced the principle of self-determination not simply because the break-up of the European empire served US national interests, but because he believed that the Poles, Czechs, Hungarians and so on all had the same right to political independence that Americans already enjoyed.

Liberals also believe that the principle of balance or natural harmony applies to the nations of the world, not just to individuals within society. The achievement of national self-determination is a means of establishing a peaceful and stable international order. Wilson believed that the First World War had been caused by an 'old order', dominated by autocratic and militaristic empires. Democratic nation-states, on the other hand, would respect the national sovereignty of their neighbours and have no incentive to wage war or subjugate others. For a liberal, nationalism does not divide nations from one another, promoting distrust, rivalry and possibly war. Rather nationalism is a force that is capable of promoting both unity within each nation and brotherhood amongst all nations on the basis of mutual respect for national rights and characteristics. At heart, liberalism looks beyond the nation to the ideas of cosmopolitanism (see p. 181) and internationalism, as discussed later.

Critics of liberal nationalism have sometimes suggested that its ideas are naive and romantic. Liberal nationalists see the progressive and liberating face of nationalism; their nationalism is rational and tolerant. However they perhaps ignore the darker face of nationalism, the irrational bonds or tribalism that distinguish 'us' from a foreign and threatening 'them'. Liberals see nationalism as a universal principle, but have less under-standing of the emotional power of nationalism, which has, in times of war, persuaded individuals to kill or die for their country, regardless of the justice of their nation's cause. Liberal nationalism is also misguided in its belief that the nation-state is the key to political and international harmony. The mistake of Wilsonian nationalism was the belief that nations live in convenient and discrete geographical areas, and that states could be constructed that coincide with these areas. In practice, all so-called 'nation-states' comprise a range of linguistic, religious, ethnic or regional groups, some of which may also consider themselves to be 'nations'. For example in 1918 the newly created nation-states of Czecho-slovakia and Poland contained a significant number of German speakers, and Czechoslovakia itself was a fusion of two major ethnic groups: the Czechs and the Slovaks. Former Yugoslavia, also created by Versailles, contained a bewildering variety of ethnic groups – Serbs, Croats, Slovenes, Bosnians, Albanians and so on – many of whom have now realised their aspiration for nationhood. In fact the ideal of a politically unified and culturally homogeneous nation-state can only be achieved by a policy of forcible deportation and an outright ban upon immigration.

## Conservative nationalism

In the early nineteenth century, conservatives regarded nationalism as a radical and dangerous force, a threat to order and political stability. However, as the century progressed, conservative statesmen such as

Disraeli, Bismarck and even Tsar Alexander III became increasingly sympathetic towards nationalism, seeing it as a natural ally in maintaining social order and defending traditional institutions. In the modern period, nationalism has become an article of faith for most conservatives. In the UK in the 1980s, Margaret Thatcher attempted to appeal to nationalist sentiments by resisting what she saw as the erosion of national sovereignty caused by an emerging 'federal Europe', and by responding triumphantly to the Falklands War of 1982. Ronald Reagan also tried to rekindle US nationalism by pursuing a more assertive foreign policy, which led to the invasion of Grenada and the bombing of Libya. George Bush continued this policy by invading Panama and sending US forces to fight in the Gulf War of 1991.

Conservative nationalism tends to develop in established nation-states, rather than ones that are in the process of nation building. Conservatives care less for the principled nationalism of universal self-determination and more about the promise of social cohesion and public order embodied in the sentiment of national patriotism. For conservatives, society is organic; they believe that nations emerge naturally from the desire of human beings to live with others who possess the same views, habits and appearance as themselves. Human beings are thought to be limited and imperfect creatures, who seek meaning and security within the national community. Therefore the principle goal of conservative nationalism is to maintain national unity by fostering patriotic loyalty and 'pride in one's country', especially in the face of the divisive idea of class solidarity preached by socialists. Indeed, by incorporating the working class into the nation, conservatives have often seen nationalism as the antidote to social revolution. Charles de Gaulle, French president from 1958 to 1969, harnessed nationalism to the conservative cause in France with particular skill. De Gaulle appealed to national pride by pursuing an independent, even anti-American defence and foreign policy, which included withdrawing French troops from NATO control. He also attempted to restore order and authority to social life and build up a powerful state, based upon the enhanced powers of the presidency. Such policies helped to maintain conservative control in France from the founding of the Fifth Republic in 1958 until the election of President Mitterand in 1981. In some respects the Thatcher government practised a British form of Gaullism by fusing an appeal based upon nationalism, or at least national independence within Europe, with the promise of strong government and firm leadership.

The conservative character of nationalism is maintained by an appeal to tradition and history; nationalism becomes thereby a defence for traditional institutions and a traditional way of life. Conservative nationalism is essentially nostalgic and backward-looking, reflecting upon a past age of national glory or triumph. This is evident in the case of British, or more accurately English nationalism, whose symbols are based very closely around the monarchy. Britain is the United Kingdom, its national anthem is 'God Save the Queen', and the Royal Family plays a prominent role in national celebrations such as Armistice Day, and on state occasions such as the opening of Parliament. Margaret Thatcher also attempted to link the UK to its past by references to 'Victorian values', which portrayed mid-nineteenth-century Britain as a 'golden age'.

Conservative nationalism is particularly prominent when the sense of national identity is felt to be threatened or in danger of being lost. The issue of immigration has kept this form of nationalism alive in many modern states, for example the UK, France and the United States. Hispanic immigration into the United States from Mexico has led some US conservatives to suggest the need for a constitutional guarantee that English will remain the United States' first language. In the UK, Enoch Powell was forced to resign from the Conservative shadow cabinet in 1968 after suggesting that further immigration into the country from the New Commonwealth would lead to racial conflict and violence. Similar views were expressed in 1990 by the former Conservative Party chairman, Norman Tebbit, who proposed that immigrants into the UK should pass what he called a 'cricket test' to establish whether they would support Britain, or England, in sporting events, or remain loyal to the teams from their country of origin.

In principle conservatives doubt that multicultural or multi-national societies can be stable and enduring, because they lack the cultural and social cohesion that only a strong national identity can generate. However in practice this involves reinventing or at least redefining national identity in such a way that immigration is either deterred or immigrants are forced to assimilate into the host culture. Such nationalism is exclusive in that it attempts to preserve a sense of nationhood by narrowing the concept of nationality itself, and drawing a very firm line between those who are members of the nation and those who are alien to it.

Although conservative politicians and parties have derived considerable political benefit from their appeal to nationalism, opponents have some-times pointed out that their ideas are based upon misguided assumptions. In the first place, conservative nationalism can be seen as a form of elite manipulation. The 'nation' is invented and certainly defined by political leaders who may use it for their own purposes. This is most evident in times of war or international crisis when the nation is mobilised to fight for the 'fatherland' by emotional appeals to patriotic duty. Furthermore conservative nationalism may also serve to promote intolerance and bigotry. By insisting on the maintenance of cultural purity and traditions, conservatives may portray immigrants, or foreigners in general, as a threat, and in the process promote, or at least legitimise, racialist and xenophobic fears.

## Expansionist nationalism

In many countries the dominant image of nationalism is one of aggression and militarism, quite the opposite of a principled belief in national self-determination. The aggressive face of nationalism became apparent in the late nineteenth century as European powers indulged in a 'scramble for Africa' in the name of national glory and their 'place in the sun'. The imperialism of the late nineteenth century differed from earlier periods of colonial expansion in that it was supported by a climate of popular nationalism: national prestige was increasingly linked to the possession of an empire and each colonial victory was greeted by demonstrations of public approval. In the UK a new word, jingoism, was coined to describe this mood of public enthusiasm for aggressive nationalism or imperial expansion. In the early twentieth century the growing rivalry of the European powers divided the continent into two armed camps, the Triple Entente, comprising the UK, France and Russia, and the Triple Alliance, containing Germany, Austria and Italy. When world war eventually broke out in August 1914, after a prolonged arms race and a succession of international crises, it provoked public rejoicing in all the major cities of Europe. Aggressive and expansionist nationalism reached its high point in the inter-war period when the authoritarian or fascist regimes of Japan, Italy and Germany embarked upon policies of imperial expansion and world domination, eventually leading to war in 1939.

What distinguished this form of nationalism from earlier liberal nationalism was its chauvinism, a belief in superiority or dominance, a term derived from the name of Nicolas Chauvin, a French soldier who had been fanatically devoted to Napoleon I. Nations are not thought to be equal in their right to self-determination; rather some nations are believed to possess characteristics or qualities that make them superior to others. Such ideas were clearly evident in European imperialism, which was justified by an ideology of racial and cultural superiority. In nineteenth century Europe it was widely believed that the 'white' peoples of Europe and America were intellectually and morally superior to the 'black', 'brown' and 'yellow' peoples of Africa and Asia. Indeed Europeans portrayed imperialism as a moral duty: colonial peoples were the 'white man's burden'. Imperialism supposedly brought the benefits of civilisation and in particular Christianity to the less fortunate and less sophisticated peoples of the world.

More particular forms of national chauvinism have developed in Russia and Germany. In Russia this took the form of pan-Slavism, sometimes called Slavophile nationalism, which was particularly strong in the late nineteenth and early twentieth centuries. The Russians are Slavs, and enjoy linguistic and cultural links with other Slavic peoples in eastern and south-eastern Europe. The prefix 'pan' means 'all' or 'every', and therefore pan-Slavism reflects the goal of Slavic unity, which the Russians have believed to be their historic mission. In the years before 1914, such ideas brought Russia into growing conflict with Austro-Hungary for control of the Balkans. The chauvinistic character of pan-Slavism derives from the belief that the Russians are the natural leaders of the Slavic people, and that the Slavs are culturally and spiritually superior to the peoples of central or western Europe. Pan-Slavism is therefore both anti-western and anti-liberal. Some have feared that the revival of Russian nationalism in the 1990s could keep such aggressive and expansionist ideas alive.

Traditional German nationalism also exhibited a marked chauvinism, which was born out of defeat in the Napoleonic Wars. Writers such as Fichte and Jahn reacted strongly against France and the ideals of its revolution, emphasising instead the uniqueness of German culture and its language, and the racial purity of its people. After unification in 1871, German nationalism developed a pronounced chauvinistic character with the emergence of pressure groups such as the Pan-German League and the Navy League, which campaigned for closer ties with German-speaking Austria and for a German empire, Germany's 'place in the sun'. Pan-Germanism was an expansionist and aggressive form of nationalism that envisaged the creation of a German-dominated Europe. German chauvinism found its highest expression in the racialist and anti-Semitic (see p. 230) doctrines developed by the Nazis. The Nazis adopted the expansionist goals of pan-Germanism with enthusiasm, but justified them in the language of biology rather than politics (this is examined more fully in Chapter 7 in connection with racialism). The Germans were portrayed as a 'master race', naturally suited to a role of world domination, while other races were considered inferior and subordinate. After 1945 West Germany espoused a very different national tradition, which openly broke with the expansionist ideals of the past. However reunification in 1990 was accompanied by a revival of far-right activism and anti-Semitic attacks, encouraging some to suggest that contemporary German nationalism has not entirely buried its past.

National chauvinism breeds from a feeling of intense, even hysterical nationalist enthusiasm. The individual as a separate, rational being is swept away on a tide of patriotic emotion, expressed in the desire for aggression, expansion and war. The right-wing French nationalist Charles Maurras (1868–1952) called such intense patriotism 'integral nationalism': individuals and independent groups lose their identity within an all-powerful 'nation', which has an existence and meaning beyond the life of any single individual. Such militant nationalism is often accompanied by militarism. Military glory and conquest are the ultimate evidence of national greatness and have been capable of generating intense feelings of nationalist commitment. The civilian population is, in effect, militarised; it is infected by the martial values of absolute loyalty, complete dedication and willing self-sacrifice. When the honour or integrity of the nation is in question, the lives of ordinary citizens become unimportant. Such emotional intensity was amply demonstrated in August 1914, and perhaps also underlies the emotional power of the *jihad*, or 'holy war', in Moslem nations.

National chauvinism has a particularly strong appeal for the isolated and powerless, for whom nationalism offers the prospect of security, self-respect and pride. Militant or integral nationalism requires a heightened sense of belonging to a distinct national group. Such intense nationalist feeling is often stimulated by 'negative integration', the portrayal of another nation or race as a threat or an enemy. In the face of the enemy, the nation draws together and experiences an intensified sense of its own identity and importance. National chauvinism therefore breeds off a clear distinction between 'them' and 'us'. There has to be a 'them' to deride or hate in order to forge a sense of 'us'. In politics, national chauvinism has commonly been reflected in racialist ideologies, which divide the world into an 'in group' and an 'out group', in which the 'out group' becomes a scapegoat for all the misfortunes and frustrations suffered by the 'in group'. It is therefore no coincidence that chauvinistic political creeds are a breeding ground for racialist ideas. Both pan-Slavism and pan-Germanism, for example, have been characterised by virulent anti-Semitism.

## Anticolonial nationalism

Nationalism may have been born in Europe, but it became a worldwide phenomenon thanks to imperialism. The experience of colonial rule helped to forge a sense of nationhood and a desire for 'national liberation' amongst the peoples of Asia and Africa, and gave rise to a specifically anticolonial form of nationalism. During the twentieth century the political geography of much of the world was transformed by anticolonialism. Although Versailles applied the principle of self-determination to Europe, it was conveniently ignored in other parts of the world, where German colonies were simply transferred to British and French control. However during the interwar period independence movements increasingly threatened the overstretched empires of the UK and France. The final collapse of the European empires came after the Second World War. India had been promised independence during the war and this was eventually granted in 1947. China only achieved genuine unity and independence in the 1949 Revolution, after fighting an eight-year war against the occupying Japanese. The Indonesian Republic was proclaimed in 1949, after a three-year war against the Netherlands. Military resistance by the Viet Minh, led by Ho Chi Minh, eventually caused the French to withdraw from Vietnam in 1954. However their departure was followed in 1961 by the arrival of the Americans, and final liberation, together with the unification of North and South Vietnam, was only achieved in 1975, after fourteen more years of war.

The nationalist struggles in South-East Asia inspired similar movements in Africa, and liberation movements sprang up under leaders such as Nkrumah in Ghana, Doctor Azikiwe in Nigeria, Julius Nyerere in what was then Tanganyika, and Hastings Banda in Nyasaland, later to become Malawi. The new-found assertiveness of African and Asian countries was expressed at the Bandung Conference of 1955, where representatives from 29 countries jointly condemned colonialism and supported a policy of Third World non-alignment. Decolonisation in Africa accelerated from the late 1950s onwards. Nigeria gained independence from the UK in 1960, and after a prolonged war against the French, Algeria achieved independence in 1962. Kenya became independent in 1963, as did Tanzania and Malawi the next year. Africa's last remaining colony, South-West Africa, finally became independent Namibia in 1990.

In a sense the colonising Europeans had taken with them the seed of their own destruction, the doctrine of nationalism. For example it is notable that many of the leaders of independence or liberation movements were western educated. It is therefore not surprising that anticolonial movements sometimes articulated their goals in the language of liberal nationalism, reminiscent of Mazzini or Woodrow Wilson. However, emergent African and Asian nations were in a very different position from the newly created European states of the nineteenth and early twentieth centuries. For these African and Asia nations the quest for political independence was closely related to their awareness of economic under-development and their subordination to the industrialised states of Europe and North America. Anticolonialism thus came to express the desire for 'national liberation' in both political and economic terms, and this has left its mark upon the form of nationalism practised in the developing world.

Most of the leaders of Asian and African anticolonial movements have been attracted to some form of socialism, ranging from the moderate and peaceful ideas represented by Gandhi and Nehru, to the revolutionary Marxism espoused by Ho Chi Minh, Che Guevara and Robert Mugabe. On the surface, as is discussed later, socialism is more clearly related to internationalism than to nationalism. Socialist ideas have nevertheless appealed powerfully to nationalists in the developing world. In the first place socialism embodies the values of community and cooperation that were already well-established in traditional, preindustrial societies. More importantly, socialism, and in particular Marxism, provided an analysis of inequality and exploitation through which the colonial experience could be understood and colonial rule challenged.

Marxism highlights a class struggle between a 'ruling class' of property owners and the oppressed and exploited working class. It also preaches the revolutionary overthrow of the class system in a 'proletarian revolution'. Such ideas had already been applied to the relationship amongst countries by Lenin (see p. 132) in *Imperialism, The Highest Stage of Capitalism* ([1916] 1970). Influenced by the work of J. A. Hobson (1902), Lenin argued that imperialism is essentially an economic phenomenon, a quest for profit by capitalist countries seeking investment opportunities, cheap labour and raw materials, and secure markets. Developing-world nationalists have applied Marxist analysis to the relationship between colonial rulers and subject peoples. The class struggle became a colonial struggle against exploitation and oppression. The overthrow of colonial rule therefore implied not only political independence but also a social revolution offering the prospect of both political and economic emancipation.

In some cases developing-world regimes have openly embraced Marxist–Leninist principles, often adapting them to their particular needs. On achieving independence, China, North Korea, Vietnam and Cambodia moved swiftly to seize foreign assets and nationalise economic resources. They founded one-party states and centrally planned economies, closely following the Soviet model. In Zimbabwe, Robert Mugabe was more pragmatic in his application of Marxism–Leninism. Zimbabwe established a mixed economy after independence in 1980 in an attempt to retain white expertise and capital, and accepted a constitution based upon western-style parliamentary democracy for the first ten years after independence. In other cases, states in Africa and the Middle East have developed a less ideological form of nationalistic socialism. This has been evident in Algeria, Libya, Zambia, Iraq and South Yemen, where one-party states were founded, usually led by powerful, 'charismatic' leaders such as Gadhafi in Libya and Saddam Hussein in Iraq. The 'socialism' proclaimed in such countries usually takes the form of an appeal to a unifying national cause or interest, in most cases economic or social development.

Anticolonialism has been a revolt against western power and influence, and has therefore not always cared to express itself in a language of liberalism and socialism borrowed from the West. In some cases western ideas have been adapted and changed beyond all recognition, as in the case of so-called 'African socialism', as practised in Tanzania, Zimbabwe and Angola. African socialism is not based on Soviet-style state socialism or western social democracy, but rather is founded upon traditional communitarian values and the desire to subordinate divisive tribal rivalries to the overriding need for economic progress. Some countries of the developing world have expressed their nationalism by cultivating links with other former colonies in an attempt to articulate a distinctive 'Third World' voice, independent from that of either the capitalist 'First World' or the communist 'Second World'. This was attempted by the Bandung Conference and was kept alive during the Cold War period by the non-aligned movement of Third World states. 'Third Worldism' reflected a fierce rejection of imperialism and a common desire for economic progress amongst countries that usually shared a colonial past. However such ties have weakened as memories of colonial rule have receded, allowing the cultural and political differences amongst developing states to become more apparent.

The post-colonial period has thrown up quite different forms of nationalism, shaped more by the rejection of western ideas and culture than by the attempt to reapply them or remain independent from them. If the West is regarded as the source of oppression and exploitation, post-colonialism must seek an anti-western voice and not merely a non-western one. In part, this is a reaction against the dominance of western, and increasingly US, culture and economic power in much of the developing world. The United States has not favoured political colonisation, but its influence reflects the worldwide dominance of the US economy, controlling investment, creating jobs and making available a wide range of western consumer goods. This so-called neocolonialism has been far more difficult to combat because it does not take an openly political form, but it has also bred fierce resentment. During the Iranian Revolution, Ayatollah Khomeini (see p. 306) dubbed the United States the 'Great Satan'. Anti-Americanism has been a prominent feature of Iranian politics since the revolution of 1979, and it has been significant in Libya under Gadhafi and also in Saddam Hussein's Iraq, especially after the invasion of Kuwait in 1990. In rejecting the West in general and the United States in particular, such forms of nationalism have increasingly looked to non-western philosophies and ideas. The growing importance of religion, and especially Islam, has given developing-world nationalism a distinctive character and a renewed potency. This is discussed in Chapter 10 in relation to religious fundamentalism.

## Beyond nationalism

A variety of political creeds can be said to look beyond the nation. This applies to any doctrine or ideology that propounds a transnational view of political identity. It is thus difficult to reconcile nationalism with feminism, since the latter holds gender or sexual differences to be of prime importance and thus implies that national ties are either of secondary importance or are politically irrelevant. Similarly, although racialism and religious fundamentalism are at times linked to nationalism, they cannot merely be viewed as subspecies of nationalism because racial and religious identities cut across national boundaries. In this sense they can be thought of as weak forms of internationalism.

Internationalism in its stronger form, however, is characterised by the more radical belief that political nationalism should be transcended because the ties that bind the peoples of the world are stronger than those that separate them. By this standard the goal of internationalism is to construct supranational structures that can command the political allegiance of *all* the peoples of the world, regardless of religious, racial, social and national differences. Such 'one worldism' has, for example, provided the basis for the 'idealist' tradition within international relations, which is characterised by a belief in universal morality and the prospect of global peace and cooperation. The German philosopher Emmanuel Kant (1724–1804) is often seen as the father of this tradition, his *Towards Eternal Peace* having envisaged a kind of 'league of nations' based on the belief that reason and morality combine to dictate that 'There should be no war'. As far as the major ideologies are concerned, this vision has been most clearly associated with liberalism and socialism, each of which has developed a particular brand of internationalism.

## Liberal internationalism

Liberals have rarely rejected nationalism in principle. They have usually been prepared to accept both that nations are natural entities, in that cultural similarities tend to build a sense of identity and common belonging, and that nations provide the most appropriate units of political rule – hence the existence of liberal nationalism. What they have not been prepared to accept, however, is that the nation constitutes the highest source of political authority: unchecked national power has very much the same drawbacks as unrestrained individual liberty. There are, broadly, two bases of liberal individualism. The first is fear of an international state of nature, and the second is commitment to the individual over the nation.

Liberals have long accepted that national self-determination is a mixed blessing. The danger of a world of sovereign nation-states lies in the scope that it allows for the pursuit of national interests, possibly at the expense of other nations. Liberal nationalists have certainly argued that constitutionalism and democracy reduce the tendency towards militarism and war, but when sovereign nations operate within conditions of 'international anarchy', self-restraint alone may not be sufficient ensure unending peace. Liberals have generally proposed two means of preventing a recourse to conquest and plunder. The first is national interdependence, aimed at promoting mutual understanding and cooperation. This is why liberals have traditionally supported the policy of free trade: economic inter-dependence means that the material cost of international conflict is so great that warfare becomes virtually unthinkable. For the nineteenth-century 'Manchester liberals' in the UK, Richard Cobden (1804–65) and John Bright (1811–89), this preference for interdependence reflected a deeper commitment to the principle of cosmopolitanism. Not only would it promote prosperity by allowing countries to specialise in producing what they are best suited to produce (the theory that economists term 'comparative advantage'), but it would also draw people of different races, creeds and languages together into what Cobden described as 'the bonds of eternal peace' (quoted in Greenleaf, 1983, p. 37).

Liberals have also proposed that national ambition should be checked by the construction of supranational bodies capable of bringing order to an otherwise lawless international scene. This argument draws on precisely the same logic as social contract theory: government is the solution to the problem of disorder. This explains Woodrow Wilson's support for the first, if flawed, experiment in world government, the League of Nations, set up in 1919, and far wider support for its successor, the United Nations, founded by the San Francisco Conference of 1945. Liberals have looked to these bodies to establish a law-governed states system to make possible the peaceful resolution of international conflicts. However liberals also recognise that law must be enforced and hence have usually endorsed the principle of collective security, the idea that aggression can best be resisted by united action by a number of states. This sympathy for supranationalism is also evident in the liberal attitude towards bodies such as the European Union. Unlike conservatives, who fear that European integration will undermine national independence and weaken national identity, liberals have been more inclined to support the idea of a 'United States of Europe', seeing it as a way in which cooperation and inter-dependence can be promoted amongst nations that nevertheless retain their distinctive traditions and identities.

The second basis for liberal internationalism stems from an overriding commitment to the individual and the principle of individualism (see p. 28). This implies that all human beings, regardless of race, creed, social background and nationality, are of equal moral worth. While liberals endorse the idea of national self-determination, by no means do they believe that it entitles nations to treat their people however they choose. Respect for the rights and liberties of the individual in that sense outranks the claims of national sovereignty. Liberal internationalism is thus char-acterised not so much by a desire to supersede the nation as a political formation, but rather by the demand that nations conform to a higher morality embodied in the doctrine of human rights. As liberals believe that these rights are universally applicable and lay down the minimum

## Cosmopolitanism

Cosmopolitanism literally means a belief in a *cosmopolis* or 'world state'. As such it implies the obliteration of national identities and the establishment of a common political allegiance, uniting all human beings. The term, however, is usually employed to refer to the more modest goal of peace and harmony amongst nations, founded upon mutual understanding, toleration and, above all, interdependence. Liberal cosmopolitanism has long been associated with support for free trade, based upon the belief that it promotes both international understanding and material prosperity. The cosmopolitan ideal is also promoted by supranational bodies that aim to encourage cooperation amongst nations rather than replace the nation-state.

conditions for a truly human existence, they should clearly also constitute the basis of international law. Such beliefs have led to the drawing up of documents such as the United Nations Declaration of Human Rights in 1948 and the European Convention on Human Rights and Fundamental Freedoms in 1956.

Critics of this form of liberal internationalism include conservatives and developing-world nationalists. The former allege that the idea of universal human rights simply fails to take account of distinctive national traditions and cultures, while the latter go further and argue that, as human rights are essentially a manifestation of western liberalism, their spread amounts to a covert form of western imperialism.

## Socialist internationalism

Socialists are more likely than liberals to reject nationalism in principle, believing both that it breeds resentment and conflict and that it has an implicitly right-wing character. Although this has not prevented modern socialists, as rulers and aspiring rulers, from reaching an accommodation with the nation-state, it has inclined them, at least in rhetoric, to treat internationalism as an article of faith if not as a core value. This has been clearest in relation to the Marxist tradition. Marxism has traditionally embraced a form of proletarian internationalism, rooted in the idea that class solidarity is more powerful and politically significant than national identity. In the *Communist Manifesto*, Marx (see p. 126) wrote:

> The working men have no country. We cannot take from them what they have not got. Since the proletariat must first of all acquire political supremacy, must rise to be the leading class of the nation, must constitute itself *the* nation, it is, so far, itself national, though not in the bourgeois sense of the word (Marx and Engels, [1848] 1968, p. 51).

Marx recognised the important national dimension of any socialist revolution; as he put it, the proletariat of each country must 'first of all settle matters with its own bourgeoisie'. Moreover he accepted that for subject peoples national liberation is a precondition for socialist revolution, a stance reflected, for instance, in his support for Polish and Irish independence. Nevertheless he did not envisage that the working class would be national 'in the bourgeois sense of the word', by which he meant that, in recognising the brotherhood of *all* proletarians, it would transcend what Engels called 'national egoism'. The *Communist Manifesto* expresses this graphically in its famous final words: 'Working men of all countries, unite!'. Socialism therefore has an intrinsically international character. Not only does proletarian class solidarity inevitably cut across national borders, but, as Marx pointed out, the emergence of world markets had turned capitalism into an international system that could only be challenged by a genuinely international movement. This is why Marx helped to found the International Working Men's Association, the so-called First International, in 1864. A Second or 'Socialist' International was set up in 1889 and revived in 1951. A Third International or 'Comintern' was formed by Lenin in 1919, while a rival Fourth International was set up in 1936 by Leon Trotsky, an arch critic of Stalin's policy of 'Socialism in One Country'.

However socialists have seldom seen proletarian internationalism as an end in itself. Their aim has not been to replace a world divided on national lines by one divided on class lines, but rather – through an international class struggle – to establish harmony and cooperation amongst all the world's peoples. Socialist internationalism is therefore ultimately based on a belief in a common humanity. This is the idea that humankind is bound together by mutual sympathy, compassion and love, based upon the belief

## Leon Trotsky (1879–1940)

Russian Marxist, political thinker and revolutionary. An early critic of Lenin and leader of the 1905 St Petersburg Soviet, Trotsky joined the Bolsheviks in 1917, becoming commissar for foreign affairs and later commissar for war. Outmanoeuvred by Stalin after Lenin's death, he was banished from the Soviet Union in 1929 and assassinated in Mexico in 1940 on Stalin's orders.

Trotsky's theoretical contribution to Marxism centres on the theory of permanent revolution, which suggested that socialism could be established in Russia without the need for the bourgeois stage of development. Trotskyism is usually associated with an unwavering commitment to internationalism and to an anti-Stalinism that highlights the dangers of bureaucratisation, as outlined in *The Revolution Betrayed* (1937).

that what human beings share with one another is greater than what divides them. From this perspective, socialists may reject nationalism not only as a species of bourgeois ideology, which conceals the contradictions upon which capitalism and all other class societies are based, but also because it encourages people to deny their common humanity. Internationalism, for a socialist, may thus imply not merely cooperation amongst nations within a framework of international law, but the more radical and utopian goal of the dissolution of the nation and the recognition that there is but one world and one people.

Criticisms of socialist internationalism fall into two categories. The first highlights the failure of international socialists to live up to their high ideals in practice. The various Internationals, for example, were hampered by deep personal and ideological rivalries, as well as by national differences. Under Stalin the Comintern became simply a tool through which the Soviet Union could pursue its own foreign policy goals, national interest masquerading as internationalism. The Socialist International has survived as a mere talking shop for moderate socialist leaders and is devoid of policy significance. The second category of criticisms emphasises the damage done to socialism by its failure to recognise and tap the enduring strength of political nationalism. The tendency to dismiss nationalism as an artificial and doomed force has repeatedly encouraged socialists to overestimate the appeal of the internationalist ideal. Nowhere was this more dramatically demonstrated than in the effective collapse of the Second International in August 1914, when the proletariats of Europe, and many of their socialist parties, succumbed eagerly at the prospect of war and national glory. Nationalism proved to be substantially more potent than the prospect of social revolution.

## Nationalism in the twenty-first century

Few political ideologies have been forced to endure prophesies of their imminent demise for as long as nationalism. As early as 1848 Marx proclaimed that 'National differences and antagonisms between peoples are daily more and more vanishing', and looked to their complete disappearance once the supremacy of the proletariat was established. Similarly the death of nationalism as the project of nation building was widely proclaimed after the First World War, following the reconstruction of Europe according to the principle of national self-determination, and after the Second World War, as a result of decolonisation in Africa, Asia and elsewhere. Once a world of nation-states had been constructed, what further role would there be for nationalism? Moreover as the twentieth century progressed it appeared that the nation had been made redundant by the progressive internationalisation of economic and political life. International organisations – from the United Nations to the European Union and from the World Trade Organisation to the International Monetary Fund – have come to dominate world politics, leaving fewer and fewer decisions in the hands of individual nations. This phenomenon has increasingly been described as 'globalisation'.

Globalisation refers to the emergence of a complex web of global interconnectedness that means that our lives are increasingly shaped by events that occur and decisions that are made at great distances from us. In reducing the significance of territorial boundaries, it has turned the world into, in Marshall McLuhan's words, a 'global village'. Globalisation has had a far-reaching impact on both the nation-state and political doctrines rooted in the idea of national distinctiveness. It has, for instance, led to the emergence of an integrated global economy, meaning that material prosperity is often more determined by the investment decisions of multinational corporations than it is by the actions of national governments. In cultural terms, with the growth of air travel, foreign tourism, satellite television and the internet, globalisation means the spread of a market-driven society, sometimes seen as the 'McDonaldisation' of the world. Can nations any longer be regarded as meaningful entities when people in different parts of the world watch the same films and television programmes, eat the same food, enjoy the same sports and so on? Given the remorseless nature of such developments, surely the twenty-first century is going to witness the final eclipse of political nationalism.

Nevertheless at least two factors point to the continued political significance of the nation. First, there is the possibility that precisely by weakening traditional civil and national bonds, globalisation may fuel the emergence of ethnically based and possibly more aggressive nationalisms. If the conventional nation-state is no longer capable of generating meaningful collective identities, 'particularisms' based on region, religion, ethnicity or race may develop to take its place. This has already occurred most dramatically in an upsurge of ethnic conflict in many parts of the former Soviet bloc, particularly in former Yugoslavia, but is also evident in the centrifugal nationalisms that have taken root in states such as the UK, Spain, Italy and Belgium.

Second, globalisation may invest the national project with a new meaning and significance, that of mapping out a future for nations in an increasingly globalised and interdependent world. In this sense globalisation may not so much make nations irrelevant as force them to reinvent themselves, continuing to provide societies with a source of social cohesion and identity but within an increasingly fluid and competitive context. In their different ways, states such as Singapore, Malaysia, Australia, New

Zealand and Canada have undergone a process of self-affirmation, as they have attempted to refashion their national identities by fusing elements from their past with an essentially future-looking orientation.

## Further reading

Alter, P., *Nationalism* (London: Edward Arnold, 1989). A good and clear introduction to the origins and development of nationalist ideas and the different forms of nationalism.

Hobsbawm, E. J., *Nations and Nationalism since 1780* (Cambridge and New York: Cambridge University Press, 1990). A good and accessible introduction to the subject.

Hutchinson, J. and A.D. Smith (eds), *Nationalism* (Oxford and New York: Oxford University Press, 1994). A wide-ranging and useful collection of readings that examine debates on the nature, development and significance of nationalism.

Kedourie, E., *Nationalism*, revised edition (London: Hutchinson, 1985). A classic account of nationalism from a critical perspective that stresses the importance of self-determination.

Smith, A.D., *National Identity* (Harmondsworth: Penguin, 1991). An important contribution to debates on the origins and formation of nations.

# Chapter 6

# Anarchism

## Origins and development

The word 'anarchy' comes from Greek and literally means 'without rule'. The term 'anarchism' has been in use since the French Revolution, and was initially employed in a critical or negative sense to imply a breakdown of civilised or predictable order. Indeed pejorative meanings continue to be attached to the term. In everyday language, anarchy is usually equated with chaos and disorder; and in the popular imagination anarchists are not uncommonly seen as bomb-toting terrorists. Needless to say anarchists themselves fiercely reject such associations. It was not until Pierre-Joseph Proudhon (see p. 199) proudly declared in *What is Property?* ([1840] 1971), 'I am an anarchist', that the word was clearly associated with a positive and systematic set of political ideas. Anarchists do advocate the abolition of law and government, but in the belief that a more natural and spontaneous social order will develop. As Proudhon suggested, 'society seeks order in anarchy'. The link with violence is also misleading. At times anarchists have openly, even proudly, supported bombings and terrorism. However most anarchists believe violence to be mistaken and counter-productive, and many follow the ideas of Tolstoy and Gandhi and regard any form of violence as morally unacceptable.

Anarchist ideas have sometimes been traced back to Taoist or Buddhist ideas, to the Stoics and Cynics of Ancient Greece, or to the Diggers of the English Civil War. However the first, and in a sense classic, statement of anarchist principles was produced by William Godwin (see p. 192) in his *Enquiry Concerning Political Justice* ([1793] 1971), although Godwin never described himself as an anarchist. During the nineteenth century, anarchism was a significant component of a broad but growing socialist movement. In 1864 Proudhon's followers joined with Marx (see p. 126) to set up the International Workingmen's Association, or First International. The International collapsed in 1871 because of growing antagonism between Marxists and anarchists led by Michael Bakunin (see p. 195). In the late nineteenth century, anarchists sought mass support amongst the landless peasants of Russia and southern Europe and, more successfully, through anarcho-syndicalism, amongst the industrial working classes.

Syndicalism was a form of revolutionary trade unionism, popular in France, Italy and Spain, which made anarchism a genuine mass movement in the early twentieth century. The powerful CGT union in France was dominated by anarchists before 1914, as was the CNT in Spain, which claimed a membership of over two million during the Civil War. Anarcho-syndicalist movements also emerged in Latin America in the early twentieth century, especially in Argentina and Uruguay, and syndicalist ideas influenced the Mexican Revolution, led by Emiliano Zapata. However the spread of authoritarianism and political repression gradually undermined anarchism in both Europe and Latin America. The victory of General Franco in the Spanish Civil War, 1936–9, brought an end to anarchism as a mass movement. The CNT was suppressed and anarchists, along with left-wingers in general, were persecuted. The influence of anarchism was also undermined by the success of Lenin and the Bolsheviks in 1917, and thus by the growing prestige of communism within the socialist and revolutionary movements.

Anarchism is unusual amongst political ideologies in that it has never succeeded in winning power, at least at the national level. No society or nation has been modelled according to anarchist principles. Hence it is tempting to regard anarchism as an ideology of less significance than, say, liberalism, socialism, conservatism or fascism, each of which has proved itself capable of winning power and reshaping societies. The nearest anarchists have come to achieving power was during the Spanish Civil War, when they briefly controlled parts of eastern Spain and set up workers' and peasants' collectives throughout Catalonia. Consequently anarchists have looked to historical societies that reflect their principles, such as the cities of Ancient Greece or Medieval Europe, or to traditional peasant communes such as the Russian *mir*. Anarchists have also stressed the non-hierarchic and egalitarian nature of many traditional societies, for instance the Nuer in Africa, and supported experiments in small-scale, communal living within western society.

As a political movement, anarchism has suffered from three major drawbacks. First, its goal, the overthrow of the state and all forms of political authority, is often considered to be simply unrealistic. Certainly the evidence of modern history from most parts of the world suggests that economic and social development is usually accompanied by a growth in the role of government, rather than its diminution or disappearance.

Second, in opposing the state and all forms of political authority, anarchists have rejected the conventional means of exercising political influence: forming political parties, standing for elections, seeking public office and so on. Anarchists have therefore been forced to rely upon less orthodox methods, often based upon a faith in mass spontaneity rather than political organisation. Third, anarchism does not constitute a single, coherent set of political ideas, or a single movement. Although anarchists are united in their opposition to the institutions of the state, and indeed other forms of coercive authority, they arrive at this conclusion from very different philosophical perspectives, and disagree, often fundamentally, about the nature of an anarchic society.

## Against the state – central themes

The defining feature of anarchism is its opposition to the state and the accompanying institutions of government and law. Anarchists have a preference for stateless society in which free individuals manage their affairs by voluntary agreement, without compulsion or coercion. Such a preference has been expressed by very different philosophical traditions, by liberal individualists on the one hand, and by communitarian socialists on the other. In that sense anarchism can be thought of as a point of overlap between liberalism and socialism, the point at which both political creeds, in their different ways, reach antistatist conclusions. Anarchism itself thus has a dual character: it can be interpreted as either 'ultraliberalism' or 'ultrasocialism'. As a result it is sometimes seen to lack the bedrock of unifying values and principles that typically distinguish one ideology from another. Nevertheless anarchists, although from very different political traditions, are united by a series of broader ideological positions. The most significant of these are the following:

- Antistatism
- Natural order
- Anticlericalism
- The free economy.

### Antistatism

Sébastien Faure, in *Encyclopédie anarchiste*, defined anarchism as 'the negation of the principle of Authority'. The anarchist case against authority is simple and clear: authority is an offence against the principles of liberty and equality. Human beings are free and autonomous creatures, who should treat each other with respect and sympathy. The power of one person over another enslaves, oppresses and limits life. It gives rise to a 'psychology of power', based upon a pattern of 'dominance and submission', a society in which, according to the US anarchist and social critic Paul Goodman (1911–72), 'many are ruthless and most live in fear'. Strictly speaking anarchists do not object to all forms of authority; for instance they may accept that the views of doctors or teachers deserve particular respect because of the specialist knowledge or learning such people possess. However, even the authority of the doctor or teacher is dangerous: knowledge can be abused and exploited in order to maintain the prestige of the educated over the ignorant. Anarchists are nevertheless firmly opposed to any form of authority that is compulsory or coercive, such as political authority, especially when it is backed up by the machinery of the modern state.

All other political ideologies believe that the state fulfils some worthy or worthwhile purpose within society. For instance liberals regard the state as the protector of individual rights; conservatives revere the state as a symbol of order and social cohesion; socialists have seen it as an instrument of reform and the source of social justice. Anarchists, in contrast, believe that such views seriously misunderstand the nature of political authority and the state, and also fail to appreciate the negative and destructive forces that are embodied in the institutions of law and government. The flavour of this anarchist critique is conveyed by one of Proudhon's famous diatribes:

> To be governed is to be watched over, inspected, spied on, directed, legislated, regimented, closed in, indoctrinated, preached at, controlled, assessed, evaluated, censored, commanded; all by creatures that have neither the right, nor the wisdom, nor the virtue. (quoted in Marshall, 1993, p. 245)

The state is a sovereign body that exercises supreme authority over all individuals and associations living within a defined geographical area. Anarchists emphasise that, unlike the authority of a doctor or teacher, the authority of the state is absolute and unlimited: law can restrict public behaviour, limit political activity, regulate economic life, interfere with private morality and thinking, and so on. The authority of the state is also compulsory. Anarchists reject the liberal notion that political authority arises from voluntary agreement, through some form of 'social contract', and argue instead that individuals become subject to state authority either by being born in a particular country or through conquest. Furthermore the state is a coercive body whose laws must be obeyed because they are backed up by the threat of punishment. For the Russian-born US anarchist Emma Goldman (1869–1940), government was symbolised by 'the club,

## Perspectives on . . .

### The state

**Liberals** see the state as a neutral arbiter amongst the competing interests and groups in society, a vital guarantee of social order. While classical liberals treat the state as a necessary evil and extol the virtues of a minimal or nightwatchman state, modern liberals recognise the state's positive role in widening freedom and promoting equal opportunities.

**Conservatives** link the state to the need to provide authority and discipline and to protect society from chaos and disorder, hence their traditional preference for a strong state. However conservative support for a pragmatic balance between the state and civil society has diminished as new right minimal statism has spread.

**Socialists** have adopted contrasting views of the state. Some have seen it as an oppressive weapon used to uphold economic inequality, as in the crude Marxist belief that the state is an instrument of class rule. Others, however, regard the state as an embodiment of the common good and thus approve of interventionism in either its social-democratic or state-collectivist form.

**Anarchists** reject the state outright, believing it to be an unnecessary evil. The sovereign, compulsory and coercive authority of the state is seen as nothing less than legalised oppression operating in the interests of the powerful, propertied and privileged.

**Fascists**, particularly in the Italian tradition, see the state as a supreme ethical ideal, reflecting the undifferentiated interests of the national community, hence their belief in totalitarianism (see p. 233). The Nazis, however, saw the state more as a vessel that contains, or tool that serves, the race or nation.

**Feminists** have viewed the state as an instrument of male power, the patriarchal state serving to exclude women from, or subordinate them within, the public or 'political' sphere of life. Liberal feminists nevertheless regard the state as an instrument of reform that is susceptible to electoral pressures.

**Fundamentalists** have adopted a broadly positive attitude towards the state, seeing it as a means of bringing about social, moral and cultural renewal. The fundamentalist state is therefore regarded as a political manifestation of religious authority and wisdom.

the gun, the handcuff, or the prison'. The state can deprive individuals of their property, their liberty and ultimately, through capital punishment, their lives. The state is also exploitative in that it robs individuals of their property through a system of taxation, once again backed up by the force of law and the possibility of punishment. Anarchists often argue that the state acts in alliance with the wealthy and privileged, and therefore serves to oppress the poor and weak. Finally, the state is destructive. 'War', as Randolph Bourne (1886–1918) suggested, 'is the health of the State'. Individuals are required to fight, kill and die in wars that are invariably precipitated by a quest for territorial expansion, plunder or national glory by one state at the expense of others.

The basis of this critique of the state lies in the anarchist view of human nature. Despite the fact that anarchists subscribe to a highly optimistic if not utopian view of human potential, they are often deeply pessimistic about the corrupting influence of political authority and economic inequality. Human beings who would otherwise be cooperative, sympathetic and sociable, become nothing less than oppressive tyrants when raised up above others by power, privilege or wealth. In other words anarchists replace the liberal warning that 'power tends to corrupt and absolute power corrupts absolutely' (Lord Acton) with the more radical and alarming warning that power in any shape or form will corrupt absolutely. The state, as a repository of sovereign, compulsory and coercive authority, is therefore nothing less than a concentrated form of evil. This theory, moreover, reflects the general anarchist belief that human nature is plastic: human beings can be either 'good' or 'evil' depending on the political and social circumstances in which they live. Nevertheless this theory of the state has attracted criticism. Critics of anarchism have argued that it is difficult to sustain a theory of human nature that allows that people are entirely peaceful and cooperative in certain circumstances, but absolutely corrupt and oppressive in other circumstances. Another line of criticism has been that the assumption that state oppression stems from individual corruption is circular, in that it is unable to explain how political authority arose in the first place.

## Natural order

Anarchists not only regard the state as evil, but also believe it to be unnecessary. William Godwin sought to demonstrate this by, in effect, turning the most celebrated justification for the state – social contract theory – on its head. The social contract arguments of Hobbes (see p. 72) and Locke (see p. 38) suggest that a stateless society, the 'state of nature', amounts to a civil war of each against all, making orderly and stable life impossible. The source of such strife lies in human nature, which

## William Godwin (1756–1836)

UK philosopher and novelist. Godwin was a Presbyterian minister who lost his faith and eventually became a professional writer, *Caleb Williams* (1794) being his most successful novel. He led an intellectual circle that included his wife, Mary Wollstonecraft (see p. 251) and a group of aspiring writers, among whom were Wordsworth and Shelley, his son-in-law.

Godwin's political reputation was established by *Enquiry Concerning Political Justice* ([1773] 1971) which, by developing a thorough-going critique of authoritarianism, constituted the first full exposition of anarchist beliefs. Godwin developed an extreme form of liberal rationalism that amounted to an argument for human perfectibility based on education and social conditioning. Though an individualist, Godwin believed that humans are capable of genuinely disinterested benevolence.

according to Hobbes and Locke is essentially selfish, greedy and potentially aggressive. Only a sovereign state can restrain such impulses and guarantee social order. In short, order is impossible without law. Godwin, in contrast, suggested that human beings are essentially rational creatures, inclined by education and enlightened judgement to live in accordance with truth and universal moral laws. He thus believed that people have a natural propensity to organise their own lives in a harmonious and peaceful fashion. Indeed in his view it is the corrupting influence of government and unnatural laws, rather than any 'original sin' in human beings, that creates injustice, greed and aggression. Government, in other words, is not the solution to the problem of order, but its cause.

Anarchists have often sympathised with the famous opening words of Jean-Jacques Rousseau's (see p. 163) *Social Contract* ([1762] 1913), 'Man was born free, yet everywhere he is in chains.' At the heart of anarchism lies an unashamed utopianism, a belief in the natural goodness, or at least potential goodness, of humankind. From this perspective, social order arises naturally and spontaneously; it does not require the machinery of 'law and order'. This is why anarchist conclusions have only been reached by political thinkers whose views of human nature are sufficiently optimistic to sustain the notions of natural order and spontaneous harmony. For example collectivist anarchist, drawing on socialist assumptions, have generally stressed the human capacity for cooperative and gregarious behaviour, while individualist anarchists highlight the importance of enlightened human reason, in line with the liberal tradition. On the other hand conservatives, who believe that human beings to be fundamentally imperfect and corrupt, believe that at best anarchism is a utopian dream.

## Utopianism

A utopia (from the Greek *outopia*, meaning 'nowhere', or *eutopia*, meaning 'good place') is literally an ideal or perfect society. Although utopias of various kinds can be envisaged, most are characterised by the abolition of want, the absence of conflict and the avoidance of oppression and violence. Utopianism is a style of political theorising that develops a critique of the existing order by constructing a model of an ideal or perfect alternative. Good examples are anarchism and Marxism. Utopian theories are usually based on assumptions about the unlimited possibilities of human self-development. However utopianism is often used as a pejorative term to imply deluded or fanciful thinking, a belief in an unrealistic and unachievable goal.

For many anarchists, order is implicit in nature itself: it is not something that needs to be achieved or constructed, but something that, if humans refrain from interfering with it, will simply emerge or blossom. This is expressed in the Buddhist emphasis upon interdependence and oneness. It is also reflected in the Taoist idea of a natural balance between the forces of *yin*, representing the feminine, the passive, the dark, the soft, and *yang*, representing the masculine, the active, the bright and the hard. Life should thus be lived in accordance with natural rhythms and harmonies, rather than in accordance with human artifice and contrivance. The most influential modern version of such ideas is found in the notion of ecology, particular the 'social ecology' of thinkers such as Murray Bookchin (see p. 287). Social ecology is discussed more fully in Chapter 9 in relation to eco-anarchism.

## Anticlericalism

Although the state has been the principal target of anarchist hostility, the same criticisms apply to any other form of compulsory authority. Indeed anarchists have sometimes expressed as much bitterness towards the church as they have towards the state, particularly in the nineteenth century. This perhaps explains why anarchism has prospered in countries with strong religious traditions, such as Catholic Spain, France, Italy and the countries of Latin America, where it has helped to articulate anticlerical sentiments.

Anarchist objections to organised religion serve to highlight broader criticisms of authority in general. Religion, for example, has often been seen as the source of authority itself. The idea of God represents the notion of a 'supreme being' who commands ultimate and unquestionable authority. For anarchists such as Proudhon and Bakunin, an anarchist political philosophy had to be based upon the rejection of Christianity because only then could human beings be regarded as free and independent. Moreover, anarchists have suspected that religious and political authority usually work hand in hand. Bakunin ([1910] 1977, p. 82) proclaimed that 'The abolition of the Church and the State must be the first and indispensable condition of the true liberation of society'. Religion is seen by anarchists as one of the pillars of the state; it propagates an ideology of obedience and submission to both spiritual leaders and earthly rulers. As the Bible says, 'give unto Caesar that which is Caesar's'. Earthly rulers have often looked to religion to legitimise their power, most obviously in the doctrine of the divine right of kings.

Finally, religion seeks to impose a set of moral principles upon the individual and to establish a code of acceptable behaviour. Religious belief requires conformity to standards of 'good' and 'evil', which are defined and policed by figures of religious authority such as priests, bishops or popes. The individual is thus robbed of personal autonomy and the capacity to make his or her own moral judgements. Nevertheless anarchists do not reject the religious impulse altogether. There is a clear mystical strain within anarchism. Anarchists can be said to hold an essentially spiritual conception of human nature, a utopian belief in the virtually unlimited possibilities of human self-development and in the bonds that unite humanity, and indeed all living things. Early anarchists were sometimes influenced by millenarianism (see p. 22), a belief in the return of Christ and the establishment of the Kingdom of God after 'a thousand years'. Modern anarchists have often been attracted to religions such as Taoism and Zen Buddhism, which offer the prospect of personal insight and preach the values of toleration, respect and natural harmony.

## The free economy

Anarchists have rarely seen the overthrow of the state as an end in itself, but have also been interested in challenging the structure of social and economic life. Bakunin argued that 'political power and wealth are inseparable'. In the nineteenth century, anarchists usually worked within the working-class movement and subscribed to a broadly socialist social philosophy. Capitalism was understood in class terms: a 'ruling class' exploits and oppresses 'the masses'. However this 'ruling class' was not interpreted in narrow economic terms, but was seen to encompass all those who command wealth, power or privilege in society. It therefore includes kings and princes, politicians and state officials, judges and police officers, bishops and priests, as well as industrialists and bankers. Bakunin, for example, argued that in every developed society three social groups can be identified: a vast majority who are exploited; a minority who are

## Michael Bakunin (1814–76)

Russian anarchist and revolutionary. Bakunin was born into a prosperous aristocratic family. He renounced a military career and after philosophical studies was drawn into political activism by the 1848–9 revolutions. By the 1860s he had renounced Slav nationalism for anarchism and spent the rest of his life as an agitator and propagandist, famous for his interest in secret societies and his endless appetite for political intrigue.

Bakunin's anarchism was based on a belief in human sociability, expressed in the desire for freedom within a community of equals and in the 'sacred instinct of revolt'. He embraced a view of collectivism as self-governing communities of free individuals, which put him at odds with Marx and his followers. However Bakunin's real importance is more as the founder of the historical anarchist movement than as an original thinker or an anarchist theoretician.

exploited but also exploit others in equal measure; and 'the supreme governing estate', a small minority of 'exploiters and oppressors pure and simple'. Hence nineteenth-century anarchists identified themselves with the poor and oppressed and sought to carry out a social revolution in the name of the 'exploited masses', in which both capitalism and the state would be swept away.

However it is the economic structure of life that most keenly exposes tensions within anarchism. Although many anarchists acknowledge a kinship with socialism, based upon a common distaste for property and inequality, others have defended property rights and even revered competitive capitalism. This highlights the distinction between the two major anarchist traditions, one of which is collectivist and the other individualist. Collectivist anarchists advocate an economy based upon cooperation and collective ownership, while individualist anarchists support the market and private property.

Despite such fundamental differences, anarchists nevertheless agree about their distaste for the economic systems that have dominated both the capitalist West and the communist East during the twentieth century. All anarchists oppose the 'managed capitalism' that has predominated in western countries. Collectivist anarchists argue that state intervention has merely propped up a system of class exploitation and given capitalism a human face. Individualist anarchists suggest that intervention has distorted the competitive market and created economies dominated by both public and private monopolies. Anarchists have been even more united in their disapproval of Soviet-style 'state socialism'. Individualist anarchists object to the violation of property rights and individual freedom that they argue occurs in a planned economy. Collectivist anarchists argue that 'state socialism' is a contradiction in terms. State socialism is seen as a system of exploitation in which a ruling class of capitalists has simply been replaced by a new ruling class of state and party officials. Anarchists of all kinds have a preference for an economy in which free individuals manage their own affairs without the need for state ownership or regulation, whether through a system of 'anarcho-capitalism' or one of 'anarcho-communism'.

## Collectivist anarchism

The philosophical roots of collectivist anarchism lie in socialism rather than liberalism. Anarchist conclusions can be reached by pushing the ideas of socialist collectivism to their limits. Collectivism (see p. 107) is, in essence, the belief that human beings are social animals, better suited to working together for the common good than striving for individual self-interest. Collectivist anarchism stresses the human capacity for social solidarity, that human beings are naturally sociable, gregarious and cooperative. The natural and proper relationship amongst people is therefore one of sympathy, affection and harmony. When people are linked together by a common humanity, they have no need to be regulated or controlled by government: as Bakunin proclaimed, 'Social solidarity is the first human law; freedom is the second law'.

Anarchists are sometimes criticised for holding a naive and hopelessly optimistic view of human nature. In reality anarchists have seldom asserted that people are 'naturally good', but rather that they have the capacity for solidarity and cooperation. If human beings are social creatures, their characters and qualities are formed by a process of social interaction and experience. Human nature is fashioned by environmental factors rather than by any innate 'goodness' or 'badness'. Human beings will be greedy and aggressive if brought up in an unjust and oppressive society; but they will be caring and cooperative if brought up in a society where justice and equality reign. This helps to explain the enduring interest that anarchists have taken in education, and their desire to liberate education from any association with 'schooling', regimentation or discipline – what Paul Goodman (1964) called 'compulsory miseducation'. Many anarchists would sympathise with the goal of 'deschooling society', as preached by writers such as Goodman and Ivan Illich.

Peter Kropotkin (see p. 200) attempted to provide a biological foundation for social solidarity in *Mutual Aid* ([1897] 1914). Kropotkin set out to re-examine Darwin's theory of evolution, which had been used by social thinkers such as Herbert Spencer (1820–1903) to support the idea that humankind is naturally competitive and aggressive. Kropotkin did not accept that biology favours competition and struggle, but argued instead that successful species are ones that harness collective energies and possess the capacity for 'mutual aid' or cooperation. The process of evolution has therefore strengthened human sociability, favouring cooperation rather than competition. Kropotkin suggested that mutual aid is best reflected in the structure of city life in Ancient Greece and Medieval Europe.

## Anarchism and Marxism

A number of obvious parallels exist between collectivist anarchism and Marxism. Both regard capitalism as a system of class exploitation and injustice. Both exhibit a preference for the collective ownership of wealth and the communal organisation of social life. Both believe that a fully communist society would be anarchic. Marx expressed this belief in the famous prediction that the state will 'wither away' once the class system is abolished. Anarchists and Marxists therefore agree that human beings have the ultimate capacity to order their affairs without the need for political authority.

On the other hand there are major differences between these two political traditions, reflected in the antagonism that led to the break-up of the First International in 1872. Anarchists have been critical of Marxism for a number of reasons. In the first place, anarchists have recoiled from the scientific pretensions of Marxism, in particular from the ideas of historical materialism. Anarchists reject the central role that Marxists accord to economic life, and prefer to appeal to the utopian hopes and ideals of the masses, rather than to their material or class interests. Many anarchists see Marxism as a form of economic determinism, which portrays human beings as puppets controlled by impersonal historical forces, rather than as masters of their own destiny. Secondly, anarchists have been critical of the Marxist belief that the proletariat is the 'revolutionary class'. Anarchists have often worked within working-class movements, but have rarely seen the industrial working class as uniquely oppressed or the sole agent of revolutionary change.

Anarchists believe class exploitation to be merely one form of oppression and have highlighted the revolutionary potential of a wide variety of other social groups, including the rural peasantry, ethnic minorities, the urban underclass, students and so on. Thirdly, anarchists have disagreed with Marxists about the issue of political organisation. Following Lenin (see p. 132), many Marxists have been committed to the idea of a 'vanguard party', capable of leading the working class towards class consciousness and revolution. Anarchists, in contrast, place their faith in the spontaneous instincts of the masses and see the idea of a revolutionary party as elitist and a recipe for dictatorship.

However the most bitter disagreement between Marxists and anarchists centres upon their rival conceptions of the transition from capitalism to communism. Marxists believe in the need for a 'dictatorship of the proletariat', a transitional period between a proletarian revolution and the achievement of full communism, during which the proletariat will have to arm and organise itself against the threat of counter-revolution. In Marxist theory the state reflects the interests of the ruling or dominant class in society. A proletarian revolution will overthrow the 'bourgeois state' and establish a temporary 'proletarian state', which will endure only so long as class antagonisms persist. Anarchists, however, do not see the state simply as an instrument of class rule: they regard it as an independent and oppressive body in itself, and draw no distinction between a bourgeois and a proletarian state. Genuine revolution, for an anarchist, requires not only the overthrow of capitalism but also the immediate overthrow of all forms of state power. The state cannot be allowed to 'wither away', it must be abolished. Anarchists believe that this explains the tragedy of the Russian Revolution. In practice the proletarian state stubbornly refused to wither away, rather it became the cornerstone of the Soviet conception of socialism. Thus when anarchist sailors at the Kronstadt naval base mutinied in 1921 in protest against increasing repression, they were massacred by a Bolshevik government employing the machinery of the newly created workers' state.

## Mutualism

The anarchist belief in social solidarity has been used to justify various forms of cooperative behaviour. At one extreme it has led to a belief in pure communism, but it has also generated the more modest ideas of mutualism, associated with Pierre-Joseph Proudhon. In a sense Proudhon's libertarian socialism stands between the individualist and collectivist traditions of anarchism, Proudhon's ideas sharing much in common with those of US individualists such as Josiah Warren (1798–1874). In *What is Property?*, Proudhon came up with the famous statement that 'Property is theft', and condemned a system of economic exploitation based upon the accumulation of capital. Nevertheless, unlike Marx, Proudhon was not opposed to all forms of private property, distinguishing between property and what he called 'possessions'. In particular he admired the independence and initiative of smallholding peasants, craftsmen and artisans. Proudhon therefore sought to establish a system of property ownership that would avoid exploitation and promote social harmony.

Mutualism is a system of fair and equitable exchange, in which individuals or groups can bargain with one another, trading goods and services without profiteering or exploitation. Social interaction is therefore

## Pierre-Joseph Proudhon (1809–65)

French anarchist. Proudhon was a largely self-educated printer, who was drawn into radical politics in Lyons before settling in Paris in 1847. As a member of the 1848 Constituent Assembly, Proudhon famously voted against the constitution 'because it was a constitution'. He was later imprisoned for three years, after which, disillusioned with active politics, he concentrated on writing and theorising.

Proudhon's best-known work, *What is Property?* ([1840] 1970) attacked both traditional property rights and communism, and argued instead for mutualism, a cooperative productive system geared towards need rather than profit and organised within self-governing communities. Nevertheless, towards the end of his life Proudhon sought an alliance with the labour movement, and in *The Federal Principle* (1863) acknowledged the need for a minimal state to 'set things in motion'.

voluntary, mutually beneficial and harmonious, requiring no regulation or interference by government. Proudhon's followers tried to put these ideas into practice by setting up mutual credit banks in France and Switzerland, which provided cheap loans for investors and charged a rate of interest only high enough to cover the cost of running the bank but not so high that it made a profit. Proudhon's own views were largely founded upon his admiration for small communities of peasants or craftsmen, notably the watchmakers of Switzerland, who had traditionally managed their affairs on the basis of mutual cooperation.

## Anarcho-communism

More radically, a belief in social solidarity can lead in the direction of collectivism and communism. Sociable and gregarious human beings should lead a shared and communal existence. For example labour is a social experience, people work in common with fellow human beings and the wealth they produce should therefore be owned in common by the community, rather than by any single individual. In this sense property is theft: it represents the exploitation of workers who alone create wealth, by employers who merely own it. Furthermore private property encourages selfishness and, particularly offensive to the anarchist, promotes conflict and social disharmony. Inequality in the ownership of wealth fosters greed, envy and resentment, and therefore breeds crime and disorder.

Proudhon believed that communism could only be brought about by an authoritarian state, but anarcho-communists such as Kropotkin and Errico Malatesta (1853–1932) argued that true communism requires the abolition

### Peter Kropotkin (1842–1912)

Russian geographer and anarchist theorist. The son of a noble family who first entered the service of Tsar Alexander II, Kropotkin encountered anarchist ideas whilst working in the Jura region on the French–Swiss border. After imprisonment in St Petersburg in 1874 he travelled widely in Europe, returning to Russia after the 1917 Revolution.

Kropotkin's anarchism was imbued with the scientific spirit and based upon a theory of evolution that provided an alternative to Darwin's. By seeing mutual aid as the principal means of human and animal development, he claimed to provide an empirical basis for both anarchism and communism. Kropotkin's major works include *Mutual Aid* (1897), *Fields, Factories and Workshops* (1901) and *The Conquest of Bread* (1906).

of the state. Anarcho-communists admire small, self-managing communities along the lines of the medieval city-state or the peasant commune. Kropotkin envisaged that an anarchic society would consist of a collection of largely self-sufficient communes, each owning its wealth in common. Such communes would be held together by natural bonds of compassion and solidarity, rather than regulations or laws. Kropotkin suggested that law does not prevent crime, but positively promotes it. Laws that protect private property and the government are both useless and harmful, and once political oppression and economic injustice are abolished, laws to protect the person will simply become unnecessary. Kropotkin proposed that the antisocial instincts that may live on in some individuals would be most effectively restrained by 'liberty and fraternal care'. In his view, prisons and punishment merely serve to corrupt and deprave human beings, thereby promoting further crime.

## Anarcho-syndicalism

Although mutualism and anarcho-communism exerted significant influence within the broader socialist movement in the late nineteenth and early twentieth centuries, anarchism only developed into a mass movement in its own right in the form of anarcho-syndicalism. Syndicalism is a form of revolutionary trade unionism, drawing its name from the French word *syndicat*, meaning union or group. Syndicalism emerged first in France and was expressed by the powerful CGT union in the period before 1914. Syndicalist ideas spread to Italy, Latin America, the United States and, most significantly, Spain, where they were supported by the country's largest union, the CNT.

Syndicalist theory drew upon socialist ideas and advanced a crude notion of class war. Workers and peasants were seen to constitute an oppressed class, and individualists, landlords, politicians, judges and the police were portrayed as exploiters. Workers could defend themselves by organising syndicates or unions, based upon particular crafts, industries or professions. In the short term these syndicates could act as conventional trade unions, raising wages, shortening hours and improving working conditions. However syndicalists were also revolutionaries, who looked forward to the overthrow of capitalism and the seizure of power by the workers. In *Reflections on Violence* ([1908] 1950), Georges Sorel (1847–1922), the influential French syndicalist theorist, argued that such a revolution would come about through a general strike, a 'revolution of empty hands'. Sorel believed that the general strike was a 'myth', a symbol of working class power, capable of inspiring popular revolt.

Although syndicalist theory was at times unsystematic and confused, it nevertheless exerted a strong attraction for anarchists who wished to spread their ideas among the masses. As anarchists entered the syndicalist movement they developed the distinctive ideas of anarcho-syndicalism. Two features of syndicalism inspired particular anarchist enthusiasm. First, syndicalists rejected conventional politics as corrupting and pointless. Working-class power, they believed, should be exerted through direct action, boycotts, sabotage and strikes, and ultimately a general strike. Second, anarchists saw the syndicates as a model for the decentralised, non-hierarchic society of the future. Syndicates typically exhibited a high degree of grass-roots democracy and formed federations with other syndicates, either in the same area or in the same industry.

Although anarcho-syndicalism enjoyed genuine mass support, at least until the Spanish Civil War, it failed to achieve its revolutionary objectives. Beyond the rather vague idea of the general strike, anarcho-syndicalism did not develop a clear political strategy or a theory of revolution, relying instead upon the hope of a spontaneous uprising of the exploited and oppressed. Other anarchists have criticised syndicalism for concentrating too narrowly upon short-term trade union goals and therefore for leading anarchism away from revolution and towards reformism.

## Radical democracy

Although collectivist anarchists usually favour democratic organisation, they are resolute critics of conventional models of democracy. Liberal democracy is based on the principles of consent and representation, and so is rooted in a distinction, unacceptable for anarchists, between government and the people. Anarchists have deep misgivings about both consent and representation. In liberal theory, consent refers to the agreement of the governed to be ruled, suggesting that political authority arises 'from below', and therefore rests upon popular legitimacy. Anarchists, on the other hand, believe that to consent to be governed is, in effect, to conspire for one's own oppression, since government itself is a violation of personal autonomy. Similarly liberals see representation as the very stuff of democracy because it establishes a link between government and the people in the form of popular accountability. For anarchists, however, representation is a mere facade, an attempt to disguise from ordinary citizens the oppressive and exploitative nature of political rule. Not only does voting every few years amount to a meaningless ritual, but it also strengthens elites and channels political discontent in a constitutional direction. As anarchists have warned: however you vote, the government always wins the election.

Anarchists have been drawn to radical models of democracy developed by thinkers such as Rousseau. Rousseau's ideas marked a departure from the dominant, liberal conception of democracy and came to have an impact on the anarchist and Marxist traditions, as well as, later, on the new left. For Rousseau, democracy was ultimately a means through which human beings could achieve freedom, which he defined as 'obedience to a law one prescribes to oneself'. In other words citizens are only 'free' when they participate directly and continuously in shaping the life of their community. However anarchists have been more critical of Rousseau's idea of the 'general will', the belief that there is an indivisible collective interest in society, arguing that it is irreconcilable with personal autonomy and that it has typically been used to legitimise political rule. Participatory or direct democracy nevertheless offers a model of popular self-government that attracts anarchist support so long as it is combined with radical decentralisation. Anarchists favour small-scale or 'human-scale' communities because they allow people to manage their own affairs through face-to-face interaction, rather than through depersonalised and bureaucratic processes. To this end anarchists have endorsed the commune as the model of social organisation, its virtue being that it is based on a high level of decentralisation, participation and political equality.

## Individualist anarchism

The individualist tradition of anarchism has been particularly influential in the United States, where it has been supported by a political culture that emphasises rugged and self-sufficient individualism and also a deep distrust of government. A strong libertarian tradition developed during the nineteenth century in the writings of Josiah Warren and Benjamin Tucker (1854–1939). The late twentieth century witnessed a revival of interest in libertarian ideas and the emergence of an anarcho-capitalist wing of the US new right, reflected in the formation of a Libertarian Party. The philosophical basis of individualist anarchism lies in the liberal idea of the sovereign individual. In many ways anarchist conclusions are reached by pushing classical liberal thinking to its logical extreme. At the heart of liberalism is a belief in the primacy of the individual and the central importance of individual freedom. Classical liberals understand freedom in negative terms: it is the absence of constraints upon the individual. However the state, by definition a sovereign, compulsory and coercive body, necessarily restricts that freedom. The individual and the state are therefore always in conflict. Quite simply, the individual cannot be sovereign in a society ruled by law and government.

Although these arguments are liberal in inspiration, significant differences exist between liberalism and individualist anarchism. First, while liberals accept the importance of individual liberty, they do not believe this can be guaranteed in a stateless society. Liberal thinkers such as John Locke have argued that law exists to protect and enlarge liberty, rather than constrain it. Such a belief is based upon the assumption that, if not restrained by government, self-seeking individuals will abuse one another by theft, intimidation, violence and even murder. Anarchists, in contrast, believe that individuals can conduct themselves peacefully and harmoniously without the need for government to 'police' society and protect them from their fellow human beings. Anarchists differ from liberals because they believe that free individuals can live and work together constructively because they are rational and moral creatures. Reason dictates that where conflict exists it should be resolved by arbitration or debate and not by violence.

Secondly, liberals believe that government power can be tamed or controlled by the development of constitutional and representative institutions. Constitutions claim to protect the individual by limiting the power of government and creating checks and balances amongst its various institutions. Regular elections are designed to force government to be accountable to the general public, or at least a majority of the electorate. Anarchists dismiss the idea of limited, constitutional or representative government. They regard constitutionalism (see p. 41) and democracy as simply facades, behind which naked political oppression operates. All laws infringe individual liberty, whether the government that enacts them is constitutional or arbitrary, democratic or dictatorial. In other words all states are an offence against individual liberty.

## Egoism

The boldest statement of anarchist convictions built upon the idea of the sovereign individual is found in Max Stirner's *The Ego and His Own* ([1845] 1971). Like Marx, the German philosopher Stirner (1806–56) was deeply influenced by ideas of Hegel (1770–1831), but the two arrived at fundamentally different conclusions. Stirner's theories represent an extreme form of individualism (see p. 28). The term 'egoism' can have two meanings. It can suggest that individuals are essentially concerned about their ego or 'self', that they are self-interested or self-seeking, an assumption that would be accepted by thinkers such as Hobbes or Locke. Self-interestedness, however, can generate conflict amongst individuals and justify the existence of a state, which would be needed to restrain each individual from harming or abusing others.

Stirner saw egoism as a philosophy that places the individual self at the centre of the moral universe. The individual, in Stirner's view, should simply act as he or she chooses, without any consideration for laws, social conventions, religious or moral principles. Such a position amounts to a form of nihilism, literally a belief in nothing, the rejection of all political, social and moral principles. This is a position that clearly points in the direction of both atheism and an extreme form of individualist anarchism. However, as Stirner's anarchism also dramatically turned its back on the principles of the Enlightenment and contained few proposals about how order could be maintained in a stateless society, it had relatively little impact on the emerging anarchist movement. His ideas nevertheless influenced Nietzsche (see p. 217) and twentieth-century existentialism.

## Libertarianism

The individualist argument was more fully developed by US libertarian thinkers such as Henry David Thoreau (1817–62), Lysander Spooner (1808–87), Benjamin Tucker and Josiah Warren. Thoreau's quest for spiritual truth and self-reliance led him to flee from civilised life and live for several years in virtual solitude, close to nature, an experience described in *Walden* ([1854] 1983). In his most political work, *Civil Disobedience* ([1849] 1983), Thoreau approved of Jefferson's liberal motto, 'That government is best which governs least', but adapted it to conform with his own anarchist sentiment: 'That government is best which governs not at all'. For Thoreau, individualism leads in the direction of civil disobedience: the individual has to be faithful to his or her conscience and do only what each believes to be right, regardless of the demands of society or the laws made by government. Thoreau's anarchism placed individual conscience above the demands of political obligation. In Thoreau's case this led him to disobey a US government he thought to be acting immorally in both upholding slavery and waging war against other countries.

Benjamin Tucker took libertarianism (see p. 89) further by considering how autonomous individuals could live and work with one another without the danger of conflict or disorder. Two possible solutions to this problem are available to the individualist. The first emphasises human rationality and suggests that when conflicts or disagreements develop they can be resolved by reasoned discussion. This, for example, was the position adopted by Godwin, who believed that truth will always tend to displace falsehood. The second solution is to find some sort of mechanism through which the independent actions of free individuals could be brought into harmony with one another.

Extreme individualists such as Josiah Warren and Benjamin Tucker believed that this could be achieved through a system of market exchange. Warren thought that individuals have a sovereign right to the property they themselves produce, but are also forced by economic logic to work with others in order to gain the advantages of the division of labour. He suggested that this could be achieved by a system of 'labour for labour' exchange, and set up 'time stores' through which one person's labour could be exchanged for a promise to return labour in kind. Tucker argued that 'Genuine anarchism is consistent Manchesterism', referring to the free-trade, free-market principles of Richard Cobden (1804–65) and John Bright (1811–89). By the late nineteenth century, individualist anarchists in the United States had come to suggest that the 'invisible hand' of the market was capable of ordering all social interaction, relieving the need for political organisation altogether.

## Anarcho-capitalism

The revival of interest in free-market economics in the second half of the twentieth century has led to increasingly radical political conclusions. New right conservatives, attracted to classical economics, wish to 'get government off the back of business' and allow the economy to be disciplined by market forces, rather than managed by an interventionist state. Right-wing libertarians such as Robert Nozick (see p. 97) revived the idea of a 'minimal state', whose principal function is to protect individual rights. Other thinkers, for example Ayn Rand, Murray Rothbard and David Friedman, have pushed free-market ideas to their limit and developed the notion of anarcho-capitalism. They argue that government can be abolished and be replaced by unregulated market competition. Property should be owned by sovereign individuals, who may choose if they wish to enter into voluntary contracts with others in the pursuit of self-interest. The individual thus remains free and all social interaction is regulated by the market, beyond the control of any single individual or group.

Anarcho-capitalists go well beyond the ideas of free-market liberalism. Liberals believe that the market is an effective and efficient mechanism for delivering most goods, but argue that it also has its limits. Some services, such as the maintenance of domestic order, the enforcement of contracts and protection against external attack, are 'public goods', which must be provided by the state because they cannot be supplied through market competition. Anarcho-capitalists, however, believe that all human wants can be satisfied by the market. For example Rothbard (1978) recognised that in an anarchist society individuals will seek protection from one another, but argued that such protection can be delivered competitively by privately-owned 'protection associations' and 'private courts', without the need for a police force or a state court system.

Indeed, according to anarcho-capitalists, profit-making protection agencies would offer a better service than the present police force because competition would provide consumers with a choice, forcing agencies to be cheap, efficient and responsive to consumer needs. Similarly private courts would be forced to develop a reputation for fairness in order to attract custom from individuals wishing to resolve a conflict. Most importantly, unlike the authority of public bodies, the contracts thus made with private agencies would be entirely voluntary, regulated only by impersonal market forces. Radical though such proposals may sound, the policy of privatisation has already made substantial advances in many western countries. In the United States, several states already use private prisons and experiments with private courts and arbitration services are well-established. In the UK, private security and protection agencies have become commonplace, and schemes such as 'Neighbourhood Watch' have helped to transfer responsibility for public order from the police to the community.

## Roads to anarchy

Anarchists have been more successful in describing their ideals in books and pamphlets than they have been at putting them into practice. Quite commonly, anarchists have turned away from active politics, concentrating instead upon writing or on experiments in communal or cooperative living. Anarchists have not only been apolitical, turning away from political life, but also positively antipolitical, repelled by the conventional processes and machinery of politics. The problem confronting anarchism is that if the state is regarded as evil and oppressive, any attempt to win government power or even influence government must be corrupting and unhealthy. For example electoral politics is based upon a model of representative democracy, which anarchists firmly reject. Political power is always oppressive, regardless of whether it is acquired through the ballot box or at the point of a gun. Similarly anarchists are disenchanted by political parties, both parliamentary and revolutionary parties, because they are bureaucratic and hierarchic organisations. The idea of an anarchist government, an anarchist party or an anarchist politician is therefore a contradiction in terms. As there is no conventional 'road to anarchy', anarchists have been forced to explore less orthodox means of political activism.

## Revolutionary violence

In the nineteenth century anarchist leaders tried to rouse the 'oppressed masses' into insurrection and revolt. Michael Bakunin, for example, led a conspiratorial brotherhood, the Alliance for Social Democracy, and took part in anarchist risings in France and Italy. Other anarchists, for example Malatesta in Italy, the Russian Populists and Zapata's revolutionaries in Mexico, worked for a peasant revolution. However anarchist risings ultimately failed, partly because they were based upon a belief in spontaneous revolt rather than careful organisation. By the end of the nineteenth century, many anarchists had turned their attention to the revolutionary potential of the syndicalist movement, and during the twentieth century anarchism increasingly lost support to the better organised and more tightly disciplined communist movement.

Nevertheless some anarchists continued to place particular emphasis on the revolutionary potential of terrorism and violence. Anarchist violence has been prominent in two periods in particular, in the late nineteenth century, reaching its peak in the 1890s, and again in the 1970s. Anarchists have employed 'clandestine violence', often involving bombings or assassinations, designed to create an atmosphere of terror or apprehension. Amongst its victims were Tsar Alexander II, King Humbert of Italy, Empress Elizabeth of Austria and Presidents Carnot of France and MacKinley of the United States. The typical anarchist terrorist was either a single individual working alone, such as Emile Henry, who was guillotined in 1894 after placing a bomb in the Café Terminus in Paris, or clandestine groups such as the People's Will in Russia, which assassinated Alexander II. More recently, anarchist violence has been undertaken by the Baader-Meinhof group in West Germany, the Italian Red Brigades and the Angry Brigade in the UK.

The use of violence to achieve political ends has been endorsed or accepted by political groups and movements of various kinds. However violence is usually regarded as a tactical consideration rather than an act of principle. It is a means to an end, not an end in itself. Revolutionary socialists, for example, have often accepted that bloodshed is a regrettable but necessary feature of any successful revolution. Conservatives are prepared to allow the state to use force, especially when national security or public order is under threat. Anarchist violence, however, is different. Bombings and assassinations have been thought to be just and fair in themselves and not merely a way of exerting political influence.

Anarchists have seen violence as a form of revenge or retribution. Violence originates in oppression and exploitation, perpetrated by politicians, industrialists, judges and the police against the working masses. Anarchist violence merely mirrors the everyday violence of society and directs it towards those who are really guilty. It is therefore a form of 'revolutionary justice'. For example the Red Brigades in Italy set up 'people's courts' and held 'proletarian trials' before assassinating victims such as former Italian Prime Minister Aldo Moro. Violence is also seen as a way of demoralising the ruling classes, encouraging them to loosen their grip upon power and privilege. Finally, violence is a way of raising political consciousness and stimulating the masses to revolt. Russian populists believed violence to be a form of 'propaganda by the deed', a demonstration that the ruling class is weak and defenceless, which, they hoped, would stimulate popular insurrection amongst the peasants. The idea that violence can be inspiring was expressed first by Georges Sorel and more recently by the Martinique-born French revolutionary theorist Frantz Fanon (1925–61), who argued that acts of violence would help liberate colonial peoples from their sense of impotence and inferiority. In a preface to Fanon's *The Wretched of the Earth* ([1961] 1965, p. 19), the French philosopher Jean-Paul Sartre (1905–80) argued that 'to shoot down a European is to kill two birds with one stone, to destroy an oppressor and the man he oppresses at the same time: there remains a dead man and a free man'.

In practice anarchist violence has been counterproductive at best. Far from awakening the masses to the reality of their oppression, political violence has normally provoked public horror and outrage. There is little doubt that the association between anarchism and violence has damaged the popular appeal of the ideology. Furthermore violence seems an unpromising way of persuading the ruling class to relinquish power. Violence and coercion challenge the state on territory upon which its superiority is most clearly overwhelming. Terrorist attacks in both the 1890s and the 1970s merely encouraged the state to expand and strengthen its repressive machinery, usually with the backing of public opinion.

## Direct action

Short of a revolutionary assault on existing society, anarchists have often employed tactics of direct action. Direct action is political action taken outside the constitutional and legal framework, and may range from passive resistance to terrorism. Anarcho-syndicalists, for example, refused to engage in conventional, representative politics, preferring instead to exert direct pressure on employers by boycotting their products, sabotaging machinery and organising strike action. From the anarchist point of view, direct action has two advantages. The first is that it is uncontaminated by the processes of government and the machinery of the state. Political discontent and opposition can therefore be expressed openly and honestly, it is not diverted in a constitutional direction and cannot be 'managed' by professional politicians.

The second strength of direct action is that it is a form of popular political activism that can be organised on the basis of decentralisation and participatory decision making. This is sometimes seen as the 'new politics', which turns away from established parties, interest groups and representative processes towards a more innovative and theatrical form of protest politics. The clear impact of anarchism can be seen in the tendency of so-called 'new' social movements such as the feminist, environmental, gay rights, animal rights and antiroads movements to engage in this form of 'antipolitical' politics. Nevertheless direct action also has its drawbacks. Notably it may damage public support by leaving political groups and movements that employ it open to the charge of 'irresponsibility' or 'extremism'. Moreover, although direct action attracts media and public attention, it may restrict political influence because it defines the group or movement as a political 'outsider' that is unable to gain access to the process of public policy making.

## Pacifism

In practice most anarchists see violence as tactically misguided, while others, following Godwin and Proudhon, regard it as abhorrent in principle. These latter anarchists have often been attracted to the principles of non-violence and pacifism developed by Leo Tolstoy (1828–1910) and Mahatma Gandhi (1869–1948), both of whom, if in different ways, expressed ideas that were sympathetic to anarchism. In his political writings the Russian novelist Tolstoy developed the image of a corrupt and false modern civilisation. He suggested that salvation could be achieved by living according to religious principles and returning to a simple, rural existence, based upon the traditional life-style of the Russian peasantry. Communes were founded to spread Tolstoy's teachings, central to which was the principle of non-violence. For Tolstoy, Christian respect for life required that no person would 'employ violence against anyone, and under no consideration'.

Gandhi campaigned against racial discrimination and led the movement for India's independence from the UK, eventually granted in 1947. His political method was based upon the idea of *satyagraha*, or non-violent resistance, influenced both by the teachings of Tolstoy and Hindu religious principles. Although not an anarchist theorist, Gandhi believed that government represents 'violence in a concentrated form' because it is based upon compulsion and coercion. He worked for a life founded upon the principle of love, which he regarded as the 'law of our being'. His ideal community was the traditional Indian village, a society both self-governing and largely self-sufficient. Its symbol, the spinning wheel, which is both the source of its livelihood and a mark of its independence, has been incorporated into the Indian flag.

The principle of non-violence was crucial to Gandhi's philosophy for two reasons. First, it reflected the sanctity of all human life, indeed of all living beings. A society regulated by love must, for Gandhi, be based upon compassion and respect. Second, non-violence was a political strategy. To refrain from the use of force, especially when subjected to intimidation and provocation, demonstrates the strength and moral purity of one's convictions. In the campaign against British rule, non-violent resistance was a powerful weapon, mobilising popular support for independence within India itself and around the world. Such tactics were also employed by Martin Luther King and the civil rights movement in the United States in the 1960s and by the peace movement during the 1980s. Anarchists who have been attracted to the principles of pacifism have often shied away from mass political activism, preferring instead to build model communities that reflect the principles of cooperation and mutual respect. They hope that anarchist ideas will be spread not by political campaigns and demonstrations, but through the stark contrast between the peacefulness and contentment enjoyed within such communities, and the 'quiet desperation', in Thoreau's words, that typifies life in conventional society.

## Anarchism in the twenty-first century

It would be easy to dismiss the whole idea of anarchism in the twenty-first century as a mere fantasy. After all, anarchism cannot be said to have existed as a significant political movement since the early twentieth century, and even then it failed to provide the basis for political reconstruction in any major society. However the enduring significance of anarchism is perhaps less that it has provided an ideological basis for acquiring and retaining political power, and more that it has challenged, and thereby fertilised, other political creeds. Anarchists have highlighted the coercive and destructive nature of political power, and in so doing have countered statist tendencies within other ideologies, notably liberalism, socialism and conservatism. In fact anarchism has had a growing influence upon modern political thought. Both the new left and the new right, for instance, have exhibited libertarian tendencies, which bear the imprint of anarchist ideas. The new left encompassed a broad range of movements that were prominent in the 1960s and early 1970s, including student activism, anticolonialism, feminism and environmentalism. The unifying theme within the new left was the goal of 'liberation', understood to mean personal fulfilment, and it endorsed an activist style of politics that was based upon popular protest and direct action, clearly influenced by anarchism. The new right also emphasises the importance of individual freedom, but believes that this can only be guaranteed by market competition. Anarcho-capitalists have sought to highlight what they see as the evils of state intervention, and have been prominent in the rediscovery of free-market economics.

Does this mean that anarchism in the twenty-first century is destined to be nothing more than a pool of ideas from which other political thinkers and traditions can draw at will? Is anarchism now only of philosophical importance? A more optimistic picture of anarchism's future can be painted. In some respects the continuing practical significance of anarchism is merely concealed by its increasingly diverse character. In addition to, and in some ways in place of, established political and class struggles, anarchists have come to address issues such as ecological and antiroads protests, consumerism, urban redevelopment, the application of new technology and the reexamination of sexual relations. To argue that anarchism is irrelevant because it has long since lost the potential to become a mass movement perhaps misses the point. As the world becomes increasingly complex and fragmented, it may be that it is mass politics itself that is dead. From this perspective, anarchism, by virtue of its association with values such as individualism, participation, decentralisation and equality, may be better equipped than many other political creeds to respond to the challenges of postmodernity.

## Further reading

Carter, A., *The Political Theory of Anarchism* (London: Routledge & Kegan Paul, 1971). A useful and straightforward examination of the anarchist ideas that contrasts anarchism with more orthodox political theory.

Marshall, P., *Demanding the Impossible: A History of Anarchism* (London: Fontana, 1993). A very comprehensive, authoritative and engagingly enthusiastic account of the full range of anarchist theories and beliefs.

Miller, D., *Anarchism* (London: Dent, 1984). An excellent and insightful introduction to anarchist ideas and theories.

Purkis, J. and J. Bowen, *Twenty-first Century Anarchism: Unorthodox Ideas for a New Millennium* (London: Cassell, 1997). An interesting collection of essays that consider anarchist ideas and actions in the late twentieth century.

Woodcock, G., *Anarchism: A History of Libertarian Ideas and Movements* (Harmondsworth and New York: Penguin, 1962). For some time the standard work on anarchism as an idea and movement; authoritative and still worth consulting.

# Chapter 7

# Fascism

## Origins and development

The term 'fascism' derives from the Italian *fasces*, meaning a bundle of rods carried before consuls in Ancient Rome to signify their authority. By the 1890s the word *fascia* was being used in Italy to refer to a political group or band, usually of revolutionary socialists. It was not until Mussolini (see p. 225) employed the term to describe the paramilitary armed squads he formed during and after the First World War that *fascismo* acquired a clearly ideological meaning. Nevertheless in political debate the words 'fascism' and 'fascist' are often employed with little precision. They are usually used pejoratively and are sometimes just all-purpose terms of political abuse. 'Fascist' and 'dictator', for example, are commonly used as if they are interchangeable, to refer to anyone who possesses or expresses intolerant or illiberal views. However fascism should not be equated with mere repression. Fascist thinkers have been inspired by a specific range of theories and values, and the fascist regimes that emerged in the 1920s and 1930s developed historically new forms of political rule.

Whereas liberalism, conservatism and socialism are nineteenth-century ideologies, fascism is a child of the twentieth century, some would say specifically of the period between the two world wars. Indeed fascism emerged very much as a revolt against modernity, against the ideas and values of the Enlightenment and the political creeds that it spawned. The Nazis in Germany, for instance, proclaimed that '1789 is Abolished'. In Fascist Italy slogans such as 'Believe, Obey, Fight' and 'Order, Authority, Justice' replaced the more familiar principles of the French Revolution, 'Liberty, Equality and Fraternity'. Fascism came not only as a 'bolt from the blue', as O'Sullivan (1983) put it, but also attempted to make the political world anew, quite literally to root out and destroy the inheritance of conventional political thought.

Although the major ideas and doctrines of fascism can be traced back to the nineteenth century, they were fused together and shaped by the First World War and its aftermath, in particular by a potent mixture of war and revolution. Fascism emerged most dramatically in Italy and Germany. In Italy a Fascist Party was formed in 1919, its leader, Benito Mussolini, was appointed prime minister in 1922, and by 1926 a one-party Fascist state had been established. The National Socialist German Workers' Party, known as the Nazis, was also formed in 1919, and under the leadership of Adolf Hitler (see p. 219) it consciously adopted the style of Mussolini's Fascists. Hitler was appointed German chancellor in 1933 and in little over a year had turned Germany into a Nazi dictatorship.

During the same period democracy collapsed or was overthrown in much of Europe, often being supplanted by right-wing, authoritarian or openly fascist regimes. A nationalist coup turned the newly independent Lithuania into a dictatorship in 1926, and the two other Baltic States, Estonia and Latvia, followed suit in 1934. By 1938 Czechoslovakia was the only remaining democracy in eastern and central Europe, with Hungary and Romania moving steadily towards fascism and collaboration with Nazi Germany. In Portugal a dictatorship was set up under Salazar in 1928, and in Spain the Nationalist victory in the Civil War, 1936–9, led to the establishment of the Franco dictatorship. Regimes that bear some relationship to fascism have also developed outside Europe, notably in the 1930s in Imperial Japan and in Argentina under Perón, 1945–55.

The origins and meaning of fascism have provoked considerable historical interest and often fierce disagreements. It seems unlikely that any single factor on its own can account for the rise of fascism, but rather that fascism emerged out of a complex range of historical forces that were present during the interwar period. In the first place, democratic government had only recently been established in many parts of Europe, and democratic political values had not replaced older, autocratic ones. Moreover democratic governments, representing a coalition of interests or parties, often appeared weak and unstable when confronted by economic or political crises. In such circumstances the rival attraction of strong leadership brought about by personal rule cast a strong appeal. Secondly, European society had been disrupted by the experience of industrialisation, which had particularly threatened a lower middle class of shopkeepers, small businessmen, farmers and craftsmen, who were squeezed between the growing might of big business on the one hand and the rising power of organised labour on the other. Fascist movements drew their membership and support largely from such lower middle class elements. In a sense fascism was a 'revolt of the lower middle classes', a fact that helps to explain the hostility of fascism to both capitalism and communism.

Thirdly, the period after the First World War was deeply affected by the Russian Revolution and the fear amongst the propertied classes that social revolution was about to spread throughout Europe. Fascist groups undoubtedly drew both financial and political support from business interests. As a result Marxist historians have interpreted fascism as a form of counterrevolution, an attempt by the bourgeoisie to cling on to power by lending support to fascist dictators. Fourthly, the world economic crisis of the 1930s often provided a final blow to already fragile democracies. Rising unemployment and economic failure produced an atmosphere of crisis and pessimism that could be exploited by political extremists and demagogues. Finally, the First World War had failed to resolve international conflicts and rivalries, leaving a bitter inheritance of frustrated nationalism and the desire for revenge. Nationalist tensions were strongest in those 'have not' nations that had either, like Germany, been defeated in war, or had been deeply disappointed by the terms of the Versailles peace settlement, for example Italy and Japan. In addition, the experience of war itself had generated a particularly militant form of nationalism and imbued it with militaristic values.

Fascist regimes were not overthrown by popular revolt or protest but by defeat in the Second World War. Since 1945 fascist movements have achieved only marginal success, encouraging some to believe that fascism was a specifically interwar phenomenon, linked to the unique combination of historical circumstances that characterised that period (Nolte, 1965). Others, however, regard fascism as an ever-present danger, seeing its roots in human psychology, or as Erich Fromm (1984) called it, 'the fear of freedom'. Modern civilisation has produced greater individual freedom but with it the danger of isolation and insecurity. At times of crisis individuals may therefore flee from freedom, seeking security in submission to an all-powerful leader or a totalitarian state. Political instability or an economic crisis could therefore produce conditions in which fascism could revive. Fear, for example, has been expressed about the possible growth of neofascism in some parts of eastern Europe since the collapse of communist rule, 1989–91. Economic backwardness, political instability and nationalist rivalries have provided fertile ground for fascist movements in the past and it would be dangerous to discount the possibility of a resurgence of fascism in the future. The prospects for fascism are discussed in the final section of the chapter.

## Strength through unity – central themes

Fascism is a difficult ideology to analyse, for a number of reasons.

In the first place its negative features are often more pronounced than its positive ones. Fascists themselves are often clearer about what they oppose than what they support. As pointed out earlier, fascism arose essentially as a reaction or revolt against the ideas and values that had dominated politics since the French Revolution. Fascism thus has the character of an antiphilosophy – it is antirational, antiliberal, anticonservative, anti-capitalist, antibourgeois, anticommunist and so on. However fascism is not merely the negation of established beliefs and principles. In a sense it represents the darker side of western political thought, the central and enduring values of which were not abandoned but rather transformed or turned upside down. For example in fascism 'freedom' came to mean complete submission, 'democracy' was equated with dictatorship, and 'progress' implied constant struggle and war. Moreover, despite an undoubted inclination towards nihilism, war and even death, fascism saw itself as a creative force, a means of constructing a new civilisation through 'creative destruction'. Indeed this conjunction of birth and death, creation and destruction can be seen as one of the characteristic features of fascism.

The second difficulty is that it is sometimes doubted if fascism can be classified as an ideology. Lacking a rational and coherent core, fascism appears to be, as Hugh Trevor-Roper put it, 'an ill-assorted hodge-podge of ideas' (Woolf, 1981, p. 20). This impression has certainly been strengthened by the fascist tendency to despise abstract thinking and revere action; for example Mussolini's favourite slogans included 'Action not Talk' and 'Inactivity is Death'. Although it attracted the support of philosophers such as Giovani Gentile (1875–1944) and Martin Heidegger (1889–1976), fascism was above all a movement; its major ideologists, such as Hitler and Mussolini, were essentially propagandists, interested in ideas and theories very largely because of their power to illicit an emotional response and spur the masses into action. Hitler himself preferred to describe his ideas as a *Weltanschauung*, or 'world view', rather than a systematic ideology. In this sense a world view constitutes a complete, almost religious set of attitudes that demand commitment and faith, rather than invite reasoned analysis and debate. Nevertheless fascism is not merely a bid for power at any cost under whatever slogans or principles that appear to be convenient. As well as being a political movement and a form of rule, fascism is also an ideology, that it is characterised by a distinctive body of ideas and theories, even if these constitute more a collection of myths than a systematic belief system.

Thirdly, so complex has fascism been as a historical phenomenon that it has been difficult to identify its core principles or a 'fascist minimum'. Where does fascism begin and where does it end? Which movements and regimes can be classified as genuinely fascist? Doubt, for instance, has been cast on whether Action Française in France, Franco's Spain, Perón's Argentina and even Hitler's Germany can be classified as fascist, and disagreement continues about the character of modern movements such as Le Pen's Front National in France and Zhirinovsky's Liberal-Democratic Party in Russia. Amongst the attempts to define the ideological core of fascism have been Bernst Nolte's (1965) theory that it is a bid to 'resist transcendence', A. J. Gregor's (1969) belief that it looks to construct 'the total charismatic community', Roger Griffin's (1993) assertion that it constitutes 'palingenetic ultra-nationalism' (palingenesis meaning rebirth) and Roger Eatwell's (1996) proposal that it is a 'holistic-national radical Third Way'. While each of these undoubtedly highlights an important feature of fascism, it is difficult to accept that any single-sentence formula can sum up a phenomenon as resolutely shapeless as fascist ideology. Perhaps the best we can hope to do is identify a collection of themes that, when taken together, constitute fascism's structural core. The most significant of these include the following:

- Anti-rationalism
- Struggle
- Leadership and elitism
- Socialism
- Militant nationalism.

## Anti-rationalism

The emphasis in fascism upon action and movement reflects a rejection of human reason and intellectual life in general. Conventional political ideas were based upon a belief in rationalism (see p. 32), for example liberals and socialists both believe that the world can be understood and transformed through the exercise of rational analysis. In the late nineteenth century, however, thinkers had started to reflect upon the limits of human reason and draw attention to other, perhaps more powerful, drives and impulses. Friedrich Nietzsche, for instance, proposed that human beings are motivated by powerful emotions, their 'will' rather than the rational mind, and in particular by what he called the 'will to power'. Sigmund Freud (1865–1939), the Austrian psychologist and father of modern psychoanalysis, also highlighted the extent to which human behaviour is driven by non-rational passions, in his view by *libido*, the desire for sexual gratification.

The French syndicalist, Georges Sorel (1847–1922) was one of the first to apply antirationalism to politics. In his *Reflections on Violence* ([1908] 1950), Sorel highlighted the importance of 'political myths', which are not passive descriptions of political reality but 'expressions of the will' that

---

### Friedrich Nietzsche (1844–1900)

German philosopher. A professor of Greek at Basel at the age of twenty five, Nietzsche abandoned theology for philology and became increasingly interested in the ideas of Schopenhauer (1788–1860) and the music of Wagner (1813–83). Deteriorating health and growing insanity after 1889 brought him under the control of his sister, Elizabeth, who edited and distorted his writings.

Nietzsche's complex and ambitious work stressed the importance of will, especially the 'will to power', and anticipated modern existentialism in emphasising that people create their own world and make their own values – 'God is dead'. A fierce critic of Christianity and an opponent of egalitarianism and nationalism, his ideas have influenced anarchism and feminism as well as fascism. Nietzsche's best known writings include *Thus Spoke Zarathustra* (1883–4), *Beyond Good and Evil* (1886) and *On the Genealogy of Morals* (1887).

---

engaged the emotions and provoked action. For example Sorel believed that the proletariat could be roused from its slumbers and awakened to its revolutionary potential by 'the myth of the General Strike', a force far more potent than any amount of rational analysis and debate. Fascism reflects a similar 'politics of the will'. Intellectual life is devalued, even despised: it is cold, dry and lifeless. Fascism instead addresses the soul, the emotions and the instincts. Its ideas possess little coherence or rigour, but seek to exert a mythic appeal. However fascism is not mere irrationalism. What is distinctive about fascism is not its appeal to non-rational drives and emotions, but rather the specific range of beliefs and values through which it attempts to engage the emotions and generate political activism.

The distrust of reason and the intellect within fascism is also related to a belief in vitalism. Vitalism is associated with the French philosopher Henri Bergson (1859–1941), and advances the theory that living organisms derive their characteristic properties from a universal 'life force'. The purpose of human existence is therefore to give expression to the life force, rather than to allow it to be confined or corrupted by the tyranny of cold reason or soulless calculation. Such ideas were particularly influential in Nazi Germany, and gave rise to a cult of the body and the near-worship of sporting prowess and physical activity. They also led the Nazis to embrace a form of ecological politics based on Walter Darré's peasant ideology of *Blut und Boden* ('Blood and Soil'), discussed more fully in Chapter 9 in relation to right-wing ecologism. The Nazis conducted experiments in organic farming, and Hitler himself was drawn to ideas such as astrology and vegetarianism. This is not to suggest, however, that an emphasis upon the life force or the spirit of nature is necessarily linked to fascism. Such ideas nevertheless take on fascist overtones when they are associated with a belief in struggle and a reverence for strength for its own sake.

## Struggle

The ideas that the UK biologist Charles Darwin (1809–82) developed in *On the Origin of Species* ([1859] 1972) had a profound effect not only on the natural sciences, but also, by the end of the nineteenth century, upon social and political thought. The image of species developing through a process of 'natural selection' was developed by the liberal philosopher and sociologist Herbert Spencer (1820–1903) into the idea of the 'survival of the fittest', the belief that competition amongst individuals would reward those who work hard and are talented, and punish the lazy or incompetent. The notion that human existence is based upon competition or struggle was particularly attractive in the period of intensifying international rivalry that eventually led to war in 1914. Social Darwinism had a considerable impact upon emerging fascism. In the first place, fascists regarded struggle as the natural and inevitable condition of both social and international life. Only competition and conflict guarantee human progress and ensure that the better and stronger will prosper. As Hitler told German officer cadets in 1944, 'Victory is to the strong and the weak must go to the wall'. If the testing ground of human existence is competition and struggle, then the ultimate test is war, which Hitler described as 'an unalterable law of the whole of life'. Fascism is perhaps unique amongst political ideologies in regarding war as good in itself, a view reflected in Mussolini's belief that 'War is to men what maternity is to women'.

Darwinian thought also invested fascism with a distinctive set of political values, which equate 'goodness' with strength and 'evil' with weakness. When the victory of the strong is glorified, power and strength are worshipped for their own sake. Similarly weakness is despised and elimination of the weak and inadequate is positively welcomed: they must be sacrificed for the common good, just as the survival of a species is more important than the life of any single member of that species. Fascism therefore stands against the moral principles traditionally preached by humanism and the major religions, in particular the values of caring, sympathy and compassion. These values encourage a debilitating sympathy for weakness. Weakness and disability must not be tolerated, they should be eliminated. This was most graphically illustrated by the programme of eugenics, or selective breeding, introduced by the Nazis in Germany, whereby mentally and physically handicapped people were first forcibly sterilised and then, between 1939 and 1941, systematically murdered. The attempt by the Nazis to exterminate European Jewry from 1941 onwards was, in this sense, an example of racial eugenics. In contrast

## Adolf Hitler (1889–1945)

German Nazi dictator. The son of an Austrian customs official, Hitler joined the German Worker's Party (later the NSDAP or Nazis) in 1919, becoming its leader in 1921. He became chancellor in 1933 and declared himself *Führer* (Leader) of Germany the following year. His regime was marked by relentless military expansionism and the attempt to exterminate European Jewry.

By no means an original thinker, in *Mein Kampf* (My Struggle) Hitler nevertheless drew together expansionist German nationalism, racial anti-Semitism (see p. 230) and a belief in relentless struggle into a near-systematic Nazi programme. The central feature of his world-view was a theory of history that highlighted the endless battle between the Germans and the Jews, respectively representing the forces of good and evil.

to traditional humanist or religious values, fascists thus respect a very different set of martial values: loyalty, duty, obedience and self-sacrifice.

Finally, fascism's conception of life as an 'unending struggle' gave it a restless and expansionist character. National qualities can only be cultivated through conflict and demonstrated by conquest and victory. This was clearly reflected in Hitler's foreign policy goals, as outlined in *Mein Kampf* ([1925] 1969): '*Lebensraum* [living space] in the East', and the ultimate prospect of world domination. Once in power in 1933, Hitler embarked upon a programme of rearmament in preparation for expansion in the late 1930s. Austria was annexed in the Anschluss of 1938; Czechoslovakia was dismembered in the spring of 1939; and Poland invaded in September 1939, provoking war with the UK and France. In 1941 Hitler launched Operation Barbarossa, the invasion of the Soviet Union. Even when facing imminent defeat in 1945, Hitler did not abandon social Darwinism, but declared that the German nation had failed him and gave orders, never fully carried out, for a fight to the death and, in effect, the annihilation of Germany.

## Leadership and elitism

Fascism also stands apart from conventional political thought in its hostility to the very idea of equality. Once again, fascists built upon nineteenth-century foundations. The idea of the *Übermensch* – the 'overman' or 'superman', a supremely gifted or powerful individual – is often associated with the work of Friedrich Nietzsche, and particularly *Thus Spoke Zarathustra* ([1884] 1961). While Nietzsche portrayed the 'superman' as an individual who rises above the 'herd instinct' of conventional morality and lives according to his own will and desires, fascists were attracted to the idea of a supreme and unquestionable leader. The idea of equality was also criticised in the early twentieth century by classical elitists such as Mosca (1858–1941), Pareto (1848–1923) and Michels (1875–1936). They argued, albeit in different ways, that the rule of elites is inevitable and therefore neither democracy, which is based upon the idea of political equality, nor socialism, which promises economic equality, is possible.

Fascism is both elitist and ferociously patriarchal; its ideas were founded upon the belief that elite rule is natural and desirable. Human beings are born with radically different abilities and attributes, a fact that emerges as those with the rare quality of leadership rise, through struggle, above those capable only of following. Fascists believe that society is composed broadly of three kinds of people. First, there is a supreme, all-seeing leader who possesses unrivalled authority. Second, there is an elite, exclusively male and distinguished by its heroism, vision and the capacity for self-sacrifice. In Germany this role was ascribed to the SS, which originated as a bodyguard but developed during Nazi rule into a state within a state. Third, there are the masses, who seek guidance and direction, and whose destiny is unquestioning obedience.

Fascist regimes placed enormous emphasis upon the role of the leader. Mussolini styled himself *Il Duce* and Hitler adopted the title *Der Führer*, both meaning simply 'the Leader'. In Japan a more traditional concept of leadership persisted in the form of the absolute authority of Emperor Hirohito. Fascist leaders emancipated themselves from any constitutionally defined notion of political leadership. The leader was the symbolic embodiment of the people. At the Nuremburg Rallies the Nazi faithful chanted 'Adolf Hitler is Germany, Germany is Adolf Hitler'. In Italy the principle that 'Mussolini is always right' became the core of fascist dogma. The leader's authority is absolute and unquestionable because he, and he alone, understands the 'real' will of the people, their 'general will'. It is through the leader that the people become articulate: he defines their interests and needs, and awakens them to their destiny.

The 'leader principle', or in German the *Führerprinzip*, is the guiding principle of a fascist state. The leader possesses both unlimited constitutional power and unquestionable ideological authority. The leader should enjoy direct, personal contact with his people, typically organised through mass meetings, popular demonstrations and plebiscites. Intermediate institutions such as elections, parliaments and parties must either be abolished or weakened to prevent them from challenging or distorting the leader's will. In fascist theory, a 'true' democracy is therefore an absolute dictatorship. In this way fascists fused the notions of absolutism and popular sovereignty into a form of 'totalitarian democracy' (Talmon, 1952).

## Authority

**Liberals** believe that authority arises 'from below' through the consent of the governed. Though a requirement of orderly existence, authority is rational, purposeful and limited, a view reflected in a preference for legal-rational authority and public accountability.

**Conservatives** see authority as arising from natural necessity, being exercised 'from above' by virtue of the unequal distribution of experience, social position and wisdom. Authority is beneficial as well as necessary, in that it fosters respect and loyalty and promotes social cohesion.

**Socialists**, typically, are suspicious of authority, which is regarded as implicitly oppressive and generally linked to the interests of the powerful and privileged. Socialist societies have nevertheless endorsed the authority of the collective body, however expressed, as a means of checking individualism and greed.

**Anarchists** view all forms of authority as unnecessary and destructive, equating authority with oppression and exploitation. Since there is no distinction between authority and naked power, all checks on authority and all forms of accountability are entirely bogus.

**Fascists** regard authority as a manifestation of personal leadership or charisma, a quality possessed by unusually gifted (if not unique) individuals. Such charismatic authority is, and should be, absolute and unquestionable, and is thus implicitly, and possibly explicitly, totalitarian in character.

**Fundamentalists** see authority as a reflection of unequal access to religious wisdom, authority being, at heart, an essentially moral quality possessed by enlightened individuals. Since such authority has a charismatic character it is difficult to challenge or reconcile it with constitutionalism (see p. 41).

## Socialism

At times both Mussolini and Hitler portrayed their ideas as a form of 'socialism'. Mussolini had previously been an influential member of the Italian Socialist Party and editor of its newspaper, *Avanti*, while the Nazi Party espoused a philosophy it called national socialism. To some extent this represented a cynical attempt to elicit support from urban workers. However it also reflected a profound distaste for capitalism amongst lower-middle-class fascist activists, who deeply resented the power of big business and financial institutions. Socialist or 'leftist' ideas were therefore prominent in German grass-roots organisations such as the SA, or Brownshirts, which recruited from amongst the lower middle classes. In a number of ways fascism and capitalism are ideologically incompatible. Fascism places the community above the individual; Nazi coins, for example, bore the inscription 'Common Good before Private Good'. Capitalism, on the other hand, is based upon the pursuit of self-interest and therefore threatens to undermine the cohesion of the nation or race. Fascists also despise the materialism that capitalism fosters: the desire for wealth or profit runs counter to the idealistic vision of national regeneration or world conquest that inspires fascists. Finally, capitalism is thought to be 'plutocratic', dominated by wealth and money, while fascists believe that leadership should be based upon nobility, honour and a sense of duty.

Fascist socialism is anti-individualistic and antibourgeois. It seeks to subordinate capitalism to the ideological objectives of the fascist state, a goal most systematically expressed through the doctrine of corporatism, which is discussed more fully below in connection with Italian fascism. Oswald Mosley, leader of the British Union of Fascists, argued that 'Capitalism is a system by which capital uses the nation for its own purposes. Fascism is a system by which the nation uses capital for its own purposes'. However historians have disagreed about how this conflict between profit and ideology was resolved in practice. On the one hand, both the Italian and German regimes tried to bend big business to their political ends by policies of nationalisation and state regulation. After 1936, for example German capitalism was reorganised under Hermann Göring's Four Year Plan, in an attempt to create a 'war economy'. Moreover the war that Hitler unleashed in 1939, which resulted in the wholesale destruction of German industry, complied more easily with Hitler's ideological objectives than it did with German capitalism's quest for profit. On the other hand fascist regimes cultivated the support of big business and were even prepared to silence leftist elements within their own ranks, as the Nazis did with the purge of the SA and the murder of its leader Ernst Röhm in the 'Night of the Long Knives' in 1934. German capitalism also thrived in the 1930s as Germany rearmed in preparation for war.

Fascist socialism is also profoundly anticommunist. Its objective has in part been to seduce the working class away from Marxism and Bolshevism, which preach the insidious, even traitorous, idea of international working-class solidarity and uphold the misguided values of cooperation and equality. Fascists are dedicated to national unity and integration, they want the allegiances of race and nation to be stronger than those of social class. As such they wish to imbue the working class with nationalist and social Darwinian values.

Fascists nevertheless do not believe in a social revolution; their ideas about the organisation of economic life are, at best, vague and sometimes inconsistent. Rather fascism seeks to bring about a revolution of the psyche, a 'revolution of the spirit', aimed at creating a new type of human being (always understood in male terms): the 'new man' or 'fascist man'. He is to be a hero, motivated by duty, honour and self-sacrifice, prepared to dissolve his personality in the social whole, and if necessary to die for the glory of his nation or race. This extreme form of collectivism (see p. 107) marks fascism out as the antithesis of liberalism: while liberals preach the primacy of the individual, fascists wish to obliterate the individual altogether and establish the dominance of the community or social group. It is this prospect of unqualified social cohesion, or as the Nazis promised 'Strength through Unity', that has given fascism its popular appeal at times of crisis, dislocation and disorder.

## Militant nationalism

Fascism inherited a tradition of chauvinistic and expansionist nationalism that had developed in the years before the First World War: nations were regarded not as equal and interdependent entities, but as natural rivals in a struggle for dominance. Fascist nationalism does not preach respect for distinctive cultures or national traditions, but asserts the superiority of one nation or race over all others, most boldly expressed in the ideas of Aryanism, the belief that the German people are a 'master race'. Between the wars such militant nationalism was fuelled by a sense of bitterness and frustration. Italy, a victor in the First World War, had failed to achieve territorial gains at Versailles. Germany had been both defeated in war and, Germans believed, humiliated at Versailles by reparations, the loss of territory and the deeply resented 'war guilt clause'.

Fascism seeks to promote more than mere patriotism, the love of one's country; it wishes to establish an intense and militant sense of national identity, what has been called 'integral nationalism'. Fascism embodies a sense of messianic or fanatical mission: the prospect of national regeneration and the rebirth of national pride. Indeed the popular appeal that fascism has exerted has largely been based upon the promise of national greatness. According to Griffin (1993), the mythic core of generic fascism is the conjunction of the two ideas of 'palingenesis', or rebirth, and populist ultranationalism. All fascist movements therefore highlight the moral bankruptcy and cultural decadence of modern society, but proclaim the possibility of rejuvenation, offering the image of the nation 'rising phoenix-like from the ashes'. While fascism may be a revolt against modernity, it does not succumb to reaction or the allure of tradition. Instead it fuses myths about a glorious past with the image of a future characterised by renewal and reawakening, hence the idea of the 'new' man.

However in practice national regeneration invariably means asserting of power over other nations through expansionism, war and imperialism. Nazi Germany looked to build an empire in eastern Europe, '*Lebensraum* in the East*'; Italy was seeking to find an African empire when it invaded Abyssinia in 1934; and Japan occupied Manchuria in 1931 in order to found a 'co-prosperity' sphere in a new Japanese-led Asia. These empires were to be autarkic, based upon strict economic self-sufficiency. In contrast to the liberal belief that economic progress results from international trade and cooperation, fascists hold that economic strength is based upon independence and self-sufficiency. Conquest and colonisation are therefore a means of gaining economic security; an autarkic empire will contain vital raw materials, guaranteed markets and a plentiful supply of cheap labour. National regeneration and economic progress are therefore tied up with military power. The logic of this was most clearly understood in Germany, where Hitler ensured that rearmament and preparation for war were a consistent political priority throughout the lifetime of the Nazi regime.

## Fascism and the state

Although it is possible to identify a common set of fascist values and principles, Fascist Italy and Nazi German nevertheless represented different versions of fascism and were inspired by distinctive and sometimes rival beliefs. Fascist ideology therefore embraces two major traditions: one, following Italian fascism, emphasises the role of an all-powerful state; the other, reflected in German fascism or national socialism, is built upon the doctrine of racialism.

### Statism

The importance that Mussolini and his supporters attached to the state can be understood in the light of Italian history. Although the formal unification of Italy was completed in 1871, the country remained deeply divided. Unlike Germany, Italy did not possess a unified culture nor even a common language. Regional dialects persisted and allegiances to local towns or provinces were not easily replaced by an affection for the newly created Italy. Most obviously, there was persistent antagonism between the industrialised north and the rural and more backward south. In short, there was an Italy but no Italians. As a nationalist, Mussolini wished to create a national consciousness, to forge an Italian nation, and the

## Benito Mussolini (1883–1945)

Italian Fascist dictator. A teacher and journalist in his early life, Mussolini became a leading member of the Socialist Party before being expelled in 1914 for supporting intervention in the First World War. He founded the Fascist Party in 1919, was appointed prime minister in 1922, and within three years had established a one-party Fascist state.

Mussolini liked to portray himself as the founder of fascism, though his speeches and writings were often prepared for him by scholars. Basic to his political philosophy was the belief that human existence is only meaningful if sustained and determined by the community. This, however, required that the state be recognised as 'the universal ethical will', a notion embodied in totalitarianism (see p. 233). Outside the state, 'no human or spiritual values can exist, much less have value'.

instrument through which he proposed to achieve this objective was the Italian state. Mussolini's goal was to politicise the Italian people. In his words, 'The nation is created by the state, which gives to the people, unconscious of its own moral unity, a will and therefore an effective existence'.

The essence of Italian fascism was the totalitarian ideal, the total subordination of the individual to the state. The fascist philosopher Gentile expressed this in the formula, 'Everything for the state; nothing against the state; nothing outside the state'. The individual's political obligations should be absolute and all-encompassing. Unquestioning obedience and constant devotion were required of the citizen, and individual existence would serve the interest of the nation. This fascist theory of the state has sometimes been associated with the ideas of the German philosopher Hegel (1770–1831). Although Hegel was liberal-conservative, he did not accept the social contract theory that the state was merely a means of protecting citizens from one another. Rather it was an ethical idea, reflecting the altruism and mutual sympathy of its members. In this view the state is capable of motivating and inspiring individuals to act in the common interest, and Hegel thus believed that higher levels of civilisation would only be achieved as the state itself developed and expanded. Hegel's political philosophy therefore amounted to an uncritical reverence of the state, expressed in practice in firm admiration for the autocratic Prussian state of his day.

The state also exerted a powerful attraction for Mussolini and Italian fascists because they saw it as an agent of modernisation. Italy was less industrialised than many of its European neighbours, notably the UK, France and Germany, and many fascists equated national revival with economic modernisation. All forms of fascism tend to be backward-looking, highlighting the glories of a lost era of national greatness, in Mussolini's case Imperial Rome. However Italian fascism was also distinctively forward-looking, extolling the virtues of modern technology and industrial life. For example many fascists were attracted to futurism, an early-twentieth-century movement in the arts – led by Filippo Marinetti (1876–1944) – that glorified factories, machinery and industrial life. Mussolini hoped that an all-powerful state would help Italy break with its backwardness traditions and become an advanced industrialised country.

## Corporatism

Although fascists revere the state, this does not extend to an attempt to collectivise economic life. Fascist economic thought is seldom systematic, reflecting the fact that fascists seek to transform human consciousness rather than social structures. Its distinguishing feature is the idea of corporatism, which Mussolini proclaimed to be the 'third way' between capitalism and socialism, a common theme in fascist thought that was embraced by Mosley in the UK and Perón in Argentina. Corporatism opposes both the free market and central planning: the former leads to the unrestrained pursuit of profit by individuals, while the latter is linked to the divisive idea of class war. In contrast corporatism is based upon the belief that business and labour are bound together in an organic and spiritually unified whole. Social classes do not conflict with one another but work in harmony for the common good and the national interest. Such a view is influenced by traditional Catholic social thought, which, in contrast to the Protestant stress upon the value of individual hard work, emphasises that social classes are held together by duty and mutual obligations.

Social harmony between business and labour offers the prospect of both moral and economic regeneration. However class relations have to be mediated by the state, which is responsible for ensuring that the national interest takes precedence over narrow sectional interests. Twenty-two corporations were set up in Italy in 1927, each representing employers, workers and the government. These corporations were charged with overseeing the development of all the major industries in Italy. The 'corporate state' reached its peak in 1939 when a Chamber of *Fasces* and Corporations was created to replace the Italian parliament. In practice fascist corporatism amounted to little more than an instrument through which the Fascist state controlled major economic interests. Working-class organisations were smashed and private business was intimidated.

A more modest form of corporatism, neocorporatism or liberal corporatism, became commonplace in the West after 1945. Governments that sought to manage their economies did so by consulting powerful economic interests such as business and trade unions, creating a partnership between government and economic groups. Although some have argued that this drift towards corporatism had inevitable fascist implications, others believe that liberal corporatism works in the opposite direction, enabling economic interests to dominate government. Neoliberals, for example, reject corporatism on the grounds that it results in government 'overload', as economic interests gain privileged access to the corridors of power.

## Fascism and racialism

Not all forms of fascism involve overt racialism, and not all racialists are necessarily fascists. Italian fascism, for example, was based upon the supremacy of the Fascist state over the individual and submission to the will of Mussolini. It was therefore a voluntaristic form of fascism, in that, at least in theory, it could embrace all people regardless of race, colour or indeed country of birth. When Mussolini passed anti-Semitic laws after 1937, he did so largely to placate Hitler and the Germans, rather than for any ideological purpose. Nevertheless fascism has often coincided with, and bred from, racialist ideas. Indeed some argue that its emphasis on militant nationalism means that all forms of fascism are either hospitable to racialism, or harbour implicit or explicit racialist doctrines (Griffin, 1993). Nowhere has this link between race and fascism been so evident as in Nazi Germany, where official ideology at times amounted to little more than hysterical, pseudo-scientific anti-Semitism.

### The politics of race

A 'nation' is a cultural entity, a collection of people who share the same language, religion, traditions and so on. The term 'race', on the other hand, reflects a belief in biological or genetic differences amongst human beings. While it may be possible to drop a national identity and assume another by a process of 'naturalisation', it is clearly impossible to change one's race, determined as it is at birth, indeed before birth, by the racial identity of one's parents. The symbols of nationality – citizenship, passport, language and perhaps religion – can all be accepted by choice, voluntarily; however the symbols of race – skin tone, hair colour, physiognomy and blood – are fixed and unchangeable. The use of racial terms and categories became commonplace in the West during the nineteenth century as imperialism brought the predominantly 'white' European races into increasingly close contact with the 'black', 'brown' and 'yellow' races of Africa and Asia. These races were thought of as

---

### Racialism

Racialism is, broadly, the belief that political or social conclusions can be drawn from the idea that humankind is divided into biologically distinct 'races'. Racialist theories are thus based on two assumptions. First, that there are fundamental genetic, or species-type differences amongst the peoples of the world. Second, that these genetic divisions are reflected in cultural, intellectual and/or moral differences, making them politically or socially significant. Political racialism is manifest in calls for racial segregation (for instance apartheid) and in doctrines of 'blood' superiority or inferiority (for example Aryanism or anti-Semitism). 'Racialism' and 'racism' are often used interchangeably, but the latter is better used to refer to prejudice or hostility towards people because of their racial origin, whether or not this is linked to a developed racial theory.

---

separate human communities, biologically distinct from one another. Racialist thinkers have often denied the existence of a single human species and treated races as if they are separate species.

In reality racial categories largely reflect cultural stereotypes and enjoy little if any scientific foundation. The broadest racial classifications, for example those based upon skin colour – white, brown, yellow and so on – are at best misleading and at worst simply arbitrary. More detailed and ambitious racial theories, such as those of the Nazis, simply produced anomalies, the most glaring of which was perhaps that Adolf Hitler himself certainly did not fit the racial stereotype of the tall, broad-shouldered, blond-haired, blue-eyed Aryan commonly described in Nazi literature. The Nazis themselves, who gave the question of race more attention than most, were never fully agreed about how 'master race' should be defined. Some described it as 'Aryan', implying a racial similarity between the peoples of northern Europe, possibly extending to the peoples of the Indian subcontinent, others preferred the term 'Nordic', which incorporates the Germans but also most of the fair-skinned peoples of northern Europe. 'Germanic' was also used, but this came close to defining race in terms of culture or citizenship.

The core of racialism is the belief that racial divisions are in some way politically significant, indeed the most significant of social cleavages; more important, for example, than social class, nationality, gender and so forth. This is often reflected in the idea of racial segregation, the belief that it is natural or desirable to live, work and breed only with members of the same race. However doctrines of racial segregation are based upon very different arguments and theories. In some cases they are founded on conservative ideas of social order and cohesion. For example Enoch Powell in the UK in the 1960s and Jean-Marie Le Pen in France in the 1980s and 1990s both argued against 'non-white' immigration into their countries on the grounds that the distinctive traditions and culture of the 'white' host community would be threatened. Such views portray racial prejudice as a natural, indeed inevitable, expression of national consciousness. Multiracial and multicultural societies are therefore thought to be unstable and prone to violence and disorder.

Elsewhere racial segregation has been based upon religious or biological beliefs. The apartheid system in South Africa and the practice of segregation in the south of the United States were both justified by reference to the Bible. Nazi race theory, however, treated racial differences as essentially biological: races were openly referred to as if they are separate species. In *Mein Kampf* Hitler described racial purity as an 'iron law of Nature': each animal, he argued, 'mates only with its own species'. This led the Nazis to pursue a radical programme of eugenics, or selective breeding. In their view biological purity was the key to racial greatness, and they feared that intermarriage between Aryans and the non-Aryans would 'pollute' the racial stock and threaten the 'vital sap'. The Nuremburg Laws, passed in 1935, therefore prohibited both marriage and sexual relations between Germans and Jews.

Although belief in racial purity and genetics does not necessarily imply that a particular race is either superior or inferior to any other race, the two sets of ideas are commonly linked. Racial superiority/inferiority suggests that races possess different, biologically determined qualities that suit them not merely to live apart, but to fulfil very different social roles. It is thought that biology invests some races with intelligence, courage and the capacity to lead, while other races are thought to be congenitally subservient. The most graphic example of a political philosophy built upon the doctrine of racial superiority/inferiority was national socialism in Germany.

## National socialism

Nazi ideology was fashioned out of a combination of racial anti-Semitism and social Darwinism. Anti-Semitism had been a force in European politics, especially in eastern Europe, since the dawn of the Christian era. Its origins were largely theological: the Jews were responsible for the death of Christ, and in refusing to convert to Christianity they were both denying the divinity of Jesus and endangering their own immortal souls. The association between the Jews and evil was therefore not a creation of the Nazis, but dated back to the Christian Middle Ages, a period when the Jews were first confined in ghettoes and excluded from respectable society. However anti-Semitism intensified in the late nineteenth century. As nationalism and imperialism spread throughout Europe, Jews were subject

---

## Anti-Semitism

By tradition Semites are descendants of Shem, son of Noah, and include most of the peoples of the Middle East. Anti-Semitism refers specifically to prejudice against or hatred towards the Jews. In its earliest systematic form, anti-Semitism had a religious character, reflecting the hostility of Christians towards the Jews, based on their complicity in the murder of Jesus and their refusal to acknowledge him as the Son of God. Economic anti-Semitism developed from the Middle Ages onwards, expressing a distaste for the Jews as moneylenders and traders. The nineteenth century saw the birth of racial anti-Semitism in the works of Wagner and H. S. Chamberlain (1855–1929), who condemned the Jewish peoples as fundamentally evil and destructive. Such ideas provided the ideological basis for German Nazism and found their most grotesque expression in the Holocaust.

---

to increasing persecution in many countries. In France this led to the celebrated Dreyfus affair, 1894–1906; in Russia it was reflected in a series of pogroms carried out against the Jews by the government of Alexander III.

The character of anti-Semitism also changed during the nineteenth century. The growth of a 'science of race', which applied pseudo-scientific ideas to social and political issues, led to the Jews being thought of as a race rather than a religious, economic or cultural group. Thereafter the Jews were defined inescapably by biological factors such as hair colour, facial characteristics and blood. Anti-Semitism was therefore elaborated into a racial theory, which assigned to the Jews a pernicious and degrading racial stereotype. The first attempt to develop a scientific theory of racialism was undertaken by the French social theorist Joseph-Arthur Gobineau (1816–82), whose *Essay on the Inequality of the Human Races* ([1854] 1970) claimed to be a 'science of history'. Gobineau argued that there is a hierarchy of races, with very different qualities and characteristics. The most developed and creative race is the 'white peoples' whose highest element Gobineau referred to as the 'Aryans'. The Jews, on the other hand, were thought to be fundamentally uncreative. Unlike the Nazis, however, Gobineau was a pessimistic racialist, believing that by his day intermarriage had progressed so far that the glorious civilisation built by the Aryans had already been corrupted beyond repair.

The doctrine of racial anti-Semitism entered Germany through Gobineau's writing and took the form of Aryanism, a belief in the biological superiority of the Aryan peoples. These ideas were taken up by the composer Richard Wagner and his British-born son-in-law, H. S. Chamberlain (1855–1929), whose *Foundations of the Nineteenth Century* ([1899] 1913) had an enormous impact upon Hitler and the Nazis. Chamberlain defined the highest race more narrowly as the 'Teutons', clearly understood to mean the German peoples. All cultural development was ascribed to the German way of life, while the Jews were described as 'physically, spiritually and morally degenerate'. Chamberlain presented history as a confrontation between the Teutons and the Jews, and therefore prepared the ground for Nazi race theory, which portrayed the Jews as a universal scapegoat for all of Germany's misfortunes. The Nazis blamed the Jews for Germany's defeat in 1918, they were responsible for its humiliation at Versailles, they were behind the financial power of the banks and big business that enslaved the lower middle classes, as well as behind the working-class movement and the threat of social revolution. Hitler suggested that the Jews were responsible for an international conspiracy of capitalists and communists, whose prime objective was to weaken and overthrow the German nation.

National socialism portrayed the world in pseudo-religious, pseudo-scientific terms as a struggle for dominance between the Germans and the Jews, representing respectively the forces of 'good' and 'evil'. Hitler himself divided the races of the world into three categories. The first, the Aryans, were the *Herrenvolk*, the 'master race'; Hitler described the Aryans as the 'founders of culture' and literally believed them to be responsible for all creativity, whether in art, music, literature, philosophy or political thought. Second, there were the 'bearers of culture', peoples who were able to utilise the ideas and inventions of the German people, but were themselves incapable of creativity. At the bottom were the Jews, who Hitler described as the 'destroyers of culture', pitted in an unending struggle against the noble and creative Aryans. Hitler's world view was therefore dominated by the idea of conflict between good and evil, reflected in a racial struggle between the Germans and the Jews, a conflict that could only end in either Aryan world domination or the final victory of the Jews.

This ideology took Hitler and the Nazis in appalling and tragic directions. In the first place Aryanism, the conviction that the Aryans are a uniquely creative 'master race', dictated a policy of expansionism and war. If the Germans are racially superior they are entitled to dominate other races. Other races are biologically relegated to an inferior and subservient position. The Slavs of eastern Europe, for instance, were regarded as 'sub-humans', suited only to carrying out manual labour for the benefit of their German masters. Nazi ideology therefore dictated an aggressive foreign policy in pursuit of a racial empire and ultimately world domination. As such it contributed to a policy of rearmament, expansionism and war. Secondly, the Nazis believed that Germany could never be secure so long as its arch-enemies, the Jews, continued to exist. The Jews had to be persecuted, indeed they deserved to be persecuted because they represented evil. The logic presented in *Mein Kampf* was that German greatness could never be assured until the final elimination of the Jewish race was achieved. National socialism therefore drove Hitler from a policy of racial persecution to one of terror, and ultimately genocide and racial extermination. In 1941, with a world war still to be won, the Nazi regime embarked upon what it called the 'final solution', an attempt to exterminate the Jewish population of Europe in an unparalleled process of mass murder, which led to the death of some six million Jewish people.

## Peasant ideology

A further difference between the Italian and German brands of fascism is that the latter advanced a distinctively anti-modern philosophy. All fascisms look both to the past – in drawing on the myth of a historical 'golden age' – and to the future – in proclaiming the possibility of national rebirth – but the balance between the two varies significantly. While Italian fascism was eager to portray itself as a modernising force and to embrace the benefits of industry and technology, Nazism reviled much of modern civilisation as decadent and corrupt. This particularly applied in the case of urbanisation and industrialisation. In the Nazi view the Germans are in truth a peasant people, ideally suited to a simple existence lived close to the land and ennobled by physical labour. However life in overcrowded, stultifying and unhealthy cities had undermined the German spirit and threatened to weaken the racial stock. Such fears were expressed in the 'Blood and Soil' ideas of Walter Darré. They also explain why the Nazis extolled the virtues of *Kultur*, which embodied the folk traditions and craft skills of the German peoples, over the essentially empty products of western civilisation. This peasant ideology had important implications for foreign policy. In particular it helped to fuel expansionist tendencies by strengthening the attraction of *Lebensraum*. Only through territorial expansion could overcrowded Germany acquire the space to allow its people to resume their proper peasant existence.

This policy was based upon a deep contradiction, however. War and military expansion, even when justified by reference to a peasant ideology, cannot but be pursued through the techniques and processes of modern industrial society. The central ideological goals of the Nazi regime were conquest and empire, and these dictated the expansion of the industrial base and the development of the technology of warfare. Far from returning the German people to the land, the Hitler period therefore witnessed rapid industrialisation and the growth of large towns and cities so despised by the Nazis. Peasant ideology thus proved to be little more than rhetoric. Militarism also brought about significant cultural shifts. While Nazi art remained fixated with simplistic images of small-town and rural life, propaganda constantly bombarded the German people with images of modern technology, from the Stuka dive-bomber and Panzer tank to the V-1 and V-2 rockets.

## Totalitarianism

Fascist regimes such as those in Hitler's Germany, Mussolini's Italy and in some respects even Perón's Argentina, sought to establish radically new forms of political rule. Traditional dictatorships had subscribed to authoritarianism (see p. 82): they had suppressed political opposition and concentrated government power in the hands of a supreme leader or ruling group. Mussolini, however, proclaimed his desire to construct not a traditional authoritarian regime but a 'totalitarian state'. Whereas authoritarian states, such as autocratic monarchies or traditional dictatorships, seek to repress political activity and exclude the masses from politics, totalitarian states attempt to politicise society by mobilising popular support of the regime, typically through mass meetings, marches and demonstrations, pervasive propaganda and constant political agitation. Passive acceptance of authority is no longer sufficient; totalitarianism demands active participation and total commitment, the politicisation of the masses. As such totalitarianism requires the complete submission of the individual to the state.

Some writers have suggested that totalitarian states are characterised by a number of defining characteristics. Friedrich and Brzezinski (1963), for example, argued that totalitarian states can be identified by a 'six point syndrome'. First, they possess an official ideology, enjoying an almost religious status of infallibility. Second, these regimes are typically dominated by a single party, usually led by a single man, that controls the

### Totalitarianism

Totalitarianism is an all-encompassing system of political rule that is typically established by pervasive ideological manipulation and open terror and brutality. It differs from autocracy, authoritarianism and traditional dictatorship in that it seeks 'total power' through the politicisation of every aspect of social and personal existence. Totalitarianism thus implies the outright abolition of civil society: the abolition of 'the private'. Fascism and communism have sometimes been seen as left-and right-wing forms of totalitarianism, based upon their rejection of toleration, pluralism and the open society. However radical thinkers such as Marcuse (see p. 139) have claimed that liberal democracies also exhibit totalitarian features.

workings of government. Third, a terroristic police force eradicates political dissent by the use of coercion and intimidation. Fourth, monopoly of the means of mass communication ensures that only politically 'reliable' and ideologically 'pure' views can be expressed. Fifth, the state possesses a monopoly on the weapons of armed combat, giving it alone the capacity to use force. Sixth, totalitarian states are characterised by state control of all aspects of economic life.

Friedrich and Brzezinski claimed these features could be identified in Fascist Italy and Nazi Germany but were also evident in the Soviet Union, suggesting that totalitarianism highlights similarities between fascism and communism. Furthermore such regimes are historically new; indeed they are a distinctively twentieth-century phenomenon. The distinguishing features of totalitarianism – pervasive ideological manipulation and the use of terror – have both been facilitated by modern technology. Totalitarian states have typically employed the radio, television and cinema to spread propaganda, and maintained political control by widespread surveillance of the civilian population, a task that requires a highly efficient system of information gathering and processing.

The totalitarian ideal has a particular attraction for fascism because its central goal is the creation of 'fascist man' – loyal, dedicated and obedient, and willing to place the good of the nation or race before self-interest. There is no doubt that Nazi Germany came close to realising the ideal of total state control: political repression was brutal and effective, and Nazi ideology dominated the media, art and culture, education and youth organisations. However in Italy the Fascist state fell some way short of Mussolini's totalitarian ideal. For example the Italian monarchy survived throughout the fascist period, many local political leaders, especially in the south, continued in power, and the Catholic Church retained its privileges and independence. In some respects Italian fascism amounted to little more than the personal dictatorship of Mussolini, and although the Fascist state was clearly authoritarian, it was a poor example of a totalitarian regime. Authoritarian-populist regimes such as that in Argentina under Perón have certainly resembled totalitarian states in attempting to stimulate mass political activism, but have usually embraced broad nationalist principles rather than an official ideology, and have failed to develop efficient, all-encompassing mechanisms of political control.

The concept of totalitarianism has also been linked to the Cold War attitudes and beliefs that were generated in the aftermath of the Second World War. To some extent its attraction in the West in the 1950s and 1960s was that it drew attention to parallels between fascist and communist regimes, emphasising the repressive and brutal character of both. As such it became a vehicle for expressing anti-communist views and, in particular, hostility towards the Soviet Union. Without doubt similarities did exist between Nazi Germany and the Soviet Union, especially during the Stalinist period. However the blanket description of both as 'totalitarian' tends to conceal significant differences. For example the Soviet economy was entirely collectivised and subject to a system of central planning, whereas a capitalist economy survived throughout the Nazi period and big business often worked closely with the Nazi state. Moreover fascism and communism are ideologically divergent: fascists, for instance, preach the values of struggle, elitism and nationalism, while communists advocate cooperation, equality and international solidarity.

## Fascism in the twenty-first century

Some commentators have argued that fascism, properly understood, did not survive into the second half of the twentieth century, still less could it continue into the twenty-first century. In the classic analysis by Ernst Nolte (1965), for instance, fascism is seen as a historically-specific revolt against modernisation and the advance of nationalism, linked to the desire to preserve the cultural and spiritual unity of traditional society. Since this moment in the modernisation process has passed, all references to fascism should be made in the past tense. Hitler's suicide in the Führer bunker in April 1945, as the Soviet Red Army approached the gates of Berlin, may therefore have marked the *Götterdämmerung* of fascism, its 'twilight of the gods'. Such interpretations, however, have been far less easy to advance in view of the revival of fascism or at least fascist-type movements in the late twentieth century, although these movements have adopted very different strategies and styles.

The Front National in France, led by Jean-Marie Le Pen, attracted growing electoral support in the 1980s and 1990s for a platform largely based on resistance to immigration. In Italy, in 1994 Gianfranco Fini's Movimento Sociale of Social Italiano (MSI) attempted to ditch its fascist past by transforming itself into the Alleanza Nazionale (AN), officially embracing a 'post-Fascist' agenda. Radical nationalist and anti-foreign groups in Germany, for example the Republikaner Party, attracted increasing support following reunification in 1990 and as a result of the influx of immigrants from the former communist East. In the UK the anti-immigration 'new racism' of the National Front was revived in the 1980s and 1990s by the British National Party (BNP). As communist rule collapsed in Russia groups such as Pamyat sprang up to give expression to a combination of anti-Semitism and long-suppressed Greater Russian nationalism, an ideological stance later adopted by Vladimir Zhirinovsky's more electorally successful Liberal-Democratic Party.

In some respects the historical circumstances of the late twentieth century bear out some of the lessons of the inter-war period, namely that fascism breeds from conditions of crisis, uncertainty and disorder. Steady economic growth and political stability in the early post-war period had proved a very effective antidote to the politics of hatred and resentment so often associated with the extreme right. However the end of the 'long boom' and growing disillusionment with the capacity of established parties to tackle political and social problems opened up opportunities for right-wing extremism, drawing on fears associated with immigration and the weakening of national identity.

Two ingredients were, however, historically new. The first of these was the collapse of communism and the end of East–West hostility. The collapse of communism produced a combination of economic crisis and political instability in many parts of eastern Europe. Rather than displace long-established national rivalries and racial hatreds, communist rule had merely brought down a political ice age, and once this was removed such forces re-emerged in revitalised form. Elsewhere the ending of the Cold War stimulated a search for new political identities and orientations. The second factor is globalisation in its economic, political and cultural forms. The declining relevance of the nation-state appears to have led not to 'one-worldism' but to the growth of insular, ethnically or racially based forms of nationalism. In the past, these have often provided fertile ground for the emergence of fascism.

What kind of fascism do these fascist-type parties and groups espouse? While certain, often underground, groups still endorse a militant or revolutionary fascism that proudly harks back to Hitler or Mussolini, most of the larger parties and movements claim either to have broken ideologically with their past or deny that they are or ever have been fascist. For want of a better term, the latter can be classified as 'neofascist'. The principal way in which groups such as the Front National, the British National Party, the MSI or AN in Italy, and Russia's Liberal-Democratic Party claim to differ from fascism is in their acceptance of political pluralism and electoral democracy. In other words 'democratic fascism' is fascism divorced from principles such as charismatic leadership, totalitarianism and overt racialism. In some respects this form of fascism may be well positioned to prosper in the twenty-first century. For one thing, in reaching an accommodation with liberal democracy it appears to have buried its past and is no longer tainted with the barbarism of the Hitler and Mussolini period. For another, it still possesses the ability to advance a politics of organic unity and social cohesion in the event of the twenty-first century bringing economic crises and further political instability.

Evaluating the prospects for neofascism, however, requires that two possibilities are examined. The first is that it is questionable whether fascism can remain true to established fascist principles whilst at the same time moving towards an accommodation with liberalism. The emphasis on the organic unity of the national community gives fascism a distinctly antiliberal emphasis and puts it at odds with ideas such as pluralism, tolerance, individualism and pacifism. This creates the possibility, perhaps parallel to the development of democratic socialism, that the struggle for electoral viability will gradually force 'democratic' fascist parties progressively to abandon their traditional values and beliefs. Democracy will thus prevail over fascism. The second possibility is that the fascist accommodation with liberal democracy is essentially tactical. This implies that the genuine spirit of fascism lives on and is only being concealed by neofascists for the purpose of gaining respectability and winning power. This, after all, is the time-honoured strategy of fascism. Hitler and the Nazis, for example, continued to proclaim their support for parliamentary democracy right up to the time that they gained power in 1933. Whether neofascist parties and movements are using democracy merely as a tactical device will only be revealed if they are similarly successful.

## Further reading

Eatwell, R., *Fascism: A History* (London: Vintage, 1996). A thorough, learned and accessible history of fascism that takes ideology to be important; covers both inter-war and post-war fascisms.

Griffen, R., *The Nature of Fascism* (London: Routledge, 1993). An ambitious and thought-provoking analysis of fascism that advances a distinctive view of the 'fascist minimum'.

Griffin, R. (ed.), *Fascism* (Oxford and New York: Oxford University Press, 1995). An excellent and wide-ranging reader on fascism that documents fascist views and interpretations of them.

Laqueur, W. (ed.), *Fascism: A Reader's Guide* (Harmondsworth: Penguin, 1979). An important collection of studies of various aspects of fascism by noted authorities.

Neocleous, M., *Fascism* (Milton Keynes: Open University Press, 1997). A short and accessible overview of fascism that situates it within the contradictions of modernity and capitalism.

# Chapter 8

# Feminism

Origins and development
The politics of the personal – central themes
Sex and politics
Feminism in the twenty-first century

## Origins and development

The term 'feminism' is a twentieth-century invention and has only been a familiar part of everyday language since the 1960s. It is invariably linked to the women's movement and the attempt to advance the social role of women. As such it is associated with two basic beliefs: that women are disadvantaged because of their sex; and that this disadvantage can and should be overthrown. In this way feminists have highlighted what they see as a political relationship between the sexes, the supremacy of men and the subjection of women in most, if not all, societies. Nevertheless feminism has also been characterised by a diversity of views and political positions. The women's movement, for instance, has pursued goals that range from the achievement of female suffrage, the establishment of equal access to education and an increase in the number of women in elite positions in public life, to the legalisation of abortion, the ending of female circumcision and the abolition of restrictive or demeaning dress codes. Similarly feminists have embraced both revolutionary and reformist political strategies, and feminist theory has at times drawn upon quite different political traditions and values.

Until the 1960s gender divisions were rarely considered to be politically interesting or important. If the very different social, economic and political roles of men and women were considered at all, they were usually regarded as 'natural' and therefore inevitable. For example, men, and probably most women, accepted that some kind of male–female division of labour in society was dictated by the simple facts of biology: women are suited to a domestic and household existence by the fact that they can bear and suckle children, while the greater physical strength of men suits them to the outdoor and public world of work. Conventional political theory played its part in upholding such beliefs, usually by ignoring gender divisions altogether. Indeed feminism can be said to have exposed a 'mobilisation of

bias' that traditionally operated within political theory, by which generations of male thinkers, unwilling to examine the privileges and power that
their sex had enjoyed, succeeded in keeping the role of women off the
political agenda.

Although the term 'feminism' may be of recent origin, feminist views
have been expressed in many different cultures and can be traced back as
far as the ancient civilisations of Greece and China. Christine de Pisan's
*Book of the City of Ladies*, published in Italy in 1405, foreshadowed many
of the ideas of modern feminism in recording the deeds of famous women
of the past and advocating women's right to education and political
influence. Nevertheless it was not until the nineteenth century that an
organised women's movement developed. The first text of modern
feminism is usually taken to be Mary Wollstonecraft's (see p. 251)
*Vindication of the Rights of Women* ([1792] 1967), written against the
backdrop of the French Revolution. By the mid nineteenth century the
women's movement had acquired a central focus: the campaign for female
suffrage, the right to vote, which drew inspiration from the progressive
extension of the franchise to men. This period is usually referred to as the
'first wave' of feminism, and was characterised by the demand that women
should enjoy the same legal and political rights as men. Female suffrage
was its principal goal because it was believed that if women could vote all
other forms of sexual discrimination or prejudice would quickly disappear.

The women's movement was strongest in those countries where political
democracy was most advanced; women demanded rights that in many
cases were already enjoyed by their husbands and sons. In the United
States, a women's movement emerged during the 1840s, inspired in part by
the campaign to abolish slavery. The famous Seneca Falls convention, held
in 1848, marked the birth of the US women's rights movement. It adopted
a Declaration of Sentiments, written by Elizabeth Cady Stanton (1815–
1902), which deliberately drew upon the language and principles of the
Declaration of Independence and called, amongst other things, for female
suffrage. The National Women's Suffrage Association, led by Stanton and
Susan B. Anthony (1820–1906), was set up in 1869 and merged with the
more conservative American Women's Suffrage Association in 1890.
Similar movements developed in other western countries. In the UK an
organised movement developed during the 1850s, and in 1867 the House of
Commons defeated the first proposal for female suffrage, an amendment
to the Second Reform Act proposed by John Stuart Mill (see p. 30). The
British suffrage movement adopted increasingly militant tactics after the
formation in 1903 of the Women's Social and Political Union, led by
Emmeline Pankhurst (1858–1928) and her daughter Christabel (1880–
1958). From their underground base in Paris, the Pankhursts coordinated
a campaign of direct action in which 'suffragettes' carried out wholesale

attacks upon property and mounted a series of well-publicised public demonstrations.

'First-wave' feminism ended with the achievement of female suffrage, introduced first in New Zealand in 1893. The Nineteenth Amendment of the US constitution granted the vote to American women in 1920. The franchise was extended to women in the UK in 1918, but they did not achieve equal voting rights with men for a further decade. Ironically, in many ways winning the right to vote weakened and undermined the women's movement. The struggle for female suffrage had united and inspired the movement, giving it a clear goal and a coherent structure. Furthermore many activists naively believed that in winning suffrage rights, women had achieved full emancipation. It was not until the 1960s that the women's movement was regenerated with the emergence of feminism's 'second wave'.

The publication in 1963 of Betty Friedan's *The Feminine Mystique* did much to relaunch feminist thought. Friedan set out to explore what she called 'the problem with no name', the frustration and unhappiness many women experienced as a result of being confined to the roles of housewife and mother. 'Second-wave' feminism acknowledged that the achievement of political and legal rights had not solved the 'women's question'. Indeed feminist ideas and arguments became increasingly radical, and at times revolutionary. Books such as Kate Millett's *Sexual Politics* (1970) and Germaine Greer's *The Female Eunuch* (1970) pushed back the borders of what had previously been considered to be 'political' by focusing attention upon the personal, psychological and sexual aspects of female oppression.

## Betty Friedan (born 1921)

US feminist and political activist, sometimes seen as the 'mother' of women's liberation. Friedan's *The Feminine Mystique* (1963) is often credited with having stimulated the emergence of 'second wave' feminism. In 1966, she helped found the National Organisation of Women (NOW) and became its first president.

Friedan attacked the cultural myths that sustained female domesticity, highlighting the sense of frustration and despair that afflicted suburban American women confined to the role of housewife and mother. She aimed at broadening educational and career opportunities for women, and has been criticised by radical feminists for focusing on the needs of middle-class women and ignoring patriarchal structures in the 'private' sphere. In *The Second Stage* (1983) Friedan drew attention to the danger that the pursuit of 'personhood' might encourage women to deny the importance of children, the home and the family.

The goal of 'second-wave' feminism was not merely political emancipation but 'women's liberation', reflected in the ideas of the growing Women's Liberation Movement. Such a goal could not be achieved by political reforms or legal changes alone, but demanded, modern feminists argued, a radical and perhaps revolutionary process of social change.

The 1980s and 1990s have sometimes been described as a period of 'post-feminism', suggesting either that feminist goals have been achieved or that feminist political thought has lost its radical or critical edge. The women's movement has certainly changed, but far from weakening it has continued to expand and broaden. In the 1990s feminist organisations exist in all western countries and most parts of the developing world, gaining impetus from the Mexico Conference, which launched International Women's Year in 1975 and designated the subsequent ten years the UN Decade for Women. Since the first flowering of radical feminist thought in the late 1960s and early 1970s, feminism has developed into a distinctive and established ideology, whose ideas and values challenge the most basic assumptions of conventional political thought. However, like all other ideologies feminism embraces a broad range of traditions and even conflicting tendencies. This does not make feminism incoherent or contra-dictory, but merely reflects the breadth and diversity of the modern women's movement.

## The politics of the personal – central themes

Although feminist thought cuts across traditional ideologies, notably liberalism and socialism, it is based upon a distinctive set of theories and values. The characteristic feature of feminism is that it highlights and examines gender divisions within society and regards such divisions as political rather than natural. Gender divisions are therefore seen to reflect a 'power relationship' between men and women. Feminists have questioned how such divisions originated and have been sustained, as well as how they can be challenged and overthrown. In so doing they have not only developed a novel account of political life and relationships, but also challenged the conventional notion of what is 'political'. In particular feminists stress that private life, personal, family and sexual conduct, is highly political and is therefore an appropriate subject for political analysis. The major themes of feminist ideology are the following:

- The public/private divide
- Patriarchy
- Sex and gender
- Equality and difference.

## The public–private divide

Traditional notions of what is 'political' locate politics in the arena of public rather than private life. Politics has usually been understood as an activity that takes place within a 'public sphere' of government institutions, political parties, pressure groups and public debate. Family life and personal relationships have normally been thought to be part of a 'private sphere', and therefore to be 'non-political'. Feminists, on the other hand, insist that politics is an activity that takes place within all social groups and is not merely confined to the affairs of government or other public bodies. Politics exists whenever and wherever social conflict is found. Millett (1970, p. 23), for example, defined politics as 'power-structured relationships, arrangements whereby one group of persons is controlled by another'. The relationship between government and its citizens is therefore clearly political, but so is the relationship between employers and workers within a firm, and also relationships in the family, between husbands and wives, and between parents and children.

The definition of what is 'political' is not merely of academic interest. Feminists argue that sexual inequality has been preserved precisely because the sexual division of labour that runs through society has been thought of as 'natural' rather than 'political'. This is highlighted in the title of Jean B. Elshtain's *Public Man, Private Woman* (1981). Traditionally the public sphere of life, encompassing politics, work, art and literature, has been the preserve of men, while women have been confined to an essentially private existence, centred upon the family and domestic responsibilities. If politics takes place only within the public sphere, the role of women and the question of sexual equality are issues of little or no political importance. Women, restricted to the private role of housewife and mother, are in effect excluded from politics.

Feminists have therefore sought to break down the divide between 'public man' and 'private woman'. However they have not always agreed about what it means to remove the distinction between 'the public' and 'the private', or about how this can be achieved. For some feminists emancipation consists of being able to escape from the narrowly domestic existence of home and family. Women's liberation therefore means that women enjoy the same access as men to the public sphere, the right to an education, to pursue a career or to enter public life. Other feminists believe that emancipation can only be achieved if some, or perhaps all, of the responsibilities of private life are transferred to the state or other public bodies. For example the burden of child-rearing could be relieved by more generous welfare support for families or the provision of nursery schools or creches at work. Indeed child-rearing could become entirely the responsibility of the community, as in the kibbutz system in Israel.

However, what distinguishes 'second-wave' feminists from their 'first-wave' predecessors is a refusal to accept that politics stops at the front door, as summed up in the slogan 'the personal is the political'. Female oppression is thought to operate in all walks of life and in many respects originates in the family itself. Modern feminists have therefore been concerned to analyse what can be called 'the politics of everyday life'. This includes the process of conditioning through which children are socialised into accepting 'masculine' and 'feminine' roles, the distribution of housework within the family and also the politics of personal and sexual conduct.

## Patriarchy

Feminists believe that gender, like social class, race or religion, is a significant social cleavage. Indeed some argue that gender is the deepest and most politically important of social divisions. Feminists have therefore advanced a theory of 'sexual politics', in much the same way that socialists have preached the idea of 'class politics'. They also refer to 'sexism' as a form of oppression, drawing a conscious parallel with 'racism' or racial oppression. However conventional political theory has traditionally ignored sexual oppression and failed to recognise gender as a politically significant category. As a result feminists have been forced to develop new concepts and theories to convey the idea that society is based upon a system of sexual inequality and oppression.

Feminists use the concept of 'patriarchy' to describe the power relationship between men and women. The term literally means 'rule by the father', and can refer narrowly to the supremacy of the husband/father within the family, and therefore to the subordination of his wife and his children. Some feminists employ patriarchy only in this specific and limited sense, to describe the structure of the family and the dominance of the father within it, preferring to use broader terms such as 'male supremacy' or 'male dominance' to describe gender relations in society at large. However feminists believe that the dominance of the father within the family symbolises male supremacy in all other institutions. Many would argue, moreover, that the patriarchal family lies at the heart of a systematic process of male domination, in that it reproduces male dominance in all other walks of life: in education, at work and in politics. Patriarchy is therefore commonly used in a broader sense to mean quite simply 'rule by men', both within the family and outside. Millett (1970, p. 25), for instance, described 'patriarchal government' as an institution whereby 'that half of the populace which is female is controlled by that half which is male'. She suggested that patriarchy contains two principles: 'male shall dominate female, elder male shall dominate younger'. A patriarchy is therefore an hierarchic society, characterised by both sexual and generational oppression.

The concept of patriarchy is nevertheless broad. Feminists may believe that men have dominated women in all societies, but accept that the form and degree of oppression has varied considerably in different cultures and at different times. At least in western countries, the social position of women significantly improved during the twentieth century as a result of the achievement of the vote and broader access to education, changes in marriage and divorce law, the legalisation of abortion and so on. However in parts of the developing world patriarchy still assumes a cruel, even gruesome form: 80 million women, mainly in Africa, are subject to the practice of circumcision; bride murders still occur in India, and the persistence of the dowry system ensures that female children are often unwanted and sometimes allowed to die.

Feminists disagree, however, about whether the institution of patriarchy has been universal. Some argue that ancient societies were matriarchal, indicated by the fact that pagan religions often practised Goddess worship. However the archaeological evidence for ancient matriarchies is at best inconclusive, and although the practice of Goddess worship may suggest that the female sex was respected and valued in ancient times, it does not prove that women ever dominated men, or even lived as their equals. To some extent the attempt to find evidence of matriarchal societies reflects a desire to prove that the institution of patriarchy is not inevitable, and can therefore be overthrown. However, even if all contemporary and historical societies are patriarchal, this does not demonstrate that male domination is either natural or inevitable.

In order to challenge and eventually abolish patriarchy, feminists must understand how the institution originated and how it is maintained. The difficulty with understanding patriarchy is that male domination operates at many different levels and in all social institutions. It is evident, for instance, in the structure of the traditional family and the process of conditioning that takes place within it, in cultural stereotypes of women as mothers, housewives or sex objects, in the under-representation of women in senior positions in politics, business, the professions and public life, and in the physical intimidation and violence employed by men to control women.

Feminists do not therefore have a single or simple analysis of patriarchy. Some believe that it is rooted in the family and a process of gender socialisation, others believe that better education and broader career opportunities can rectify inequality. In the eyes of some feminists the economic system is the source of oppression while others believe that women are controlled by male violence and the fear of rape. At the heart of these divisions lies quite different views about the importance of nature and nurture in conditioning human behaviour. Are human beings born with a fixed and unchangeable character, or are they moulded and shaped by social experience? If feminists seek to liberate women from patriarchy, they must be able to distinguish between the biological and unchangeable elements in human nature, and those attitudes and forms of behaviour that are conditioned by society and can therefore be altered.

## Sex and gender

The most common of all antifeminist arguments simply asserts that gender divisions in society are 'natural', that men and women merely fulfil the social roles that nature designed them for. Thus a woman's physical and anatomical make-up suits her to a subordinate and domestic role in society; in short, 'biology is destiny'. In practice all such biological arguments are hollow. A woman's brain may be, as male chauvinists point out, smaller than a man's, but in proportion to her body it is relatively larger, which is usually a more accurate indication of intelligence. Women are generally physically less powerful than men, with less developed musculatures. To some extent this simply reflects social factors: men have been encouraged to undertake physical and outdoor work, to participate in sport and to conform to a stereotypical 'masculine' physique. However, although physical strength is important in agricultural or industrialising societies, it has little value in developed societies where tools and machinery are far more efficient than human strength. The heavily muscled male may therefore simply be redundant in a technological world of robots and microchips. In any case, physical hard work, for which the male body may be better suited, has traditionally been undertaken by people of low status, not by those in authority.

However the biological factor that is most frequently linked to women's social position is their capacity to bear children. Without doubt, child bearing is unique to the female sex, together with the fact that women menstruate and have the capacity to suckle babies. However in no way do such biological facts necessarily disadvantage women nor determine their social destiny. Women may be mothers, but they need not accept the responsibilities of motherhood: nurturing, educating and raising children by devoting themselves to home and family. The link between childbearing and child rearing is cultural rather than biological: women are expected to stay at home, bring up their children and look after the house because of the structure of traditional family life. Domestic responsibilities could be undertaken by the husband, or they could be shared equally between husband and wife in so-called 'symmetrical families'. Moreover child rearing could be carried out by the community or the state, or it could be undertaken by relatives, as in 'extended families'.

In addition it is misleading to regard childbirth as a social disadvantage that disqualifies women from playing a role in public life or pursuing a career. In developing countries childbirth often causes only the briefest of interruptions in a woman's working life. More significantly, the capacity to bear children could carry with it high social status, being a symbol of creativity and a guarantee of the survival of the human species. Indeed some feminists argue that patriarchy has its origins in male fears about women's power, represented by women's sexuality, their fertility and their power as mothers. As a result men have sought to control women by confining them to domestic or household responsibilities, so constraining or neutralising this power.

Nevertheless, although biology may not dictate destiny, it cannot be denied that physical differences do exist between men and women. Just how profound these natural differences are is an issue of crucial importance for feminists, who seek to enhance the role of women and build a non-sexist society. In order to examine this issue, feminists have usually distinguished between sex and gender. 'Sex' refers to biological factors that distinguish 'men' from 'women', and are therefore unalterable. 'Gender', on the other hand, is a cultural term and refers to the different roles that society ascribes to men and women, and therefore distinguishes between 'masculine' and 'feminine' stereotypes. Patriarchal ideas blur the distinction between sex and gender, and assume that all social distinctions between men and women are rooted in biology or anatomy. Feminists insist that there is no necessary or logical link between sex and gender, and in contrast emphasise that gender differences are entirely cultural and hence are imposed upon individuals by society.

Most feminists believe that sex differences between men and women are relatively minor and neither explain nor justify gender distinctions. As a result human nature is thought to be essentially androgynous, incorporating the characteristics of both sexes. All human beings, regardless of sex, possess the genetic inheritance of a mother and a father, and therefore embody a blend of both male and female attributes or traits. Such a view accepts that sex differences are biological facts of life but insists that they have no social, political or economic significance. Women and men should not be judged by their sex, but as individuals, as 'persons'. The goal of feminism is therefore the achievement of 'personhood'. Gender differences are entirely artificial and can be obliterated. As Simone de Beauvoir (see p. 257) pointed out, 'Women are made, they are not born'.

Gender differences are manufactured by society, which conditions women to conform to a stereotype of 'feminine' behaviour, requiring them to be passive and submissive, suited to a life of domestic and family responsibilities. In precisely the same way, men are encouraged to be 'masculine', assertive, aggressive and competitive, prepared for a world of work, politics and public life. In a patriarchal society women are moulded according to men's expectations and needs, they are encouraged to conform to one of a number of female stereotypes, all the creation of men: the mother, the housewife, the Madonna, the whore. In so doing the personalities of both sexes are distorted. Women are encouraged to suppress the masculine side of their nature; they must not be noisy, assertive or ambitious. In turn men are forced to deny their feminine side, to repress their emotional, sensitive and gentle impulses: 'big boys don't cry'.

## Perspectives on . . .

### Gender

**Liberals** have traditionally regarded differences between women and men as being of entirely private or personal significance. In public and political life all people are considered as individuals, gender being as irrelevant as ethnicity or social class.

**Conservatives** have traditionally emphasised the social and political significance of gender divisions, arguing that they imply that the sexual division of labour between women and men is natural and inevitable. Gender is thus one of the factors that gives society its organic and hierarchical character.

**Socialists**, like liberals, have rarely treated gender as a politically significant category. When gender divisions are significant it is usually because they reflect and are sustained by deeper economic and class inequalities.

**Fascists** view gender as a fundamental division within humankind. Men naturally monopolise leadership and decision making, while women are suited to an entirely domestic, supportive and subordinate role.

**Feminists** usually see gender as a cultural or political distinction, in contrast to biological and ineradicable sexual differences. Gender divisions are therefore a manifestation of male power. Feminist separatists may nevertheless believe that gender differences reflect a psycho-biological gulf between female and male attributes and sensibilities.

**Fundamentalists** usually regard gender as a God-given division, and thus as one that is crucial to social and political organisation. Patriarchal structures and the leadership of males therefore tend to be regarded as natural and desirable.

## Equality and difference

Although the goal of feminism is the overthrow of patriarchy and the ending of sexist oppression, feminists have sometimes been uncertain about what this means in practice and how it can be brought about. Traditionally, women have demanded equality with men, even to the extent that feminism is often characterised as a movement for the achievement of sexual equality. However equality can have very different implications. For instance with which men do women wish to be equal? Male society is itself hierarchical, it embodies significant class and racial divisions. Nineteenth-century feminists were usually middle-class women who wished to enjoy the privileges and rights enjoyed by their husbands and sons: middle-class men. Moreover, in what do women wish to be equal? Feminists are divided on this point. Liberal feminists argue that women should enjoy legal and political equality with men, they should possess equal rights, enabling them to compete on equal terms with men, regardless of sex. Socialist feminists, however, argue that equal rights may be meaningless unless women also enjoy social equality, which may require the abolition of both sexual and class oppression.

However some feminists regard the very notion of equality as either misguided or simply undesirable. To want to be equal to a man may imply that women are 'male identified', that they define their goals in terms of what men already have, that they want to be 'like men'. Feminists seek to overthrow patriarchy, but not by modelling themselves upon men, which might require them to adopt the competitive and aggressive behaviour that characterises male society. For many feminists 'liberation' means the desire to develop and achieve fulfilment as women; in other words to be 'woman identified'.

Some feminists thus subscribe to a 'pro-woman' position, which holds that sex differences do have political and social importance. Such a view is sometimes called essentialism: it suggests that the essential natures of women and men are fundamentally different. The aggressive and competitive nature of men and the creative and emotional character of women are thought to reflect hormonal and other genetic differences, rather than simply the structure of society. To idealise androgyny or personhood and ignore sex differences is therefore a mistake. Women should recognise and celebrate the distinctive characteristics of the female sex, they should seek liberation not as sexless 'persons' but as developed and fulfilled women.

This has led to the emergence of cultural feminism, which reveres women's crafts, art and literature, and highlights those experiences that are unique to women and promote a sense of 'sisterhood', such as childbirth, motherhood and menstruation. Such an analysis presents a very different picture of men. If male aggression and chauvinism are thought to be biologically determined rather than socially conditioned, men are 'the enemy', men are incorrigible: they cannot be redeemed, nor can they be adapted to life in a non-sexist society. As a result some feminists insist upon separatism from men and male society, a decision that has profound consequences for their political strategies and their personal and sexual behaviour.

## Sex and politics

Feminism is a cross-cutting ideology, encompassing three principle traditions: liberal, socialist and radical. It is difficult, however, to develop feminist arguments on the basis of conservative or right-wing political perspectives. Conservatives believe that society is essentially organic, that it has developed out of natural necessity and reflects natural patterns and forces. The patriarchal structure of society and the sexual division of labour between 'public' man and 'private' woman is therefore thought to be natural and inevitable. Women are born to be housewives and mothers, and rebellion against this fate is both pointless and wrong. At best conservatives can argue that they support sexual equality on the ground that women's family responsibilities are every bit as important as men's public duties. Men and women are therefore 'equal but different'.

A form of reactionary feminism has nevertheless emerged in certain circumstances. This has occurred when the traditional status and position of women has been threatened by rapid social change, as in inter-war Germany. National socialism was virulently antifeminist: the role of women was summed up in the Nazi slogan *Kinder, Kirche, Küche* ('Children, Church, Kitchen'). A cult of motherhood developed during the Nazi period, with medals being given to mothers of large families, and national celebrations being held on the anniversary of Hitler's mother's birthday. Women were nevertheless drawn to the Nazi cause, and its women's organisation, National Socialist Womanhood, gained a membership of over 2.3 million by 1939. This was because the process of industrialisation imposed a double burden upon German women. During the 1920s women were increasingly recruited into the workforce, usually into poorly paid, low-status jobs, but were at the same time expected to maintain their traditional domestic role as housewives and mothers. National socialism was attractive precisely because it promised to re-establish the distinction between the public and private spheres of life, protecting women from the world of work and enhancing the status of women's traditional family role. In effect women sought emancipation and security by abandoning the public sphere and reclaiming control of family and domestic life.

Similar attitudes are inhibiting the spread of feminism in parts of the developing world. In Moslem countries in particular there is a firmly established demarcation between the social status of men and that of women, reflected in the institution of polygamy, the use of the veil and the imposition of other dress codes, and sometimes the enforced seclusion of women in the home. There is therefore strong cultural resistance to feminist ideas that challenge traditional moral and religious principles and so appear alien and intrinsically western. Nevertheless growing attention has been devoted to the role of women, both because of the creeping influence of western values, especially in urban areas, and the reassertion of strict Islamic laws in countries such as Iran, Pakistan and Sudan, where fundamentalism (see p. 299) has been strong. For example the appointment of Benazir Bhutto as prime minister of Pakistan in 1988 provoked fierce controversy throughout the Islamic world about whether a woman could be the head of government in an Islamic state. In some places a form of Moslem feminism has emerged. This is particularly evident in Iran, where women have sometimes supported the reimposition of a strict dress code and the exclusion of women from public life, in the hope that such measures will re-establish respect for women and so enhance their social status through a form of Islamic feminism.

## Liberal feminism

Early feminism, particularly the 'first wave' of the women's movement, was deeply influenced by the ideas and values of liberalism. The first major feminist text, Wollstonecraft's *Vindication of the Rights of Women* ([1792] 1967), argued that women should be entitled to the same rights and privileges as men on the ground that they are 'human beings'. She claimed that the 'distinction of sex' would become unimportant in political and social life if women gained access to education and were regarded as rational creatures in their own right. John Stuart Mill's *On the Subjection of Women* ([1869] 1970), written in collaboration with Harriet Taylor, proposed that society should be organised according to the principle of 'reason' and that 'accidents of birth' such as sex should be irrelevant. Women would therefore be entitled to the rights and liberties enjoyed by men, and in particular the right to vote.

'Second-wave' feminism also has a significant liberal component. Liberal feminism has dominated the women's movement in the United States; its major spokesperson has been Betty Friedan, whose *The Feminine Mystique* marked the resurgence of feminist thought in the 1960s. The 'feminine mystique' to which Friedan referred is the cultural myth that women seek security and fulfilment in domestic life and 'feminine' behaviour, a myth that serves to discourage women from entering

## Mary Wollstonecraft (1759–97)

UK social theorist and feminist. Drawn into radical politics by the French Revolution, Wollstonecraft was part of a creative and intellectual circle that included her husband, the anarchist William Godwin (see p. 192). She died giving birth to her daughter Mary, who later married the poet Shelley and wrote *Frankenstein*.

Wollstonecraft's feminism drew upon an Enlightenment liberal belief in reason and a radical humanist commitment to equality. She stressed the equal rights of women, especially in education, on the basis of the notion of 'personhood'. However her work developed a more complex analysis of women as the objects and subjects of desire, and also presented the domestic sphere as a model of community and social order.

employment, politics and public life in general. She highlighted what she called 'the problem with no name', by which she meant the sense of despair and deep unhappiness many women experience because they are confined to a domestic existence, unable to gain fulfilment in a career or through political life. In 1966 Friedan helped to found and became the first leader of the National Organisation of Women (NOW), which has developed into a powerful pressure group and the largest women's organisation in the world.

The philosophical basis of liberal feminism lies in the principle of individualism (p. 28), the belief that the human individual is all important and therefore that all individuals are of equal moral worth. Individuals are entitled to equal treatment, regardless of their sex, race, colour, creed or religion. If individuals are to be judged, it should be on rational grounds, on the content of their character, their talents, or their personal worth. Liberals express this belief in the demand for equal rights: all individuals are entitled to participate in, or gain access to, public or political life. Any form of discrimination against women in this respect should clearly be prohibited. Wollstonecraft, for example, insisted that education, in her day the province of men, should be opened up to women. J.S. Mill argued in favour of equal citizenship and political rights. Indeed the entire suffrage movement was based upon liberal individualism and the conviction that female emancipation would be brought about once women enjoy equal voting rights with men. Similarly Friedan's work and the activities of groups such as NOW have aimed at breaking down the remaining legal and social pressures that restrict women from pursuing careers and being politically active. NOW, for instance, campaigned in the 1970s and 1980s in favour of the Equal Rights Amendment (ERA), which would have prohibited any form of discrimination on grounds of sex, and also supports the legalisation of abortion on the grounds that an unwanted pregnancy undermines a woman's autonomy over her own body and damages her career and educational prospects.

However liberal feminism is essentially reformist: it seeks to open up public life to equal competition between women and men, rather than to challenge what many feminists see as the patriarchal structure of society itself. In particular liberal feminists generally do not wish to abolish the distinction between the public and private spheres of life. Reform is necessary, they argue, but only to ensure the establishment of equal rights in the public sphere: the right to education, the right to vote, the right to pursue a career and so on. Significant reforms have undoubtedly been achieved in the industrialised West, notably the extension of the franchise, the 'liberalisation' of divorce law and abortion, equal pay and so forth. Nevertheless far less attention has been given to the private sphere, the sexual division of labour and distribution of power within the family.

Liberal feminists have usually assumed that men and women have different natures and inclinations, and therefore accept that, at least in part, women's leaning towards family and domestic life is influenced by natural impulses and so reflects a willing choice. This certainly applied in the case of nineteenth-century feminists, who regarded the traditional structure of family life as 'natural', but it is also evident in the work of modern liberal feminists such as Friedan. In *The Second Stage* (1983) Friedan discussed the problem of reconciling the achievement of 'person-hood', made possible by opening up broader opportunities for women in work and public life, with the need for love, represented by children, home and the family. Friedan's emphasis upon the continuing and central importance of the family in women's life has been criticised by more radical feminists as contributing to a 'mystique of motherhood'.

At a deeper level, radical feminists have drawn attention to the limitations of individualism as the basis for gender politics. In the first place, an individualist perspective draws attention away from the structural character of patriarchy, in which women are subordinated not as individuals who happen to be denied rights or opportunities, but as a sex that is subject to systematic and pervasive oppression. Secondly, the stress in individualism upon 'personhood' may make it more difficult for women to think and act collectively on the basis of their common gender identity, their 'sisterhood'. Thirdly, liberal individualism may only *appear* to rise above gender differences. In viewing humans beings as individuals, liberalism seems to transcend gender and other social identities, enabling people to be valued on the basis of personal talents and achievements. However this may at best depoliticise sexual relations by, in effect, making gender invisible, and at worst it may foist male attributes and aspirations on women, because the allegedly sexless 'individual' invariably embodies concealed male norms. Treating people equally may thus mean treating women like men.

Finally, the demand for equal rights, which lies at the core of liberal feminism, has principally attracted those women whose education and social background equip them to take advantage of wider educational and career opportunities. For example nineteenth-century feminists and the leaders of the suffrage movement were usually educated, middle-class women who had the opportunity to benefit from the right to vote, pursue a career or enter public life. The demand for equal rights assumes that all women would have the opportunity to take advantage of, for example, better educational and economic opportunities. In reality, women are judged not only by their talents and abilities, but also by social and economic factors. If emancipation simply means the achievement of equal rights and opportunities for women and men, other forms of social disadvantage, for example social class and race, are ignored. Liberal feminism may therefore reflect the interests of white, middle-class women in developed societies, but fail to address the problems of working-class women, black women and women in the developing world.

## Socialist feminism

Although some early feminists subscribed to socialist ideas, socialist feminism only became prominent in the second half of the twentieth century. In contrast to their liberal counterparts, socialist feminists do not believe that women simply face political or legal disadvantages that can be remedied by equal legal rights or the achievement of equal opportunities. Rather socialist feminists argue that the relationship between the sexes is rooted in the social and economic structure itself, and that nothing short of profound social change, some would say a social revolution, can offer women the prospect of genuine emancipation. As a United Nations report pointed out in 1980: 'While women represent 50 per cent of the world population, they perform nearly two thirds of all working hours, receive one-tenth of world income and own less than 1 per cent of world property'.

The central theme of socialist feminism is that patriarchy can only be understood in the light of social and economic factors. The classic statement of this argument was developed in Friedrich Engels' *The Origins of the Family, Private Property and the State* ([1884] 1976). Engels (1820–95), the lifelong friend and collaborator of Karl Marx (see p. 126), suggested that the position of women in society had fundamentally changed with the development of capitalism and the institution of private property. In pre-capitalist societies, family life had been communistic, and 'mother right' – the inheritance of property and social position through the female line – was widely observed. Capitalism, however, being based upon the ownership of private property by men, had overthrown 'mother right' and brought about what Engels called 'the world historical defeat of the female sex'. Like many subsequent socialist feminists, Engels believed that female oppression operated through the institution of the family. 'The first class oppression that appears in history', Engels argued, 'coincides with the development of the antagonism between men and women in monogamous marriage, the first class oppression coincides with that of the female sex by the male' (ibid., p. 129).

The 'bourgeois family' is patriarchal and oppressive because men wish to ensure that their property will be passed on only to *their* sons. Men achieve undisputed paternity by insisting upon monogamous marriage, a restriction that is rigorously applied to wives, depriving them of other sexual partners, but, as Engels noted, is routinely ignored by their husbands. Women are compensated for this repression by the development of a 'cult of femininity', which extols the attractions of romantic love but in reality is an organised hypocrisy designed to protect male privileges and property. Engels did not go as far as to offer a detailed description of what family life would be like in a socialist society. However he clearly believed that marriage should be dissolvable, and that once private property is abolished its patriarchal features, and perhaps also monogamy, will disappear. Other socialist feminists have proposed that the traditional, patriarchal family should be replaced by a system of communal living and 'free love', as advocated by early utopian socialists such as Fourier and Owen.

Although Engels' ideas were based upon the dubious anthropology of L. H. Morgan, most socialist feminists agree that the confinement of women to a domestic sphere of housework and motherhood serves the economic interests of capitalism. Some have argued that women constitute a 'reserve army of labour', which can be recruited into the workforce when there is a need to increase production, but easily shed and returned to domestic life during a depression, without imposing a burden upon employers or the state. In addition, as temporary workers women are conditioned to accept poorly paid, low-status jobs, which has the advantage of helping to depress wage rates without posing a threat to 'men's jobs'. At the same time women's domestic labour is vital to the health and efficiency of the economy. In bearing and rearing children, women are producing labour power for the next generation and thus guaranteeing future production. Women are also responsible for socialising, conditioning and even educating children, thereby ensuring that they develop into disciplined and obedient workers.

Similarly, in their role as housewives, women relieve men of the burden of housework and child-rearing, allowing them to concentrate their time and energy upon paid and productive employment. In that sense the sexual division of labour between men, who undertake waged labour in factories or offices, and women, who carry out unwaged domestic work, promotes economic efficiency. Furthermore housewives are responsible for getting their husbands to work on time, properly dressed and well fed, ready for a hard day's work. The traditional family provides the worker with a powerful incentive to find and keep a job because he has a wife and children to support. In addition the family provides the worker with a necessary cushion against the alienation and frustrations of life as a 'wage slave'. Indeed conventional family life provides the husband–father with considerable compensations: for example he enjoys the status of being the 'breadwinner' and is granted leisure and relaxation at home, while the housewife–mother is employed in 'trivial' domestic labour.

Some feminists have argued that it is the unwaged nature of domestic work that accounts for its low social status and leaves women financially dependent upon their husbands, thus establishing systematic social inequality. The campaign for 'wages for housework', associated in the UK with Costa and James (1972), suggested that women would gain economic independence and enjoy enhanced social status if their labour, like that of men, is recognised as productive and worthwhile by being paid. This argument has also been used to suggest that prostitution should be accepted as legal and waged employment. However most socialist feminists argue that emancipation requires that women be afforded a broader range of social and economic opportunities, rather than merely being paid for fulfilling their traditional social roles as housewives or sex objects.

Although socialist feminists agree that the 'women's question' cannot be separated from social and economic life, they are profoundly divided about the nature of that link. Gender divisions clearly cut across class cleavages, creating tension within socialist feminist analysis about the relative importance of gender and social class, and raising particularly difficult questions for Marxist feminists. Orthodox Marxists insist upon the primacy of class politics over sexual politics. Engels, for example, believed that the 'bourgeois family', which had subordinated women, arose as a consequence of private property and was therefore a by-product of capitalism. This suggests that class exploitation is a deeper and more significant process than sexual oppression. Women are oppressed not by men, but by the institution of private property, by capitalism. It also suggests that women's emancipation will be a by-product of a social revolution in which capitalism is overthrown and replaced by socialism. Women seeking liberation should therefore recognise that the 'class war' is more important than the idea of a 'sex war'. Hence feminists should devote their energies to the labour movement rather than support a separate and divisive women's movement.

However, modern socialist feminists have found it increasingly difficult to accept the primacy of class politics over sexual polities. For them, sexual oppression is every bit as important as class exploitation. Writers such as the UK socialist feminist Juliet Mitchell (b. 1940) subscribe to modern Marxism, which accepts the interplay of economic, social, political and cultural forces in society, rather than orthodox Marxism, which insists upon the primacy of material or economic factors. This is why Mitchell refuses to analyse the position of women in simple economic terms and has increasingly given attention to the cultural and ideological roots of patriarchy. In *Woman's Estate* (1971) she suggested that women fulfil four social functions: (1) they are members of the workforce and are active in production; (2) they bear children and thus reproduce the human species; (3) they are responsible for socialising children; and (4) they are sex objects. Liberation requires that women achieve emancipation in each of these areas, and not merely that the capitalist class system be replaced by socialism.

Disenchantment with orthodox Marxism is also a result of the disappointing progress that feminism made in state socialist societies. After the Russian Revolution, the notion that social equality should lead to equality between the sexes was advocated by Alexandra Kollontai. Kollontai (1872–1952), who was commissar for social affairs and the only woman in Lenin's government, favoured the abolition of the conventional family and its replacement by a system of open sexuality. However her radical ideas were increasingly marginalised after the rise of Stalin, and female emancipation in the Soviet Union came to mean little more than the recruitment of women into the workforce, made possible by the provision of state facilities to look after children. Moreover little attention was given to the sexual division of labour. In the Soviet Union, for example, women were substantially under-represented in the upper echelons of political and professional life, and those who wished to pursue careers were still expected to fulfil their traditional household and family responsibilities. The most important exception to this is Cuba, where the Family Code requires husbands and wives to take equal responsibility for housework and childcare.

## Radical feminism

One of the distinctive features of 'second-wave' feminism is that many feminist writers moved beyond the perspectives of existing political ideologies. Gender differences in society were regarded for the first time as important in themselves, needing to be understood in their own terms. Liberal and socialist ideas had already been adapted to throw light upon the position of women in society, but neither acknowledged that gender is the most fundamental of all social divisions. During the 1960s and 1970s, however, the feminist movement sought to uncover the influence of patriarchy not only in politics, public life and the economy, but in all aspects of social, personal and sexual existence. This trend was evident in the pioneering work of Simone de Beauvoir, and was developed by early radical feminists such as Eva Figes and Germaine Greer (b. 1939).

Figes's *Patriarchal Attitudes* (1970) drew attention not to the more familiar legal or social disadvantages suffered by women, but to the fact that patriarchal values and beliefs pervade the culture, philosophy, morality and religion of society. In all walks of life and learning, women are portrayed as inferior and subordinate to men, a stereotype of 'femininity' being imposed upon women by men. In *The Female Eunuch* (1970), Greer suggested that women are conditioned to a passive sexual role, which has repressed their true sexuality as well as the more active and adventurous side of their personalities. In effect women have been castrated and turned into sexless objects by the cultural stereotype of the 'eternal feminine'. Greer's work was influenced by new left writers such as Wilhelm Reich (1897–1957) and Herbert Marcuse (see p. 139), who had proclaimed the need for 'sexual liberation' and criticised the repressive nature of conventional society.

However it was with the work of activists such as the US writer Kate Millett (b. 1934) and the Canadian author Shulamith Firestone (b. 1945) that radical feminism developed a systematic theory of sexual oppression that clearly stood apart from established liberal and socialist traditions. The central feature of radical feminism is the belief that sexual oppression is the most fundamental feature of society and that other forms of injustice – class exploitation, racial hatred and so on – are merely secondary.

## Simone de Beauvoir (1906–86)

French novelist, playwright and social critic. De Beauvoir taught philosophy at the Sorbonne from 1931 to 1943, and later became an independent writer and social theorist. *The Second Sex* (1949) had a massive influence on the feminist movement by effectively reopening the issue of gender politics and foreshadowing some of the themes later developed by radical feminists. De Beauvoir was a long-time companion of Jean-Paul Sartre (1905–80).

De Beauvoir insisted that women's position was determined by social and not natural factors, and developed a complex critique of patriarchal culture. Her work highlights the extent to which the masculine is represented as the positive or the norm, while the feminine is portrayed as 'other'. Such 'otherness' fundamentally limits women's freedom and prevents them from expressing their full humanity. De Beauvoir placed her faith in rationality and critical analysis as the means of exposing this process and of giving women responsibility for their own lives.

Gender is thought to be the deepest social cleavage and the most politically significant; more important, for example, than social class, race or nation. Radical feminists have therefore insisted that society be understood and described as 'patriarchal' to highlight the central role of sex oppression, just as socialists use the term 'capitalist' to draw attention to the significance of economic exploitation. Patriarchy thus refers to a systematic, institutionalised and pervasive process of gender oppression.

In *Sexual Politics* (1970) Millett described patriarchy as a 'social constant' running through all political, social and economic structures and found in every historical and contemporary society, as well as in all major religions. The different roles of men and women have their origin in a process of 'conditioning': from a very early age boys and girls are encouraged to conform to very specific gender identities. This process takes place largely within the family, 'patriarchy's chief institution', but it is also evident in literature, art, public life and the economy. Millett proposed that patriarchy should be challenged through a process of 'consciousness raising', an idea influenced by the Black Power movement of the 1960s and early 1970s. Through discussion and education women would become increasingly aware of the sexism that pervades and structures this society, and would therefore be better able to challenge it. Women's liberation thus required a revolutionary change: the institution of the family would have to be destroyed and the psychological and sexual oppression of women that operates at all levels of society would have to be overthrown.

Firestone's *The Dialectic of Sex* (1972) attempted a still more ambitious explanation of social and historical processes in terms of sexual divisions. Firestone adapted Marxist theory to the analysis of the role of women by substituting the category of sex for that of social class. According to Firestone, sex differences do not merely arise from social conditioning, but from biology. The basic fact that women bear babies has led to a 'natural division of labour' within what she called 'the biological family'. Society could be understood not, as Marx had claimed, through the process of production, but rather through the process of reproduction. In bearing children, women are constantly at the mercy of biology, and therefore, like children, are dependent upon men for their physical survival. Nevertheless Firestone did not accept that patriarchy is either natural or inevitable.

Women, Firestone argued, can only achieve emancipation if they transcend their biological nature and escape from the 'curse of Eve'. Just as Marx believed that history had developed to the point that it was possible to envisage the abolition of class conflict, so Firestone believed that modern technology opened up the prospect of genuine sexual equality by relieving women of the burden of pregnancy and childbirth. Pregnancy can be avoided by contraception or be terminated by abortion, but new technology also creates the possibility of avoiding pregnancy by artificial reproduction in test tubes and the transfer of child-rearing responsibilities to social institutions. In other words the biological process of reproduction can be carried out in laboratories by use of cybernetics, allowing women, for the first time in history, to escape from the biological family and enter society as the true equals of men.

Although Millett saw the roots of patriarchy in social conditioning, while Firestone located them in biology, they agreed that liberation requires that gender differences between men and women be diminished and eventually abolished. They both believed that the true nature of the sexes is equal and identical, a fact presently concealed either by the influence of patriarchal culture or the misfortune that women are born with wombs. Both accepted that human nature is essentially androgynous. However, radical feminism encompasses a number of divergent elements, some of which emphasise the fundamental and unalterable difference between women and men. An example of this is the 'pro-woman' position, particularly strong in France and the United States. In sharp contrast to Firestone's belief that women need to be liberated from the curse of childbirth and child-rearing, this position extols the positive virtues of fertility and motherhood. Women should not try to be 'more like men'. Instead they should recognise and embrace their sisterhood, the bonds that link them to all other women. The pro-woman position therefore accepts that women's attitudes and values are different from men's, but implies that in certain respects women are superior, possessing the qualities of creativity, sensitivity and caring, which men can never fully appreciate or develop. Such ideas have been associated in particular with ecofeminism, which is examined in Chapter 9.

The acceptance of unalterable differences between men and women has led some feminists towards cultural feminism, a retreat from the corrupting and aggressive male world of political activism into an apolitical, woman-centred culture and life style. Conversely other feminists have become politically assertive and even revolutionary. If sex differences are natural, then the roots of patriarchy lie within the male sex itself. 'All men' are physically and psychologically disposed to oppress 'all women'; in other words 'men are the enemy'. This clearly leads in the direction of feminist separatism. Men constitute an oppressive 'sex-class' dedicated to aggression, domination and destruction; the female 'sex-class' is therefore the 'universal victim'. For example Susan Brownmiller's *Against Our Will* (1975) emphasised that men dominate women through a process of physical and sexual abuse. Men have created an 'ideology of rape', which amounts to a 'conscious process of intimidation by which all men keep all women in a state of fear' (p. 15). Brownmiller argued that men rape because they can, because they have the 'biological capacity to rape', and that even men who do not rape nevertheless benefit from the fear and anxiety that rape provokes amongst all women.

Feminists who have pursued this line of argument also believe that it has profound implications for women's personal and sexual conduct. Sexual equality and harmony is simply impossible because all relationships between men and women must involve oppression. Heterosexual women are therefore thought to be 'male identified', incapable of fully realising their true nature and becoming 'woman identified'. This has led to the development of political lesbianism, which holds that sexual preferences are an issue of crucial political importance for women. Only women who remain celibate or choose lesbianism can regard themselves as 'woman-identified women', capable of finally escaping from male oppression. As Ti-Grace Atkinson put it, 'feminism is the theory; lesbianism is the practice'. However the issues of separatism and lesbianism have deeply divided the women's movement. The majority of feminists see such uncompromising positions as a distorted reflection of the misogyny, or woman-hating, that pervades traditional male society. Instead they remain faithful to the goal of sexual equality and the belief that it is possible to establish harmony between women and men in a non-sexist society. Hence they believe that sexual preference is strictly a matter of personal choice and not a question of political commitment.

## Feminism in the twenty-first century

In some respects feminist theory reached a high-point of creativity and radicalism in the late 1960s and early 1970s. Since that time the women's movement appears to have undergone a decline, and it has become fashionable to discuss the emergence of 'post-feminism'. Without doubt feminism has confronted a number of difficulties in the late twentieth century. In the first place there have been clear splits and divisions within the women's movement – between reformist and revolutionary feminists, between radical and socialist feminists, and over highly controversial issues such as separatism and lesbianism. The modern women's movement is heterogeneous and therefore lacks a coherent or unified structure. Although united by a common desire to advance the role of women, feminists disagree about how this can be achieved and about what this means in practice. Will women be liberated by the enactment of laws that guarantee equal rights or forbid sexual discrimination? Does emancipation require equal representation amongst the ranks of the privileged or powerful? Should the state provide more generous welfare support or childcare facilities? Can the position of women only be advanced by a social revolution, or some kind of sexual revolution? Such a broad range of political strategies and goals is, however, no more bewildering than that found within socialist ideology. Indeed it may merely serve to highlight the fact that feminism has developed from a political movement into a political ideology that, like other ideologies, encompasses a range of often-competing traditions.

A further problem is that, since the late 1970s, feminism has operated in an increasingly hostile political environment. In Islamic countries the advance of fundamentalism has been reflected in pressure for the exclusion of women from politics and public life, the abolition of their legal rights and a return to the veil. A conservative backlash against feminism has also been evident in the industrialised West. Both the Thatcher and the Reagan administrations in the 1980s, for instance, were openly antifeminist in their call for the restoration of 'family values' and in their emphasis upon women's traditional role as mother and housewife. The new right has tried to reassert 'pro-family' patriarchal values and ideas, not only because they are seen to be 'natural' but also because they are viewed as a guarantee of social order and stability. For example the responsibility for controlling and disciplining children is placed firmly in the hands of mothers, who are 'neglecting their children' if they put their own education or careers before their family duties. The rise in crime and vandalism amongst young people is therefore blamed upon working mothers; and in both the United States and the UK single mothers in particular have been demonised as providers of inadequate parenting and a threat to traditional family relationships. These are examples of what Susan Faludi referred to in *Backlash* (1991) as the 'blame it on feminism' syndrome. At the same time, however, such antifeminism also pays the women's movement a backhanded compliment. The attempt to reassert conventional social and religious values reflects the success of feminism in encouraging women to question established attitudes and rethink traditional sex roles.

Feminism in the twenty-first century also faces the problem that many of its original goals have been achieved or are being achieved, which is the basis of the post-feminism critique. Just as the right to vote was won in the early years of the twentieth century, so 'second-wave' feminism successfully campaigned in many countries for the legalisation of abortion, equal pay legislation, anti-discrimination laws and wider access to education and political and professional life. Some have even suggested the victory of feminism can be seen in the emergence of a new breed of man, no longer the chauvinist bigot of old, but the 'new man', who has come to terms with the 'feminine' elements of his make-up and is prepared to share domestic and family responsibilities within the 'symmetrical family'. The so-called men's movement has in fact argued that matters have gone further still, that men have become the victims of gender politics and are no longer its beneficiaries. This perspective suggests that the advance of feminism has simply gone 'too far'. Confronted by the decline of traditional 'male' occupations, faced with growing competition from women in the workplace and at home, and deprived of their status as 'breadwinners', there is a danger that men, particularly young men, will retreat into a culture of non-achievement, unable to cope with a future that is female.

In the face of these challenges the women's movement has certainly undergone a process of deradicalisation. The militant and revolutionary wing of the movement has been increasingly marginalised, and feminist literature reflects clear evidence of revisionism. Friedan's *The Second Stage* (1983) and Greer's *Sex and Destiny* (1985) both celebrated the importance of childbearing and motherhood, and drew criticism from more radical feminists for lending support to traditional gender stereotypes. Moreover new feminist thinkers are generally more iconoclastic and less politically radical than their counterparts in the 1960s and 1970s. For instance Camille Paglia (1990) has attacked the image of women as 'victims', and insisted on the need for women to take greater responsibility for their own sexual and personal conduct.

The central illusion of post-feminism is that the most obvious forms of sexist oppression have been overcome, and therefore that society is no longer patriarchal. Without doubt an increasing number of women go out to work, in many western countries a clear majority of married women. However, despite anxiety about male non-achievement, it is still women who are predominantly employed in poorly paid, low-status and often part-time jobs. Although legal, political and sometimes social reforms have been introduced, a substantial difference continues to persist between the roles of women and men in all contemporary societies. This suggests that the institution of patriarchy remains deeply and stubbornly entrenched in the social and cultural fabric of life, and feminism will survive as long as patriarchy persists. Feminism's chief challenge for the twenty-first century is to establish a viable and coherent 'third wave' that is capable of making sense of the changing nature of gender relations and of exploding the myth of post-feminism.

## Further reading

Bryson, V., *Feminist Political Theory: An Introduction* (Basingstoke: Macmillan, 1992). A thorough and accessible introduction to the development and range of feminist theories.

Coole, D., *Women in Political Theory: From Ancient Misogyny to Contemporary Feminism*, 2nd edn (Hemel Hempstead: Harvester Wheatsheaf, 1993). A fascinating account of attitudes to women in western political thought that highlights the different forms that misogyny has taken.

Elstain, J. B., *Public Man, Private Woman: Women in Social and Political Thought* (Oxford: Martin Robertson, 1981). A critical examination, from a feminist perspective, of the notions of public and private as they appear in the theories of major western thinkers.

Randall, V., *Women and Politics: An International Perspective*, 2nd edn (Basingstoke: Macmillan, 1987). A comparative analysis of male dominance in society and of debates about and changes in women's political situation.

Schneir, M., *The Vintage Book of Feminism: The Essential Writings of the Contemporary Women's Movement* (London: Vintage, 1995). A useful and comprehensive collection of writings from major contemporary feminist theorists.

# Chapter 9

# Ecologism

Origins and development
Return to nature – central themes
Nature and politics
Ecologism in the twenty-first century

## Origins and development

The term 'ecology' was coined by the German zoologist Ernst Haeckel in 1866. Derived from the Greek *oikos*, meaning household or habitat, he used it to refer to 'the investigations of the total relations of the animal both to its organic and its inorganic environment'. Since the early years of the twentieth century, ecology has been recognised as a branch of biology that studies the relationship amongst living organisms and their environment. It has, however, increasingly been converted into a political term by the use made of it, especially since the 1960s, by the growing green movement. Considerable confusion nevertheless surrounds the title of this 'new' ideology.

'Green' has been used since the 1950s to indicate sympathy for environmental issues or projects, and since the late 1970s it has been adopted by a growing number of environmental parties, the first being the German Greens (Die Grünen). However the emergence of green parties has meant that the term has been linked to the specific ideas and policies of such parties, rather than to the principles of the larger environmental movement. 'Environmentalism', also used since the 1950s, refers to ideas and theories that are characterised by the central belief that human life can only be understood in the context of the natural world. As such it covers a wide variety of beliefs – scientific, religious, economic and political – rather than a particular set of policies, such as those endorsed by the contemporary green movement. However the drawback of 'environment-alism' is that it is sometimes used to refer to a moderate or reformist approach to the environment that responds to ecological crises but without fundamentally questioning conventional assumptions about the natural world. The virtue of 'ecologism' is that, in stressing the central importance of ecology, it highlights an approach to political understanding that is qualitatively different from the conventional ones. In calling for radical socio-political change and a fundamental rethinking of the relationship between human beings and the natural world, ecologism has developed into an ideology in its own right.

The idea that the relationship between humans and nature is politically important is of relatively recent origin. Until the 1960s nature was regarded by most political thinkers as nothing more than an 'economic resource', available for human beings to exploit, more or less efficiently. What has changed this view has been the growing realisation that in exploiting nature human beings have placed their own survival in jeopardy. Rachel Carson's *The Silent Spring* (1962), a critique of the damage done to wildlife and the human world by the increased use of pesticides and other agricultural chemicals, is often considered to have been the first book to draw attention to a developing ecological crisis. The Earth's human population has continued to expand: 5.3 billion people live in the world today and it is estimated that this figure will grow to 8.5 billion by the year 2025. At the same time human beings in all parts of the world, but particularly in the industrialised West, have demanded higher standards of living and greater affluence, which can only be achieved by utilising greater quantities of the Earth's resources. The result of this has been that the natural resources available on the planet to feed, sustain and satisfy its human population are running out and in some cases are close to exhaustion. In addition the Earth itself and all its species have increasingly been blighted by pollution and waste, the by-products of human economic activity.

Although modern environmental or green politics did not emerge until the 1960s, ecological ideas can be traced back to much earlier times. Many have suggested that the principles of contemporary ecologism owe much to ancient pagan religions, which stressed the concept of an Earth Mother, and also to eastern religions such as Hinduism, Buddhism and Taoism. However, to a large extent ecologism was, and remains, a reaction against the process of industrialisation. This was evident in the nineteenth century when the spread of urban and industrial life created a profound nostalgia for an idealised rural existence, as conveyed by novelists such as Thomas Hardy and political thinkers such as the UK libertarian socialist William Morris (1834–96) and Peter Kropotkin (see p. 200). This reaction was often strongest in those countries that had experienced the most rapid and dramatic process of industrialisation. By the late nineteenth century, for example, in little more than 30 years Germany had become an industrial power capable of challenging the economic might of the UK and the United States. This experience deeply scarred German political culture, creating powerful myths about the purity and dignity of peasant life and giving rise to a strong 'back to nature' movement amongst German youth. Such romantic pastoralism was to be exploited in the twentieth century by nationalists and fascists.

The growth of ecologism in the late twentieth century has been provoked by the further and more intense advance of industrialisation and urbanisation. Environmental concern has become more acute because of the fear that economic growth is endangering both the survival of the human race and the very planet it lives upon. Such anxieties have been expressed in a growing body of literature, including Ehrlich and Harriman's *How to be a Survivor* (1971), and Goldsmith *et al.*'s *Blueprint for Survival* (1972), the unofficial UN report *Only One Earth* (1972) and the Club of Rome's *The Limits to Growth* (1972). At the same time, a new generation of activist pressure groups have developed, for example Greenpeace and Friends of the Earth, which highlight environmental issues such as the dangers of nuclear power, pollution and the dwindling reserves of fossil fuels. Together with established and much larger groups such as the Worldwide Fund for Nature, this has led to the emergence of a well-publicised and increasingly powerful environmental movement. From the 1980s onwards environmental questions have been kept high on the political agenda by green parties, which now exist in most industrialised countries.

Environmental politics has clearly drawn attention to issues such as pollution, conservation, acid rain, the greenhouse effect and global warming, but ecologists refuse to accept that they merely constitute another single-issue lobby group. In the first place the environmental movement has addressed a far broader range of issues. The Greens in Germany, for instance, have campaigned on the role of women, defence and disarmament, the welfare state and unemployment, and the need for a re-examination of Germany's Nazi past, as well as on narrower environmental issues. More significantly, ecologists have developed a radically new set of concepts and values with which to understand and explain the world. Ecologism stands apart from traditional political creeds because it starts from an examination of what they have tended to ignore: the interrelationships that bind humans to all living organisms and, more broadly, to the 'web of life' (Capra, 1996). For this reason it is difficult or even impossible to slot ecologism into the established left–right political divide or to understand it in terms of established doctrines and philosophies. As the German Green slogan puts it: 'neither left nor right, but ahead'.

## Return to nature – central themes

Ecologists have criticised the most basic assumption upon which conventional political thought is based. Traditional doctrines and ideologies are 'anthropocentric', or human-centred. They commit, ecologists believe, the sad, even comic mistake of believing that human beings are the centrepiece of existence. David Ehrenfeld (1978) called this the 'arrogance of humanism'. For example the categories in which conventional thought analyses the world are those of human beings and their groups, for instance the individual, social class, the nation and humanity. Moreover, its abiding values are ones which reflect human needs and interests – liberty, equality, justice, order, and so on. Ecologists argue that this exclusive concern with human beings has distorted and damaged the relationship between the human species and its natural environment. Instead of preserving and respecting the Earth and the diverse species that live upon it, human beings have sought to become, in the words of John Locke (see p. 38), 'the masters and possessors of nature'.

All major ideologies thus embody an anthropocentric bias. Ecologists claim that they merely promise different ways of exploiting nature for the convenience and benefit of humankind. The conventional left–right divide in politics, the conflict between collectivism and individualism, reflects different views about the ownership of wealth – common ownership versus private ownership, socialism versus capitalism. However both positions are dedicated to the same goal: greater material affluence, achieved by ever more efficient exploitation of the natural world. Political debate is therefore reduced to a discussion of how the goal of economic growth can best be achieved, and about who should benefit from it. As a result nature has been portrayed as separate from human life, inhospitable to it, and even hostile. Nature has to be 'conquered', 'battled against' or 'risen above'. However, in the process, the natural world has not only been despoiled, but the human species itself has been brought close to destruction.

Ecologism represents a new style of politics. It starts not from a conception of 'humanity' or human needs, but from a vision of nature as a network of precious but fragile relationships between living species, including the human species, and the natural environment. Humankind no longer occupies centre stage, but is regarded as an inseparable part of nature. Human beings are therefore required to practise humility, moderation and gentleness, and to abandon the misguided dream that science and technology can solve all their problems. In order to give expression to this vision, ecologists have been forced to search for new concepts in the realm of science or rediscover ancient ones from the realms of religion and mythology. The central themes of ecologism are the following:

- Ecology
- Holism
- Sustainability
- Environmental ethics
- Postmaterialism.

## Ecology

The central principle of all forms of green thought is ecology. Ecology, as explained earlier, literally means the study of organisms 'at home' or 'in their habitats', and developed as a distinct branch of biology out of a growing recognition that plants and animals are sustained by self-regulating natural systems – ecosystems – composed of both living and non-living elements. Simple examples of an ecosystem are a field, a forest, a pond or even a puddle. In a pond, for instance, the sediment lying at the bottom contains nutrients that support various kinds of plant life. These plants provide oxygen and food, which sustain the fish and insects living in the pond. When the plants and animals die their bodies decompose, releasing nutrients back into the sediment in what is a continuous process of recycling. All ecosystems tend towards a state of harmony or balance through a system of self-regulation. Food and other resources are recycled and the population size of animals, insects and plants adjusts naturally to the available food supply. However such ecosystems are not 'closed' or entirely self-sustaining; each interreacts with other ecosystems. A lake may constitute an ecosystem, but it also needs to be fed with fresh water from tributaries and receive warmth and energy from the sun. In turn the lake provides water and food for species living along its shores, including human communities. The natural world is therefore made up of a complex web of ecosystems, the largest of which is the global ecosystem, commonly called the 'ecosphere' or 'biosphere'.

The development of scientific ecology radically altered our understanding of the natural world and the place of human beings within it. Ecology conflicts quite dramatically with the notion of humankind as 'the master' of nature, and instead suggests that each human community, indeed the entire human species, is sustained by a delicate network of interrelationships that have hitherto been ignored. Humankind currently faces the prospect of environmental disaster precisely because, in its passionate and blinkered pursuit of material wealth, it has, quite simply, upset the 'balance of nature' and endangered the very ecosystems that make human life possible.

For example, since the beginning of the nineteenth century, the world's population has increased fivefold, and currently 220 000 babies are born each day, 150 every minute. The Earth has become overburdened with an exploding human population, which has given little thought to how its new members are going to be fed, clothed and housed. Finite and irreplaceable fuel resources such as coal, oil and natural gas are, it is argued, being used up with reckless abandon. Even if the consumption of oil remains at 1985 levels, it is estimated that the reserves will last only between 40 and 80 years. The tropical rain forests, which help clean the air

## Nature

**Liberals** see nature as a resource to satisfy human needs, and thus rarely question human dominion over nature. Lacking value in itself, nature is invested with value only when it is transformed by human labour, or when it is harnessed to human ends.

**Conservatives** often portray nature as threatening even cruel, characterised by an amoral struggle and harshness that also shapes human existence. Humans may be seen as part of nature within a 'great chain of being', their superiority nevertheless being enshrined in their status as custodians of nature.

**Socialists**, like liberals, have viewed and treated nature as merely a resource. However a romantic or pastoral tradition within socialism has also extolled the beauty, harmony and richness of nature, and looks to human fulfilment through a closeness to nature.

**Anarchists** have often embraced a view of nature that stresses unregulated harmony and growth. Nature therefore offers a model of simplicity and balance, which humans would be wise to apply to social organisation in the form of social ecology.

**Fascists** have often adopted a dark and mystical view of nature that stresses the power of instinct and primal life forces, nature being able to purge humans of their decadent intellectualism. Nature is characterised by brutal struggle and cyclical regeneration.

**Feminists** generally hold nature to be creative and benign. By virtue of their fertility and disposition to nurture, women are often thought to be close to nature and in tune with natural forces, while men, creatures of culture, are out of step or in conflict with nature.

**Ecologists**, particularly deep ecologists, regard nature as an interconnected whole, embracing humans and non-humans as well as the inanimate world. Nature is sometimes seen as a source of knowledge and 'right living', human fulfilment coming from a closeness to and respect for nature, not from the attempt to dominate it.

and regulate the Earth's climate, will be completely eradicated within 50 years if the current rate of deforestation continues. Moreover factories and power stations are polluting the rivers, lakes and forests that provide human beings with food, fuel, water and other vital resources. Finally, atomic technology has the capacity both to wipe out the human species and to destroy the planet upon which it lives.

Ecologism provides a radically different vision of nature and the place of human beings within it, one that is 'ecocentric' or nature-centred rather than anthropocentric. However green or environmental thinkers have applied ecological ideas in different ways and sometimes drawn quite different conclusions. The most important distinction in the environmental movement is between what the Norwegian philosopher Arne Naess (1973) termed 'shallow ecology' and 'deep ecology'. The 'shallow' perspective accepts the lessons of ecology but harnesses them to human needs and ends. In other words it preaches that if we conserve and cherish the natural world, it will continue to sustain human life. This view is reflected in a particular concern with issues such as controlling population growth, cutting back on the use of finite, non-renewable resources and reducing pollution.

'Deep' ecologists dismiss shallow ecologism as a thinly concealed form of anthropocentricism, arguing that its central objective is to maintain the health and prosperity of people who live in developed countries. The 'deep' perspective completely rejects any lingering belief that the human species is in some way superior to, or more important than, any other species, or indeed nature itself. It offers the challenging idea that the purpose of human life is to help sustain nature, not the other way around. What Naess (1989) called 'ecosophy' thus represents a fundamentally new world view based upon philosophical ecology, as well as an entirely novel moral vision. For their part shallow ecologists, or as they prefer, 'humanistic' ecologists, criticise deep ecology for subscribing to 'irrational' or mystical doctrines and for advocating starkly unrealistic solutions that are, in any event, likely to have little appeal to human populations. The alternative idea of 'social ecology' is considered later in the chapter in connection with eco-anarchism.

## Holism

Traditional political ideologies have never looked seriously at the relationship between humankind and nature. They have typically assumed that human beings are the masters of the natural world, and have therefore regarded nature as little more than an economic resource. In that sense they have been part of the problem and not part of the solution. In *The*

*Turning Point* (1982) Fritjof Capra traced the origin of such ideas to the scientists and philosophers of the seventeenth century, such as Rene Descartes and Isaac Newton. The world had previously been seen as organic; however these seventeenth-century philosophers portrayed it as a machine, whose parts could be analysed and understood through the newly discovered scientific method, which involved testing hypotheses against 'the facts' by careful, reproducible experiments. Science enabled remarkable advances to be made in human knowledge and provided the basis for the development of modern industry and technology. So impressive were the fruits of science that intellectual inquiry in the modern world has been dominated by scientism, the belief that scientific method provides the only reliable means of establishing truth. However Capra argued that orthodox science, what he referred to as the 'Cartesian–Newtonian paradigm', amounts to the philosophical basis of the contemporary environmental crisis. Science treats nature as a machine, and like any other machine it can be tinkered with, repaired, improved upon or even replaced. If human beings are to learn that they are part of the natural world rather than its masters, Capra suggested that this fixation with the 'Newtonian world-machine' must be overthrown and replaced by a new paradigm.

In searching for this new paradigm, ecological thinkers have been attracted to a variety of ideas and theories, drawn from both modern science and ancient myths and religions. However the unifying theme amongst these ideas is the notion of holism. The term 'holism' was coined in 1926 by Jan Smuts, a Boer general and twice prime minister of South Africa. He used it to describe the idea that the natural world could only be understood as a whole and not through its individual parts. Smuts believed that science commits the sin of reductionism: it reduces everything it studies to separate parts and tries to understand each part in itself. In contrast holism is based upon the belief that 'the whole' is more important than its individual 'parts'; indeed it suggests that each part only has meaning in relation to other parts, and ultimately in relation to 'the whole'.

In medical science, for example, disease has traditionally been understood and treated as a defect of a particular organ or even of specific cells within the body, not as an imbalance within the life of the patient as a whole. Attention has therefore been paid to the treatment of physical symptoms while psychological, social or environmental factors have tended to be ignored. In the case of heart disease, conventional medicine has made remarkable advances, for instance in correcting or replacing defective heart valves, transplanting human hearts and even developing artificial hearts. However it often neglects psychological factors such as stress and social and environmental factors such as smoking, diet and pollution, which may have caused the condition in the first place. A holistic approach to health therefore tries to treat the 'whole person', understanding injuries and disease as only physical symptoms of what may be a complex range of physical, psychological, social and environmental factors. Such holistic principles have deeply impressed environmental thinkers intent upon discovering new approaches to social, economic and political problems. Indeed holism implies that the traditional division of human knowledge into separate compartments – science, philosophy, history, politics and so on – is redundant. For example economics can no longer be regarded simply as the study of the production and consumption of goods. A holistic approach to economics requires that the environmental cost of production, its spiritual or moral value, and its political consequences must also be taken into account.

Although many see science as the culprit in teaching humans how to plunder the riches of nature more effectively, others have suggested that modern science may perhaps offer a new paradigm for human thought. Capra, for example, argued that the Cartesian–Newtonian view of the world has now been abandoned by many scientists, particularly by physicists like himself. During the twentieth century, with the development of 'new physics', physics moved a long way beyond the mechanistic and reductionist ideas of Newton. The breakthrough was achieved at the beginning of the twentieth century by the German-born US physicist Albert Einstein (1879–1955), whose theory of relativity fundamentally challenged the traditional concepts of time and space. Einstein's work was taken further by quantum theory, developed by physicists such as Niels Bohr and Verner Heisenberg. New physics emerged out of advances in subatomic research and has come to abandon the idea of absolute or objective knowledge. In its place Heisenberg proposed the 'uncertainty principle'. The physical world is understood not as a collection of individual molecules, atoms or even particles, but as a system, or more accurately a network of systems.

A systems view of the world concentrates not upon individual building blocks, but upon the principles of organisation within the system. It therefore stresses the relationships within the system and the integration of its various elements within the whole. Such a view had very radical implications. Objective knowledge, for example, is impossible because the very act of observing alters what is being observed. The scientist is not separate from his or her experiment but is intrinsically related to it; subject and object are therefore one. Similarly the concepts of cause and effect have had to be revised because changes are seen to develop within a system out of a network of factors, rather than as a consequence of a single, linear cause. Capra suggested that such a systems view of life has already revolutionised physics, is in the process of changing other sciences, and can equally well be applied to the study of social, political or environmental questions. In short new physics could provide a paradigm capable of replacing the now redundant mechanistic and reductionist world view.

An alternative and particularly fertile source of new concepts and theories has been religion. In *The Tao of Physics* (1975), Capra drew attention to important parallels between the ideas of modern physics and those of eastern mysticism. He argued that religions such as Hinduism, Taoism and Buddhism, particularly Zen Buddhism, have long preached the unity or oneness of all things, a discovery that western science has only made in the twentieth century. Many in the green movement have been attracted by eastern mysticism, seeing in it both a philosophy that gives expression to ecological wisdom and a way of life that encourages compassion for fellow human beings, other species and the natural world. Other writers believe that ecological principles are embodied in mono-theistic religions such as Christianity, Judaism and Islam, which regard both humankind and nature as products of divine creation. Jonathan Porritt, a former director of Friends of the Earth, has, for instance, described the Earth as 'the most powerful embodiment of God's work that we have', suggesting that it is a religious duty to cherish and preserve the planet. He has suggested that human beings will only act in harmony with nature if they come to see themselves as God's stewards on Earth.

However, perhaps the most influential concept for modern greens has been developed by looking back to pre-Christian spiritual ideas. Primitive religions often drew no distinction between human and other forms of life, and indeed little distinction between living and non-living objects. All things are alive, stones, rivers, mountains and even the Earth itself, often conceived of as 'Mother Earth'. The idea of an Earth Mother has been particularly important for ecologists trying to articulate a new relationship between human beings and the natural world, especially so for those sympathetic to ecofeminism, examined later in the chapter. In *Gaia: A New Look at Life on Earth* (1979) James Lovelock developed the idea that the planet itself is alive and gave it the name 'Gaia', after the Greek goddess of the Earth. Lovelock (see p. 274) defined Gaia as 'Earth's biosphere, atmosphere, oceans and soil' and argued that Gaia constitutes a living organism that acts to maintain its own existence. Lovelock claimed this on the basis that the Earth exhibits precisely the kind of self-regulating behaviour that characterises other forms of life. Gaia has achieved 'home-ostasis', a state of dynamic balance, despite dramatic changes that have taken place in the solar system. The most dramatic evidence for this is the fact that although the sun has warmed up by more than 25 per cent since life began, the temperature on Earth and the composition of its atmosphere have remained virtually unchanged. A quite small change in the proportion of oxygen in the atmosphere, or in the Earth's average temperature, would endanger all forms of life on the planet. In his essay 'Man and Gaia' (1988,

## James Lovelock (born 1919)

Canadian atmospheric chemist, inventor and environmental theorist. An independent scientist who lives in Cornwall, Lovelock cooperated with NASA in their space programme, advising on ways of looking for life on Mars.

Lovelock's influence on the green movement stems from his portrayal of the Earth's biosphere as a complex, self-regulating, living 'being', which he named Gaia (at the suggestion of the novelist William Golding). Although the Gaia hypothesis extends the ecological idea by applying it to the Earth as an ecosystem and offers a holistic approach to nature, Lovelock supports technology and industrialisation and is an opponent of 'back to nature' mysticism and ideas such as Earth worship. His major writings include *Gaia: A New Look at Life on Earth* (1979) and *The Ages of Gaia: A Biography of our Living Earth* (1989).

p. 63), Lovelock warned that 'To destroy such a large chunk of the living ecosystem when we do not properly understand how it all works is like pulling apart the control system of a modern aircraft while in mid-flight'.

The idea of Gaia has developed into an 'ecological ideology' that conveys the powerful message that human beings must respect the health of the planet and act to conserve its beauty and resources. It also contains a revolutionary vision of the relationship between the animate and inanimate world. Lovelock suggested that the Earth itself is alive and sees the living and the non-living world as one. He points out, for example, that much of the soil and rock on Earth are made up of reprocessed plants, insects and other forms of life, and that in turn they provide support for the plants and species living today. However the Gaia philosophy does not always correspond to the concerns of the environmental movement. Shallow ecologists have typically wished to change policies and attitudes in order to ensure the continued survival of the human species. Gaia, however, is non-human, and the Gaia theory suggests that the health of the planet matters more than that of any individual species presently living upon it. Lovelock has suggested that those species that have prospered have been ones that have helped Gaia to regulate its own existence, while any species that poses a threat to the delicate balance of Gaia, as humans currently do, is likely to be extinguished.

## Sustainability

Ecologists argue that the ingrained assumption of conventional political creeds, articulated by virtually all mainstream political parties ('grey parties'), is that human life has unlimited possibilities for material growth and prosperity. People in many parts of the world enjoy a standard of living that would have been unimaginable 50 or 100 years ago. Science and technology constantly solve old problems such as poverty and disease, and open up new possibilities through television and videos, computers and robots, air travel and even space travel. From an ecocentric perspective, however, the promise of unlimited prosperity and material affluence, 'growth mania' as Herman Daly (1974) called it, is not only misguided but also a fundamental cause of environmental disaster. Indeed green thinkers commonly lump capitalism and communism together and portray them both as examples of 'industrialism'. Green economics therefore requires orthodox assumptions about the nature and purpose of economic activity to be rethought, particularly in relation to our view of the Earth and the resources it contains.

A particularly influential metaphor for the environmental movement has been the idea of 'spaceship Earth', because this emphasises the notion of limited and exhaustible wealth. The idea that Earth should be thought of as a spaceship was first suggested by Kenneth Boulding (1966). From the perspective of deep ecology, the drawback of this theory is that it embodies the anthropocentric assumption that the planet exists to serve human needs: the Earth is a vessel, our vessel. Nevertheless the concept of spaceship Earth does serve to redress the conventional belief in unlimited resources and unbounded possibilities. Boulding argued that human beings have traditionally acted as though they live in a 'cowboy economy', an economy with unlimited opportunities, like the American west during the frontier period. Boulding suggested that this encourages, as it did in the American west, 'reckless, exploitative, and violent behaviour'. However a spaceship is a capsule, and therefore possesses finite resources. In the future 'spaceman economy', human beings will have to live within limits and pay closer attention to the spaceship that is propelling them through space.

---

## Industrialism

The term industrialism, as used by environmental theorists, relates to a 'super-ideology' that encompasses capitalism and socialism, left-wing and right-wing thought. As an economic system, industrialism is characterised by large-scale production, the accummulation of capital and relentless growth. As a philosophy, it is dedicated to materialism, utilitarian values, absolute faith in science and a worship of technology. Industrialism is thus seen by many ecologists as 'the problem'. Ecosocialists, however, blame capitalism rather than industrialism (which ignores important issues such as the role of ownership, profit and the market), while ecofeminists argue that industrialism has its origins in patriarchy.

Living in a spaceship requires an understanding of the ecological processes that sustain life. Most importantly, human beings must recognise that spaceship Earth is a closed system. Open systems receive energy or inputs from outside, for example all ecosystems on Earth – ponds, forests, lakes and seas – are sustained by the sun. Such open systems are self-regulating, and tend to establish a natural balance or a steady state. However closed systems, as the Earth itself becomes when it is thought of as a spaceship, show evidence of 'entropy'. Entropy is a measure of the degree of disorder or disintegration within a system. All closed systems tend to decay or disintegrate because they are not sustained by external inputs. They rely on their own resources and these become exhausted and cannot be renewed. Ultimately, however wisely and carefully human beings behave, the Earth, the sun, and indeed all planets and stars, will be exhausted and die. For example energy cannot be recycled indefinitely; each time energy is transformed some of it is lost, until finally none remains. When the 'entropy law' is applied to social and economic issues it produces very radical conclusions.

The green movement has drawn particular attention to what it sees as the 'population timebomb'. Such concerns are not new: as early as 1798 the British economist and cleric Thomas Malthus (1766–1834) warned that population growth would inevitably lead to mass starvation because food production is limited. However Malthus failed to appreciate how scientific methods of farming would succeed in feeding an ever-growing population. Nevertheless contemporary greens believe that Malthus's ecological ideas are not false, but were simply ahead of their time. Population growth is a problem in itself, but also one that makes every other environmental problem more serious. The proportion of the spaceship that each person occupies is getting smaller: in other words human beings are increasingly living in expanding but overcrowded cities, and less and less unspoilt countryside is available for recreation and leisure. More seriously, population growth accelerates the effects of entropy. With one million people being added to the world's population every five days, human beings are outstripping the land and other resources available on Earth and increasing their output of poisonous waste.

No issue reflects the law of entropy more clearly than the 'energy crisis'. Industrialisation and mass affluence have been made possible by the exploitation of coal, gas and oil reserves, which have provided fuel for power stations, factories, motor cars, aeroplanes and so on. These fuels are fossil fuels, formed by the decomposition or compaction of organisms that died in prehistoric times. They are also non-renewable, once used up they cannot be replaced. In *Small is Beautiful* (1973), E. F. Schumacher argued that human beings have made the mistake of regarding energy as an 'income' that is being constantly topped-up each week or each month,

## Fritz (Ernst Friedrich) Schumacher (1911–1977)

German-born UK economist and environmental theorist. Schumacher moved to Britain in 1930 as an Oxford Rhodes scholar, going on to gain practical experience in business, farming and journalism, before re-entering academic life. He was an economic adviser to the British Control Commission in Germany (1946–50) and the National Coal Board (1950–70).

Schumacher's seminal *Small is Beautiful: A Study of Economics as if People Mattered* (1973) championed the cause of human-scale production, and advanced a 'Buddhist' economic philosophy (economics 'as if people mattered') that stresses the importance of morality and 'right livelihood'. Though an opponent of industrial giantism, Schumacher believed in 'appropriate' scale production, and was a keen advocate of 'intermediate' technology.

rather than as 'natural capital' that they are forced to live off. This mistake has allowed energy demands to soar, especially in the industrialised West, at a time when finite fuel resources are close to depletion and very unlikely to last to the end of the next century. As the spaceship draws to the close of the 'fossil fuel age' it approaches disintegration because as yet, there are no alternative sources of energy to compensate for the loss of coal, oil and gas. Conserving what remains of our fossil fuel stocks means driving fewer cars, using less electricity and, in short, accepting a more meagre standard of living.

Human beings have not simply depleted natural resources through overpopulation and overconsumption, they have also polluted and poisoned the spaceship with an ever-increasing quantity of waste. Fossil fuels, for example, are 'dirty' forms of energy that, when burnt, release dangerous sulphuric and nitric acids into the atmosphere, causing acid rain, as well as carbon dioxide, which has been associated with global warming. The issue of global warming has stimulated fierce academic controversy. Some scientists have linked the $0.5^{0}C$ rise in world temperature during the twentieth century to the increased emission of 'greenhouse gases' since the industrial revolution. Gases such as carbon dioxide warm the atmosphere by trapping heat radiated back from the Earth's surface, causing sea levels to rise and thus threatening low-lying coastal areas. Global warming also affects agricultural and vegetation patterns throughout the world. The production of synthetic chemicals too has devastated both human and non-human life. For example the escape of poisonous gases in 1984 from a factory owned by the US company Union Carbide in Bhopal, in central India, caused an official death toll of 2352, though some have estimated that the actual figure could have been as high as 10 000.

Ecological economics is not only about warnings and threats, it is also about solutions. Entropy may be an inevitable process; however its effects can be slowed down or delayed considerably if governments and private citizens respect ecological principles. Ecologists argue that the human species will only survive and prosper if it recognises that it is only one element of a complex biosphere, and that only a healthy, balanced biosphere will sustain human life. Policies and actions must therefore be judged by the principle of 'sustainability', the capacity of a system, in this case the biosphere itself, to maintain its health and continue in existence. Sustainability sets clear limits upon human ambitions and material dreams because it requires that production does as little damage as possible to the fragile global ecosystem. For example the current use of fossil fuels is clearly not sustainable – coal, oil and natural gas will simply run out. Consequently a sustainable energy policy must be based upon a dramatic reduction in the use of fossil fuels and a search for alternative, renewable energy sources such as solar energy, wind power and wave power. These are by their very nature sustainable and can be treated as 'income' rather than 'natural capital'. Greens have therefore suggested that the 'fossil fuel age' must give way to a coming 'solar age', and have encouraged governments to step up the research and development of renewable energy sources.

Sustainability, however, requires not merely the more enlightened use of natural resources, but also an alternative approach to economic activity. This is precisely what Schumacher (1973) sought to offer in his idea of 'Buddhist economics'. For Schumacher, Buddhist economics is based upon the principle of 'right livelihood' and stands in stark contrast to conventional economic theories, which assume that individuals are nothing more than 'utility maximisers'. Buddhists believe that, in addition to generating goods and services, production facilitates personal growth by developing skills and talents, and helps to overcome egocentredness by forging social bonds and encouraging people to work together. Such a view moves economics a long way from its present obsession with wealth creation, an obsession that, ecologists believe, has paid little regard to either nature or the spiritual quality of human life. The principal goal of Buddhism – spiritual liberation – is not, however, irreconcilable with material prosperity. 'It is not wealth that stands in the way of liberation', Schumacher (1973, p. 47) pointed out, 'but the attachment to wealth; not the enjoyment of pleasurable things but the craving for them'. The environmental movement therefore hopes that in future economics can be used to serve humanity, rather than enslave it.

There is considerable debate about what this implies in practice. So-called 'light greens', referred to in Germany as the *realos* (realists), approve of the idea of 'sustainable growth': in effect, getting richer but at a slower pace. This holds that the desire for material prosperity can be balanced against its environmental costs. One way in which this could be achieved would be through changes to the tax system, either to penalise and discourage pollution or to reduce the use of finite resources. Schumacher's version of this position stressed the value of 'technology with a human face' and advocated a system of small-scale or 'human-scale' production to replace what he believed to be the dehumanising world of large cities and mass production. However 'dark greens', in Germany the *fundis* (fundamentalists), argue that such views are simply not radical enough. The notion of sustainable growth simply pays lip service to environmental fears whilst allowing human beings to carry on as if nothing is wrong. If, as the dark greens insist, the origin of the ecological crisis lies in materialism, consumerism and a fixation with economic growth, the solution lies in 'zero growth' and the construction of a 'post-industrial age' in which people live in small rural communities and rely upon craft skills. This means a fundamental and comprehensive rejection of industry and modern technology, literally a 'return to nature'.

## Environmental ethics

Ecological politics, in all its forms, is concerned with extending moral thinking in a number of novel directions. This is because conventional ethical systems are clearly anthropocentric. Utilitarianism, for example, evaluates 'good' and 'evil' in terms of the pleasure and pain that human beings experience. As 'utility maximisers', humans act – and should act – in whatever way will gain them the greatest happiness or the least unhappiness. If the non-human world – other species in the animal kingdom, as well as trees, plants, the land and so on – has any value at all, it is a strictly instrumental value, a means to achieve human ends or satisfy human interests. The same is true of the labour theories of value developed by thinkers such as John Locke, David Ricardo (1772–1823) and Karl Marx (see p. 126). In these, the non-human world is invested with value only to the extent that it is 'mixed' with human labour, or because interaction between human beings and nature through labour promotes the development of human skills and sensibilities.

One ethical issue that even humanist or shallow ecologists extensively grapple with is the question of our moral obligations towards future generations. It is in the nature of environmental matters that many of the consequences of our actions will not be felt until decades or even centuries to come. Why should we care about the depletion of fossil fuels if we are not going to be around when they run out? Why worry about the accummulation of nuclear waste if the generations that will have to deal with it have yet to be born? Clearly a concern with our own interests and perhaps those of our immediate family and friends only stretches a little way into the future. Ecologists are therefore forced to extend the notion of human interests to encompass the human species as a whole, making no distinction between the present generation and future generations, the living and the still to be born. Such 'futurity' may be justified in different ways. Ecoconservatives, for instance, may link it to tradition and continuity, to the notion that the present generation is merely the 'custodian' of the wealth that has been generated by past generations and so should conserve it for the benefit of future generations. Ecosocialists, on the other hand, may hold that a concern for future generations merely reflects the fact that compassion and a love for humanity extend through time, just as they cut across national, ethnic, gender and other boundaries.

An alternative approach to environmental ethics involves applying moral standards and values developed in relation to human beings to other species and organisms. The most familiar attempt to do this is in the form of 'animal rights'. The case for animal welfare was put forward by Peter Singer in *Animal Liberation* (1976). Singer argued that an altruistic concern for the well-being of other species derives from the fact that as sentient beings they are capable of suffering. As a utilitarian, he pointed out that animals, like humans, have an interest in avoiding physical pain, and he therefore condemned any attempt to place the interests of humans above those of animals as 'speciesism', an arbitrary and irrational prejudice not unlike sexism or racism. However altruistic concern for other species does not imply equal treatment, and Singer's argument does not apply to non-sentient life forms such as trees, rocks and rivers, which do not possess value.

The more radical idea that humans and animals can enjoy the same moral status was advanced by the US philosopher Tom Regan in *The Case for Animal Rights* (1983), on the ground that all creatures that are 'the subject of a life' qualify for rights. Such a position makes it very difficult, and perhaps impossible, to draw a clear distinction between the animal and human worlds. Nevertheless Regan acknowledged that as some rights are invested in human beings by virtue of the fact that they are capable of rational thought and moral autonomy, they can only be applied selectively to animals, notably to 'normal mammalian animals aged one or more'. However this individualist, rights-based approach to environmental ethics fails to satisfy deep ecologists, who have attempted to advance a more holistic or all-encompassing moral vision.

The moral stance of deep ecology is that nature has value in its own right, that is, intrinsic value. From this perspective, environmental ethics have nothing to do with human-instrumentality and cannot be articulated simply through the extension of human values to the non-human world. Goodin (1992), for instance, attempted to develop a 'green theory of value', which holds that resources should be valued precisely because they result from natural processes rather than from human activities. However, since this value stems from the fact that the natural landscape helps people to see 'some sense and pattern in their lives' and to appreciate 'something larger' than themselves, it embodies a residual humanism that fails to satisfy some deep ecologists. A classic statement of their more radical position is articulated in Aldo Leopold's *Sand County Almanac* ([1948] 1968, p. 225) in the form of the 'land ethic': 'A thing is right when it tends to preserve the integrity, stability and beauty of the biotic community. It is wrong when it tends otherwise'. Nature itself is thus portrayed as an ethical community, meaning that human beings are nothing more than 'plain citizens' who have no more rights and are no more deserving of respect than any other member of the community. Such a moral stance implies 'biocentric equality', the principle that all organisms and entities in the ecosphere are of equal moral worth, each of them being part of an interrelated whole. Arne Naess (1989) expressed this as an 'equal right to live and bloom'. Critics of deep ecology nevertheless argue either that this position is based on an unrealistic, indeed Arcadian view of nature that ignores, for instance, the food chain and the struggle for survival, or that this value-in-nature stance fails to recognise that morality is a human invention and that what makes nature 'natural' is precisely that it is amoral.

## Postmaterialism

Since one of the consistent themes of ecologism is rejection of self-seeking behaviour and material greed, it has sought to develop an alternative philosophy based upon personal fulfilment and a balance with nature. Indeed the growth of concern about environmental issues since the 1960s is commonly associated with the phenomenon of postmaterialism (Inglehart, 1977). Postmaterialism is a theory that explains the nature of political concerns and values in terms of levels of economic development. It is loosely based upon Abraham Maslow's (1908–70) 'hierarchy of needs', which places the need for esteem and self-actualisation above material or economic needs. Postmaterialism holds that while conditions of material scarcity breed egoistical and acquisitive attitudes, conditions of widespread prosperity allow individuals to express more interest in postmaterial or 'quality of life' issues. These are typically concerned with morality, political justice and personal fulfilment, and include feminism, world peace, racial harmony, ecology and animal rights. In this sense ecologism can be seen as one of the 'new' social movements that sprang up in the second half of the twentieth century, broadly committed to a new left agenda that rejected the hierarchical, materialist and patriarchal values of conventional society.

However, to a greater extent than any of the other new social movements, ecologism has indulged in radical and innovative thinking about the nature of human sensibilities and self-realisation. All ecologists, for example, would have some sympathy with the view that human development has become dangerously unbalanced: human beings are blessed with massive know-how and material wealth, but possess precious little 'know-why'. Humankind has acquired the ability to fulfil its material ambitions but not the wisdom to question whether these ambitions are sensible, or even sane. As Schumacher (1973) warned, 'Man is now too clever to survive without wisdom'. However some shallow or humanistic ecologists have serious misgivings when this quest for wisdom draws ecologism into the realms of religious mysticism or New Age ideas. Murray Bookchin (see p. 287), for instance, portrayed such tendencies as a form of 'anti-humanism', arguing that in creating a mythologised 'Nature', they represent a failure of human self-confidence and almost entirely neglect social concerns. Many greens, particularly those who subscribe to deep ecology, have nevertheless embraced world views that are quite different from those that have traditionally dominated political thought in the developed West. This, they argue, is the basis of the 'paradigm shift' that ecologism aims to bring about, and without which it is doomed to repeat the mistakes of the 'old' politics because it cannot move beyond its concepts and assumptions.

Deep ecologists are usually happy to acknowledge that there is, in a sense, a spiritual dimension to their view of politics. A closeness to nature is not merely a theoretical stance or an ethical position, it is, at heart, a human experience, the achievement of 'environmental consciousness'. The Australian philosopher Warwick Fox (1990) claimed to go beyond deep ecology in embracing 'transpersonal ecology', the essence of which is the realisation that 'things are', that human beings and all other entities are part of a single unfolding reality. For Naess, self-realisation is attained through a broader and deeper 'identification with others'. Such ideas have often been shaped by eastern religions, most profoundly by Buddhism, which has been portrayed as an ecological philosophy in its own right. One of the key doctrines of Buddhism is the idea of 'no self', the notion that the individual ego is a myth or delusion and that awakening or enlightenment involves transcending the self and recognising that each person is linked to all other living things, and indeed to the universe itself.

This can be developed into a kind of holistic individualism, in which freedom comes to be equated with the experience of 'being' and the realisation of organic wholeness. Such ideas were advanced by the German psychoanalyst and social philosopher Eric Fromm (1900–80) in *To Have and To Be* (1979). Fromm portrayed 'having' as an attitude of mind that seeks fulfilment in acquisition and control, and is clearly reflected in consumerism and the materialistic society. In contrast 'being' derives satisfaction from experience and sharing, and leads to personal growth and spiritual awareness. However, as Fromm pointed out, a 'being-orientated' existence requires not only radical socio-political change but nothing less than the transformation of humankind.

## Nature and politics

Deep ecologists typically dismiss conventional political creeds as merely different versions of anthropocentrism, each embodying an anti-nature bias. They claim to have developed an entirely new ideological paradigm (though many reject the term 'ideology' because of its association with human-centred thinking), developed though the radical application of ecological and holistic principles. Nevertheless other ecological or environmental thinkers have drawn inspiration, to a greater or lesser extent, from established political traditions. Such a stance is based on the belief that these traditions contain values and doctrines that are capable of accommodating a positive view of non-human nature, and of shedding light on why the ecological crisis has come about and how it can be tackled. In this sense ecologism, like nationalism and feminism, can be regarded as a cross-cutting ideology. At different times conservatives, fascists, socialists, anarchists, feminists and liberals have claimed a special sympathy with the environment. However they have enlisted ecological ideas in support of very different political goals.

### Right-wing ecologism

Although modern green politics is associated with causes and concerns that are generally viewed as left wing – such as belief in decentralisation and direct action and opposition to hierarchy and materialism – the earliest manifestations of political ecology, as Anna Bramwell (1989) pointed out, had an essentially right-wing orientation. This was most dramatically demonstrated by the emergence of a form of fascist ecologism during the Nazi period in Germany. Its principle exponent was Walter Darré, who was minister of agriculture under Hitler from 1933 to 1942, and also held the post of Nazi peasant leader. The experience of rapid industrialisation in late-nineteenth-century Germany had created a strong 'back to the land' movement, which was especially attractive to students and young people. The German Youth Movement developed out of the *Wandervoegel*, bands of German students who took to the forests and mountains to escape from the alienation of urban life. Darré's own ideas were a mixture of Nordic racialism (see p. 228) and the idealisation of peasant or rural life, fused into an agrarian philosophy of 'Blood and Soil' that overlapped at several points with national socialism. Nazism, for instance, was associated with a form of vitalism, which places heavy emphasis on the role of the 'life force' and so is at odds with any form of materialism. As peasant leader, Darré was responsible for introducing the hereditary farm law, which gave owners of small and medium-size farms complete security of tenure, and also for setting up the National Food Estate to market agricultural produce with the intention of keeping food prices high and maintaining rural prosperity.

Despite his links with the Nazis, Darré's ideas have much in common with the modern green movement. In the first place he was convinced that only a life lived close to nature and on the land could be truly fulfilling, and he therefore wished to recreate a peasant Germany. Such ideas have been echoed by modern ecologists such as Edward Goldsmith (1988). Moreover Darré became a powerful advocate of organic farming, which uses only natural fertilisers such as animal manure. Darré believed in an organic cycle of animal–soil–food–humans, which he discovered in the works of the Austrian philosopher and educationalist Rudolph Steiner (1861–1925) and the anthroposophy movement. Organic farming reflects ecological principles and has become a major plank in the idea of environmentally friendly agriculture. During the Third Reich, Darré's peasant ideology helped the Nazis to secure committed support in the German countryside. However, though a scientific racialist, Darré himself was never a Nazi and publicly distanced himself from the *Führerprinzip,* or leader principle, and also from talk of expansion and empire. In reality the Nazi regime did little to fulfil Darré's dreams of a sturdy, peasant Germany. Despite Hitler's attachment to the idea of 'Blood and Soil', his obsession with military expansion intensified the process of industrialisation in Germany and brought poverty to the countryside.

On the 'soft right', conservatives have also evinced a sympathy for environmental issues. For example in her famous 'green speech' in 1988, Margaret Thatcher described the Conservatives in the UK as 'the guardians and trustees of the Earth'. Ecoconservatism reflects a romantic and nostalgic attachment to a rural way of life threatened by the growth of towns and cities. It is clearly a reaction against industrialisation and the idea of 'progress'. It does not envisage the construction of a post-industrial society, founded upon the principles of cooperation and ecology, but a return to or the maintenance of a more familiar pre-industrial one. Such environmental sensibilities typically focus upon the issue of conservation and upon attempts to protect what is seen as the natural heritage – woodlands, forests and so on, as well as the architectural and social heritage. The conservation of nature is therefore linked to a defence of traditional values and institutions. In this light, ecology stands for a return to the feudal past, with the land in the hands of a small minority and political control imposed from above. For example Edward Goldsmith, the father of British environmentalism, has argued that an ecological society would involve the resurrection of traditional order within the family and the community – in effect the establishment of strong authoritarian government.

## Ecosocialism

There is a distinct socialist strand within the green movement, and this is particularly pronounced amongst the German Greens, many of whose leaders have been former members of far-left groups. Ecosocialism often draws upon Marxist analysis, and has usually sought to distance itself from the quasi-religious ideas that are influential elsewhere in the environmental movement. For example Rudolph Bahro (1982), a leading German ecosocialist, argued that capitalism is the root cause of environmental problems. The natural world has been despoiled by industrialisation, but this is merely a consequence of capitalism's search for profit. Capitalism is thus characterised not only by class conflict but also by the progressive destruction of the natural environment. Both human labour and the natural world are exploited because they are treated simply as economic resources. Any attempt to improve the environment must therefore involve a radical process of social change, some would say a social revolution. However Marx's own position in relation to the natural word is a matter of some controversy. While some see his belief in the progressive development of productive forces as a classic statement of industrialism, others have argued that the depiction of labour in his early writings as the 'humanisation' of nature and the 'naturalisation' of the human, has an unmistakable ecological character.

The core theme of ecosocialism is the idea that capitalism is the enemy of the environment, whilst socialism is its friend. However, as with socialist feminism, such a formula embodies tension between two elements, this time between 'red' and 'green' priorities. If environmental catastrophe is nothing more than a by-product of capitalism, environmental problems are best tackled by abolishing capitalism, or at least taming it. Therefore ecologists should not form separate green parties or set up narrow environmental organisations, but work within the socialist movement and address the real issue: the economic system. On the other hand socialism has also been seen as another 'pro-production' political creed because it espouses exploiting the wealth of the planet for the good of all humanity, rather than just a small class of capitalists. Socialist parties have been slow to adopt environmental policies because they, like other 'grey' parties, continue to base their electoral appeal upon the promise of economic growth. As a result ecologists have often been reluctant to subordinate the green to the red, hence the proclamation by the German Greens that they are 'neither left nor right'. Indeed many ecosocialists, for example Bahro (1984), have come to the conclusion that the ecological crisis is so pressing that it must take precedence over the class struggle.

Ecosocialists argue that socialism is naturally ecological. If wealth is commonly owned by all it will be used in the interests of all, which means in the long-term interests of humanity. However it is unlikely that ecological problems can be solved simply by a change in the ownership of wealth. This was abundantly demonstrated by the experience of state socialism in the Soviet Union and eastern Europe, which produced some of the world's most intractable environmental problems. Economic priorities in the communist East, no less so than in the capitalist West, were based upon the pursuit of growth. The system of central planning also allowed public policy to be made in Moscow, many miles from the scene of any ecological disaster. In the 1960s, for example, the two principal rivers that fed the Aral Sea in Soviet Central Asia were rerouted in order to irrigate cotton and rice fields. As a result, the Aral Sea, once the fourth biggest lake in the world, has shrunk to half its original size and its shores have receded in some places by 100 kilometres, leaving a salty, polluted desert. The best publicised environmental disaster in eastern Europe was the Chernobyl nuclear explosion in the Ukraine in 1986, the scale of which at least forced the Soviet regime into greater openness about environmental problems in general. In the post-communist era, environmental protest groups have sprung up throughout the Soviet Union. However it is noticeable that, unlike the green movement in the West, these groups rarely espouse ecosocialism and are more usually linked to conservative or reactionary political doctrines.

## Eco-anarchism

Perhaps the ideology that has the best claim to being environmentally sensitive is anarchism. Some months before the publication of Rachel Carson's influential *The Silent Spring*, Murray Bookchin brought out *Our Synthetic Environment* ([1962] 1975). Many in the green movement also acknowledge a debt to nineteenth-century anarcho-communists, particularly Peter Kropotkin. Bookchin (1977) has suggested that there is a clear correspondence between the ideas of anarchism and the principles of ecology, articulated in the idea of 'social ecology', the belief that ecological balance is the surest foundation for social stability. Anarchists believe in a stateless society, in which harmony develops out of mutual respect and social solidarity amongst human beings. The richness of such a society is founded upon its variety and diversity. Ecologists also believe that balance or harmony spontaneously develops within nature, in the form of

## Murray Bookchin (born 1921)

US anarchist social philosopher and environmental thinker. Bookchin was a radical activist in the American labour movement of the 1930s, and was one of the very earliest social thinkers to take environmental issues seriously. He is professor emeritus of the Institute of Social Ecology in Vermont.

Bookchin's contribution to anarchism is linked to an emphasis on the potential for non-hierarchic cooperation within conditions of post-scarcity, and on ways of promoting decentralisation and community within modern societies. As the leading proponent of 'social ecology', he propounds the view that ecological principles can be applied to social organisation and argues that the environmental crisis is a result of the breakdown of the organic fabric of both society and nature. Bookchin's major works include *Post-scarcity Anarchism* (1971), *The Ecology of Freedom* (1982) and *Remaking Society* (1989).

ecosystems, and that these, like anarchist communities, require no external authority or control. The anarchist rejection of government within human society thus parallels the ecologists' warnings about human 'rule' within the natural world. Bookchin therefore likened an anarchist community to an ecosystem, and suggested that both are distinguished by respect for the principles of diversity, balance and harmony.

Anarchists have also advocated the construction of decentralised societies, organised as a collection of communes or villages. Life in such communities would be lived close to nature, each community attempting to achieve a large degree of self-sufficiency. Such communities would be economically diverse, they would produce food and a wide range of goods and services, and therefore contain agriculture, craftwork and small-scale industry. Self-sufficiency would make each community dependent upon its natural environment, spontaneously generating an understanding of organic relationships and ecology. In Bookchin's view, decentralisation would lead to 'a more intelligent and more loving use of the environment'. A society regulated by spontaneous sympathy amongst human beings is therefore likely to encourage an ecological balance between human beings and the natural world.

Without doubt the conception that many ecologists have of a post-industrial society has been influenced by the writings of Kropotkin and William Morris. The green movement has also adopted ideas such as decentralisation, participatory democracy and direct action from anarchist thought. However, even when anarchism is embraced as providing a vision of an ecologically sound future, it is seldom accepted as a means of getting there. Anarchists believe that progress will only be possible when the government and all forms of political authority are overthrown. In contrast many in the green movement see government as an agency through which collective action can be organised and therefore as the most likely means through which the environmental crisis can be addressed, at least in the short term. They fear that dismantling or even weakening government may simply give free rein to those forces that generated industrialisation and blighted the natural environment in the first place.

## Ecofeminism

The idea that feminism offers a distinctive and valuable approach to green issues has grown to such a point that ecofeminism has developed into one of the major philosophical schools of environmentalist thought. Its basic theme is that ecological destruction has its origins in patriarchy: nature is under threat not from humankind but from men and the institutions of male power. Feminists who adopt an androgynous or sexless view of human nature argue that patriarchy has distorted the instincts and sensibilities of men by divorcing them from the 'private' world of nurturing, home making and personal relationships. The sexual division of labour thus inclines men to subordinate both women and nature, seeing themselves as 'masters' of both. From this point of view ecofeminism can be classified as a particular form of social ecology. However many ecofeminists subscribe to essentialism, in that their theories are based upon the belief that there are fundamental and ineradicable differences between women and men.

Such a position is adopted, for instance, by Mary Daly in *Gyn/Ecology* (1979). Daly argued that women would liberate themselves from patriarchal culture if they aligned themselves with 'female nature'. The notion of an intrinsic link between women and nature is not a new one. Pre-Christian religions and 'primitive' cultures often portrayed the Earth or natural forces as a Goddess, an idea resurrected in some respects in the Gaia hypothesis. Modern ecofeminists, however, highlight the biological basis for women's closeness to nature, in particular the fact that they bear children and suckle babies. The fact that women cannot live separate from natural rhythms and processes in turn structures their politico-cultural orientation. Traditional 'female' values are therefore reciprocity, cooperation and nurturing, values that have a 'soft' or ecological character. The idea that nature is a resource to be exploited or a force to be subdued is more abhorrent to women than men, because they recognise that nature operates in and through them and intuitively sense that personal fulfilment stems from acting with nature rather than against it. The overthrow of patriarchy therefore promises to bring with it an entirely new relationship between human society and the natural world.

However, if there is an essential or 'natural' bond between women and nature, the relationship between men and nature is quite different. While women are creatures of nature, men are creatures of culture: their world is synthetic or man-made, a product of human ingenuity rather than natural creativity. In the male world, then, intellect is ranked above intuition, materialism is valued over spirituality, and mechanical relationships are emphasised over holistic ones. In politico-cultural terms this is reflected in a belief in self-striving, competition and hierarchy. The implications of this for the natural world are clear. Patriarchy, in this view, establishes the supremacy of culture over nature, the latter being nothing more than a force to be subdued, exploited or risen above. Ecological destruction and gender inequality are therefore part of the same process in which 'cultured' men rule over 'natural' women.

## Ecologism in the twenty-first century

The prospects for ecologism in the twenty-first century would appear to be firmly linked to the state of the environmental crisis and the general level of understanding about environmental issues and problems. As evidence of the blighting of nature increases – through changing weather patterns resulting from global warming, reduced levels of male fertility caused by pollution, the eradication of animal and plant species, and so on – the search for an alternative to growth-obsessed industrialism will surely intensify. The fluctuating fortunes of green parties and single-issue environmentalist groups provide no reliable indication of the strength of ecological ideas and values. One of the problems confronting green parties is that their mainstream and much larger rivals have taken up 'eco-friendly' positions that were once exclusively theirs. Similarly the membership and activist base of single-issue environmental groups does not reflect the number of fellow-travellers in society at large nor the wider adoption of ecological practices such as recycling and the use of organic foods. This perspective suggests that humankind will have no choice in the twenty-first century but to reverse the policies and practices that have brought both the human species and the natural world close to destruction.

A number of problems confront ecological theory, however. In the first place it is difficult to see how ecologism can become a global ideology. As far as developing-world states are concerned, its strictures appear to deny them the opportunity to catch up with the West. Western states developed through large-scale industrialisation, the exploitation of finite resources, pollution and so forth, practices they now seek to deny to the developed world. However the industrialised West is no more likely than the developing world fully to adopt ecological priorities since this would mean that it, as the major consumer of energy and resources, would have to forego the prosperity it already enjoys. Secondly, difficulties surround the antigrowth message of ecologism. The politics of sustainable or zero growth may either be so unattractive to populations that it is electorally impossible, or misconceived, as Bramwell argued in *The Fading of the Greens* (1994), because the environmental crisis can only be tackled by advanced and materially prosperous societies. Thirdly, greenism may simply be an urban fad, a form of post-industrial romanticism. This suggests that environmental awareness is merely a temporary reaction to industrial progress and is likely to be restricted to the young and the affluent.

Perhaps the most daunting challenge facing ecologism is the very scale of the changes it calls for. Ecologism, at least in the guise of deep ecology, is more radical than socialism, fascism, feminism or any of the other political creeds examined in this book. It does not merely demand the transformation of the economic system or the reordering of power relations within the political system, it also seeks to establish nothing less than a new mode of being, a different way of experiencing and understanding existence. What is more its theories, values and sensibilities are entirely at odds with those that have traditionally dominated industrialised societies. The problem of ecologism is therefore that it is based upon a philosophy that is deeply alien to the culture that it must influence if it is to be successful. However this may also be the source of its appeal.

## Further reading

Bramwell, A., *Ecology in the 20th Century: A History* (New Haven and London: Yale University Press, 1989). A highly influential study of the intellectual and political history of the ecological movement; detailed and provocative.

Dobson, A., *Green Political Thought* (London: HarperCollins, 1990). An accessible and very useful account of the ideas behind green politics.

Dobson, A., *The Green Reader* (London: André Deutsch, 1991). An excellent collection of short extracts from important texts by ecological thinkers; a good basis for further reading.

Eckersley, R., *Environmentalism and Political Theory: Towards an Ecocentric Approach* (London: UCL Press, 1992). A detailed and comprehensive examination of the impact of environmentalist ideas on contemporary political thought.

Marshall, P., *Nature's Web: Rethinking Our Place on Earth* (London: Cassell, 1995). A history of ecological ideas that serves as a compendium of the various approaches to nature in different periods and from different cultures.

# Chapter 10

# Religious Fundamentalism

## Origins and development

The word 'fundamentalism' derives from the Latin *fundamentum*, meaning base. The term was first used in debates within American Protestantism in the early twentieth century. Between 1910 and 1915 evangelical Protestants published a series of pamphlets entitled *The Fundamentals*, upholding the inerrancy or literal truth of the Bible in the face of 'modern' interpretations of Christianity. In its contemporary usage, however, fundamentalism (see p. 299) is associated with all the world's major religions – Islam, Judaism, Hinduism, Sikhism and Buddhism, as well as Christianity – and is viewed as a particular kind of religio-political movement or project, rather than as simply the assertion of the literal truth of sacred texts (although this remains a feature of certain forms of fundamentalism).

The term fundamentalism is highly controversial. For many it implies repression and intolerance, fundamentalism being seen as the enemy of liberal values and personal freedom. This tendency was intensified by the collapse of communism, which encouraged many in the developed West to believe that religious fundamentalism, and especially Islamic fundamentalism, had displaced Marxism as the principal threat to world order. The end of the Cold War had thus given rise to a global 'clash of civilisations' (Huntington, 1993). As fundamentalism has come to be associated with inflexibility, dogmatism and authoritarianism, many of those who are classified as fundamentalists reject the term as simplistic or demeaning. However, unlike alternative terms such as 'traditionalism', 'conservatism', 'orthodoxy' and 'revivalism', fundamentalism has the advantage that it conveys the distinctive character of the political phenomenon.

The upsurge in religious fundamentalism in the final decades of the twentieth century has confounded advocates of the so-called secularisation thesis (the belief that modernisation, and particularly industrialisation, are invariably accompanied by the victory of reason over religion and the displacement of spiritual values by material ones). In many parts of the world, religious movements appear to have gained a renewed potency. Moreover, in its fundamentalist guise this religious revivalism has assumed an overtly political form. The claim that religious fundamentalism should be treated as an ideology in its own right is based on its assertion that religion is inseparable from law and politics, reflected in attempts to regenerate and comprehensively reconstruct society.

Despite its backward-looking emphasis and evident anti-modernism, religious fundamentalism is very much a creature of the modern world. Indeed most commentators treat it as a distinct modern phenomenon and deny that it has historical parallels. Possible exceptions to this include the German preacher and Anabaptist, Thomas Müntzer (1489–1525), who led the Peasants' War, and the French Protestant reformer, Jean Calvin (1509– 64), who founded a theocracy in Geneva that allowed him to control almost all the city's affairs. Similarly the Puritans played a major role in initiating the English Revolution of the seventeenth century, and demonstrated their 'this-worldly' concern to establish a new political and social system by sailing to North America to found a New England.

What makes the fundamentalisms that have sprung up in the late twentieth century unique is their ambiguous relationship with the process of modernisation. Religious fundamentalism is characterised by the fact that it constitutes a revolt against modernity but also draws on many of the weapons, views and spirit of the modern world. While decrying the degeneration and corruption of contemporary society, it embraces modern technology, electronic communication, the machinery of the modern state and even, at times, nuclear missiles. Thus religious fundamentalism, in Bhikhu Parekh's (1994) words, is an 'illegitimate child of modernity'. It is difficult to generalise about the causes of the fundamentalist upsurge because in different parts of the world it has taken different doctrinal forms and displayed contrasting ideological features. What is clear, however, is that fundamentalism arises in deeply troubled societies, particularly societies afflicted by an actual or perceived crisis of identity. Amongst the factors that have contributed to such crises in the late twentieth century, four are particularly relevant to religious fundamentalism: secularisation, post-colonialism, the failure of revolutionary socialism, and globalisation.

Secularisation – the spread of worldly or rationalistic ideas and values in place of religious or sacred ones – has contributed to a decline of traditional religion and a weakening of what is seen as the 'moral fabric' of society. In that sense fundamentalism represents a moral protest against decadence and hypocrisy; it aims to restore 'rightful' order and re-establish the link between the human world and the divine. Such moral conservatism has been very evident in the so-called new Christian right in the United States, prominent since the 1970s, and has been an important component of Islamic fundamentalism in countries such as Iran, Egypt, Turkey, Pakistan and Afghanistan. The impact of post-colonialism helps to explain why, although fundamentalism can be found across the globe, its most potent and influential manifestations have been found in the developing world. As a reaction against post-colonial modernity, religious fundamentalism has the advantage that it offers an indigenous and therefore non-western basis for national reconstruction. Political Islam has been particularly significant in this respect, most notably during the Iranian 'Islamic Revolution' of 1979, when it served to articulate anti-westernism in general, and specific hostility towards the United States as the 'Great Satan'.

A further reason for the spread of religious fundamentalism has been the failure of revolutionary socialism. Religious fundamentalism has been particularly successful in articulating the aspirations of the urban poor and the lower middle classes in developing states, groups that until the 1970s were more likely to be attracted to some brand of socialism and in many cases to Marxism–Leninism. Thus Lebanese resistance to Israel in the 1980s and 1990s has been led by groups linked to Iran, for example Heizbollah (Party of God) and Amal (Hope), while amongst the Palestinians the traditional dominance of the Palestinian Liberation Organisation has been severely threatened by the rise of fundamentalist groups such as Hamas.

Finally, fundamentalism has drawn strength from the advance of globalisation. Globalisation has undermined the capacity of 'civic' nationalism to establish secure and stable political identities. Religion has therefore tended to replace the nation as the principal source of collective identity, meaning that fundamentalism has emerged as a sub-variety of ethnic nationalism. This has been particularly significant in parts of the world where national identity has been challenged or threatened. Fundamentalism as ethnic mobilisation can, for instance, be seen in the militant Buddhism of the Sinhalese in Sri Lanka, in the Jewish settler movement in Israel, in Hindu and Sikh extremism in India, and in the resistance of Ulster Protestants to a united Ireland. The implications of globalisation for fundamentalism are nevertheless complex. In an increasingly interdependent world the capacity to reconstruct society according to particular national, religious or indeed political blueprints is limited. The emergence of so-called 'pragmatic fundamentalism' in Iran since the death in 1988 of Ayatollah Khomeini (see p. 306) highlights the practical constraints upon fundamentalist in power. The point at which pragmatism (see p. 11) calls the fundamentalist credentials of a regime into question is, however, another matter.

## Back to basics – central themes

Religious fundamentalism is an untypical political ideology in two senses. First, it cuts across a variety of, perhaps all, religions, regardless of their doctrinal and structural differences. To study religious fundamentalism as a single, coherent entity is to treat as secondary the substantial differences that divide the religions of the world – whether they believe in a single god, many small gods or no god at all; whether they have a holy book, a variety of scriptures or place faith in an oral tradition; how they view morality and social conduct, and so forth. Moreover, while some fundamentalisms have been associated with violence and anti-constitutional political action, others have supported law-abiding and peaceful behaviour. Such differences draw attention to the fact that religious fundamentalism is essentially a *style* of political thought rather than a *substantive* collection of political ideas and values. For example, while most forms of fundamentalism are entirely at odds with liberal individualism, Protestant fundamentalism in North America embraces 'rugged individualism' as an article of faith. In the same way the Koran's rejection of usury and interest-based banking makes it difficult for Islamic fundamentalists to accept market economics, while the new Christian right in the United States have enthusiastically endorsed *laissez-faire* capitalism. To the extent that religious fundamentalism's central or core themes can be identified, they follow from its tendency to recognise certain principles as essential or unchallengeable 'truths', regardless of their content.

Second, given religion's traditional concern with sacred, spiritual or 'other-worldly' matters, it is odd to suggest that religious doctrines and values can constitute a political ideology. Of course there is nothing new about ideology drawing from the pool of religious ideas. Ethical socialists have often looked to Christianity, Islam, Judaism and other religions to provide a basis for their value system. Conservatives have traditionally applauded religion for providing society with a bedrock of shared values and a common culture. Anarchists have seen in Taoism and Buddhism models of natural harmony, while ecologists have been inspired by their emphasis on the oneness of life, also emphasised by paganism and nature religions.

However fundamentalism is different in that it treats religious ideas not as a means of defending or embellishing political doctrines, but as the very stuff of political thought itself. As a programme for the comprehensive restructuring of society on religious lines and according to religious principles, fundamentalism deserves to be classified as an ideology in its own right. Nevertheless some interpret fundamentalism as a subspecies of nationalism, and it is difficult to deny that in certain cases fundamentalism operates as a form of religious nationalism. However, at least in its more radical forms, religious fundamentalism goes well beyond the reassertion of national or ethnic distinctiveness, and in the case of Islam in particular it has a marked transnational dimension. The characteristic themes of religious fundamentalism are the following:

- Religion and politics
- The fundamentalist impulse
- Anti-modernism
- Militancy.

## Religion and politics

The core theme of fundamentalism is a rejection of the distinction between religion and politics. In effect, in Khomeini's words, 'Politics is religion'. Religion may be the basis of politics, but what is religion? In its most general sense a religion is an organised community of people bound together by a shared body of beliefs concerning some kind of transcendent reality, usually expressed in a set of approved activities and practices. What transcendent means here is difficult to define, as it may refer to anything from a supreme being, a creator God, to the experience of personal liberation, as in the Buddhist theory of nirvana, literally meaning 'extinction'. Social theorists have also profoundly disagreed about the nature of religion.

The French sociologist Emile Durkheim (1858–1917) argued that religion encompasses what societies regard as 'sacred' as opposed to what they think of as 'profane', its central function being that it creates a collective consciousness that binds all adherents together into a single 'moral community'. In Marx's (see p. 126) view, religion represents a protest against a dehumanising social world and human alienation; it is 'the sigh of the oppressed creature, the heart of a heartless world'. In characterising it as 'the opium of the people' Marx linked religion to ideology in the sense of 'false consciousness'; however, this means that religion gives the proletariat illusions that help to sustain it in its misery, not that religion is crudely foisted on the working class in the form of ruling-class ideology. The German sociologist Max Weber (1864–1920) highlighted the ability of religious beliefs and movements to help shape social change. In particular he argued that the 'Protestant ethic', which emphasises personal salvation and the importance of work, had laid down the foundations for the development of capitalism in northern Europe.

The impact of religion on political life has progressively been restricted by the spread of liberal culture and ideas, the industrialised West, naturally, having the taken the lead in this process. Nevertheless liberal secularism is by no means an anti-religious tendency. Rather it is concerned to establish a 'proper' sphere and role for religion. A key feature of liberal culture is the so-called public/private distinction. This establishes a strict separation between a public sphere of life regulated by collective rules and subject to political authority, and a private sphere in which people are free to do as they like. The great virtue of this distinction, from a liberal perspective, is that it guarantees individual liberty by constraining government's ability to interfere in personal or private affairs. However it also has important implications for religion, which is fenced into a private arena, leaving public life to be organised on a strictly secular basis. In bringing about the 'privatisation of religion', secularisation has extended the public/private divide into a distinction between politics and religion. The clearest manifestation of this is the separation of church and state, which is constitutionally enshrined in the United States and elsewhere, and even substantially observed in states such as the UK, where 'established' churches continued to enjoy formal privileges in relation to the state.

Much of the spirit of religious fundamentalism is captured in its rejection of the public/private divide. On one level fundamentalism is a manifestation of the politics of identity. The expansion of a public realm organised on a secular and rationalistic basis has gradually weakened traditional social norms, textures and values and has left many bereft of identity, or as Eric Hobsbawm (1994) put it, 'orphans' in the modern world. The intensity and zeal that typically characterises fundamentalism establishes religion as the primary collective identity, giving its members and supporters the rootedness and sense of belonging that they would otherwise lack. More significantly, it is precisely religious fundamentalism's refusal to accept that religion is merely a private or personal matter that establishes its ideological credentials. To treat religion only as a personal or spiritual matter is to invite evil and corruption to stalk the public domain, hence the spread of permissiveness, materialism, corruption, greed, crime and immorality. The fundamentalist solution is simple: the world must be made anew, existing structures must be replaced with a comprehensive system founded upon religious principles and embracing law, politics, society, culture and the economy.

However the perceived corruption of the secular public realm may give rise to one of two responses. The first, sometimes called 'passive' fundamentalism, takes the route of withdrawal and attempts to construct communities of believers untainted by the larger society. Groups such as the Amish in the United States and the Haredim, the ultra-orthodox Jews of Israel, undoubtedly believe that religion dictates social, economic and political principles, but they are generally more concerned with their own observation of these principles than with the comprehensive regeneration

## Perspectives on . . .

### Religion

**Liberals** see religion as a distinct 'private' matter linked to individual choice and personal development. Religious freedom is thus essential to civil liberty and can only be guaranteed by a strict division between religion and politics, and between church and state.

**Conservatives** regard religion as a valuable (perhaps essential) source of stability and social cohesion. As it provides society with a set of shared values and the bedrock of a common culture, overlaps between religion and politics, and church and state are inevitable and desirable.

**Socialists** have usually portrayed religion in negative terms, as at best a diversion from the political struggle and at worst a form of ruling-class ideology (leading in some cases to the adoption of state atheism). In emphasising love and compassion, religion may nevertheless provide socialism with an ethical basis.

**Anarchists** generally regard religion as an institutionalised source of oppression. Church and state are invariably linked, with religion preaching obedience and submission to earthly rulers while also prescribing a set of authoritative values that rob the individual of moral autonomy.

**Fascists** have sometimes rejected religion on the grounds that it serves as a rival source of allegiance or belief, and that it preaches 'decadent' values such as compassion and human sympathy. Fascism nevertheless seeks to function as a 'political' religion, embracing its terminology and internal structure – devotion, sacrifice, spirit, redemption and so on.

**Fundamentalists** view religion as a body of 'essential' and unchallengeable principles, which dictate not only personal conduct but also the organisation of social, economic and political life. Religion cannot and should not be confined to the 'private' sphere but finds its highest and proper expression in the politics of popular mobilisation and social regeneration.

of society. The second response is 'active' fundamentalism, which takes the route of opposition and combat, and which alone should be considered an ideology on the ground that only it adopts an overtly political stance. However the notion of politics that it adopts is a distinctly conventional one. In marked contrast to feminists, who have also challenged the public/ private divide, religious fundamentalists view politics in terms of government policy and state action. Far from regarding politics as inherently corrupt, they usually look to seize, or at least exert influence over, the modern state, seeing it as an instrument of moral regeneration. Critics of fundamentalism nevertheless argue that it is precisely this determination to remove the distinction between religion and politics that invests in fundamentalism a totalitarian impulse. A state founded upon religious principles is, almost by definition, unencumbered by constraints that arise out of the notion of the public/private divide. However the degree to which particular fundamentalisms have succumbed to this totalitarian impulse varies greatly.

## The fundamentalist impulse

In its broadest sense, fundamentalism refers to a commitment to ideas and values that are seen as 'basic' or 'foundational'. Since fundamental beliefs are regarded as the core of a theoretical system, as opposed to peripheral and more transitory beliefs, they usually have an enduring and unchanging character, and are linked to the system's original or 'classical' form. Fundamentalism can therefore be seen as the opposite of relativism, the denial that there are any objective or 'absolute' standards, as reflected in the belief that statements can only be judged in relation to their contexts. By this standard, certain political ideologies, notably fascism and communism, can be placed nearer the fundamentalist end of the fundamentalism–relativism spectrum, while liberalism in particular, disposed as it is towards scepticism by its commitment to reason and toleration, can be placed near the relativist end. All ideologies, however, contain elements of fundamentalism. In the sense that fundamentalism implies keeping faith with original or 'classical' ideas, it is also possible to classify some traditions within an ideology as fundamentalist and others as not. In this respect, fundamentalism is the opposite of revisionism. Classical Marxism, which aimed to abolish and replace capitalism, has thus been seen as a form of fundamentalist socialism, while social democracy is portrayed as revisionist socialism by virtue of having modified its rejection of private property, the market, material incentives and so on.

In the case of religious fundamentalism, the 'fundamentals' have usually, but not always, been derived from the content of sacred texts, supported by the assertion of their literal truth. Indeed scriptural literalism was a central feature of American Protestant fundamentalism, which, for example, has continued to preach creationism or 'creation science', the belief that humankind was created by God, as described in the Book of Genesis, and the outright rejection of the Darwinian theory of evolution. Such tendencies can be found in all three 'religions of the book' – Christianity, Islam and Judaism – each of which possesses sacred texts that have been claimed to express the revealed word of God. Nevertheless, though often

## Fundamentalism

Fundamentalism is a style of thought in which certain principles are recognised as essential 'truths' that have unchallengeable and overriding authority, regardless of their content. Substantive fundamentalisms therefore have little or nothing in common, except that their supporters tend to evince an earnestness or fervour born out of doctrinal certainty. Although it is usually associated with religion and the literal truth of sacred texts, fundamentalism can also be found in political creeds. Even liberal scepticism can be said to incorporate the fundamental belief that all theories should be doubted (apart from its own). Although the term is often used pejoratively to imply inflexibility, dogmatism and authoritarianism, fundamentalism may also give expression to selflessness and a devotion to principle.

related, religious fundamentalism should not be equated with scriptural literalism. In the first place all sacred texts contain a complex and diverse range of ideas, doctrines and principles. To treat a sacred text as a political ideology, as a moral and political programme for the regeneration of society and the mobilisation of the masses, it is necessary to extract out its 'fundamentals'. These are a set of simple and clean principles that provide an exact and unambiguous definition of religious identity. In John Garvey's (1993) words, fundamentalism constitutes 'a kind of stripped-down religion that travels light and fast'.

Secondly, in contrast with the ultra-orthodox, whose principle goal is to 'live by the book', fundamentalists have supported an 'activist' reading of texts that enables them to reduce the complexity and profundity of scripture to a theo-political project. In Islam this is described as 'dynamic interpretation'. Selectivity and interpretation, however, create the problem of how one version of scripture or doctrine can be upheld over other versions. Fundamentalists have usually resolved this problem by reflecting on *who* is doing the interpreting. In this respect, clerical position and religious office may be of secondary importance; more significantly the 'true' interpreter must be a person (invariably male) of deep faith and moral purity, as well as an activist whose spiritual insight has been deepened through the experience of struggle. This is why religious fundamentalism is invariably associated with charismatic leadership, which gives it, critics argue, an implicitly authoritarian character.

The great strength of fundamentalism, as demonstrated by the proliferation of fundamentalist movements in the late twentieth century, is its capacity to generate political activism and mobilise the faithful. Fundamentalism thus operates on both psychological and social levels. Psychologically, its appeal is based upon its capacity to offer certainty in an uncertain world. Being religious, it addresses some of the deepest and most perplexing problems confronting humankind; being fundamentalist, it provides solutions that are straightforward, practical and above all absolute. Socially, while its appeal has extended to the educated and professional classes, religious fundamentalism has been particularly successful in addressing the aspirations of the economically and politically marginalised. Together with offering a secure identity and the prospect of social order, in the developing world in particular, it has displaced socialism as the creed of political renewal and social justice. However, amongst the limitations of fundamentalism is the fact that its simplicity and stripped-down character prevent it from dealing with complex problems or developing comprehensive solutions. Lacking a political blueprint, fundamentalists in power, as in Iran, have been forced to improvise and borrow from existing political traditions, and nowhere have fundamentalist movements and leaders been able to develop a coherent form of 'fundamentalist economics'.

## Anti-modernism

The most prominent feature of religious fundamentalism is that it dramatically turns its back on the modern world. Modernisation appears to be equated with decline and decay, typified by the spread of god-less secularism, and regeneration can only be brought about by returning to the spirit and traditions of some long-past 'golden age'. Unfortunately, however, this image is simplistic and in certain respects misleading. Religious fundamentalism is selectively traditional but also selectively modern; its relationship to modernity is characterised by a mixture of resentment and envy. One face of fundamentalism is undoubtedly its strident anti-modernism. This is most evident in its endorsement of 'traditional' values, which amounts to a form of moral conservatism. Western society, having succumbed to the cult of the individual and a passion for personal gratification, is seen as amoral at best and thoroughly degenerate at worst. Permissiveness, adultery, prostitution, homosexuality and pornography are only some of the symptoms of this moral pollution. Nothing less than a moral gulf divides liberal individualism from religious fundamentalism, the former encouraging people to make their own moral choices while the latter demands that they conform to a prescribed and divinely ordained moral system. Islamic fundamentalists therefore call for the reintroduction of ancient *Shari'a* law and Christian fundamentalists attempt to combat the spread of permissiveness and materialism by a return to 'family' or 'religious' values.

Fundamentalism should not be mistaken for conservatism or traditionalism, however. Despite overlaps between conservatism and fundamentalism and the ease with which they have sometimes constructed alliances, notably in the United States through organisations such as Moral Majority, the two differ in terms of both temper and aspirations. Conservatism is modest and cautious, where fundamentalism is strident and passionate; conservatism is disposed to protect elites and defend hierarchy, while fundamentalism embodies populist and egalitarian inclinations; conservatism favours continuity and tradition, while fundamentalism is radical and sometimes openly revolutionary. Traditionalism refers to the belief that inherited institutions and practices, particularly those with a long and continuous history, provide the best guide for human conduct. As such, fundamentalism has little in common with traditionalism, inclined as it is to favour 'novel' interpretations of religious teachings and to call for comprehensive social regeneration. There is a closer affinity between fundamentalism and the reactionary radicalism of the new right. Nevertheless fundamentalism is more clearly reactive than reactionary: behind the rhetoric of moral traditionalism, it is perhaps orientated more towards a purified future than towards an idealised past. The tendency within fundamentalism towards charismatic leadership, populism and psychosocial regeneration has also led some to suggest parallels with fascism; however this risks ignoring the degree to which fundamentalism is animated by genuinely religious passions.

The clearest evidence that fundamentalists are not just dyed-in-the-wool reactionaries is found in their enthusiasm for particular aspects of modernity. For instance fundamentalists across the globe have shrewdly exploited the advantages of modern techniques of mass communication, not least in the case of the 'televangelists' of the United States. This contrasts markedly with the revivalist and ultra-orthodox movements that have turned against the 'unredeemed' world and retreated from it by resurrecting pre-modern ways and practices. The fundamentalist

---

## Populism

Populism (from the Latin *populus*, meaning 'the people') has been used to describe both distinctive political movements and a particular tradition of political thought. Movements or parties described as populist have been characterised by their claim to support the common people in the face of 'corrupt' economic or political elites. As a political tradition, populism reflects the belief that the instincts and wishes of the people provide the principal legitimate guide to political action. Populist politicians therefore make a direct appeal to the people and claim to give expression to their deepest hopes and fears, all intermediary institutions being distrusted. Although populism may be linked to any cause or ideology, it is often seen as implicitly authoritarian, 'populist' democracy being the enemy of 'pluralist' democracy.

accommodation with modernity is not merely a cynical exercise. The willingness to accept technology, science, the machinery of the modern state and even nuclear weapons suggests sympathy for the spirit of modernity, respect for this-worldly rationalism rather than a descent into other-worldly mysticism. Early interest in Iran, for instance, in the idea of 'Islamic science' quickly gave way to an acceptance of conventional, and therefore western, science. Similarly the search for 'Islamic economics' soon developed into the application of market principles derived from economic liberalism. Finally, it is significant that fundamentalists advance an essentially modernist view of religion, relying more heavily upon 'dynamic' interpretation than upon faith in inherited structures and traditions. As Parekh (1994, p. 121) put it, fundamentalism 'reconstitutes religion within the limits of modernity, even as it copes with modernity within the limits of religion'.

## Militancy

While religious fundamentalists have embraced a conventional, state-centred view of politics, they have pursued a highly distinctive style of political activity: one that is vigorous, militant and sometimes violent. Fundamentalists are usually happy to see themselves as militants, in the sense that militancy implies the zeal and passion of one who is engaged in combat. Where does this militancy come from, and what are its implications? Fundamentalist militancy derives from a variety of sources. In the first place, there is a tendency for conflicts involving religion to be intense because religion deals with core values and beliefs. Those who act in the name of religion are inspired by what they believe to be a divinely ordained purpose, which clearly takes precedence over all other considerations. This perhaps helps to explain why religious wars have been so common throughout history.

A second factor is that fundamentalism in particular is a form of politics of identity: it serves to define who a people are and gives them a collective identity. All forms of politics of identity, whether based on social, national, ethnic or religious distinctiveness, tend to be based upon divisions between 'them' and 'us', between an 'out-group' and an 'in-group'. Certainly, religious fundamentalism has been associated with the existence of a hostile and threatening 'other', which serves both to create a heightened sense of collective identity and to strengthen its oppositional and combative character. This demonised 'other' may take various guises, from secularism and permissiveness to rival religions, westernisation, Marxism and imperialism. A third and related factor is that fundamentalists generally possess a Manichaean world view, one that emphasises conflict between light and darkness, or good and evil. If 'we' are a chosen people acting according to the will of God, 'they' are not merely people with whom we disagree, but a body actively subverting God's purpose on Earth, representing nothing less than the 'forces of darkness'. Political conflict, for fundamentalists, is therefore a battle or war, and ultimately either the believers or the infidels must prevail.

One of the consequences of this militancy is a willingness to engage in extra-legal, anti-constitutional political action. Nonetheless, although God's law outranks human law, fundamentalists do not necessarily disregard the latter, as the new Christian right's firm support for law and order demonstrates. The most controversial issue, however, is the fundamentalist use of violence. While the popular image of fundamentalists as bombers and terrorists is unbalanced and misleading as it ignores the fact that fundamentalist protest is overwhelmingly peaceful and usually legal, it is impossible to deny a link with violence. Examples, sadly, are legion. Amongst the political leaders who have been assassinated are Anwar Sadat by Islamic fundamentalists in 1981, Indira Gandhi by militant Sikhs in 1984 and Yitzak Rabin by a Jewish fanatic in 1995; other victims have included the Japanese and Italian translators of Salman Rushdie's *The Satanic Verses*, both of whom were stabbed to death in 1991. Islamic groups such as Heizbollah and Hamas have carried out concerted campaigns of terror in Lebanon and Israel respectively; communitarian violence has been perpetrated by, amongst others, militant Buddhists in Sri Lanka, Jewish fundamentalists in Israel's occupied territories and Islamic terrorists in Algeria; and anti-abortion extremists have furthered their crusade through bombings and murder.

The most common fundamentalist justification for such acts is that, as they are intended to eradicate evil, they fulfil the will of God. Islamic suicide bombers, for example, believe that in sacrificing their lives in the cause of Allah they will immediately be despatched to heaven. The incidence of violence amongst fundamentalist groups is almost certainly increased by the heightened expectations and revolutionary fervour provoked by apocalypticism, the belief that we are living in what is seen as 'end-time'. Fundamentalist movements have often subscribed to millenarianism (see p. 22), a belief in the imminent establishment of a thousand-year Kingdom of God, and articulated messianic expectations that are based on the hope of the return of God to Earth.

## The family of fundamentalisms

As Marty (1988) pointed out, the various fundamentalisms can be seen to constitute a hypothetical 'family'. Nevertheless its family members differ from one another in at least three crucial ways. First, they derive from very different religions. Although all religions have spawned fundamentalist or fundamentalist-type movements, certain religions may be more prone than others to fundamentalist developments, or place fewer obstacles in the way of emerging fundamentalism. In this respect Islam and Protestant Christianity have been seen as most likely to throw up fundamentalist movements, as both are based on a single sacred text and hold that believers have direct access to spiritual wisdom, rather than this being concentrated in the hands of accredited representatives (Parekh, 1994, pp. 123–4). Second, fundamentalisms emerge in very different societies. The impact and nature of fundamentalist movements is thus conditioned by the social, economic and political structures of the society in which they arise. Third, fundamentalisms differ according to the political causes they are associated with. These broadly fall into three categories. Religious fundamentalism can be used as a means of achieving comprehensive political renewal, which is particularly attractive to marginalised or oppressed peoples; as a way of shoring up an unpopular leader or government by creating a unified political culture; or as a means of strengthening a threatened national or ethnic identity.

## Islamic fundamentalism

Islam is the world's second largest religion and its fastest growing. There are over 750 million Moslems in the world today, spread over more than 70 countries. The strength of Islam is concentrated geographically in Asia and Africa; it is estimated, for example, that over half the population of Africa will soon be Moslem. However, it has also spread into Europe and elsewhere. Islam is not, and never has been, just a 'religion'. Rather it is a complete way of life, with instructions on moral, political and economic behaviour for individuals and nations alike. The 'way of Islam' is based upon the teachings of the Prophet Muhammad (*ca* 570–632 AD), as revealed in the Koran, which is regarded by all Moslems as the revealed word of God, and the Sunna, or 'beaten path', the traditional customs observed by devout Moslems and said to be based upon the Prophet's own life. There are two principal sects within Islam, which developed within 50 years of Muhammad's death in 632 AD. The Sunni sect represents the majority of Moslems, while the Shi'ite or Shia sect contains just over one tenth of the Moslem world.

Throughout the history of Islam there has been a conflict between religion and politics, between Islamic leaders who were often secular-minded and flexible in their application of Islamic principles to political life, and fundamentalists who believe in strict adherence to the principles and life-style of the Prophet. Fundamentalism in Islam does not mean a belief in the literal truth of the Koran, for this is accepted by all Moslems, and in that sense all Moslems are fundamentalists. Rather it means an intense and militant faith in Islamic beliefs as the overriding principles of social life and politics, as well as of personal morality. Islamic fundamentalists wish to establish the primacy of religion over politics. In practice this means the founding of an 'Islamic state', a theocracy ruled by spiritual rather than temporal authority, and applying the *Shari'a*, divine Islamic law, based upon principles expressed in the Koran. The *Shari'a* lays down a code for legal and righteous behaviour, including a system of punishment for most crimes as well as rules of personal conduct for both men and women. In common with other religions, Islam contains doctrines and beliefs that can justify a wide range of political causes. This is particularly true of Islamic economic ideas. The Koran, for example, upholds the institution of private property, which some have claimed endorses capitalism. However it also prohibits usury or profiteering, which others have argued indicates sympathy for socialism.

The revival of Islamic fundamentalism in the twentieth century commenced with the founding of the Moslem Brotherhood in Egypt in 1928. Although Egypt had gained nominal independence in 1922 and full independence was recognised in 1936, the UK retained a powerful economic and military presence in the country. The Brotherhood was founded by Hassan al Banna with a view to revitalising what he believed to be a corrupted Islamic faith and providing the faithful with a political voice, a party of Islam. The Brotherhood sought to found an Islamic government that would provide an alternative to both capitalist and socialist forms of development. Such a government would transform the social system by applying Islamic principles to economic and political life as well as personal morality. This process of spiritual purification would also involve the final liberation of Egypt from foreign control, and the Brotherhood envisaged the ultimate liberation and unity of all Islamic peoples. The Brotherhood spread into Jordan, Sudan and Syria, where it set up branches containing mosques, schools, youth clubs and even business enterprises. It trained young people physically and militarily to prepare them for the coming *jihad*, or holy war, through which they would achieve their objectives.

The political appeal of Islam for the Brotherhood was that, unlike liberalism, socialism and conventional forms of nationalism, it had not been inherited or borrowed from the West. The desire for independence was understood to involve a process of spiritual purification because colonial peoples needed to regain self-respect and purge themselves of western ideas and influences. In preaching a return to traditional institutions and principles, Islamic fundamentalists therefore expressed a powerful desire for political and cultural independence from the West. This was evident in the fact that the Moslem Brotherhood was founded in Ismailiya, which at the time was the headquarters of the Suez Canal Company and an important base for British troops. The other Arab countries to which fundamentalist ideas spread were also under either UK or French control.

Nevertheless fundamentalism remained on the fringe of Arab politics while Arab leaders either looked to the West or, after the rise of Gamal Nasser in Egypt, supported some form of Arab socialism. Nasser nationalised the Suez Canal in 1956 and, after surviving military intervention from the UK, France and Israel, became the undisputed leader of the Arab world. Nasser's socialism encouraged him to forge a close diplomatic relationship with the Soviet Union and to suppress the Moslem Brotherhood. However Egypt's defeat in the Arab–Israeli war of 1967 greatly discredited the ideas of Arab socialism and provided an opportunity for the growth of the fundamentalist movement. Despite the ending of colonial rule, the countries of the Middle East and North Africa were acutely aware of their continued economic dependence on the West or the Soviet Union, and of their political impotence, symbolised by the survival of the state of Israel. In those circumstances, resurgent nationalism once again took the form of Islamic fundamentalism. Since the 1970s fundamentalist groups sprang up in most Islamic countries and attracted growing support amongst the young and the politically committed.

## Ayatollah Ruhollah Khomeini (1900–89)

Iranian cleric and political leader. The son and grandson of Shi'ite clergy, Khomeini received a religious education and eventually became one of the foremost scholars in the major theological centre in Qom. He came to national prominence in 1944 by attacking the secular policies of Shah Rezapahlavi and was expelled from Iran in 1964. Khomeini's return from exile in 1979 sparked the popular revolution that overthrew the shahdom, leaving the Ayatollah (literally, 'gift of God') as the supreme leader of the world's first Islamic state until his death.

Although Khomeini raised the idea of Islamic government as early as the 1940s, his notion of institutionalised clerical rule, the basis of an 'Islamic republic', did not emerge until the late 1960s. He acknowledged that this was based upon a novel interpretation of Islamic doctrine, as the realisation of political Islam was to occur in the absence of the Prophet's successor. Khomeini's world view was rooted in a clear division between the oppressed, understood largely as the poor and excluded of the Third World, and the oppressors, seen as the twin Satans: the United States and the Soviet Union, capitalism and communism, the West and the East. Islam thus became a theo-political project aimed at regenerating the Islamic world by ridding it of occupation and corruption from outside.

The focal point of this process hass been Iran, where in 1979 a popular revolution brought Ayatollah Khomeini to power and led to Iran being the first country to declare itself an 'Islamic Republic'. The Iranian example has inspired fundamentalist groups in many parts of the world. In 1981 the Moslem Brotherhood assassinated President Sadat of Egypt; and the leaders of several Islamic countries, for example Pakistan and Sudan, under growing pressure from fundamentalists, introduced *Shari'a* law. Fundamentalism has been particularly prominent in the Lebanon, divided as it was in the 1980s by civil war between Christians and Moslems, and occupied by Israel in the south and by Syria in the north. Parts of Beirut fell under the control of fundamentalist groups such as the Iranian-backed Hezbollah or 'Party of God', which carried out a number of well-publicised kidnappings of Western hostages.

Islam was also a significant component of the Gulf War of 1991. In many ways Saddam Hussein was slow to grasp the political potential of Islamic fundamentalism. The Ba'athist movement, which he led, espoused an ideology based upon a fusion of socialism and pan-Arab nationalism, inspired by the example of Nasser. By declaring war against Iran in 1980, Saddam was attempting to destroy radical Islamic fundamentalism and hence enjoyed the support of both the West and conservative Gulf states. However, on the eve of the Gulf War Saddam openly embraced Islamic principles, declaring the coming war to be a *jihad* between 'true believers' and 'the infidel'. The words 'God is Great' were added to the Iraqi flag and the motto of the Ba'athist party was changed to 'The Believers stride forward'. The subsequent advance of Islamism in the 1990s has taken a variety of forms. In the case of Turkey, constitutional fundamentalism became increasingly prominent through the growing parliamentary strength of the Welfare Party, while in 1997 the Taliban guerrillas seized power in Afghanistan, representing the forces of revolutionary fundamentalism.

Political Islam has also had growing influence within western countries. This was evident as long ago as 1929 with the formation of the Black Muslims in the United States, which under the leadership of Malcolm X (1926–65) developed into the radical Black Power movement during the 1960s. More recently the impact of Islam has been demonstrated in the conflict over the publication of Salman Rushdie's *The Satanic Verses*. Moslems in the UK and elsewhere campaigned to ban this book, which they believed insulted the Prophet and denigrated Islamic principles. In 1988 Khomeini issued a *fatwa*, or religious order, condemning Rushdie to death. The Rushdie affair in the UK indicates the potential that exists for the growth of fundamentalist ideas within cultures that are perceived as intolerant and insensitive to racial minorities. At the same time it under-

lines the gulf that has developed between the values of Islamic fundamentalism and those of western liberal democracy.

## Shi'ite fundamentalism

Iran has come to symbolise the revival of political Islam, and
fundamentalist groups in countries such as the Lebanon, Pakistan,
Afghanistan and the UK look to Iran for spiritual and political leadership.
The majority of Iran's population are members of the Shi'ite sect, the
smaller of the two Islamic sects. The division of Islam into two sects is
politically significant because the temper and political aspirations of the
two have traditionally diverged. The split was provoked by differences
over the question of the Prophet Muhammad's successors. The Sunnis
believed that only the first four caliphs or deputies who succeeded
Muhammad, the 'Rightly Guided Caliphs', had received divine wisdom.
The last of these was the Prophet's cousin, Ali, and the Sunnis thought that
Ali's successors should be determined by a consensus amongst the ulama,
or notable clerics. However a leader so chosen could no longer be regarded
as divine or infallible. In contrast the Shi'ites believed that divine wisdom
continued to be transmitted to the descendants of Ali and Fatima, one of
the Prophet's daughters. As a result the Shi'ites have held that each
succeeding imam, or religious leader, is immaculate and infallible, and
therefore commands absolute religious and political authority.

Sunnis have tended to see Islamic history as a gradual movement away
from the ideal community, which existed during the life of Muhammad
and his four immediate successors. Shi'ites, though, believe that divine
guidance is always available in the teachings of the infallible imam, or that
divine wisdom is about to re-emerge into the world with the return of the
'hidden imam', or the arrival of the mahdi, a leader directly guided by
God. Shi'ites see history moving towards the goal of an ideal community,
not away from it. Such ideas of revival or imminent salvation have given
the Shi'ite sect a messianic and emotional quality that is not enjoyed by the
traditionally more sober Sunnis. The religious temper of the Shi'ite sect is
also different from that of the Sunnis. Shi'ites believe that it is possible for
an individual to remove the stains of sin through the experience of
suffering and by leading a devout and simple life. The prospect of spiritual
salvation has given the Shi'ite sect its characteristic intensity and emotional
strength. When such religious zeal has been harnessed to a political goal it
has generated fierce commitment and devotion. The Shi'ite sect has
traditionally been more political than the Sunni sect. It has proved
especially attractive to the poor and the downtrodden, for whom the
re-emergence of divine wisdom into the world has represented the
purification of society, the overthrow of injustice and liberation from
oppression.

Although Iran, known before 1935 as Persia, has been a sovereign state since the fifteenth century, during the twentieth century it came under the growing influence of foreign countries that were keen to exploit its oil reserves. First the UK and then the United States manipulated Iranian politics in order to safeguard their business investments. Under Shah Rezakhan and, after 1941, his son, Shah Rezapahlavi, the country embarked upon a programme of modernisation, in close collaboration with western oil companies. In the 1970s Iran experienced a dramatic resurgence of fundamentalism, stimulated by reaction against the materialism and secular culture promoted by the Shah, and the continuing domination of Iran by western, and particularly US, interests. The movement focused around the leadership of Ayatollah Khomeini, who coordinated resistance to the Shah from his Paris home. In 1979 a growing wave of popular demonstrations forced the Shah to flee the country and prepared the way for Khomeini's return. Iran was declared an Islamic Republic and power fell into the hands of the Islamic Revolutionary Council, comprising 15 senior clerics, dominated by Khomeini himself. All legislation passed by the popularly elected Islamic Consultative Assembly has to be ratified by the Council for the Protection of the Constitution, on which sit six religious and six secular lawyers, to ensure that it conforms to Islamic principles.

In effect Iran became an absolutist theocracy under the unquestioned leadership of Khomeini. Iran exhibited a fierce religious consciousness, reflected in popular antipathy to the 'Great Satan', the United States, and the application of strict Islamic principles to social and political life. For example in 1981 the wearing of a headscarf and *chador*, loose-fitting clothes, became obligatory for all women in Iran, Moslems and non-Moslems alike. Restrictions on polygamy were removed, contraception was banned, adultery punished by public flogging or execution, and the death penalty was introduced for homosexuality. Both Iranian politics and society were thoroughly 'Islamised' and Friday prayers in Tehran became an expression of official government policy and a focal point of political life. The religious nationalism generated by the Islamic Revolution reached new heights when Iran was invaded by Iraq in 1980. Popular resistance to Iraq was organised by the Islamic Revolutionary Guards, who enlisted volunteers, many of them young boys, inspired to fight by a potent combination of patriotism and religious fervour. Iraq had not only invaded Iran, but had committed an offence against the 'Government of God' and therefore against Islam itself.

The abrupt end of the Iran–Iraq War in 1988 and the death of Ayatollah Khomeini the next year paved the way for more moderate forces to surface within Iran. The Iranian economy had been devastated by the massive cost of the eight-year war and the lack of foreign trade and investment.

Economic revival would be impossible unless Iran's diplomatic isolation from the industrialised West was brought to an end. The gradual emergence of Hashemi Rafsanjani, speaker of the Iranian parliament (the Islamic Consultative Assembly), and his election as president in 1989 marked a more pragmatic and less ideological turn in Iranian politics. Militant Islam nevertheless reasserted itself through the Taliban victory in Afghanistan, which resulted in the imposition of strict theocratic rule and the exclusion of women from education, the economy and public life in general.

The Iranian Revolution demonstrates the remarkable political power of Islam in general and of Shi'ite fundamentalism in particular. It has dramatically altered the political balance in North Africa and throughout the Middle East. Indeed political Islam now constitutes a major alternative, and a significant threat, to the dominance of western ideologies in many parts of the world. However the survival of revolutionary zeal in Iran itself was closely tied up with the patriotic war fought against invading Iraq and the continuing messianic influence of Khomeini himself. Once these factors were removed, Iran gradually began to recognised that exclusive and militant fundamentalism is unworkable in an increasingly interdependent world.

## Christian fundamentalism

With about 1500 million adherents, Christianity is the world's largest religion. From its origins in Palestine, it was spread via the Roman Empire throughout Europe and was later exported to North America by European settlers. Despite attempts to extend Christianity further by conquest and missionary endeavour, by 1900 about 83 per cent of the world's Christians still lived in the West. However, while during the twentieth century Christian belief declined in the West, especially in Europe, vigorous growth occurred in the developing world, meaning that the majority of Christians now live in Africa, Asia and Latin America.

Christianity began as a movement within Judaism. It was distinguished by the belief that Jesus was the messiah prophesied in the Old Testament, and his life and teachings are described in the New Testament. Although all Christians acknowledge the authority of the Bible, three main divisions have emerged: the Catholic, Orthodox and Protestant churches. Roman Catholicism is based on the temporal and spiritual leadership of the pope in Rome, seen as unchallengeable since the doctrine of papal infallibility was promulgated in 1870. Eastern Orthodox Christianity emerged from the split with Rome in 1054 and developed into a number of autonomous churches, the Russian Orthodox Church and the Greek Orthodox Church being the most significant. Protestantism embraces a variety of movements that during the Reformation of the sixteenth century rejected Roman authority and established reformed national forms of Christianity. The most influential Protestant movements were Lutheranism in Sweden and parts of Germany, Calvinism in Geneva and Scotland, and Anglicanism in England. Although there are many doctrinal divisions amongst Protestants, Protestantism tends to be characterised by the belief that the Bible is the sole source of truth and by the idea that it is possible for people to have a direct relationship with God.

Since the Reformation the political significance of Christianity has declined markedly. The advance of liberal constitutionalism was in part reflected in the separation of church and state, and in the thoroughgoing secularisation of political life. Christianity, at least in the developed West, adjusted to these circumstances by increasingly becoming a personal religion, geared more to the spiritual salvation of the individual than to the moral and political regeneration of society. This in turn helped to shape the character of Christian fundamentalism in the late twentieth century. Confronted by stable social, economic and political structures, rooted in secular values and goals, fundamentalists have been mainly content to work within a pluralist and constitutional framework. Rather than seeking to establish a theocracy, they have usually campaigned around single issues, or concentrated their attention on moral crusading.

One of the causes that Christian fundamentalism has helped to articulate is ethnic nationalism. This has been evident in Northern Ireland, where an upsurge in evangelical Protestantism has been one of the consequences of 'the troubles' since 1969. Largely expressed through Ian Paisley's breakaway Free Presbyterian Church and organised politically by the Democratic Unionist Party (DUP), Ulster fundamentalism largely operates by equating the idea of a united Ireland with the victory of Catholicism and Rome. Although Paisley himself has never actively promoted violence, he has warned that, should reunification go ahead, he would lead the Protestant community in armed resistance. By appealing to working-class Protestants as well as fundamentalists, Paisley and his supporters have succeeded, as Steve Bruce (1993, p. 57) put it, in keeping 'the iron in the soul of Ulster unionism' and blocking political moves that might ultimately lead to the establishment of a united Ireland. However, the theological basis of Paisleyite resistance is drawn heavily from the United States, the birthplace of evangelical Protestantism and home of the most influential Christian fundamentalist movement, the new Christian right.

## The new Christian right

In terms of the number of church-going Christians, the United States is easily the most religious of western countries. About 60 million American citizens claim to have been 'born again' and half of these describe themselves as fundamentalists. This largely reflects the fact that from its earliest days America provided a refuge for religious sects and movements wishing to escape from persecution. During the nineteenth century a fierce battle was fought within American Protestantism between modernists, who adopted a liberal view of the Bible, and conservatives (later 'fundamentalists') who took a literal view of it. Nevertheless such religious passions and views were largely confined to the private world of the family and the home. Religious groups were rarely drawn into active politics, and when they were, they were rarely successful. The introduction of prohibition, 1920–33, was a notable exception to this. The new Christian right, which emerged in the late 1970s, was therefore a novel development in that it sought to fuse religion and politics in attempting to 'turn America back to Christ'.

The 'new Christian right' is an umbrella term that describes a broad coalition of groups that are primarily concerned with moral and social issues and are intent on maintaining or restoring what they see as 'Christian culture'. Two main factors explain its emergence. The first is that in the post-war period the United States, as elsewhere, experienced a significant extension of the public sphere. For instance in the early 1960s the Supreme Court ruled against the use of prayers in American schools (because it was contrary to the First Amendment, which guarantees religious freedom), civil rights legislation led to employment quotas and the enforced desegregation of schools through bussing, and, particularly as part of Lyndon Johnson's 'Great Society' initiative, there was a proliferation of welfare, urban development and other programmes. The result of this was that many 'God-fearing' southern conservatives felt that their traditional values and way of life were being threatened, and that the Washington-based liberal establishment was to blame.

The second factor was the increasingly political prominence of groups representing blacks, women and homosexuals, whose advance threatened traditional social structures, particularly in rural and small-town America. As the new Christian right emerged in the 1970s to campaign for the restoration of 'traditional family values', its particular targets thus included 'affirmative action' (positive discrimination in favour of blacks), feminism (particularly the proposed Equal Rights Amendment) and the gay rights movement. In the 1980s and 1990s this politics of morality increasingly coalesced around the anti-abortion issue.

A variety of organisations emerged to articulate these concerns, often mobilised by noted televangelists. These included the Religious Round Table, Christian Voice, American Coalition for Traditional Values and the most influential of all, Moral Majority, formed by Jerry Falwell in 1980. Although Catholics were prominent in the anti-abortion movement, new

Christian right groups drew particularly from the ranks of evangelical Protestants who as 'Bible believers' subscribed to scriptural inerrancy, and often claimed to be 'born again' in the sense that they had undergone a personal experience of conversion to Christ. Divisions nevertheless exist amongst evangelicals, for instance between those who style themselves as fundamentalists and tend to keep apart from non-believing society, and charismatics, who believe that the Holy Spirit can operate through individuals giving them the gifts of prophesy and healing. During the 1980s Moral Majority and other such groups provided campaign finance and organised voter-registration drives with a view to targeting liberal or 'pro-choice' Democrats and encouraging Republicans to embrace a new social and moral agenda based on opposition to abortion and calls for the restoration of prayers in US schools. Ronald Reagan's willingness to embrace this agenda in the 1980s meant that the new Christian right became an important component of a new Republican coalition that placed as much emphasis on moral issues as it did on traditional ones such as the economy and foreign policy.

Since the late 1980s, however, the limitations of political Protestantism have become increasingly apparent. In the first place the movement was damaged by a series of financial and sexual scandals involving televangelists such as Jimmy Swaggart. More importantly, although Reagan eagerly adopted the rhetoric of the Christian right, apart from making 'pro-life' appointments to the Supreme Court he failed to deliver on its moral agenda. Anxiety amongst evangelicals was further heightened by the fact that Reagan's successor, George Bush, was not 'one of them' (until 1980, for instance, he supported abortion) and also broke his campaign promise not to put up taxes. This prompted the Christian right to put up its own candidate for the presidency, leading to televangelst Pat Robertson's unsuccessful 1992 bid for the Republican nomination.

Robertson's failure and Reagan and Bush's unwillingness to deliver highlight the two principal stumbling blocks encountered by the movement. In addition to the Christian right's inability to extend its political base beyond the white evangelical Protestant community, mainstream parties in pluralistic societies such as the United States cannot afford to be exclusively linked to any single social, ethnic or religious interest. In response to these problems, elements of the evangelical movement have adopted more militant strategies. In the case of Operation Rescue, set up by Randal Terry in 1987 to fight abortion, this has meant the adoption of peaceful civil disobedience tactics that are consciously modelled on those employed by the civil rights movement in the 1960s. Conversely the so-called militias, which claim to be influenced by shady groups such as the Christian Patriots, have resorted to a campaign of terrorism, exemplified by the Oklahoma bombing in the spring of 1995.

## Other fundamentalisms

Islam and Protestant Christianity have been distinguished by their capacity to throw up comprehensive programmes of political renewal, albeit with very different characters and ambitions. In most cases, however, other fundamentalist movements have been more narrowly concerned with helping to clarify or redefine national or ethnic identity. In this sense many fundamentalisms can be seen as subvarieties of ethnic nationalism. This has usually occurred as a reaction to a change in national identity, occasioned by the growth of rival ethnic or religious groups or actual or threatened territorial changes. The attraction of religion rather than the nation as the principal source of political identity is that it provides a supposedly primordial and seemingly unchangeable basis for the establishment of group membership, which is why it tends to be associated with the emergence of an enclave culture. The fundamentalism of Ulster Protestants – whose religion gives their national identity, their 'Britishness', an ethnic substance – is very different from the fundamentalism of US evangelicals, which has little bearing on their ethnicity. Hindu, Sikh, Jewish and Buddhist fundamentalism also resemble forms of ethnic mobilisation.

Hinduism, the principal religion of India, appears on the surface to be relatively inhospitable to fundamentalism. It is the clearest example of an ethnic religion where emphasis is placed on custom and social practice rather than formal texts or doctrines, which are anyway remarkably diverse. Little scope is therefore left for protest against the expansion of the public realm, since the public/private distinction is at odds with the very spirit of Hinduism. Nevertheless, although marginal in comparison with secular parties such as the Congress Party, a fundamentalist movement emerged out of the struggle for Indian independence and gained greater support after the achievement of independence in 1947. Its key goal was to challenge the multicultural, multi-ethnic mosaic of India by making Hinduism the basis of national identity. This was not expressed in demands for the expulsion of 'foreign' religions and culture so much as in a call for the Hinduisation of Moslem, Sikh, Jain and other communities. Particularist and ethnic groups have flourished in India since the decline of Congress and the collapse of the Nehru–Gandhi dynasty in the mid-1980s, Hindu fundamentalists and their principal political voice, the Bharatiya Janata Party (BJP), being the clearest beneficiaries. The most dramatic demonstration of Hindu militancy came in 1992 with the destruction of the ancient Babri Masjid mosque in Ayodhya, believed to have been built on the birthplace of the god Rama. Electoral progress has also been impressive, with the BJP becoming the largest party in the Indian parliament in 1996. However the weakness of Hindu fundamentalism is that, in common with most ethnic movements, it has struggled to build alliances with other groups and movements and is unable to extend its political base beyond its own enclave.

Sikh fundamentalism is different in that it is associated with the struggle to found an independent nation-state, not with the remaking of national identity within an existing one. As such it overlaps with the concerns of liberal nationalism, and is distinguished from the latter only by its vision of the nation as an essentially religious entity. Sikh nationalists thus look to establish 'Khalistan', located in present-day Punjab, with Sikhism as the state religion and its government obliged to ensure its unhindered flourishing. Just as Hindu nationalism has a markedly anti-Islamic character, Sikh nationalism is in part defined by its antipathy towards Hinduism. This was evident in the seizing of the Golden Temple in Amritsar in 1982 by the Damdami Taksal, under its militant leader Bhindranwale, and in the assassination of Indira Gandhi two years later, following the storming of the temple. The separate upsurges in Hindu, Sikh and Islamic fundamentalism in the Indian subcontinent are undoubtedly interconnected developments. Not only have they created a chain reaction of threats and resentments, but they have also inspired one another by closely linking ethnic identity to religious fervour.

Both Jewish and Buddhist fundamentalisms are also closely linked to the sharpening of ethnic conflict. In contrast with the ultra-orthodox Jews, some of whom have refused to accept Israel as the Jewish state prophesied in the Old Testament, Jewish fundamentalists have transformed Zionism into a defence of the 'Greater Land of Israel', characterised by territorial

## Zionism

Zionism (Zion is Hebrew for the Kingdom of Heaven) is the movement for the establishment of a Jewish homeland, usually seen as located in Palestine. The idea was first advanced in 1897 by Theodore Herzl (1860–1904) at the World Zionist Congress in Basle. It was a direct consequence of anti-Semitism (see p. 230), in that it was seen as the only means of protecting the Jewish people from persecution. Chaim Weizmann (1874–1952), later the first president of Israel, was influential in insisting that a Jewish nation could only be recreated in Palestine. Early Zionists had secularist and nationalistic aspirations, often associated with socialist sympathies. Since the foundation of the state of Israel in 1948, however, Zionism has come to be associated both with the continuing promise of Israel to provide a home for all Jews and with attempts to promote sympathy for Israel and defend it against its enemies. In the latter sense it has been recruited to the cause of fundamentalism, and according to Palestinians it has acquired an expansionist, anti-Arab character.

aggressiveness. In the case of Israel's best known fundamentalist group, Gushmun Emunim (Bloc of the Faithful), this has been expressed in a campaign to build Jewish settlements in territory occupied in the Six Day War of 1968 and then formally incorporated into Israel. More radical groups such as Katch (Thus), led until his assassination in 1990 by Rabbi Meir Kahane, proclaimed that Jews and Arabs can never live together and so look to the expulsion of all Arabs from what they see as the 'promised land'.

The spread of Buddhist nationalism in Sri Lanka has largely occurred as a result of growing tension between the majority and largely Buddhist Sinhalese population and the minority Tamil community, comprising Hindus, Christians and Moslems. Although on the surface – by virtue of its commitment to individual responsibility, religious toleration and non-violence – Buddhism is the least fundamentalist of the major religions (Dalai Lama, 1996), the Theravada Buddhism of Southern Asia has supported fundamentalist-type developments when nationalism and religious revivalism have been intertwined. In Sri Lanka the drive for the Sinhalisation of national identity, advanced by militant groups such as the People's Liberation Front, have been expressed in the demand that Buddhism be made a state religion. Such pressures, however, have merely fuelled Tamil separatism, and since the late 1970s they have given rise to the terrorist campaign waged by the Tamil Tigers.

## Religious fundamentalism in the twenty-first century

Is religious fundamentalism destined to survive into the twenty-first century, or will it ultimately be viewed as a phenomenon peculiar to the late twentieth century? The question of the future of fundamentalism raises two starkly different scenarios. The first questions the long-term viability of any religiously based political creed in the modern world, and highlights the particular limitations of fundamentalism as a political project. According to this view, fundamentalist religion is essentially a *symptom* of the difficult adjustments that modernisation brings about, but it is ultimately doomed because it is out of step with the principal thrust of the modernisation process. Modernisation as westernisation is destined to prevail because it is supported by the trend towards economic globalisation and the spread of liberal democracy. Religion will therefore be restored to its 'proper' private domain, and public affairs will once again be contested by secular political creeds.

This analysis suggests that the theo-political project that lies at the heart of fundamentalism will gradually fade, with religious groups becoming mere components of broader nationalist movements. The emergence of a western-dominated global system may allow for the survival of civic nationalism, orientated around the goal of self-determination, but it suggests that there is little future for militant ethnic nationalisms, especially when they are based upon religious distinctiveness. The limitations of fundamentalism will thus become particularly apparent if fundamentalists succeed in winning power and are confronted with the complex tasks of government. Lacking a clear political programme or a coherent economic philosophy, fundamentalism as an ideology of protest will survive, if it survives at all, only as rhetoric or as the 'founding myth' of a regime.

The rival view holds that religious fundamentalism offers a glimpse of the 'postmodern' future. From this perspective it is secularism and liberal culture that are in crisis. Their weakness, dramatically exposed by fundamentalism, is their failure to address deeper human needs and their inability to establish authoritative values that give social order a moral foundation. Far from the emerging global system fostering uniformity modelled on western liberal democracy, a more likely scenario is that the twentieth-century battle between capitalism and communism will give way to some form of clash of civilisations. Competing transnational power blocs will emerge, and religion is likely to provide them with a distinctive politico-cultural identity. In this version, fundamentalism is seen to have strengths rather than weaknesses. Religious fundamentalists have already demonstrated their adaptability by embracing the weapons and spirit of the modern world, and the very fact that they are not encumbered by tradition but travel 'fast and light' enables them to reinvent their creeds in response to the challenges of postmodernity.

## Further reading

Ahmed, A. and H. Donnan, *Islam, Globalisation and Postmodernity* (London and New York: Routledge, 1994). A useful collection of essays examining both the nature of political Islam and its relationship to modernity.

Hadden, J. K. and A. Shupe (eds), *Prophetic Religions and Politics: Religion and Political Order* (New York: Paragon House, 1986). A useful collection of essays by noted sociologists of religion that examines a wide range of movements across the globe.

Hiro, D., *Islamic Fundamentalism* (London: Paladin, 1988). A good and accessible account of the development and impact of fundamentalist Islam.

Marty, M. E. and R. S. Appleby (eds), *Fundamentalisms and the State: Remaking Polities, Economies, and Militance* (Chicago and London: University of Chicago Press, 1993). Part of the massively comprehensive, authoritative yet accessible six-volume Fundamentalism Project. Other volumes that are of interest include *Fundamentalism Observed* (1991) and *Accounting for Fundamentalisms* (1994).

Parekh, B., 'The Concept of Fundamentalism' in A. Shtromas (ed.), *The End of 'isms'? Reflections on the Fate of Ideological Politics after Communism's Collapse* (Oxford, and Cambridge, Mass.: Blackwell, 1994). A clear and insightful introduction to the nature of fundamentalism and the modernisation process.

# Chapter 11

# Conclusion: Ideology without End?

The end of politics
The end of ideology
The end of history
The end of modernity

Political ideology has been an essential component of world history for over two hundred years. Ideology sprang out of the upheavals – economic, social and political – through which the modern world took shape, and has been intimately involved in the continuing process of social transformation and political development. Although ideology emerged first in the industrialising West, it has subsequently appeared throughout the globe, creating a worldwide language of political discourse. However opinion has been deeply divided about the role that ideology has played in human history. Has ideology served the cause of truth, progress and justice, or has it generated distorted and blinkered world views, resulting in intolerance and oppression?

This debate goes back to the nineteenth century and the firm distinction that Marx (see p. 126) drew between 'ideology' and 'science'. The notion that science provides an objective and value-free method of advancing human knowledge, so releasing humanity from enslavement to irrational ideologies, has been one of the enduring myths of modern times. Science is not the antithesis of ideology, but can perhaps be seen as an ideology in its own right. For instance science has been linked to the interests of powerful social forces, in particular those represented by industry and technology. It has contributed to a profound process of social change and become, in a sense, the ruling ideology of industrial society. Ideology, from this point of view, is simply a means by which a social group or an entire society achieves a measure of self-consciousness, by establishing a common identity or a set of collective goals. As such ideology should not be thought of as liberating or oppressive, nor as true or false. It can be any of these things. The character of ideology is shaped by the historical forces from which it emerges and is fashioned by the social and political needs it serves. Ideology has therefore come to be an indispensable and ineradicable feature of the human condition. Nevertheless it is remarkable how often political thinkers have proclaimed that ideology has been, or should be, brought to an end.

## The end of politics

One of the earliest versions of this argument was the assertion that politics can disappear or will be abolished. In its broadest sense, politics is a social activity that occurs whenever conflict is present. Politics involves the expression of rival opinions or opposing interests; in essence it is the attempt to resolve any form of social conflict. It therefore takes place when disagreements emerge within a family, when antagonism occurs between communities or social classes, and also when conflict breaks out amongst nations or states. Politics, then, can only end when conflict is replaced by spontaneous harmony and agreement. Some political thinkers have believed this to be possible.

Marxists and anarchists have been the most prominent exponents of the idea of the 'end of politics'. Marxists believe that the major divisions in society are economic, and that they take the form of class conflict between capitalists and workers, or between the rich and the poor. However if wealth is owned in common by all, the source of class conflict is removed and with it the need for politics, a view that Marx expressed in his famous prediction that, with the achievement of full communism, the state will 'wither away'. As ideology, in Marx's view, constitutes the ideas of the ruling class, this too will wither away. The mere fact that this goal has never been achieved does not prove that it cannot be achieved, but it is certainly a utopian vision. Even if all significant conflicts are agreed to be economic, the ability to satisfy material needs is restricted by the fact that economic resources are limited. Universal prosperity has probably always been a hopeless dream, but this is now underlined by a growing awareness of the environmental 'limits to growth'. Moreover the experience of consumerism in the affluent West offers little support for the belief that material needs can ever be satisfied: the more people have, the more they seem to want. If politics is about 'who gets what', it is difficult to envisage it ever coming to an end.

## The end of ideology

In other cases thinkers have accepted that politics may persist, but have predicted the 'end of ideology'. The most influential statement on this position was made by Daniel Bell in *The End of Ideology* (1960). Bell was impressed by the fact that after the Second World War politics in the West was characterised by broad agreement amongst major political parties and

## Daniel Bell (born 1919)

US academic and essayist. As professor of sociology at Harvard University, Bell developed an analysis of modern society that had a broad political as well as an academic impact. In the 1960s, with Irving Kristol, he founded the journal *The Public Interest*, which has attacked the philosophy of 'big' government, and helped to give neoconservatism intellectual credibility in the United States.

In *The End of Ideology* (1960), Bell drew attention to the exhaustion of rationalist approaches to social and political issues, and, in the Afterword to the 1988 edition, he warned against tyranny of utopian end-states. *The Coming of Post-Industrial Society* (1973) highlighted the emergence of 'information societies' dominated by a new 'knowledge class' of scientists and professionals. In *The Cultural Contradictions of Capitalism* (1976), Bell analysed the growing tension between the need for rationality and efficiency to sustain production and capitalism's tendency to strengthen values such as 'feeling', personal gratification and self-expression.

the absence of ideological division or debate. Fascism and communism had both lost their appeal, while the remaining parties disagreed only about which of them could best be relied upon to deliver economic growth and material prosperity. In effect, economics had triumphed over politics. Politics was reduced to technical questions about 'how' to deliver affluence, and had ceased to address moral or philosophical questions about the nature of the 'good society'. To all intents and purposes ideology had become an irrelevance.

However the process to which Bell drew attention was not the 'end of ideology' so much as the emergence of a broad ideological consensus amongst major parties and therefore the suspension of ideological debate. In the immediate post-war period, representatives of the three major western ideologies – liberalism, socialism and conservatism – came to accept the common goal of 'managed capitalism'. This goal, however, was itself ideological, for example it reflected an enduring faith in market economics, private property and material incentives, tempered by a belief in social welfare and economic intervention. In effect an ideology of 'welfare capitalism' or 'social democracy' had triumphed over its rivals, although this triumph proved to be only temporary. The 1960s witnessed the rise of more radical new left ideas, a revival of interest in Marxist and anarchist thought and the growth of modern ideologies such as feminism and ecologism. The onset of economic recession in the 1970s provoked renewed interest in long-neglected, free-market doctrines and stimulated the development of new right theories, which also challenged the post-war consensus.

Finally, the 'end of ideology' thesis focused attention exclusively upon developments in the industrialised West and ignored the fact that communism remained firmly entrenched in the Soviet Union, eastern Europe, China and elsewhere, and that revolutionary political movements were operating in Asia, Africa and parts of Latin America.

## The end of history

A more recent and broader perspective has been adopted by Francis Fukuyama in his essay 'The End of History' (1989). Unlike Bell, Fukuyama did not suggest that political ideas had become irrelevant, but that one particular set of ideas, western liberalism, had triumphed over all its rivals. Fascism was defeated in 1945, and Fukuyama clearly believes that the collapse of communist rule in eastern Europe in 1989 marked the passing of Marxism–Leninism as an ideology of world significance. By the 'end of history', Fukuyama meant that the history of ideas has ended, and with it, fundamental ideological debate. Throughout the world there is broad agreement on the desirability of liberal democracy, by which he means a market or capitalist economy and an open, competitive political system. Without doubt, the eastern European revolutions of 1989–91 and the dramatic reform of surviving communist regimes such as China have profoundly altered the worldwide balance of ideological debate. However it is far less certain that this process amounts to the 'end of history'.

One difficulty with the idea of the 'end of history' is that no sooner had it been proclaimed than new ideological forces rose to the surface. While liberal democracy may have made impressive progress during the twentieth century, as the century draws to its close there is undoubted evidence of the revival of very different ideologies, notably political Islam, whose influence extends from the Moslem countries of Asia and Africa into the former Soviet Union and also the industrialised West. It is possible, for example, that the 'death of communism' in the Soviet Union and eastern Europe may prepare the way for the revival of nationalism, racialism or religious fundamentalism, rather than lead to a smooth and inevitable transition towards liberal democracy.

Underlying Fukuyama's thesis is the optimistic belief, inherited from classical liberalism, that industrial capitalism offers all members of society the prospect of social mobility and material security, encouraging every citizen to regard it as reasonable and attractive. In other words it is possible for a broad, even universal, agreement to be achieved about the nature of the 'good society'. This can nevertheless only be achieved if a society can be constructed that is capable both of satisfying the interests of all major social groups and of fulfilling the aspirations of at least a

## Perspectives on . . .

### History

**Liberals** see history as progress, brought about as each generation advances further than the last through the accumulation of knowledge and understanding. Liberals generally believe that this will happen through gradual or incremental reform, not through revolution.

**Conservatives** understand history in terms of tradition and continuity, allowing little scope for progress. The lessons of the past provide guidance for present and future conduct. Reactionary conservatives believe that history is marked by decline, and wish to return to an earlier and preferred time.

**Socialists** are committed to a progressive view of history, which places heavy emphasis on the scope for social and personal development. Marxists believe that class conflict is the motor of history and that a classless, communist society is history's determinant end-point.

**Fascists** generally view history as a process of degeneration and decay, a decline from a past 'golden age'. They nevertheless subscribe to a cyclical theory of history that holds out the possibility of national rebirth and regeneration, usually through violent struggle and war.

**Fundamentalists** have an ambivalent attitude towards history. Although they tend to see the present as morally and spiritually corrupt in comparison with an idealised past, they conceive of social regeneration in modernist terms, thus rejecting conservative traditionalism.

substantial majority of individual citizens. Despite the undoubted vigour and efficiency that the capitalist market has demonstrated, it certainly cannot be said that capitalism has treated all social classes or all individuals alike. Ideological conflict and debate are thus unlikely to end in the late twentieth century with the ultimate worldwide triumph of liberalism, any more than they did with the 'inevitable' victory of socialism that was widely predicted at the end of the nineteenth century.

## The end of modernity

Yet another form of 'endism' is the belief that, as the established features of modern society have crumbled, the political creeds and doctrines that it threw up have been rendered irrelevant. This notion is usually advanced through the ideas of postmodernity or postmodernism. The central theme of postmodernism was summed up by Jean-François Lyotard in *The Postmodern Condition* (1984) as 'incredulity towards meta-narratives'. In this view conventional creeds and the major ideological traditions are based on universal theories of history that view society as a coherent totality, hence they are seen as metanarratives. Political debate during the 'modern' period thus took the form of contested universalism, each ideology claiming to offer a version of truth that is applicable to all individuals and all societies. In turn these tendencies have been linked to the 'Enlightenment project' of rationalism and progress (Gray, 1997). The classic metanarratives are therefore liberalism and Marxism.

The postmodern condition, however, is one that highlights the importance of difference, dialogue and debate, in which truth is seen as merely a social construct that is applicable only to particular individuals, groups and societies and never to the universal. Some argue that this means that democracy, particularly deliberative democracy, has emerged as perhaps the only stable and enduring principle in the postmodern political landscape. Others predict that the postmodern future is increasingly likely to be dominated by intolerant and authoritarian particularisms, political doctrines that offer an escape from the burdens of uncertainty and personal responsibility.

However the very assertion of an 'end of modernity', an 'end of history', or an 'end of ideology' or an 'end of politics' is itself ideological. Each of these theses is essentially an attempt to portray one particular set of political ideas and values as superior to all its rivals, and to do so by predicting its ultimate triumph. The mandate of history is called upon to validate a single ideology or creed, be it Marxist socialism, welfare capitalism, western liberalism or deliberative democracy, and so to discredit every other political creed. Rather than heralding the final demise of ideology, such assertions merely demonstrate that ideological debate is alive and well, and that ideology is a continuing and unending process.

---

## Postmodernism

Postmodernism is a controversial and confusing term that was first used to describe experimental movements in western arts, architecture and cultural development in general. As a tool of social and political analysis, postmodernism highlights the shift away from societies structured by industrialisation and class solidarity to increasingly fragmented and pluralistic 'information' societies, in which individuals are transformed from producers to consumers, and individualism replaces class, religious and ethnic loyalties. Postmodernists argue that there is no such thing as certainty; the idea of absolute and universal truth must be discarded as an arrogant pretence. Emphasis is instead placed on discourse, debate and democracy.

## Further reading

Collins, P., *Ideology After the Fall of Communism* (London: Bowerdean, 1993). A short but useful examination of the likely developments in ideological thinking after the fall of the Berlin Wall in 1989.

Gray, J., *Endgames: Questions in Late Modern Political Thought* (Oxford, and Malden, Mass.: Blackwell, 1997). A fascinating and insightful discussion of the condition of the major ideological traditions as they confront the collapse of the 'Enlightenment project'.

Shtromas, A. (ed.), *The End of 'isms'?: Reflections on the Fate of Ideological Politics after Communism's Collapse* (Oxford, and Cambridge, Mass.: Blackwell, 1994). A collection of considered and carefully argued essays on the state of and future prospects for the politics of ideology after the collapse of communism.

Smart, B., *Postmodernity* (London and New York: Routledge, 1993). A short, critical introduction to this controversial and often misunderstood concept.

# Glossary of Terms

*When a term is discussed more fully in a box in the main text of the book, a page reference is given after the definition in the glossary.*

**Absolutism**  A form of government in which political power is concentrated in the hands of a single individual or small group, in particular, an absolute monarchy.

**Alienation**  To be separated from one's genuine or essential nature; used by Marxists to describe the process whereby under capitalism labour is reduced to being a mere commodity and work becomes a depersonalised activity rather than a creative and fulfilling one.

**Altruism**  Concern for the interests and welfare of others, based either upon enlightened self-interest or a belief in a common humanity.

**Anarchy**  Literally, without rule; anarchy is often used pejoratively to suggest instability or even chaos.

***Ancien régime***  Literally, old order; usually linked to the absolutist structures that predated the French Revolution.

**Androgyny**  The possession of both male and female characteristics; used to imply that human beings are sexless persons in the sense that sex is irrelevant to their social role or political status.

**Anomie**  A weakening of values and normative rules, associated with feelings of isolation, loneliness and meaninglessness.

**Anthropocentrism**  A belief that human needs and interests are of overriding moral and philosophical importance; the opposite of ecocentrism.

**Anti-Semitism**  Prejudice or hatred towards Jews; anti-Semitism may take religious, economic or racial forms (see p. 230).

**Atomism**  A belief that society is made up of a collection of self-interested and largely self-sufficient individuals, or atoms, rather than social groups.

**Autarky**  Economic self-sufficiency, brought about either through expansionism aimed at securing markets and sources of raw materials or by withdrawal from the international economy.

**Authoritarianism** A belief that strong central authority, imposed from above, is either desirable or necessary, and therefore demands unquestioning obedience (see p. 82).

**Authority** The right to exert influence over others by virtue of an acknowledged obligation to obey (see p. 221).

**Autonomy** Literally, self-government; the ability to control one's own destiny by virtue of enjoying independence from external influences.

**Bourgeois ideology** A Marxist term denoting ideas and theories that serve the interests of the bourgeoisie by disguising the contradictions of capitalist society.

**Bourgeoisie** A Marxist term denoting the ruling class of a capitalist society, the owners of productive wealth.

**Capitalism** An economic system in which wealth is owned by private individuals or businesses and goods are produced for exchange, according to the dictates of the market.

**Charisma** Charm or personal power; the ability to inspire loyalty, emotional dependence or even devotion in others.

**Chauvinism** Uncritical and unreasoned dedication to a cause or group, typically based upon a belief in its superiority, as in 'national chauvinism' or 'male chauvinism'.

**Christian democracy** An ideological tradition within European conservatism that is characterised by a commitment to the social market and qualified economic intervention.

**Citizenship** Membership of a state; a relationship between the individual and the state based on reciprocal rights and responsibilities.

**Civil liberty** The private sphere of existence, belonging to the citizen not to the state; freedom from government.

**Civil society** A realm of autonomous associations and groups, formed by private citizens and enjoying independence from the government; civil society includes businesses, clubs, families and so on.

**Class-consciousness** A Marxist term denoting an accurate awareness of class interests and a willingness to pursue them; a class-conscious class is a class-*for*-itself.

**Classical liberalism** A tradition within liberalism that seeks to maximise the realm of unconstrained individual action, typically by establishing a minimal state and relying upon market economies.

**Collectivisation**   The abolition of private property and the establishment of a comprehensive system of common or public ownership, usually through the mechanisms of the state.

**Collectivism**   A belief that human ends are best achieved through collaborative or collective effort, highlighting the importance of social groups (see p. 107).

**Colonialism**   The theory or practice of establishing control over a foreign territory, usually by settlement or economic domination.

**Communism**   The principle of the common ownership of wealth; communism is often used more broadly to refer to movements or regimes that are based on Marxist principles.

**Communitarianism**   A belief that the self or person is constituted through the community in the sense that there are no 'unencumbered selves' (see p. 148).

**Conflict**   Opposition or competition between two or more forces, arising either from the pursuit of incompatible goals or a clash of rival opinions.

**Consensus**   An agreement on basic issues or principles that may permit disagreement about matters of detail or emphasis.

**Constitutionalism**   The belief that government power should be exercised within a framework of rules (a constitution) that define the duties, powers and functions of government institutions and the rights of the individual (see p. 41).

**Contract**   An agreement entered into voluntarily and on mutually acceptable terms.

**Cooperation**   Working together; collective effort intended to achieve mutual benefit.

**Corporatism**   The theory (linked to either fascist or liberal theory) that the major economic interests – business and labour – are or should be incorporated into the processes of government.

**Cosmopolitanism**   Literally, a belief in a world state; more usually, a commitment to fostering harmony and understanding amongst nations (see p. 181).

**Cultural nationalism**   A form of nationalism that places primary emphasis on the regeneration of the nation as a distinctive civilisation rather than on self-government.

**Decentralisation**   The expansion of local autonomy through the transfer of powers and responsibilities away from national or central bodies.

**Deep ecology**  A green ideological perspective that rejects anthropocentrrism and gives priority to the maintenance of nature, and is associated with values such as biocentric equality, diversity and decentralisation.

**Deliberative democracy**  A form of democracy that emphasises the role of discourse and debate in helping to define the public interest.

**Democracy**  Rule by the people; democracy implies both popular participation and government in the public interest, and can take a wide variety of forms.

**Democratic centralism**  The Leninist principle of party organisation, based upon a supposed balance between freedom of discussion and strict unity of action.

**Determinism**  A belief that human actions and choices are entirely conditioned by external factors; determinism implies that free will is a myth.

**Devolution**  The transfer of power from central government to subordinate regional bodies, without (unlike federalism) leading to shared sovereignty.

**Dialectic**  A process of development in which interaction between two opposing forces leads to a further or higher stage; historical change resulting from internal contradictions within a society.

**Dialectical materialism**  The crude and deterministic form of Marxism that dominated intellectual life in orthodox communist states.

**Dictatorship of the proletariat** A Marxist term denoting the transitionary phase between the collapse of capitalism and the establishment of full communism, characterised by the establishment of a temporary proletarian state.

**Direct action**  Political action taken outside the constitutional and legal framework; direct action may range from passive resistance to terrorism.

**Direct democracy**  Popular self-government, characterised by the direct and continuous participation of citizens in the tasks of government.

**Discourse**  Human interaction, especially communication; discourse may disclose or illustrate power relationships.

**Divine right**  The doctrine that earthly rulers are chosen by God and thus wield unchallengeable authority; divine right is a defence for monarchical absolutism.

**Ecocentrism**  A theoretical orientation that gives priority to the maintenance of ecological balance rather than the achievement of human ends.

**Ecology**  The study of the relationship between living organisms and the environment; ecology stresses the network of relationships that sustain all forms of life.

**Economic liberalism**   A belief in the market as a self-regulating mechanism that tends naturally to deliver general prosperity and opportunities for all.

**Egalitarianism**   A theory or practice based on the desire to promote equality; egalitarianism is sometimes seen as the belief that equality is the primary political value.

**Egoism**   Concern for one's own interest or welfare, selfishness; or the belief that each individual is the centre of his or her own moral universe, and is thus entitled to function as a morally autonomous being.

**Elitism**   A belief in rule by an elite or minority; elite rule may be thought to be desirable – the elite possessing superior talents or skills – or inevitable, egalitarian ideas such as democracy and socialism being simply impractical.

**Enlightenment, the**   An intellectual movement that reached its height in the eighteenth century and challenged traditional beliefs in religion, politics and learning in general in the name of reason and progress.

**Environmentalism**   A belief in the political importance of the natural environment; environmentalism is often used (in contrast to ecologism) to denote a reformism approach to nature that reflects human needs and concerns.

**Equality**   The principle that human beings are of identical worth or are entitled to be treated in the same way; equality can have widely differing applications (see p. 111).

**Ethnicity**   A sentiment of loyalty towards a particular population, cultural group or territorial area; bonds that are cultural rather than racial.

**Ethnic nationalism**   A form of nationalism that is fuelled primarily by a keen sense of ethnic distinctiveness and the desire to preserve it.

**Eugenics**   The theory or practice of selective breeding, achieved either by promoting procreation amongst 'fit' members of a species or preventing procreation by the 'unfit'.

**Eurocommunism**   A form of deradicalised communism that attempts to blend Marxism with liberal-democratic principles.

**False consciousness**   A Marxist term denoting the delusion and mystification that prevents subordinate classes from recognising the fact of their own exploitation.

**Federalism**   A territorial distribution of power based on the sharing of sovereignty between central (usually national) bodies and peripheral ones.

**Feudalism**   A system of agrarian-based production that is characterised by fixed social hierarchies and a rigid pattern of obligations.

**Fraternity**   Literally, brotherhood; bonds of sympathy and comradeship between and amongst human beings.

**Free market**   The principle or policy of unfettered market competition, free from government interference.

**Free trade**   A system of trading between states that is unrestricted by tariffs or other forms of protectionism.

**Freedom (or liberty)**   The ability to think or act as one wishes, a capacity that can be associated with the individual, a social group or a nation (see p. 31).

**Fundamentalism**   A belief in the original or most basic principles of a creed, often associated with fierce commitment and sometimes reflected in fanatical zeal (see p. 299).

**Gender**   A social and cultural distinction between males and females, as opposed to sex, which refers to biological and therefore ineradicable differences between men and women (see p. 247).

**General will**   The genuine interests of a collective body, equivalent to the common good; the will of all provided each person acts selflessly.

**Globalisation**   A complex web of interconnectedness through which life is increasingly shaped by decisions or events taken at a distance.

**Government**   The machinery through which collective decisions are made on behalf of the state, usually comprising a legislature, executive and judiciary.

**Hegemony**   The ascendency or domination of one element of a system over others; for Marxists, hegemony implies ideological domination.

**Hierarchy**   A gradation of social positions or status; hierarchy implies structural or fixed inequality in which position is unconnected with individual ability.

**Historical materialism**   A Marxist theory that holds that material or economic conditions ultimately structure law, politics, culture and other aspects of social existence.

**Holism**   A belief that the whole is more important than its parts; holism implies that understanding is gained by studying relationships among the parts.

**Human nature**   The essential and innate character of all human beings, what they owe to nature rather than to society (see p. 74).

**Human rights**   Rights to which people are entitled by virtue of being human; universal and fundamental rights.

**Humanism**    A philosophy that gives moral priority to the achievement of human needs and ends.

**Idealism**    A view of politics that emphasises the importance of morality and ideals; philosophically, idealism can imply that ideas are more 'real' than the material world.

**Ideology**    A more or less coherent set of ideas that provides the basis for some kind of organised political action (see p. 15).

**Imperialism**    The extension of control by one country over another, whether by overt political means or through economic domination.

**Individualism**    A belief in the central importance of the human individual as opposed to the social group or collective (see p. 24).

**Individuality**    Self-fulfilment achieved through the realisation of an individual's distinctive or unique identity and qualities; that which distinguishes one person from all others.

**Industrialism**    An economic theory or system based on large-scale factory production and the relentless accummulation of capital (see p. 275).

**Integral nationalism**    An intense, even hysterical nationalist enthusiasm that absorbs individual identity into that of the nation.

**Internationalism**    A theory or practice of politics that is based on transnational or global cooperation; the belief that nations are artificial and unwanted formations.

**Jingoism**    A mood of nationalist enthusiasm and public celebration provoked by military expansion or imperial conquest.

**Justice**    A moral standard of fairness and impartiality; social justice is the notion of a fair or justifiable distribution of wealth and rewards in society.

**Keynesianism**    A theory (developed by J. M. Keynes) or policy of economic management, associated with regulating aggregate demand and achieving full employment.

**Labourism**    A tendency exhibited by socialist parties to serve the interests of the organised labour movement rather than pursue broader ideological goals.

*Laissez-faire*    The doctrine that economic activity should be entirely free from government interference, an extreme belief in the free market.

**Law**    Established and public rules of social conduct, backed up by the machinery of the state: the police, courts and prisons.

**Left** A broad ideological disposition that is characterised by sympathy for principles such as liberty, equality, fraternity and progress.

**Legitimacy** The acceptance that political authority is rightful and therefore that those subject to it have a moral obligation to obey.

**Leninism** Lenin's theoretical contributions to Marxism, notably his belief in the need for a revolutionary or vanguard party to raise the proletariat to class consciousness.

**Liberal democracy** A form of democracy that incorporates both limited government and a system of regular and competitive elections; liberal democracy is also used as a regime type.

**Libertarianism** A belief that the individual should enjoy the widest possible realm of freedom; libertarianism implies the removal of both external and internal constraints upon the individual (see p. 89).

**Majoritarianism** A belief in majority rule; majoritarianism implies either that the majority dominates the minority, or that the minority *should* defer to the judgement of the majority.

**Managerialism** The theory that a governing class of managers, technocrats and state officials – those who possess technical and administrative skills – dominates all industrial societies, both capitalist and communist.

**Market** A system of commercial exchange between buyers and sellers, controlled by impersonal economic forces: 'market forces'.

**Market socialism** An economic system based upon self-managing cooperative enterprises operating within a context of market competition.

**Meritocracy** Literally, rule by those with merit, merit being intelligence plus effort; a society in which social position is determined exclusively by ability and hard work.

**Militancy** Heightened or extreme commitment; a level of zeal and passion typically associated with struggle or war.

**Militarism** The achievement of ends by military means, or the extension of military ideas, values and practices to civilian society.

**Millenarianism** A belief in a thousand-year period of divine rule; political millenarianism offers the prospect of a sudden and complete emancipation from misery and oppression (see p. 22).

**Modernisation** The process of social and political change through which modern industrial societies came about; the emergence of a capitalist economic order and a liberal-democratic political system.

**Modern liberalism**   A tradition within liberalism that provides (in contrast to classical liberalism) a qualified endorsement for social and economic intervention as a means of enlarging liberty.

**Monetarism**   The theory that inflation is caused by an increase in the supply of money: 'too much money chasing too few goods'.

**Monism**   A belief in only one theory or value; monism is reflected politically in enforced obedience to a unitary power and is thus implicitly totalitarian.

**Mutualism**   A system of voluntary, mutually beneficial and harmonious exchange, in which individuals or groups bargain with one another, trading goods and services without profiteering or exploitation.

**Myth, political**   A belief that has the capacity to provoke political action by virtue of its emotional or symbolic power rather than through an appeal to reason.

**Nation**   A collection of people bound together by shared values and traditions, a common language, religion and history, and usually occupying the same geographical area (see p. 160).

**National socialism**   A form of fascism practised in Hitler's Germany and characterised by totalitarian terror, genocidal anti-Semitism and expansionist racism.

**Nationalisation**   The extension of state or public ownership over private assets or industries.

**Nation-state**   A sovereign political association within which citizenship and nationality overlap; one nation within a single state.

**Natural aristocracy**   The idea that talent and leadership are innate or inbred qualities that cannot be acquired through effort or self-advancement.

**Natural rights**   God-given rights that are fundamental to human beings and are therefore inalienable (they cannot be taken away).

**Negative freedom**   The absence of external restrictions or constraints upon the individual, allowing freedom of choice.

**Neoconservatism**   A modern version of social conservatism that emphasises the need to restore order, return to traditional or family values or revitalise nationalism.

**Neoliberalism**   An updated version of classical political economy that is dedicated to market individualism and minimal statism.

**Neo-Marxism** An updated and revised form of Marxism that rejects determinism, the primacy of economics and the privileged status of the proletariat.

**New left** An ideological movement that seeks to revitalise socialist thought by developing a radical critique of advanced industrial society, stressing the need for decentralisation, participation and personal liberation.

**New right** An ideological trend within conservatism that embraces a blend of market individualism and social authoritarianism.

**Nihilism** Literally a belief in nothing, the rejection of all moral and political principles; nihilism is sometimes, but not necessarily, associated with destruction and the use of violence.

**Normative** The prescription of a moral standard of what 'should', 'ought' or 'must' be, rather than a descriptive statement of what 'is'.

**One nation conservatism** The tradition of conservative reformism, characterised by a belief in paternal duty and a fear of wide social inequality.

**Order** Settled, predictable and peaceful social circumstances in which personal security is upheld.

**Organicism** A belief that society operates like an organism or living entity, the whole being more than a collection of its individual parts.

**Orthodoxy** Adherence to an established or conventional view, usually enjoying 'official' sanction or support.

**Pacifism** The principled rejection of war and all forms of violence as fundamentally evil.

**Pan-nationalism** A style of nationalism that is dedicated to unifying a disparate people either through expansionism or political solidarity ('pan' means all or every).

**Pastoralism** A belief in the virtues of rural existence: simplicity, community and a closeness to nature, in contrast to the allegedly corrupting influence of urban and industrialised life.

**Paternalism** Authority exercised from above for the guidance and support of those below, modelled on the relationship between fathers and children.

**Patriarchy** Literally, rule by the father; patriarchy is often taken more generally to describe the dominance of men and the subordination of women in society at large.

**Patriotism** Literally, love of one's fatherland; a psychological attachment and loyalty to one's nation or country (see p. 165).

**Permissiveness** The willingness to allow people to make their own moral choices; permissiveness suggests that there are no authoritative values.

**Pluralism** A belief in diversity or choice, or the theory that political power is or should be widely and evenly dispersed (see p. 36).

**Politics** An activity related to the institution of the state or the machinery of government; more broadly, the processes through which social conflict is expressed and possibly resolved.

**Populism** A belief that popular instincts and wishes are the principal legitimate guide to political action, often reflecting distrust of or hostility towards political elites (see p. 301).

**Positive freedom** Self-mastery or self-realisation; the achievement of autonomy and the development of human capacities.

**Postmaterialism** The theory that as material affluence spreads, 'quality of life' issues and concerns tend to displace economic ones.

**Postmodernism** An intellectual movement that rejects the idea of absolute and universal truth, and usually emphasises discourse, debate and democracy (see p. 324).

**Pragmatism** Behaviour shaped in accordance with practical circumstances and goals rather than ideological objectives (see p. 11).

**Privatisation** The transfer of state assets from the public to the private sector, reflecting a contraction of the state's responsibilities.

**Progress** Moving forward, usually implying improvement; progress is based upon the belief that human history is marked by the advance of knowledge and the achievement of higher levels of civilisation.

**Proletariat** A Marxist term denoting a class that subsists through the sale of its labour power; strictly speaking, the proletariat is not equivalent to the working class (manual workers).

**Property** The ownership of physical goods or wealth, whether by private individuals, groups of people or the state.

**Protectionism** Import restrictions such as quotas and tariffs that are designed to protect domestic producers from foreign competitors.

**Race**  A collection of people who share a common genetic inheritance and are thus distinguished from others by biological factors.

**Racialism**  A belief that racial divisions are politically significant, either because races should live apart or because they possess different qualities and are thus suited to different social roles (see p. 228).

**Radical democracy**  A form of democracy that favours decentralisation and participation: the widest possible dispersal of political power.

**Radical feminism**  A form of feminism that holds gender divisions to be the most politically significant of social cleavages, and believes that they are rooted in the structures of domestic life.

**Radicalism**  A belief in fundamental or far-reaching change, as opposed to moderate or incremental reforms.

**Rationalism**  A belief that the world can be understood and explained through the exercise of human reason, based upon assumptions about its rational structure (see p. 32).

**Reactionary**  Resistance to change or a desire to return to a former system, based upon the belief that human history is marked by descent or decay.

**Reformism**  A belief in gradual, piecemeal improvements, opposed to both revolution and reaction; a reform is an action or policy designed to remedy a problem or grievance.

**Relativism**  A belief that moral or factual statements can only be judged in relation to their contexts, because there are no objective or 'absolute' standards.

**Representative democracy**  A limited and indirect form of democracy that is based on the selection (usually by election) of those who will rule on behalf of the people.

**Revisionism**  The revision or reworking of a political theory that departs from earlier interpretations in an attempt to present a 'corrected' view.

**Revolution**  A fundamental and irreversible change, often a brief but dramatic period of upheaval; systemic change.

**Right**  A broad ideological disposition that is characterised by sympathy for principles such as authority, order, hierarchy and duty.

**Rights**  Moral entitlements to act or be treated in a particular way.

**Science**  A method of acquiring knowledge through a process of careful observation and the testing of hypotheses by reproducible experiments.

**Scientism**   The belief that scientific method is the only value-free and objective means of establishing truth, and is applicable to all fields of learning.

**Secularism**   A belief that religion should not intrude into secular (worldly) affairs, usually reflected in the desire to separate church from state.

**Separatism**   The quest to secede from a political formation with a view to establishing an independent state.

**Shallow ecology**   A green ideological perspective that harnesses the lessons of ecology to human needs and ends, and is associated with values such as sustainability and conservation.

**Social class**   A social division based upon economic or social factors; a social class is a group of people who share a similar socio-economic position.

**Social contract**   A (hypothetical) agreement amongst indivuduals through which they form a state in order to escape from the disorder and chaos of the 'state of nature'.

**Social democracy**   A moderate or reformist brand of socialism that favours a balance between the market and the state, rather than the abolition of capitalism.

**Social ecology**   The theory that human society operates according to ecological principles, implying a belief in natural harmony and the need for a balance between humankind and nature.

**Social revolution**   A qualitative change in the structure of society; for Marxists a social revolution involves a change in the mode of production and the system of ownership.

**Sovereignty**   The principle of absolute or unrestricted power expressed either as unchallengeable legal authority or unquestionable political power.

**Stalinism**   A centrally planned economy supported by systematic and brutal political oppression, based on the structures of Stalin's Russia.

**State**   An association that establishes sovereign power within a defined territorial area, usually possessing a monopoly of coercive power (see p. 190).

**State of nature**   A pre-political society characterised by unrestrained freedom and the absence of established authority.

**State socialism**   A form of socialism in which the state controls and directs economic life, acting, in theory, in the interests of the people.

**Statism**   A belief that the state is the most appropriate means of resolving problems and of guaranteeing economic and social development.

**Supranationalism**  The ability of bodies with transnational or global jurisdiction to impose their will upon nation-states.

**Surplus value**  A Marxist term denoting the value that is extracted from the labour of the proletariat by the mechanism of capitalist exploitation.

**Sustainability**  The ability of a system to maintain its health and continue in existence; the central principle of green economics.

**Syndicalism**  A form of revolutionary trade unionism that is based upon a crude notion of class war and emphasises the use of direct action and the general strike.

**Thatcherism**  The free-market/strong state ideological stance associated with Margaret Thatcher; the UK version of the new right political project.

**Theocracy**  Literally, rule by God; the principle that religious authority should prevail over political authority, usually through the domination of church over state.

**Third way**  The notion of an alternative form of economics to both state socialism and free-market capitalism, sought at different times by conservatives, socialists and fascists.

**Toleration**  Forbearance; a willingness to accept views or action with which one is in disagreement.

**Toryism**  An ideological stance within conservatism that is characterised by a belief in hierarchy, an emphasis upon tradition and support for duty and organicism (see p. 86).

**Totalitarian democracy**  An absolute dictatorship that masquerades as a democracy, typically based on the leader's claim to a monopoly of ideological wisdom.

**Totalitarianism**  An all-encompassing process of political rule in which the state penetrates and controls all social institutions, thus abolishing civil society and 'private' life (see p. 233).

**Tradition**  A practice or institution that has endured through time and has therefore been inherited from an earlier period.

**Traditionalism**  A belief that inherited institutions and practices, particularly those with a long and continuous history, provide the best guide for human conduct.

**Utilitarianism**  A moral and political philosophy that evaluates 'goodness' in terms of pleasure and pain, and ultimately seeks to achieve 'the greatest happiness for the greatest number'.

**Utility**   Use-value; in economics, utility describes the satisfaction that is gained from the consumption of material goods and services.

**Utopianism**   A belief in the unlimited possibilities of human development, typically embodied in the vision of a perfect or ideal society, a utopia (see p. 193).

**Violence**   Destructive action undertaken against property or person.

**Vitalism**   The theory that living organisms derive their characteristic properties from a universal 'life-force'; vitalism implies an emphasis upon instinct and impulse rather than intellect and reason.

**Welfarism**   A belief that the state or community has a responsibility to ensure the social well-being of its citizens, usually reflected in the emergence of a welfare state.

**West, the**   The parts of the world that are distinguished culturally by common Greco-Roman and Christian roots, socially by the dominance of industrial capitalism, and politically by the prevalence of liberal democracy.

**Xenophobia**   A fear or hatred of foreigners; pathological ethnocentrism.

**Zionism**   The movement for the establishment of a Jewish homeland, now linked to the defence of the interests and the territorial integrity of Israel (see p. 315).

# Bibliography

Adams, I. (1989) *The Logic of Political Belief: A Philosophical Analysis*. London and New York: Harvester Wheatsheaf.

Adams, I. (1993) *Political Ideology Today*. Manchester: Manchester University Press.

Ahmed, A. and H. Donnan (1994) *Islam, Globalisation and Postmodernity*. London and New York: Routledge.

Alter, P. (1989) *Nationalism*. London: Edward Arnold.

Anderson, B. (1983) *Imagined Communities: Reflections on the Origins and Spread of Nationalism*. London: Verso.

Arblaster, A. (1984) *The Rise and Decline of Western Liberalism*. Oxford: Basil Blackwell.

Arendt, H. (1951) *The Origins of Totalitarianism*. London: Allen & Unwin.

Aristotle (1962), *The Politics*, trans. T. Sinclair. Harmondsworth: Penguin (Chicago, Ill.: University of Chicago Press, 1985).

Aughey, A., G. Jones and W. T. M. Riches (1992) *The Conservative Political Tradition in Britain and the United States*. London: Pinter.

Bahro, R. (1982) *Socialism and Survival*. London: Heretic Books.

Bahro, R. (1984) *From Red to Green*. London: Verso/New Left Books.

Bakunin, M. (1977) 'Church and State', in G. Woodcock (ed.), *The Anarchist Reader*. London: Fontana.

Barker, R. (1997) *Political Ideas in Modern Britain: In And After the 20th Century*, 2nd edn. London and New York: Routledge.

Barry, N. (1987) *The New Right*. London: Croom Helm.

Beauvoir, S. de (1968) *The Second Sex*, trans. H. M. Parshley. New York: Bantam.

Bell, D. (1960) *The End of Ideology*. Glencoe, Ill.: Free Press.

Bellamy, R. (1992) *Liberalism and Modern Society: An Historical Argument*. Cambridge: Polity Press.

Benn, T. (1980) *Arguments for Democracy*. Harmondsworth: Penguin.

Bentham, J. (1970) *Introduction to the Principles of Morals and Legislation*, ed. J. Burns and H. L. A. Hart. London: Athlone Press (Glencoe, Ill.: Free Press, 1970).

Berki, R. N. (1975) *Socialism*. London: Dent.

Berlin, I. (1969) 'Two Concepts of Liberty', in *Four Essays on Liberty*. London: Oxford University Press.

Bernstein, E. (1962) *Evolutionary Socialism*. New York: Schocken.

Bobbio, N. (1996) *Left and Right*. Oxford: Polity Press.

Bookchin, M. (1975) *Our Synthetic Environment*. London: Harper & Row.

Bookchin, M. (1977) 'Anarchism and Ecology', in G. Woodcock (ed.), *The Anarchist Reader*. London: Fontana.

Boulding, K. (1966) 'The Economics of the Coming Spaceship Earth', in H. Jarrett (ed.), *Environmental Quality in a Growing Economy*. Baltimore: Johns Hopkins Press.

Bourne, R. (1977) 'War is the Health of the State', in G. Woodcock (ed.), *The Anarchist Reader*. London: Fontana.

Bracher, K. D. (1985) *The Age of Ideologies: A History of Political Thought in the Twentieth Century*. London: Methuen.

Bramwell, A. (1989) *Ecology in the Twentieth Century: A History*. New Haven, CT, and London: Yale University Press.

Bramwell, A. (1994) *The Fading of the Greens: The Decline of Environmental Politics in the West*. New Haven, CT: Yale University Press.

Brownmiller, S. (1975) *Against Our Will: Men, Women and Rape*. New York: Simon & Schuster.

Bruce, S. (1993) 'Fundamentalism, Ethnicity and Enclave', in M. Marty and R. S. Appleby (eds), *Fundamentalism and the State*. Chicago, Ill. and London: Chicago University Press.

Bryson, V. (1992) *Feminist Political Theory: An Introduction*. Basingstoke: Macmillan.

Burke, E. (1968) *Reflections on the Revolution in France*. Harmondsworth: Penguin.

Burke, E. (1975) *On Government, Politics and Society*, ed. B. W. Hill. London: Fontana.

Burnham, J. (1960) *The Managerial Revolution*. Harmondsworth: Penguin (Bloomington: Indiana University Press, 1960).

Capra, F. (1975) *The Tao of Physics*. London: Fontana.

Capra, F. (1982) *The Turning Point*. London: Fontana (Boston, Mass.: Shambhala, 1983).

Capra, F. (1996) *The Web of Life: A New Synthesis of Mind and Matter*. London: HarperCollins.

Carson, R. (1962) *The Silent Spring*. Boston, Mass.: Houghton Mifflin.

Carter, A. (1971) *The Political Theory of Anarchism*. London: Routledge & Kegan Paul.

Cecil, H. (1912) *Conservatism*. London and New York: Home University Library.

Chamberlain, H. S. (1913) *Foundations of the Nineteenth Century*. New York: John Lane.

Charvert, J. (1982) *Feminism*. London: Dent.

Club of Rome. See Meadows *et al.* (1972).

Collins, P. (1993) *Ideology After the Fall of Communism*. London: Bowerdean.

Constant, B. (1988) *Political Writings*. Cambridge: Cambridge University Press.

Coole, D. (1993) *Women in Political Theory: From Ancient Misogyny to Contemporary Feminism*, 2nd edn. Hemel Hempstead: Harvester Wheatsheaf.

Costa, M. D. and S. James (1972) *The Power of Women and the Subordination of the Community*. Bristol: Falling Wall Press.

Crewe, I. (1989) 'Values: The Crusade that Failed', in D. Kavanagh and A. Seldon (eds), *The Thatcher Effect*. Oxford: Oxford University Press.

Crick, B. (1962) *A Defence of Politics*. Harmondsworth: Penguin.

Critchley, T. A. (1970) *The Conquest of Violence*. London: Constable.

Crosland, C. A. R. (1956) *The Future of Socialism*. London: Cape (Des Plaines, Ill.: Greenwood, 1977).

Dahl, R. (1961) *Who Governs? Democracy and Power in an American City*. New Haven, CT: Yale University Press.

Dalai Lama (1996) *The Power of Buddhism*. London: Newleaf.

Daly, H. (1974) 'Steady-state economics vs. growthmania: a critique of orthodox conceptions of growth, wants, scarcity and efficiency', in *Policy Sciences* vol. 5, pp. 149–67.

Daly, M. (1979) *Gyn/Ecology: The Meta-Ethics of Radical Feminism*. Boston, Mass.: Beacon Press.

Darwin, C. (1972) *On the Origin of Species*. London: Dent.

Dickinson, G. L. (1916) *The European Anarchy*, London: Allen & Unwin.

Dobson, A. (1990) *Green Political Thought*. London: HarperCollins.

Dobson, A. (1991) *The Green Reader*. London: André Deutsch.

Downs, A. (1957) *An Economic Theory of Democracy*. New York: Harper & Row.

Eagleton, T. (1991) *Ideology: An Introduction*. London: Verso.

Eatwell, R. (1996) *Fascism: A History*. London: Vintage.

Eatwell, R. and N. O'Sullivan (eds) (1989) *The Nature of the Right: European and American Politics and Political Thought Since 1789*. London: Pinter.

Eatwell, R. and A. Wright (eds) (1993) *Contemporary Political Ideologies*. London: Pinter.

Eccleshall, R. *et al.* (1994) *Political Ideologies: An Introduction*, 2nd edn. London and New York: Routledge.

Eckersley, R. (1992) *Environmentalism and Political Theory: Towards an Ecocentric Approach*. London: UCL Press.

Edgar, D. (1988) 'The Free or the Good', in R. Levitas (ed.) *The Ideology of the New Right*. Oxford: Polity Press.

Ehrenfeld, D. (1978) *The Arrogance of Humanism*. Oxford: Oxford University Press.

Ehrlich, P. and A. Ehrlich (1970) *Population, Resources and Environment: Issues in Human Ecology*. London: W. H. Freeman.

Ehrlich, P. and R. Harriman (1971) *How to be a Survivor*. London: Pan.

Elshtain, J. B. (1981) *Public Man, Private Woman*. Princeton, NJ: Princeton University Press.

Engels, F. (1976) *The Origins of the Family, Private Property and the State*. London: Lawrence & Wishart (New York: Pathfinder, 1972).

Etzioni, A. (1995) *The Spirit of Community: Rights, Responsibilities and the Communitarian Agenda*. London: Fontana.

Eysenck, H. (1964) *Sense and Nonsense in Psychology*. Harmondsworth: Penguin.

Faludi, S. (1991) *Backlash: The Undeclared War Against American Women*. New York: Crown.

Fanon, F. (1965) *The Wretched of the Earth*. Harmondsworth: Penguin (New York: Grove - Weidenfeld, 1988).

Faure, S. (1977) 'Anarchy-Anarchist', in G. Woodcock (ed.), *The Anarchist Reader* London: Fontana.

Figes, E. (1970) *Patriarchal Attitudes*. Greenwich, CT: Fawcett.

Firestone, S. (1972) *The Dialectic of Sex*. New York: Basic Books.

Foley, M. (1994) (ed.) *Ideas that Shape Politics*. Manchester and New York: Manchester University Press.

Fox, W. (1990) *Towards a Transpersonal Ecology: Developing the Foundations for Environmentalism*. Boston, Mass.: Shambhala.

Freeden, M. (1996) *Ideologies and Political Theory: A Conceptual Approach*. Oxford and New York: Oxford University Press.

Friedan, B. (1963) *The Feminine Mystique*. New York: Norton.

Friedan, B. (1983) *The Second Stage*. London: Abacus (New York: Summit, 1981).

Friedman, M. (1962) *Capitalism and Freedom*. Chicago, Ill.: University of Chicago Press.

Friedman, M. and R. Friedman (1980) *Free to Choose*. Harmondsworth: Penguin (New York: Bantam, 1983).

Friedrich, C. J. and Z. Brzezinski (1963) *Totalitarian Dictatorships and Autocracy*. New York: Praeger.

Fromm, E. (1979) *To Have or To Be*. London: Abacus.

Fromm, E. (1984) *The Fear of Freedom*. London: Ark.

Fukuyama, F. (1989) 'The End of History', *National Interest*, Summer.

Galbraith, J. K. (1992) *The Culture of Commitment*. London: Sinclair Stevenson.

Gallie, W. B. (1955–6) 'Essentially Contested Context', in *Proceedings of the Aristotelian Society*, vol. 56.

Gamble, A. (1988) *The Free Economy and the Strong State*. London: Macmillan (Durham, NC: Duke University Press, 1988).

Gandhi, M. (1971) *Selected Writings of Mahatma Gandhi*, ed. R. Duncan. London: Fontana.

Garvey, J. H. (1993) 'Fundamentalism and Politics', in Martin E. Marty and R. Scott Appleby (eds), *Fundamentalisms and the State*. Chicago, Ill., and London: University of Chicago Press.

Gasset, O. Y. (1972) *The Revolt of the Masses*. London: Allen & Unwin.

Gellner, E. (1983) *Nations and Nationalism*. Oxford: Blackwell.

Giddens, A. (1994) *Beyond Left and Right: The Future of Radical Politics*. Oxford: Polity Press.

Gilmour, I. (1978) *Inside Right: A Study of Conservatism*. London: Quartet Books.

Gilmour, I. (1992) *Dancing with Dogma: Britain under Thatcherism*. London: Simon & Schuster.

Gobineau, J. A. (1970) *Gobineau: Selected Political Writings*, ed. M. D. Biddiss. New York: Harper & Row.

Godwin, W. (1971) *Enquiry Concerning Political Justice*, ed. K. C. Carter. Oxford: Oxford University Press.

Goldsmith, E. (ed.) (1972) *Blueprint for Survival*. Harmondsworth: Penguin.

Goldsmith, E. (1988) *The Great U-Turn: De-industrialising Society*. Bideford: Green Books.

Goodin, R. E. (1992) *Green Political Theory*. Oxford: Polity Press.

Goodman, P. (1964) *Compulsory Miseducation*. New York: Vintage Books.

Goodman, P. (1977) 'Normal Politics and the Psychology of Power', in G. Woodcock (ed.), *The Anarchist Reader*. London: Fontana.

Goodwin, B. (1992) *Using Political Ideas*, 3rd edn. London: John Wiley & Sons.

Gorz, A. (1985) *Farewell to The Working Class*. London: Pluto Press (Boston, Mass.: South End Press, 1982).

Gould, B. (1985) *Socialism and Freedom*. London: Macmillan, 1985 (Wakefield, NH: Longwood, 1986).

Gramsci, A. (1971) *Selections from the Prison Notebooks*, ed. Q. Hoare and G. Nowell-Smith. London: Lawrence & Wishart.

Gray, J. (1995a) *Enlightenment's Wake: Politics and Culture at the Close of the Modern Age*. London: Routledge.

Gray, J. (1995b) *Liberalism*, 2nd edn. Milton Keynes: Open University Press.

Gray, J. (1996) *Post-liberalism: Studies in Political Thought*. London: Routledge.

Gray, J. (1997) *Endgames: Questions in Late Modern Political Thought*. Cambridge and Malden, Mass.: Blackwell.

Green, T. H. (1988) *Works*, R. Nettleship (ed.). London: Oxford University Press (New York: AMS Press, 1984).

Greenleaf, W. H. (1983) *The British Political Tradition: The Ideological Heritage*, vol. 2. London: Methuen.

Greer, G. (1970) *The Female Eunuch*. New York: McGraw-Hill.

Greer, G. (1985) *Sex and Destiny*. New York: Harper & Row.

Gregor, A. J. (1969) *The Ideology of Fascism*. New York: Free Press.

Griffin, R. (1993) *The Nature of Fascism*. London: Routledge.

Griffin, R. (1995) *Fascism*. Oxford and New York: Oxford University Press.

Hadden, J. K. and A. Shupe (eds) (1986) *Prophetic Religions and Politics: Religion and Political Order*. New York: Paragon House.

Hall, J. A. (1988) *Liberalism: Politics, Ideology and the Market*. London: Paladin.

Hall, S. and M. Jacques (eds) (1983) *The Politics of Thatcherism*. London: Lawrence & Wishart.

Harrington, M. (1993) *Socialism, Past and Future*. London: Pluto Press.

Hattersley, R. (1987) *Choose Freedom*. Harmondsworth: Penguin.

Hayek, F. A. (1944) *The Road to Serfdom*. London: Routledge & Kegan Paul (Chicago, Ill.: University of Chicago Press, 1956).

Hayek, F. A. (1960) *The Constitution of Liberty*. London: Routledge & Kegan Paul.

Heath, A., R. Jowell and J. Curtice (1985) *How Britain Votes*. Oxford: Pergamon.

Hegel, G. W. F. (1942) *The Philosophy of Right*, trans. T. M. Knox. Oxford: Clarendon Press.

Hiro, D. (1988) *Islamic Fundamentalism*. London: Paladin.

Hitler, A. (1969) *Mein Kampf*. London: Hutchinson (Boston, Mass.: Houghton Mifflin, 1973).

Hobbes, T. (1968) *Leviathan*, ed. C. B. Macpherson. Harmondsworth: Penguin.

Hobhouse, L. T. (1911) *Liberalism*. London: Thornton Butterworth.

Hobsbawm, E. (1983) 'Inventing Tradition', in E. Hobsbawm and T. Ranger (eds) *The Invention of Tradition*. Cambridge: Cambridge University Press.

Hobsbawm, E. (1992) *Nations and Nationalism Since 1780: Programme, Myth and Reality*, 2nd edn. Cambridge: Cambridge University Press.

Hobsbawm, E. (1994) *Age of Extremes: The Short Twentieth Century 1914–1991*. London: Michael Joseph.

Hobson, J. A. (1902) *Imperialism: A Study*. London: Nisbet.

Holden, B. (1993) *Understanding Liberal Democracy*, 2nd edn. Hemel Hempstead: Harvester Wheatsheaf.

Honderich, T. (1991) *Conservatism*. Harmondsworth: Penguin.

Huntington, S. (1993) 'The Clash of Civilisations', *Foreign Affairs*, vol. 72, no. 3.

Hutchinson, J. and A. D. Smith (eds) (1994) *Nationalism*. Oxford and New York: Oxford University Press.

Hutton, W. (1995) *The State We're In*. London: Jonathan Cape.

Illich, I. (1973) *Deschooling Society*. Harmondsworth: Penguin (New York: Harper & Row, 1983).

Inglehart, R. (1977) *The Silent Revolution: Changing Values and Political Styles Amongst Western Publics*. Princeton, NJ: Princeton University Press.

Jefferson, T. (1979) 'The United States Declaration of Independence', in W. Laqueur and B. Rubin (eds), *The Human Rights Reader*. New York: Meridan.

Kedourie, E. (1985) *Nationalism*, revised edn. London: Hutchinson.

*Journal of Political Ideologies*. Abingdon, UK and Cambridge, Mass.: Carfax.

Keynes, J. M. (1963) *The General Theory of Employment, Interest and Money*. London: Macmillan (San Diego: Harecourt Brace Jovanovich, 1965).

Kropotkin, P. (1914) *Mutual Aid*. Boston, Mass.: Porter Sargent.

Kuhn, T. (1962) *The Structure of Scientific Revolutions*. Chicago, Ill.: Chicago University Press.

Lane, D. (1996) *The Rise and Fall of State Socialism*. Oxford: Polity Press.

Laqueur, W. (ed.) (1979) *Fascism: A Reader's Guide*. Harmondsworth: Penguin.

Larrain, J. (1983) *Marxism and Ideology*. London: Macmillan.

Leach, R. (1996) *British Political Ideologies*, 2nd edn. London: Harvester Wheatsheaf.

Lenin, V. I. (1964) *The State and Revolution*. Peking: People's Publishing House.

Lenin, V. I. (1970) *Imperialism, the Highest Stage of Capitalism*. Moscow: Progress Publishers.

Lenin, V. I. (1988) *What is to be Done?* Harmondsworth and New York: Penguin.

Leopold, A. (1968) *Sand County Almanac*. Oxford: Oxford University Press.

Letwin, S. R. (1992) *The Anatomy of Thatcherism*. London: Fontana.

Lindblom, C. (1977) *Politics and Markets*. New York: Basic Books.

Locke, J. (1962) *Two Treatises of Government*. Cambridge: Cambridge University Press.

Locke, J. (1963) *A Letter Concerning Toleration*. The Hague: Martinus Nijhoff.

Lovelock, J. (1979) *Gaia: A New Look at Life on Earth*. Oxford and New York: Oxford University Press.

Lovelock, J. (1988) 'Man and Gaia', in E. Goldsmith and N. Hilyard (eds), *The Earth Report*. London: Mitchell Beazley.

Lyotard, J.-F. (1984) *The Postmodern Condition: The Power of Knowledge*. Minneapolis: University of Minnesota Press.

MacIntyre, A. (1981) *After Virtue*. London: Duckworth.

Macmillan, H. (1966) *The Middle Way*. London: Macmillan.

Macpherson, C. B. (1973) *Democratic Theory: Essays in Retrieval*. Oxford: Clarendon Press.

Mannheim, K. (1960) *Ideology and Utopia*. London: Routledge & Kegan Paul.

Manning, D. (1976) *Liberalism*. London: Dent.

Marcuse, H. (1964) *One Dimensional Man: Studies in the Ideology of Advanced Industrial Society*. Boston, Mass.: Beacon.

Marquand, D. (1988) *The Unprincipled Society*. London: Fontana.

Marquand, D. (1992) *The Progressive Dilemma*. London: Heinemann.

Marquand, D. and A. Seldon (1996) *The Ideas that Shaped Post-War Britain*. London: Fontana.

Marshall, P. (1993) *Demanding the Impossible: A History of Anarchism*. London: Fontana.

Marshall, P. (1995) *Nature's Web: Rethinking our Place on Earth*. London: Cassell.

Marty, M.E. (1988) 'Fundamentalism as a Social Phenomenon', *Bulletin of the American Academy of Arts and Sciences*, vol. 42, pp. 15–29.

Marty, M.E. and R.S. Appleby (eds) (1993) *Fundamentalisms and the State: Remaking Politics, Economics, and Militance*. Chicago, Ill. and London: University of Chicago Press.

Marx, K. and F. Engels (1968) *Selected Works*. London: Lawrence & Wishart.

Marx, K. and F. Engels (1970) *The German Ideology*. London: Lawrence & Wishart.

McLellan, D. (1979) *Marxism After Marx*. London: Macmillan.

McLellan, D. (1980) *The Thought of Karl Marx*, 2nd edn. London: Macmillan.

McLellan, D. (1986) *Ideology*. Milton Keynes: Open University Press.

Meadows, D.H., D.L. Meadows, D. Randers and W. Williams (1972) *The Limits to Growth*. London: Pan (New York: New American Library, 1972).

Michels, R. (1958) *Political Parties*. Glencoe, Ill.: Free Press.

Miliband, R. (1969) *The State in Capitalist Society*. London: Verso (New York: Basic, 1978).

Miliband, R. (1995) *Socialism for a Sceptical Age*. Oxford: Polity.

Mill, J.S. (1970) *On the Subjection of Women*. London: Dent.

Mill, J.S. (1972) *Utilitarianism, On Liberty and Consideration on Representative Government*. London: Dent.

Miller, D. (1984) *Anarchism*. London: Dent.

Millett, K. (1970) *Sexual Politics*. New York: Doubleday.

Mitchell, J. (1971) *Women's Estate*. Harmondsworth: Penguin.

Montesquieu, C. de (1969) *The Spirit of Laws*. Glencoe, Ill.: Free Press.

More, T. (1965) *Utopia*. Harmondsworth: Penguin (New York: Norton, 1976).

Mosca, G. (1939) *The Ruling Class*, trans. and ed. A. Livingstone. New York: McGraw-Hill.

Murray, C. (1984) *Losing Ground: American Social Policy: 1950–1980*. New York: Basic Books.

Murray, C. and R. Herrnstein (1995) *The Bell Curve: Intelligence and Class Structure in American Life*. New York: Free Press.

Naess, A. (1973) 'The shallow and the deep, long-range ecology movement. A summary'. *Inquiry*, vol. 16.

Naess, A. (1989) *Community and Lifestyle: Outline of an Ecosophy*. Cambridge: Cambridge University Press.

Neocleous, M. (1997) *Fascism*. Milton Keynes: Open University Press.

Nietzsche, F. (1961) *Thus Spoke Zarathustra*, trans. R.J. Hollingdale. Harmondsworth: Penguin (New York: Random, 1982).

Nolte, E. (1965) *Three Faces of Fascism: Action Française, Italian Fascism and National Socialism.* London: Weidenfeld & Nicolson.

Nozick, R. (1974) *Anarchy, State and Utopia.* Oxford: Blackwell (New York: Basic, 1974).

Oakeshott, M. (1962) *Rationalism in Politics and Other Essays.* London: Methuen (New York: Routledge Chapman & Hall, 1981).

O'Sullivan, N. (1976) *Conservatism.* London: Dent.

O'Sullivan, N. (1983) *Fascism.* London: Dent.

Paglia, C. (1990) *Sex, Art and American Culture.* New Haven, CT.: Yale University.

Paglia, C. (1992) *Sexual Personae: Art and Decadence From Nefertiti to Emily Dickinson.* Harmondsworth: Penguin.

Parekh, B. (1994) 'The Concept of Fundamentalism', in A. Shtromas (ed.), *The End of 'isms'? Reflections on the Fate of Ideological Politics after Communism's Collapse.* Oxford, and Cambridge, Mass.: Blackwell.

Pareto, V. (1935) *The Mind and Society.* London: Cape (New York: AMS Press, 1935).

Plato (1955) *The Republic,* trans. H. D. Lee. Harmondsworth: Penguin (New York: Random, 1983).

Popper, K. (1945) *The Open Society and Its Enemies.* London: Routledge & Kegan Paul.

Poulantzas, N. (1968) *Political Power and Social Class.* London: New Left Books (New York: Routledge Chapman & Hall, 1987).

Proudhon, P. J. (1970) *What is Property?,* trans. B. R. Tucker. New York: Dover.

Purkis, J. and J. Bowen (1997) *Twenty-First Century Anarchism: Unorthodox Ideas for a New Millennium.* London: Cassell.

Ramsay, M. (1997) *What's Wrong with Liberalism? A Radical Critique of Liberal Political Philosophy.* London: Leicester University Press.

Randall, V. (1987) *Women and Politics: An International Perspective,* 2nd edn. Basingstoke: Macmillan.

Rawls, J. (1970) *A Theory of Justice.* Oxford: Oxford University Press (Cambridge, Mass.: Harvard University Press, 1971).

Regan, T. (1983) *The Case for Animal Rights.* London: Routledge & Kegan Paul.

Roemer, J. (ed.) (1986) *Analytical Marxism,* Cambridge: Cambridge University Press.

Rothbart, M. (1978) *For a New Liberty.* New York: Macmillan.

Rousseau, J. J. (1913) *The Social Contract and Discourse,* ed. G. D. H. Cole. London: Dent (Glencoe, Ill.: Free Press, 1969).

Sandel, M. (1982) *Liberalism and the Limits of Justice.* Cambridge: Cambridge University Press.

Sassoon, D. (1997) *One Hundred Years of Socialism.* London: Fontana.

Schneir, M. (1995) *The Vintage Book of Feminism: The Essential Writings of the Contemporary Women's Movement.* London: Vintage.

Schumacher, E. F. (1973) *Small is Beautiful.* London: Blond and Briggs (New York: Harper & Row, 1989).

Schumpeter, J. (1976) *Capitalism, Socialism and Democracy.* London: Allen & Unwin (Magnolia, Mass.: Petersmith, 1983).

Schwarzmantel, J. (1991) *Socialism and the Idea of the Nation*. Hemel Hempstead: Harvester Wheatsheaf.

Scruton, R. (1984) *The Meaning of Conservatism*, 2nd edn. Basingstoke: Macmillan.

Seliger, M. (1976) *Politics and Ideology*. London: Allen & Unwin (Glencoe, Ill.: Free Press, 1976).

Shtromas, A. (ed.) (1994) *The End of 'isms'? Reflections on the Fate of Ideological Politics After Communism's Collapse*. Oxford, and Cambridge, Mass.: Blackwell.

Singer, P. (1976) *Animal Liberation*. New York: Jonathan Cape.

Smart, B. (1993) *Postmodernity*. London and New York: Routledge.

Smiles, S. (1986) *Self-Help*. Harmondsworth: Penguin.

Smith, A. (1976) *An Enquiry into the Nature and Causes of the Wealth of Nations*. Chicago, Ill.: University of Chicago Press.

Smith, A. D. (1986) *The Ethnic Origins of Nations*. Oxford: Blackwell.

Smith, A. D. (1991) *National Identity*. Harmondsworth: Penguin.

Sorel, G. (1950) *Reflections on Violence*, trans. T. E. Hulme and J. Roth. New York: Macmillan.

Spencer, H. (1967) *On Social Evolution: Selected Writings*. Chicago, Ill.: University of Chicago Press.

Spencer, P. (1940) *The Man Versus the State*. London: Watts & Co.

Stirner, M. (1971) *The Ego and His Own*, ed. J. Carroll. London: Cape.

Sumner, W. (1959) *Folkways*. New York: Doubleday.

Sydie, R. A. (1987) *Natural Women, Cultured Men: A Feminist Perspective on Sociological Theory*. Milton Keynes: Open University Press.

Talmon, J. L. (1952) *The Origins of Totalitarian Democracy*. London: Secker & Warburg.

Tawney, R. H. (1921) *The Acquisitive Society*. London: Bell (San Diego: Harcourt Brace Jovanovich, 1955).

Tawney, R. H. (1969) *Equality*. London: Allen & Unwin.

Thompson, J. B. (1984) *Studies in the Theory of Ideology*. Cambridge: Polity Press.

Thoreau, D. H. D. (1983) *Walden* and *'Civil Disobedience'*. Harmondsworth: Penguin.

Tocqueville, A. de (1968) *Democracy in America*. London: Fontana (New York: McGraw, 1981).

United Nations (1972). See Ward and Dubois (1972).

United Nations (1980) *Compendium of Statistics: 1977*. New York: United Nations.

Vincent, A. (1995) *Modern Political Ideologies*, 2nd edn. Oxford: Blackwell.

Willetts, D. (1992) *Modern Conservatism*. Harmondsworth, Penguin.

Wollstonecraft, M. (1967) *A Vindication of the Rights of Women*, ed. C. W. Hagelman. New York: Norton.

Ward, B. and R. Dubois (1972) *Only One Earth*. Harmondsworth: Penguin.

Woodcock, G. (1962) *Anarchism: A History of Libertarian Ideas and Movements*. Harmondsworth and New York: Penguin.

Woolf, S. J. (1981) (ed.) *European Fascism*. London: Weidenfeld & Nicolson.

Wright, A. (1987) *Socialisms: Theories and Practices*. Oxford and New York: Oxford University Press.

# Index